DYNAMICS OF ARAB FOREIGN POLICY-MAKING IN THE TWENTY-FIRST CENTURY

Hassan Hamdan al-Alkim

Dynamics of Arab Foreign Policy-Making in the Twenty-First Century

Domestic Constraints and External Challenges

SAQI

To all those who still
Have faith in Arab unity,
To all those who still
Believe in Arab destiny,
To all those who believe
In the freedom of expression,
To all those who still believe
That there is a light at the end of the tunnel,
To all those who are
In search of truth and objectivity.

ISBN: 978-0-86356-446-8

A full CIP record for this book is available from the British Library.
A full CIP record for this book is available from the Library of Congress.

Manufactured in Lebanon

SAQI
26 Westbourne Grove, London W2 5RH, UK
www.saqibooks.com

Contents

List of Tables

List of Figures

See seperate section

List of Maps

See seperate section

Abbreviations

AKP – Justice and Development Party
GCC – Gulf Cooperation Countries
GDP – Gross Domestic Product
GNP – Gross National Product
HDI – Human Development Index
IAEA – International Atomic Energy Agency
IMF – International Monetary Fund
IPCC – Intergovernmental Panel for Climate Change
KGK – People's Congress of Kurdistan
KUNA – Kuwait News Agency
LEU – Low-Enriched Uranium
mbd – Million Barrels per Day
mcm – Million Cubic Metres
MDG – Millennium Development Goals
NGO – Non-Governmental Organizations
NPT – Non-Proliferation Treaty
OAPEC – Organization for Arab Oil Exporting Countries
OPEC – Organization for Oil Exporting Countries
OPT – Occupied Palestinian Territory
PKK – Kurdistan Workers' Party
PLO – Palestinian Liberation Organization
UAE – United Arab Emirates
UNDP – United Nations Development Project
UNRWA – The United Nations Relief and Works Agency
WMD – Weapons of Mass Destruction

Prelude

Scholars and analysts of foreign policy studies agree that foreign policy is the by-product or outcome of interactions between external and internal factors aimed at maintaining or changing the status quo. They argue that foreign policy undertakings are shaped by human and non-human factors. Foreign policy study cannot be reduced to testing generalizations that treat societies as agents subject to stimuli that produce external responses.[1]

The Arab world constitutes twenty-two independent countries with a total population of approximately 335 million people, stretching over 14 million square kilometres. The Arab world's considerable material and human potential, and its strategic location, should allow it to play a major role in world affairs. The Arab states share culture, language, history and geographic proximity and face common external threats. Yet the majority are still characterized by authoritarian regimes, social injustice, economic underdevelopment and military weakness. They suffer common characteristics such as political repression, corruption, identity crisis, ethnic and social cleavages, and dependency on the outside for security. Such factors inspired the Tunisian and Egyptian revolutions and the uprisings in Yemen, Libya, Jordan, Bahrain and Syria.

This work takes a social science approach to the investigation of the dynamics of Arab states' foreign policy-making. It is an attempt to understand the evolution of Arab politics in the troubled contemporary world. It sets out a paradigm or a road map that will help decision-makers, scholars, researchers, and students of Middle Eastern politics to understand Arab politics. The purpose of the study is as much to stimulate discussion as to present an overall indigenous cultural interpretation. Earlier versions of some of the chapters have been published in reviewed academic journals in both Arabic and English. The present work does not try to examine all variables involved, problems faced or factors determining Arab states' foreign policy undertakings. Nor does it claim to be the only comprehensive work on Arab politics since no paradigm is eternally valid. It is no more than another mile-stone added to the previous extensive and significant works by both Arab and non-Arab scholars on the road to understand contemporary Arab politics.

The main objective of this book is to examine the different, external and internal, variables shaping the Arab states' foreign policy undertakings in the contemporary post-cold war world. Numerous challenges face the Arab in the post-cold war era. While I accept the heterogeneity among the Arab countries, I here look at the Arab states as one political unit. The study is based on the assumption that the Arab states' foreign policy-makings are determined by similar external and domestic environmental variables. The attempt is to understand the ongoing political dynamics of the region. I do not predict the future of the Arab regional system, but rather analyse what is at stake. As Charles Maynes once wrote: 'no one can predict the unpredictable. All we can know is that important but unpredictable events will happen.'[2]

The work's key assumption is that, despite the Arabs' contribution to raising the strong winds of change that have swept the international world order, they themselves, until recently, have only reaped the storm. It relies on analyses and deduction, seeking to stay neutral throughout the process and arrive at objective and scientific conclusions, while also raising the level of scientific research in the Arab world. It relies on primary and secondary sources. Although the difficulties faced by the author are not unique but are those any Arab researcher faces in general, they are still worth mentioning. They include a shortage of information due to the lack of transparency in the Arab world, excessive political and social hypocrisy in Arabic reporting, and most foreign sources' lacking the indigenous cultural paradigm. Moreover, the author encountered, on the one hand, the hegemony of Western colonial culture and, on the other, Arab intellectual bias and division coupled with an absence of a culture of tolerance, which in turn has led to more social division and infighting.

The book is divided into two parts covering both the input variables and the output process. Part One looks at external and domestic variables. Chapters 1 and 2 examine the domestic constraints intended to investigate the impacts of the political, economic and social factors on the foreign policy-making process in the Arab states. The external variables are covered in Chapters 3, 4 and 5: the contemporary world order, the Arab regional system, the Arab Israeli conflict and the interactions between the Arab states and their main neighbouring countries. Part Two is dedicated to study and analyse four separate case studies as foreign policy undertakings. The choice of the case studies covered in Chapters 6, 7 and 8 was determined by their significance and importance on the macro level to enable a general comparative analysis for viewing and understanding Arab politics and its role in contemporary world affairs. Chapter 9 takes Saudi Arabia's foreign policy-making process as a case study on the micro level. Since Egypt opted for a low-profile regional foreign policy after its rehabilitation and the occupation of Iraq by the American forces since 2003, Saudi Arabia with all the potential resources and its international status found itself in the front line of Arab politics. It was unable, however, to stop the winds of change sweeping the Arab world in 2011. King Abdullah pledged five billion US dollars in support of President Mubarak maintaining power, failed to put down the Bahraini uprising, despite its military intervention, or to contain the Yemeni revolution.

The work in this book has benefited greatly from collegial and institutional support. On the collegial level, I wish to thank Shaykh Saud AlQassimi, Crown Prince of Ras Al Khaimah emirate, Shaykh Nahyan bin Mubarak Al Nahyan, the Chancellor of the United Arab Emirates University (UAEU), my colleagues at the UAEU Department of Political Science, the Dean of the Faculty of Humanities and Social Science, Professor Timothy Niblock from the University of Exeter and Dr Peter Woodward from the School of Politics and International Relations at the University of Reading for their valuable comments and continuous support to make this longstanding objective a reality. On the institutional level, all my thanks go to both the UAEU, which granted me a two-year sabbatical, and the University of Reading for hosting me and offering me a fellowship status during my stay. I wish also to extend my thanks to my family, parents, wife and children, without whose constant encouragement I would not have been able to finish this work. Last but not least, I would like to express my profound appreciation to all those who assisted me in one way or another, particularly those who translated, edited and typed all or part of this book.

Introduction: A Road Map

The Arab world's considerable material and human potential, its strategic geographical location and its oil wealth should allow it to play a major role in the contemporary world order. However, at a time when a number of Arab countries have 45 per cent of the world's proven oil reserves and invest around US$1,400 billion abroad, many still suffer from scientific, cultural and social underdevelopment. Around 70 million Arab children, out of a total population of 335 million, are deprived of their right to an education and a number of Arab states are burdened with heavy debt, amounting in 2006 to around US$800 billion. This book investigates Arab foreign policy-making in such a troubled age. It seeks to understand the dynamics of foreign policy by analysing domestic constraints and international pressure. This introduction presents a theoretical framework or a road map for study of the troubled Arab world.

Social scientists have tried to understand the political changes sweeping the world. Alvin Toffler linked globalization to the technological revolution, while others, such as John Gilbert and Marshall McLuhan, have talked about the 'abundant society' and the 'global village'. Francis Fukuyama went even further and argued that 'we may be witnessing the end of history', saluting the predominance of the Western economic and political model. In his book on the clash of civilizations, Samuel Huntington pointed out that 'the end of the cold war has not ended conflict but has rather given rise to new identities rooted in culture'.[1] He spoke of clashes between the Islamic/Confucian civilizations with the West or with each other. He attributed the rise of the East Asia to a spectacular rate of economic growth, and the resurgence of Islam to a spectacular rate of population growth. 'Overall Muslims constituted perhaps 18 per cent of the world's population in 1980 and are likely to be over 20 per cent in 2000 and 30 per cent in 2025.'[2] A study released in October 2009 revealed that the number of Muslims is 1.57 billion, making 23 per cent of the world population of 6.8 billion people.[3] George W. Bush, the former US president, used the term 'Crusade' in his talks describing his war on terror.

'Power is the ability of one person or group to change the behaviour of another person or group.'[4] Are the Arabs and Muslims currently more influenced by the dominant Western culture than the other way round, given the lackof partity between the two sides? In the second half of the twentieth century, the Arab world witnessed a tremendous scientific and cultural renaissance. Some Arab countries successfully eradicated illiteracy, and Arab culture spread and was recognizable worldwide. Yet this Islamic renaissance was paralysed, if not totally annihilated, by the unequal encounter between the East and the West, from which emerged many schisms and intellectual currents. Since the downfall of the Ottoman Empire intellectual divisions have prevailed in the Arab world.[5] Arab individuals now face an identity crisis, being no longer able to answer the legitimate questions 'Who am I?' and 'Who are we?'

Economists agree that sustainable development has the human person as its centre and main objective. From a quick reading of development indicators in the Arab world, one finds that the ranking of Arab countries in the human development report ranges from 40th for Qatar, the highest on the list, to 151st, for Yemen, the lowest, with Iraq and Somalia not included due to their particular circumstances.[6] On this basis, the researcher can state unequivocally that conditions in the Arab countries are not very different from those in other underdeveloped countries. Manifestations of underdevelopment are many and varied.

World order is described as the pattern of interaction between international actors in the political, economic, cultural and sports domains, in the form of either cooperation or conflict. After its inception upon the signing of the Treaty of Westphalia, in 1648, the contemporary world order passed through several stages, from a uni-polar to a multi-polar world, to a bi-polar, to a uni-polar, after the collapse of the Soviet Union and the Second Gulf War of 1991, and finally, today, it is once again developing towards a multi-polar world. Sweeping international changes that brought an end to the cold war era have helped the United States to impose hegemony on the world at the lowest possible cost.[7] Huntington, however, argues that the end of the cold war inspired a 'power shifting from the long predominant West to non-Western civilizations. Global politics has become multi-polar and multicivilizational.'[8] These international changes have had significant and deeply negative repercussions for the international order in general, and the Arab regional order and regimes in particular, with repeated calls being made to replace the latter with a new Middle Eastern order,[9] or a 'Greater Middle East'.[10]

On the one hand, American hegemony was imposed on international affairs and, as a result, small states lost whatever room for manœuvre they had once possessed. On the other, the structures and tools of globalization reinforced this American hegemony by promoting it economically, culturally and through the media.[11] 'Americanization' became synonymous with 'globalization', the two terms becoming inseparable, each unfathomable without the other. For example, spreading American university education and transferring its terminologies, tenets, curricula and intellectual processes involves not only the globalization of university education, but also its worldwide Americanization.[12] However, the global economic crisis prompted a retreat from globalization to localization producing a new world order (see Chapter 3). Moreover, despite the fact that this international order is in general increasingly democratic, respectful of human rights and integrated, the Arab individual's share has not even reached the lowest common denominator. The Arabs have actively contributed to making these international changes possible, starting with Egypt's shift into the Western camp under Sadat, the convergence of Arab and American interests over the Soviet invasion of Afghanistan, and some Arab governments and salafi Islamist groups (like Bin Laden's) concluding alliances with the US against the Soviet Union. Some Arab countries contributed to the cold war between the Eastern and Western blocs by offering economic and logistical support to the United States, for example by linking their currencies to the dollar, forcing OPEC to tie oil sale to the US dollar, shifting large investments to Western markets and granting the Americans military facilities, sometimes even military bases. Saudi Arabia went even further by spending large sums of money in an attempt to check the Soviet advance in the region, if not the whole world. Saudi enmity towards Communism was not limited to severing all relations with the Soviet Union and combating communist movements in the region (South Yemen, Oman and Somalia), but they even provided financial assistance, upon the Americans' request, to the Contra rebels fighting the socialist Sandinista government in Nicaragua (see Chapter 9). The overwhelming majority of Arab countries (including Syria) did not hesitate to conclude an alliance with the US in its war on Iraq, and many of them took part in the Annapolis Conference, thus providing the American initiative with an Arab umberalla, despite the inherent contradictions between it and the Arabs' own initiative.

Regional and international developments in August 1990 marked the beginning of a transformation in the Arab–Israeli conflict. The outcome of these developments culminated in the birth of new regional forces and variables determining not only regional interactions, prompting greater US involvement, but also causing regional instability and a new cold war in interregional affairs. The Arabs became the weakened party in the regional equation with Israel and Iran becoming the main players.[13] Turkey, from 2003, with the accession to power of the AKP, adopted a conciliatory approach towards regional issues, with a more lenient policy towards Arab states and issues, especially the Palestinian cause on the one hand, and voice its concerns and opinions openly, for the first time, on the political developments in Egypt, Libya, Bahrain and Syria.

The shifting balance of power in favour of Israel brought with it fragile peace agreements. As of this date, all peace treaties and negotiations between the two parties, from the Madrid Conference in 1991 to Annapolis in November 2007, were the natural outcome of the earthquake that was the Second Gulf War. This period also witnessed major transformations in international relations, the most important of which was the collapse of the Eastern bloc and the dismantling of the Soviet empire, as well as other factors that led both the Arabs and Israel to seek negotiations instead of a military confrontation. Among these factors was the growing Islamic revival, represented by Hamas and Islamic Jihad in Palestine, and the Islamic resistance in southern Lebanon, which threatened the presence of Israel but also posed a direct threat to Arab regimes in the region. Another contributing factor was the internal situation in the United States, which would make it difficult for the Americans to continue backing Israel's security for decades to come. The Americans tried to distance Israel from Arab threats and ensure its safety and stability by working to normalize its relations with Arab countries. Among the main aims of the American–Israeli meeting that took place in December 2004 was to re-engineer a political map of the Middle East that steered the Arabs towards closer links with Israel and the United States, within the framework of bilateral relations, at the expense of inter-Arab relations and various bilateral and collective economic and security agreements.[14] Arab national security is challenged not only by the Israeli threat, but also by many other domestic constraints, namely the lack of legitimacy of political regimes, water scarcity and the food insecurity due to the insufficiency of local food production and the increasing dependency on the outside market for food security. The immediate threat, however, came from within, with the growing social unrest that finally culminated in the Tunisian and Egyptian revolutions and the uprisings in other Arab countries. The changes in the Arab world since early 2011 add value to the analyses in this book about the domestic and international factors determining Arab foreign policy-making and substantiate the argument that foreign policy is the outcome of interaction between internal and external variables. For instance, the role played by the international factor through the security decision to impose a no-fly zone over Libya was detrimental.

The purpose of this study is to reach a better understanding of Arab foreign policy-making in an instable world, characterized by tremendous external pressures through the trend of globalization along with greater domestic pressures on governments to pursue foreign policy more inclined to serve local objectives. The new trend of glocalization has spurred a retreat from globalization to attend more to local immediate needs. Therefore, the situation in the developing world, including the Arab states, becomes more intense and complex. The book studies the determinants of Arab states' foreign policy during the period 1979 to 2009, although relevant material from before or after the specified periods is not neglected.

The methodology pursued in this book is based on the input–output model[15] whereby the process of foreign policy-making goes through fourfold interdependent stages: the input, the foreign policy-making apparatus, the output or undertakings, and the feedback which then becomes part of the input for decision-enhancement or change. James Rosenau divides the process into the independent variables, the intervening variables and the dependent variables. Students of foreign policy have not only failed to produce a comprehensive framework, but they differ on whether or not to include the external milieu[16] or the internal milieu in the case of the developing countries since their foreign policies are merely reactions to the international environment. The foreign policy-making process is usually done on a PESTEL model of analysis taking into account all the different variables involved: historical, geographical, social, cultural, ideological, political, legal, bureaucratic, economical and ecological emanating from both the domestic and external milieux that include both human and non-human factors. Foreign policy study, despite various attempts[17] to provide a comprehensive theoretical framework, lacks the coherence to test generalizations that treat societies as agents subject to stimuli that produce external responses.[18] Part of the difficulty in analysing determinants of foreign policy is the complexity: 'there are so many interacting sets of variables one might look at when explaining the action of states.'[19]

Foreign policy is the outcome of the interactions that take place between the internal and external factors coloured by the decision makers' perception of current events. The author has used such methodology in his previous works on the *Foreign Policy of the United Arab Emirates* (1989) and the *GCC States in an Unstable World: Foreign-Policy Dilemmas of Small States* (1994) and found it useful for a better understanding of the dynamics of Arab states' foreign policy-making. This work does not claim that the methodology that has been adopted for the study of the dynamics of foreign policy in Arab states is the only approach, but that it is possibly the most appropriate. Therefore, the analyses are intended to give the reader an initial picture of the current situation in the Arab world and to draw a road map. The variables investigated and analysed in this book are by no means the only variables determining Arab states foreign policy-making, but I claim that they are the most important. I hold the Rosenau view that the foreign policy-making process goes through three main stages: the dependent, the intervening and the independent variables plus the feedback which acts in many cases as an input as system-supporting or system challenging (see Figure 1).

The domestic milieu includes all human and non-human factors within the national border of a state whereas the external milieu includes all human and non-human factors outside the national boundaries. The book is divided into two main parts. The first part covers the input process, discussing the internal and external milieux. Chapters 1 and 2 include the discussion and investigation of intra- and inter-Arab politics and socio-economic variables. Chapters 3, 4 and 5 are dedicated to investigating the external milieu, analysing the impacts of the contemporary world order developments, the Arab regional order and the Arab–Israeli conflict. Part Two is devoted to the study of the output since, in many cases, it becomes part of the input for policy-enhancing or policy-changing. It also seeks to understand the dynamics of Arab states' policies through the discussion and investigation of the different variables involved in shaping certain foreign policy undertakings on the macro-level, to generalize the determining factors of Arab countries' foreign policy-making. Chapters 6, 7 and 8 study the Arab countries' foreign policies towards the Middle East peace process, water scarcity and the possibility of water wars in the region and the food crisis. Chapter 9 is a micro-level case study of Saudi Arabia's foreign policy-making. Saudi Arabia has been chosen simply because of the increasing Saudi role in regional and international politics.

Part One

THE INPUT PROCESS

CHAPTER I

Political Aggregations and Political Articulations

1. Introduction

It is not easy to define political underdevelopment in the Arab world, though it is possible to recognize some of its manifestations. Analysts usually start by distinguishing between politically advanced countries and those to which the economic terms 'developing countries' or 'in the process of development' apply. In this context Talcott Parsons formulated a set of factors, comprising a generality of jobs, laws, achievements, specializations, public interests and emotional neutrality. What he means by 'generality' is that the yardsticks for political mobilization and the issuing of laws are general and concern an entire community rather than specific persons to the exclusion of others. The 'achievement' factor refers to the fact that these communities rely on performance and efficiency in their evaluation, and that social connections do not play an important role in their political choices. In addition, they are advanced scientifically, because they respect specialization and are not founded on superficiality. They are also public spirited and strive to advance the public interest without, however, neglecting personal interests. They rely on logic, reason and common sense, and emotions do not play a key role in their daily lives and political activities. Some thinkers have attempted to qualify political underdevelopment without specifying particular indicators or groups: for these, a society is 'more or less modern depending on its use of new elements of power, and advanced tools, to maximize the outcome of its efforts'. They also believe that a modern society (i.e. one that is politically advanced) is the result of the historical adaptation process by institutions, with fast-changing jobs that reflect the unprecedented increase in man's knowledge, and allow him to control his environment.[1] Arab governments, Samuel Huntington argued, are overwhelmingly undemocratic: monarchies, one-party system, military junta, personal dictatorship or some combination of these, 'usually resting on limited family, clan, or tribal base and in some cases highly dependent on foreign support'.[2]

My study is based on the hypothesis that the political regimes of the majority of Arab states lack political legitimacy, are undemocratic and that inter-Arab political dynamics are characterized by competition, distrust and power struggles. The political situation in both Tunisia and Egypt, though moving towards democratization, is still unstable and difficult to predict. In an attempt to analyse and assess Arab states' foreign policy undertakings, this chapter will discuss the political process, and the analysis of political aggregations and political articulations includes political legitimacy, the democratic process and the inter-Arab political dynamics and their impacts on the dynamics of foreign policy-making. The importance of this stems from the fact that foreign policy-making is envisaged in the executive authority whereas the legislative and judicial powers are paralysed by their total dependence on the former for information and interpretations of policies.

2. Lost Political Legitimacy

Political legitimacy is linked to the degree of political development achieved by a given country. Politically advanced societies possess attributes such as diverse political (i.e. institutional) structures, democracy, a proper system of accessing power and the successive ability to achieve several objectives. On this basis, political underdevelopment might be identified as follows.

> It is the weakness of a political regime's ability to mobilize its members' and institutions' efforts for the pursuit of the higher objective. It could therefore be seen as the failure to formulate a new political value system that compels its constituent elements to acquire new constructive outlooks, and engage in participatory activities.[3]

In short, political underdevelopment is due to a political system's lack of 'row potential', including the ability to maintain contact with intermediary agencies and non-governmental organizations (NGOs), not to mention the requisite economic resources to complement this potential. This limits both the possibility and the desire to bring up a new breed of individuals and institutions, or mobilize those already available, to achieve the country's higher political objectives. Political underdevelopment also carries with it a certain lack of clarity as to what a political regime's higher political objectives are, whether in the short or the long term. A politically underdeveloped society is therefore one that is unable to have an overview of the future because it is not yet able to ascertain the scope or full range of its current political manœuvrability. Arab governments lack any bases for justifying their rule in terms of Islamic, democratic or even nationalist values.[4] It is argued that Arab states are an 'artificial creation'. Their borders were drawn by the colonial powers and do not represent naturally ordained living spaces for homogeneous ethnic, linguistic and religious groups. Arab states' borders 'often appear contrived, enclosing diverse ethnic, religious and linguistic groups that were incorporated as minorities in the post colonial era'.[5]

The Arab regimes are corrupt and brutal. Corruption constitutes the main obstacle to the development process. A questionnaire responded to by 150 officials from 60 underdeveloped countries confirmed that corruption is the main obstacle facing development.[6] Examples of corruption in the Arab world are many and cover almost all Arab countries from the Gulf States to Morocco. The Tunisian and Egyptian revolutions have unveiled this fact. The kings, presidents and emirs have enhanced their grip on the local business sector giving free rein to their associates and relatives; for example, Al-Walid Ibn Talal in Saudi Arabia, Alla'a Mubarak in Egypt, the Al-Trapolsi family in Tunisia, Al-Makhloof, Al-Shalish, Al-Asaad and Al-Akhrass in Syria or party members as in Iraq, Lebanon and Yemen. They give high priority to arms deals, not to be used, but to amass booty and plunder resources. Gulf ruling families have fleets of aircrafts that are private, but paid for with public funds.[7] The war lords in Lebanon dragged the country into fifteen years of civil war and instability and threatened the country's independence because of their foreign connections, reflecting that personal interests supersede loyalty to the state. Monopoly of power, censorship, banning political parties, outlawing trade unions, espionage, restrictions on the freedom of expression, bullying, discrimination on tribal, religious, ethnic and sectarian bases, imprisonment of oppositions, forcing opposition members into early retirement, and injustice are common to all Arab regimes, to differing degrees. Senior official posts in the foreign office, the interior and finance and the chief of staff of the armed forces are always assigned to either family members or senior personnel or close associates, regardless of their suitability for the post. Personal allegiance rather than to the state is the prerequisite. It was argued that as population increases in the Arab world, so governments become more complex, the ruling elites grow more distant from the ruled and the regimes' legitimacy face an increasing danger of gradual erosion.[8]

The political, religious and cultural terrain of the Arab world has not been fertile ground for democracy. Salama argued that Arab governments are fragile, dependent and that the political systems are scared, insecure and believe that dependence on foreign powers represents the best insurance policy for their survival.[9] The fact that contemporary Arab states are artificial and the by-product of colonial divisions has cost them legal legitimacy, and raised questions about their legitimate nature.[10] Oil in some Arab countries has freed oppressive governments from the need to raise taxes and thereby expose themselves to those pressures that raising taxes brings, such as for accountability and political participation.[11] Members of the ruling elites have become businessmen competing with the local bourgeoisie but also defending the business social strata's interests in the form of political articulations. Therefore, the ruling elites have increasingly allied themselves to the oligopolistic business group that emerged in the 1990s. The private sector has not been politically active in the Arab world. Local bourgeoisie has always been weak and dependent on governments simply because, in reality, they are compradors, not real businessmen. They tend to support the ruling party or family. Arab entrepreneurs have not been prominent in the political reform process.[12] In fact, they constitute the second social group for political recruitment to senior official posts. Arab governments followed the colonial legacy of greater dependence on minorities for political support for their unpopular policies. This is clearly manifested in the fact that minorities have always represented pools for political recruitment. The refusal of the ruling elites to share power has left Arab governments exposed to criticism, and threatens state security and stability.[13]

Reforms pursued in most Arab countries failed to confer political legitimacy or ease social unrest since they were cosmetic. Elections held in some of these countries could not 'substitute for legitimacy based on consensual political participation within the framework of clear rules of the game'.[14] Reforms adopted, despite their significance, have not changed the structural basis of power, where the executive branch still dominates, unchecked by any form of accountability.[15] On the contrary, steps taken in the so-called Arab republics to maintain power through changing the succession procedures from a scrutinized closed selection to a hereditary approach similar to the other Arab monarchies and sheikhdoms mark the decay in those political systems. The Syrian constitution was amended to open the way for the appointment of Bashar Assad, the son of the late president Hafiz Assad. Egypt, Yemen and Libya are expected to follow suit. Colonel Gaddafi has held absolute power since 1 September 1969, calling himself the King of the Kings. The Libyan people are among few peoples all over the contemporary world that have not witnessed any elections or change in ruling power for four decades. Moreover, the Libyan people have suffered the absence of a free press and partisan life or real civic institutions. There are only those institutions established by Gaddafi as propaganda machines, to praise him and glorify his book 'The Green Book'.[16] The perceived absence of political legitimacy has made efforts at developing good and transparent governance very difficult.[17] There is simply the absence of the rule of law, fuelling violent rebellions against the Gaddafi and Saleh regimes. Thus, dependency values foster negative trends that lead to isolationism and carelessness, so that political underdevelopment not only affects good political governance, but also has an impact on people, institutions, values and behaviour. 'Increasing transparency will make it difficult for governments to continue the kind of policies they so routinely carried out in the past.'[18] The global financial and domestic social crises faced by the middle class would ultimately and eventually erode the material gains of the other social strata and further weaken the legitimacy of the existing political regimes.[19] The Arab states are irrational and weak, internally violent, based on tribal solidarity, and old forms of governing principle based on the personality of the leader illustrate the fragility of their political legitimacy. Political underdevelopment in the Arab world may therefore be summarized as follows:

1. There are internal schisms and divisions, and often loyalty to one's family, tribe, sect or region supersedes loyalty to the state. 'The homogenising project of the Arab states has never been a smooth transition towards inclusion. Rather, a strong nationalistic trend developed with the objective of masking the diversity of the population and subduing its cultural, linguistic and religious heterogeneity under command structure.'[20]
2. Political elites are highly insular, rigid and self-perpetuating, regardless of the potential for social mobility at the lower and middle social levels. This means that the range of political choice and mobilization is very narrow, if not entirely closed.
3. Popular participation is weak and ineffective, and most of these states rely, as a means of political choice, on appointments or referenda that are no more than proforma exercises designed to limit the citizens' options.
4. Instability has been the hallmark of Arab states, evidenced by recurrent military coups, social unrest, uprising and revolution. This is due to the absence of political organizations capable of accommodating newcomers on the political stage, such as political parties and civil society institutions, especially those seeking to play an effective role in their country's constitutional life, which explains the youth leadership of the contemporary revolutions in Tunisia, Egypt and Yemen.
5. The reliance on security forces does not in fact produce security; rather, it has fueled the revolutions in Tunisia, Egypt, Yemen, Libya and the uprisings in other Arab countries, mainly Morocco, Syria, Algeria and Jordan. Increasing roles are given to methods and tools of social control and political repression, such as military institutions, security services and the police, at the expense of civil institutions, whether technical or bureaucratic. 'The suppression of channels through which public grievances can be heard has only further reduced the acceptability of the states to many groups within

their territory.'[21] The judiciary, despite a few attempts to assert independence, a dim light at the end of the tunnel, is in most cases controlled by the state. It is plagued by a lack of transparency and due process.[22] Reformists and human rights activists in most Arab countries have become the target of repression and are the object of legal persecution, arrests,[23] dismissals,[24] forced early retirement,[25] even sometimes murder, especially in the case of Islamists.[26] They are 'bunker regimes' to use Clement Henry Moore's words, 'repressive, corrupt and divorced from the needs and aspirations of their societies'.[27] The majority of Arabs hold the opinion that their governments are losing touch with the needs and demands of their people represents an extremely serious development, as it strikes at the heart of the regimes' legitimacy.[28] The Arab world remains on or near the bottom rung of the ladder on human rights and this weakens their position in criticizing Israeli hostility against the Palestinians – the outcries against Israeli abuses have a hollow ring.[29]

6. Observers who follow political developments in the Arab world have concluded that, in order to achieve progress, symptoms of underdevelopment have to be addressed above all else. It is impossible to do this successfully if, as a first step, serious efforts are not made to introduce political reforms. In short, the winds of change that have been sweeping the world since the 1990s have had no substantial impact on the Arab world until 2011. Instead of democratization, political openness and promotion of human rights, Arab governments have taken advantage of the American so-called 'war on terror' to get rid of the opposition, under the umbrella of international legitimacy. Globalization and Western values were said to be replacing indigenous cultural values. Saudi Arabia has a dismal record on human rights. In August 2009, both Amnesty International and Human Rights Watch issued reports chastizing the Kingdom for abuses they allege were committed in the name of anti-terror campaign.[30] It has detained indefinitely more than 9,000 people under its counterterrorism programme since 2003, offering many religious 're-education' instead of judicial review to attain their freedom.[31] Ten people involved in petitioning the King were arrested in February 2007; eight of them remain in jail without charge at the time of writing. The first trial of militants linked to al-Qaeda saw one sentenced to death and 329 others to life imprisonment or house arrest.[32] The Saudi monarch, worried about what was going on around him, issued, on 18 March 2011, royal decrees intended to imrove the standard of living, curb unemployment and fight corruption. Earlier in the month, the Saudi government sought a fatwa (religious verdict) from the religious clergy, prohibiting demonstrations against the political authority. Human Rights Watch 2009 report[33] criticized the UAE record on human rights, calling for the rule of law, judiciary independence, increased freedom level and the introduction of institutional reforms. According to

> Amnesty International: 'the scale of human rights violations is shocking. Thousands of people have had their lives turned upside down or destroyed by violations of their rights in the name of countering terrorism.'[34]

The Arab states are characterized by fragile stability and a longstanding authority crisis. The relationship between the rulers and the ruled in the Arab world is not defined in accordance with Rousseau's social contract of equality, partnership and interdependence, but on dependence whereby the rulers dictate policies, rules, laws and bylaws to maintain their power. Rousseau believed that a government can only be legitimate if it has been sanctioned by the people through the sovereign.[35] Partnership means that government is effectively controlled by the general will of its populace, with participation in decision-making processes and the right to vote, object, question and change the political elite with a peaceful transition of power.[36] Arab governments, however, are founded on a patriarchal form of governance. Peterson argued that in Saudi Arabia, as well as in other Arab countries, 'the regime is the source of prosperity and social welfare, in return for which the people implicitly leave the government to decide and carry out policies without consultation'[37], but this argument has been disputed by many of the reform-orientated messages to the Saudi king. Arab political systems are characterized by an absence of peaceful means for transformation of power, a huge gap between the people (governed) and the ruling elites (governing), a lack of democratic values, different interpretations of political legitimacy, stability and ways of influencing public opinion, and a lack of effective political participation.[38] Authoritarian controls were imposed by some Arab countries in response to the rejection of the legitimacy of the kind of state which the Arab world inherited, and to conflicts that threatened state security and stability. Political legitimacy in the Arab states is disputed and based on competition, creating internal crises, confrontations, intra-state power struggles and inter-state political feuds. Challenges take different forms. Coups d'état and allegations of attempted coups as an effective tool for regime changing are common in Arab political life. Mauritania is by no means the only Arab country where the military plays an effective role in politics. Talks were engineered by Prince Bandar in Saudi Arabia in late 2008 (see Chapter 9) and it is alleged that an abortive coup was discovered in Qatar on 30 July 2009. The coup was set up by a group of sixteen military officers led by the commander in chief of the Qatari defence forces, Hamad bin Ali Al-Attayya. It is alleged that the conspiracy was inspired by Saudi Arabia and engineered by advocates of closer Qatari–Saudi relations. Qatar over its short history has witnessed two family coups, in 1970 and 1997, and an allegation of an abortive coup d'état in 2002. For this reason, local political regimes adopt isolationism, pursue an internal policy of divide and rule, domestically apply carrots and sticks, use the different means of political socialization at their disposal to indoctrinate their local public opinion and enhance a very narrow concept of the nation-state to legitimize their existence within their defined borders at the expense of pan-Arabism or Arab unity. Challenges to state legitimacy seem to be acute in some Arab countries. Consequently, contemporary Arab regimes seek legitimacy through the persistence of disintegration,[39] social cleavages, tribalism, sectarianism, poverty, backwardness and corruption. 'Most Arab states failed to introduce democratic governance and institutions of representation that ensure inclusion, the equal distribution of wealth among various groups, or respect for cultural diversity.'[40] The state= crises so created are clearly illustrated in the case of Iraq, Lebanon, Sudan and Algeria. Sa'd El-Din Ibrahim argued that the state establishments in the Arab world failed to deal with the following:[41]

1. To protect the national independence.
2. To achieve economic development.
3. To achieve social justice.
4. To culturally reform and modernize.
5. To increase political participation.

3. The Unfinished Democracy

Democracy is a word derived from the Latin word 'democracia', a compound of two syllables 'demo' and 'cracia' that literally means the people's reign. The word has been incorporated in the English language as the rule of the people by the people and for the people. Though such a definition sounds utopian, Robert Dahl argued, in his book *Democracy and its Crisis*, that democracy is a polyarchy rule or the 'rule of many'. Western analysts have laid down a set of criteria as the basis for democracy, including the degree of political participation, transparency, elections, political parties, interest groups, separation of powers, checks and balances, respect for human rights, the rights of minorities, rule of law and the freedom of speech, press, religion, practice and movement. Among the basic criteria for determining the democratic nature of the existing political system is the free choice of the political elite which makes up the three governing circles: the legislative, the executive and the judiciary are accountable to the people through well-defined and transparent codes of governance – this constitutes one of the main features of democracy. The process of selection is left open whether through direct secret ballot, as in Britain, or indirect selection through an electoral college, as in the election of the American presidency. It is argued that democratic governance relies on three conditions: 'first is to have a set of good institutions; second is to have a body of citizens who possess a good understanding of the principles of democracy; third is to have a high quality of leadership, at least at critical moment'.[42]

In some of the Arab countries the institutionalization of political participation was hindered as the regimes secured their powers through colonial protection, mobilization of force and oil income. They began to feel that they no longer needed to sacrifice any of their prerogatives and authorities. However, despite the fact that political participation was not totally absent during this period, the region was and still is characterized by political instability. There were repeated coups d'état, social and political unrest, banning of oppositions, the continuing violation of human rights and an authoritarian code of conduct in many Arab states.

Political participation is a 'process whereby individuals engage in activity that impinges directly upon the national power and authority structure of society. This activity can be system-challenging or system-supportive.'[43] Political systems in most of the Arab world have been traditionally closed systems. The contemporary Arab status quo is a continuation of the old structure with variations between one country and another and from time to time. Theoretically it is neither democratic, nor oligarchic, nor theocratic, but a mixture of all three. Likewise it is based on a combination of political legitimacy, political rationality and victorious tribal solidarity. It is characterized by contrast: between the old and the new, the ancient norms and the contemporary values, renaissance and revolution, heritage and modernity and locality, Arabism and Islam.[44] Popular demand for democratic transformation and popular participation is a nascent and fragile development in the Arab world until 25 January 2011.[45] The degree of the formal political participation varies from one Arab country to the other (see Table 1). The institutionalization of political participation came about with the end of the colonial era in the second half of the twentieth century. Some Arab countries like Lebanon, Kuwait, Mubarak's Egypt, Morocco, Jordan and recently Iraq, Algeria and Yemen have embarked on some liberalization of their political systems, whereas others are mainly characterized by being authoritarian-technocratic-traditional and others are authoritarian-technocratic-distributive.[46] The emergence of political participation in some parts took place after regime change by revolution like in Tunisia and Egypt, a coup d'état (Mauritania), foreign intervention (Iraq) or international pressures, whilst in others it was enhanced by the ruling families' realization of the importance of engaging their people in the political process (Kuwait) to secure state's security and stability.

Table 1.1 Electoral Turnout in Eighteen Arab States (2003–2008)

State	Parliamentary	Presidential	Local
Algeria	35.5% (2007)	59.3% (2004)	—
Bahrain	72% and 73.6% (2 rounds in 2006)	—	61% (2006)
Djibouti	72.6% (2008)	78.9% (2005)	—
Egypt	28.1% (2005) 31.2% (2007)	23% (2005)	—
Iraq	76.9% (2005)	—	—
Jordan	54% (2007)	—	—
Kuwait	59.4% (2008)	—	Less than 50% (2005)
Lebanon	46.4% (2005)	—	—
Mauritania	73.4% & 69.4% (2 rounds in 2006) 98.2% & 97.6% (2 rounds in 2007)	70.1% & 67.5% (2 rounds in 2007)	73.4% & 69.4% (2 rounds in 2006)
Morocco	37% (2007)	—	54"% (2003)
Oman	62.7% (2007)	—	—
OPT*	77.6% (2006)	66.5% (2005)	—
Qatar	—	—	30% (2007)
Saudi Arabia	—	—	70% (2005)
Sudan	—	86% (2000)	—
Syria	56% (2007)	95.8% (2007)	49.5% & 37.8% (2007)
Tunisia	91.4% (2004)	91.5% (2004)	82.7% (2005)
Yemen	75.9% (2003)	65.1% (2006)	65% (2006)

*Occupied Palestinian Territories.
Source: UNDP/RBAS 2008; IPU 2008; Egypt SIS, 2008 et al.
UNDP, *Arab Human Development Report,* 2009, p. 74.

Political challenges to the Arab political systems are enormous, stemming from external threats and the domestic desire to develop. Calls for political reforms took different shape, nature and scope, some of which were violent. The changes took the form of revolution, coups d'état and evolution. The degree of response to the reform movements in the Arab world differed from republican states, as in Egypt, Algeria, Tunisia, Libya, Syria, Iraq and Yemen, to monarchies whereby reforms are either gifted or conceded to the demands of the people, as in Kuwait, Jordan and Bahrain. The reform movements of 1938 in Bahrain, Dubai and Kuwait called for the institutionalization of representative councils in these emirates. Although the ruling families reacted differently to such demands, the movements represented the seeds for change and had positive effects on political developments in these emirates.[47] However, Abdalaziz Ibn Saud, who founded the Kingdom of Saudi Arabia in 1932, opposed the reform movements in these countries. He believed that people should not be encouraged to seize power.[48] His position failed to stop the winds of change from affecting the Saudi internal political developments. One of his own sons, Prince Talal Ibn Abdul Aziz, in the late 1950s and early 1960s, called for the establishment of a democratic constitutional monarchy.[49] He reiterated his position in April 2009, warning that the kingdom was not prepared to face the challenges of the twenty-first century. Prince Talal said: 'there needs to be increased dialogue within the ruling family and calls for greater power for Ashura Council to pave the way for eventual elections.'[50]

The discovery of oil in the mid-twentieth century had dual effects. It strengthened the powers of the ruling families and promoted social and political change. Governments manipulated oil wealth through the distribution of its income,[51] allocating a large proportion of this for security expenses to maintain the status quo.[52] Oil inaugurated the increasing importance of the region in world politics and encouraged the spread of education, which inspired social changes. Such developments, accompanied by the appeal of pan-Arab nationalism, prompted new demands for power sharing. This tendency has acquired growing importance due to social and political developments since the 1950s.

The governments' responses to public demands for political participation differed from one country to the other. Some Arab states embarked on parliamentary experiments, like Lebanon, Iraq, Palestine, Algeria and to a lesser extent Egypt, Morocco, Jordan, Yemen, Mauritania, Sudan, Kuwait and Bahrain. Others adopted less radical initiatives and set up consultative bodies: for example, Syria, Oman, Qatar, UAE and Saudi Arabia. The Saudis, although they refrained until recently from launching any formal means of political participation, maintained regular contact with the 'Ulama and incorporated the new technocrats within the political infrastructure. Although power rests in royal prerogatives, 'the King needed to take into account the opinions and interests of other members of the royal family, the 'Ulama, the commercial sector and the tribal leaders'.[53]

The Arab world was not immune to world political developments. Demands for constitutional political reforms go back to the late nineteenth-century crossing from the Arab renaissance to the nationalist movement to Islamic political resurgence. The Arab world throughout history responded as a single entity to any international development. The call for reform affected the Gulf subregion as early as the 1920s. Bahrain witnessed the convention of the National Conference held in 1920 which called for the adherence to the Islamic Shari'ah, the election of Shura Majlis and the establishment of a court to deal with pearl diving issues and problems. However, the British protectorate authorities refused to concede to these demands and expelled the national movement leaders. Upon independence in 1971, Bahrain embarked immediately on constitutional democracy in response to public demands. The first National Assembly was inaugurated in December 1973. The assembly consisted of sixty members, half of whom were elected. Among the elected members, eleven belonged to Islamic groups and several were nationalists. The results of the election were alarming and unacceptable to most of the ruling families in the conservative Gulf States.[54] The Bahraini experience, however, did not last long. The parliament, because of regional pressure,[55] was dissolved on 26 August 1975. Scholars believe that, although dissolutions of parliaments in both Bahrain and Kuwait were carried out because they became critical of government policies, Saudi Arabia played a significant role in bringing these parliamentary experiments to an end.[56] According to some sources, Saudi Arabia paid $350 million for the dissolution of the Bahraini parliament.[57] Following the eviction of Iraqi forces from Kuwait, the Emir decided to set an election date to restore parliament. A prominent Kuwaiti opposition leader revealed that Saudi Arabia and the other GCC members were worried about the implications and impact of Kuwaiti democratic process on their people.[58] It is argued that Saudi Arabia is combating the Kuwaiti democratic experiment, attempting to scare the people of the other GCC countries about its instable outcomes in its petition to contain the spread of democracy.[59] 'Saudi Arabia faces growing pressures for political participation, at least from the expanding educated sector of its population.'[60] The Saudi perception of democracy always has been negative. The idea that people could influence decisions by attending the ruler's court or private congregation does not negate the fact that the Gulf States' political systems lack real and effective political participation. The Majlis system could not be described as a form of democratic representation. As Tim Niblock has observed in reference to those who have praised the representativeness of the Majlis system: 'This is incorrect, for the ability to express views to the decision-maker is not equivalent to having a share in determining what decisions are made.'[61]

The earlier parliamentary experiments in both Bahrain and Kuwait were short-lived and halted by emiri decrees. However, the Kuwaiti experience has been the longest among the GCC states. In 1921 the Emir decided, for the first time, to set up Ashura Majlis to help him run the country, but it was soon abolished. Upon independence in 1961, a body consisting of thirty-one members, twenty of whom were elected, was established. Among other achievements, this assembly enacted the Kuwaiti constitution proclaimed on 11 November 1962. The constitution demonstrates the Kuwaiti commitment to political participation. The Kuwaiti experience, however, revealed the limits to the emiri government's willingness to tolerate popular involvement in the decision-making process. The Emir dissolved the parliament three times, in 1976, in 1986 and 2009. His subsequent decision to set up an advisory national council, after 1986, was rebuffed by the opposition on grounds that it was unconstitutional.[62] The opposition accused the government of power monopoly and of circumventing democracy.[63] Kuwait was the scene of several angry pro-democracy demonstrations against the Emir's decision to freeze the only Arab Gulf parliamentary experiment. After one rancorous protest, in spring 1990, several people, including prominent figures, were arrested.[64]

Kuwait has witnessed two significant political developments since 1991. The first was the inauguration in December 1991 of the first political party in Kuwait, al-Munbar al-Dimuqraty.[65] The party was organized by members of the former democratic movement. Its formation is seen as a major challenge to the ruling al-Sabah family, although its organizers are not keen to describe the new political entity as a party.[66] The second development was the demand to grant women the right to vote.[67] Following liberation, the effort to extend them full political rights was renewed by a much larger number of Kuwaitis.[68] Since the 1992 parliamentary election, women have actually entered the public space of political activity. The idea of granting women the right to vote[69] enjoyed the support of the Emir, his crown prince, and a number of parliament members (MPs). Despite the political debates and the different point of views expressed on this issue, legislation granting equal political rights to women was finally passed in 2006. However, on the first occasion, no female candidate secured the necessary votes to be elected. In a further step enhancing the democratic life, the Kuwaiti government in January 1992 lifted restrictions imposed on the freedom of the press since 1986.[70] The Emir's 1990 promise to restore the parliament was a factor in uniting the political opposition behind the national effort to restore Kuwaiti sovereignty following the Iraqi annexation. Elections were held in 1992 in which the opposition won a majority. After Kuwait regained its sovereignty, and despite the ups and downs in the government–parliament relations, subsequent Emirs were more reluctant to use their prerogative to dissolve parliament and pursued a more conciliatory approach in dealing with crises. Sheikh Sabah al Ahmed, the incumbent Emir, chose, in 2008, to go through government reshuffles three times to avoid dissolving parliament, but on 18 March 2009 he did dissolve it and called for elections in May. The parliament resumed its practice on 29 June 2009 with four female members for the first time in Kuwaiti history.

Consideration of checks and balances helps in evaluating the democratic process in any given country. Contemporary Arab governments present a mixture of presidential and parliamentary systems. Any Arab government constitutionally adheres, at least in theory, to the contemporary principles of good governance based on separation of powers, rule of law, peaceful transformation of power, checks and balance ... and so on. In practice, however, the executive authority represented by the ruling families, party or/and military junta, holds all powers envisaged in a state. Each Arab government applies the separation of powers and the checks and balances principles by having three organs of a government – the presidency, a parliament and the judiciary – and some of them hold elections to choose the president or members of parliament, making them theoretically accountable to the people. However, they continue to lack transparency, there is an absence of the rule of law and they do not adhere to any democratic principles. It is argued that Arab countries today are characterised by:[71]

> the exclusion of civil society from decision making, the absence of political freedoms, the politicization of Islam, the absence of good governance, terrorism, the lack of peaceful rotation of power, the suppression of pluralism, obstacles young people face in attaining public office, the oppression of minorities, and stifling bureaucracy and wide corruption in governments.

Demands for reforms in the Arab world, since the early 1990s, have acquired a significant importance in its political life. The demands for greater political participation have taken different forms. They are manifested in public debates,[72] press articles,[73] conferences[74] and the presenting of memoranda to governments soliciting public demands.[75] For example, the Islamists in Saudi Arabia presented King Fahd with a memorandum in May 1991 calling for the institution of

Ashura council, more accountability to the people, the codification of all laws and regulations on the basis of Shari'ah in order to achieve social justice, and to give more consideration to qualifications and merit than to kinship.[76] The demands centre around three broad issues: the establishment of freely elected legislative bodies; more political freedoms; and respect for human rights.[77] Kuwaiti demands for the restoration of democratic life intensified with the beginning of the second Gulf crisis. People began to be critical of government policies and the way it handled problems with Iraq. The government also was accused of misusing power and of corruption. In response, the Kuwaiti Emir declared on 2 June 1991 that parliamentary elections would be held in October 1992.[78] The Kuwaiti opposition groups immediately mobilized to express their disappointment at postponing the election date so far into the future.[79] In October 1992 the opposition won thirty-one out of fifty seats in parliament. Yet the Kuwaiti experience cannot be described as a democratic form of government, on two grounds: first, the 1962 constitution grants the Emir absolute power to dissolve the parliament and suspend the application of any article of the constitution, as has been practised in the past. Second, the Emir continues to enjoy the right to appoint members of the ruling family to the key ministerial posts of defence, foreign affairs and the interior.[80] The constitution is seen from two opposing perspectives by the people and the ruling family. The former believes that it is a contract between the people and the ruling al-Sabah family. The latter sees it as gifted by the Emir who has the authority to forestall the people's political participation through the dissolution of parliament and the suspension of the articles permitting freedom of press and speech. Nevertheless, the Kuwaiti experience is the most advanced form of political participation in the GCC countries. Oman was quick to act positively. Sultan Qaboos took the initiative to reform the process of political participation in his country. On 12 November 1991, he issued royal decree number 94/91 outlining membership, functions, terms and procedures of a Consultative Majlis. The Majlis has fifty-nine members and a speaker. Members of the first three-year Majlis term were selected by the governors of the fifty-nine administrative districts. Members of the second Majlis, which convened in 1994 for a three-year term, were elected through an indirect process. Each district elects three candidates and Sultan Qaboos issues a royal decree naming the Majlis members. The speaker of the Majlis is appointed by Sultan Qaboos. The term of each member is three years, subject to renewal. The Majlis responsibilities, under article 9, include some legislative powers in social and economic fields and members were given the right to question cabinet ministers. During 1995, several of these hearings were broadcast live on television.[81] Article 10 calls for joint meetings to be held with the government twice a year. The first Majlis was inaugurated in January 1992,[82] replacing the State Consultative Council. Qaboos in 1995 became the first ruler of the GCC countries to tolerate women's political participation. Two women have been elected to the Majlis.[83] However, despite the significance of the Omani step, real political participation remains minimal. After the uprising in February 2011, Qaboos sacked three prominent government officials, reshuffled the government, introduced some economic reforms and formed a legal committee to review the Majlis laws.

Saudi Arabia's monarch King Fahd's repeated promises to establish Ashura council were not fulfilled until March 1992. At first, his response to the public demands for political participation was negative.[84] However, in an unexpected move, the Saudi monarch declared new political reforms on 1 March 1992, announcing the establishment of Ashura council, consisting of sixty appointed members. The council is empowered to question the members of the cabinet.[85] Despite the significance of the step taken, unless followed by further measures to promote effectiveness, they are no more than a symbolic gesture because: (a) the council plays only an advisory role; (b) its members are appointed by the King and therefore they are accountable to him; (c) the number of its members is not proportional to the census of the people; (d) the powers delegated to the council is conditional on the endorsement of the King and subject to his approval. In an unprecedented move, King Fahd in June 1995 set up a new government that included for the first time twenty ministers holding doctorate degrees. In February 2009 King Abdullah conducted a major cabinet reshuffle, bringing reformists and moderate religious scholars to important posts.[86]The Saudi Monarch placed increasing emphasis on yonger modernists with higher degrees[87] to draw recruits for both the cabinet and the Majlis. The move was intended to expand political participation and to draw support from the educated elite in an attempt to weaken the opposition. The policy adopted, however, seems to have failed and militancy is growing fast in the kingdom, as has been manifested in a series of attacks on American and Saudi official establishments. A clear example is the Saudi opposition in exile and the attack on the American military compounds in Riyadh and Khobar.[88]

Bahrain is the only GCC country to witness violent protests calling for the restoration of the 1975 dissolved parliament. The Emir of Bahrain, in an initial response, issued a decree establishing a Ashura council, a consultative body. Unofficially it is intended to fulfil two separate objectives: one is to divert attention from economic and policy failures, the other is to provide a platform for discussion of policy options without threatening the country's political stability.[89] The council was inaugurated at the beginning of 1993, but it did not play more than an advisory role. According to a confidential source,[90] the Emir and his crown prince are eager to prove the importance of the council in the legislative process. They promised the members that they would immediately adopt the policies recommended by the council. This would depend, however, on the nature of the policy recommended and on the royal family's intention to legitimize the significance of the step taken in the field of political participation. The government seems to have the desire to emphasize the importance of the council as a substitute for the 1975 dissolved parliament in order to weaken the domestic opposition. The Emir announced, in a speech before the Ashura council, an increase in the council's membership and an expansion of its role in areas of public concerns. He also promised to open up the council's meetings to the public. However, unless the government concedes some of its prerogatives, transfers some legislative authority to the council, and changes the method of recruitment, Bahrain will continue to face political instability that ultimately will affect stability in the region as a whole and the Gulf subregion in particular. The only rational policy option left for Bahrain is to manage its crisis peacefully through conciliation and compromise. Bahrain is faced with a dilemma between its domestic needs and fears of Iranian influence on the one hand, and Saudi hegemony on the other. As a result of the continued demands and to defuse the social unrest characterizing the Bahraini political life, Sheikh Hamed, after his succession to power, decided to introduce some reforms to the Bahraini political system, accepting a limited share of power whereby Bahrain was transferred to a kingdom, securing himself and his immediate family the right to the throne with almost supreme powers and conceding to the public the restoration of parliament consisting of members elected directly by their constituencies. Hence, Bahrain became the second GCC country to accept the idea of power sharing. However, Bahrain's experience fell short of people's aspirations for more effective democratic measures. Bahrain, being divided ethnically and by sect, still experienced social and political unrest. The public demand for the restoration of parliament took a violent form. Extremists used explosives to blow up the Diplomat and Meridian hotels and a number of shops, offices and agencies.[91] The violence culminated in the death of a number of people[92] and the imprisonment of hundreds of demonstrators.[93] In addition to demonstrations and violence, the Bahraini government revealed in June 1996 and September 2010 the discovery of an abortive coup d'état, which it claimed in both cases were engineered by shi'is with foreign support.[94] Several accused plotters confessed on television that they were members of Bahraini Hezbollah (party of God), had been trained in Iran,[95] and had smuggled arms from Kuwait in cooperation with Kuwaiti Hezbollah.[96] Iran and Bahraini militant Shi'ites have been blamed for the violence. However, the opposition includes Sunni fundamentalists and Arab nationalists. This is substantiated by the fact that the opposition includes people like Sheikh Abdulatif al-Mahmud (an outspoken Sunni) and Ahmed al-Shamlan (an Arab nationalist), both of whom were imprisoned for their political beliefs, as well as a member of the al-Khalifa ruling family living in exile in London. Inspired by the Tunisian and Egyptian revolutions, the Bahrain opposition staged a new wave of protests, which were forcibly dealt with by the Bahraini government. Financial and military support from other GCC states further complicated the situation and resulted in varying international reactions. Thus, unless the issue is addressed in a balanced manner, no peaceful end is in sight for the Bahraini predicament. The Bahraini ruling family needs to accept the power-sharing option and manage its regional foreign policy independent of both Iran and Saudi Arabia.

In response to new political trends and tendencies, some Arab countries have embarked on limited measures encouraging political participation. 'A spate of political reforms initiated by leaders has cascaded across the Arab countries.'[97] Egypt, Jordan, Algeria and Morocco have increased the pace of democratic measures, employing a multi-party system, holding parliamentary elections, and enjoying semi-independent judiciaries and a greater degree of media freedom. Since his accession to power and more recently, to keep pace with developments in the Arab world, King Mohammed V of Morocco introduced a seven-points reform initiative, which unfortunately fell short of people's aspirations, as illustrated by the ongoing demonstrations.

The Arab people are victims of their regime/state terror. Despite the fact that the democratization process in Algeria has contributed significantly to better security and enhanced political stability, corruption continues to cloud Algerian political and economic life. On the other hand, Tunisia, since Ibn Ali assumed power, saw a retreat from democracy with more political intervention in public life, security scrutiny, infringement of personal freedom, greater media control and a ban on Islamists' activities, fraud and corruption, violations of human rights[98] and further dependence on the US for regime security. Egypt, though officially having a multi-party system, is in real political terms a one dominant party system and holds parliamentary elections amid allegations of fraud and political harassment. Islamists, al-Ikhwan al-Muslimeen (the Muslim Brotherhood), enjoy the largest popularity but are denied the right to form a political party. The chance of an independent presidential candidate is remote with the rigid requirements set forth by the ruling party. In February 2009, frustration led thousands of people from across the political spectrum to gather at Cairo International Airport to give Mohammed El Baradei, the former Director General of the IAEA, a hero's welcome and to call on him to stand for presidency. Chanting supporters for an end to the Mubarak regime see him as a new man who could inject new life in the politics of the country where the vast majority do not bother to vote. El Baradei, though he expressed his willingness to take responsibility, demanded that the constitution must be amended before taking part in the forthcoming 2011 election, insisting that the process must be seen to be free and fair and calling for supervision of the judiciary as well as international monitors. However, no such change is possible without a peaceful transition of power. Article 76 of the constitution, introduced in 2005, states that any presidential candidate must have been a leader in an officially sanctioned political party for at least a year, and any independent runner must be endorsed by 250 elected officials, including 65 MPs and 25 senators, which seems impossible with Housni Mubarak's National Democratic Party dominating both parliament and the senate.[99] However, Mubarak's regime had weakened considerably, failing to stand more than eighteen days of the revolution that opened new prospects for democracy. A national referendum, held on 19 March 2011, saw constitutional amendments approved by 77.2 per cent. Despite the different degrees of tolerance and standards of living from one country to another, the grievances of the Arab people are the same, as illustrated by the social uprisings. Gaddafi, during the past forty-two years, had been assisted by a strong tyrannical and brutal security system that targeted his opponents at home and abroad.[100] The atrocities suffered by the Libyan people during their revolution forced the Arab League, for the first time, to seek international help through the UN Security Council. Saudi Arabia continues to deny its people their basic rights, as illustrated in the social segregations on the basis of gender, discrimination on ethnic, tribal and sectarian bases and economic inequality. Many parts of Saudi Arabia, despite its wealth, lack the necessary health, educational, housing and infrastructure, adequate water and power supply. Today Saudi Arabia has a very high rate of unemployment among males: it was 25 per cent in 2005 and was estimated at 13 per cent in 2008, ranking 135 in the world.[101] The UAE, once viewed as an oasis of luxury, security and peace of mind, land of opportunity and home for exiled fellow Arabs, witnessed an increased security intervention in state affairs, imprisonment of local soft opposition, violations of basic human rights,[102] deportation of foreigners and a crackdown on media liberalization.[103] The UAE president when receiving the Lebanese parliament speaker, Nabih Berri, on 13 October 2009, reiterated the UAE Arab position and pointed out that the UAE is exercising its sovereign right in accordance with its national security, but its policy is deliberately directed against certain groups on the basis of nationality or religious sect.[104] Freedom of the press in the Arab countries is restricted by the governments' rigid laws and hijacked by government officials. Despite the different degrees of tolerance from one country to another, the press in the Arab world is expected to support their governments' policies and choices. The partial indirect election of the Federal National Council (FNC) membership in the UAE was frozen in 2008. Reports Without

Borders Secretary-General Jean-Francois sent a letter to the UAE government on 17 December 2008 voicing concern about the latest version of its proposed bill to amend the press law to ensure that the 'proposed amendments do not endanger the news media'. The proposed law has provoked uproar.[105] 'Reports Without Borders urge you to reduce the size of the fines and to restrict the powers of both the National Media Council and the court to punish the media.'[106] Amazingly, the UAE authority banned fifteen prominent writers, most of them academics, from appearing in local media for no reason other than their personal convictions. On 6 March 2011, 133 UAE nationals presented the UAE President with a petition calling for an elected FNC with legislative powers. It is argued that the absence of justice makes the state nearer to what is known in development terms as a 'predatory state'.[107] Qatar tensions have been rising over press freedom. A publicly aired argument between Doha Centre for Media Freedom and its political sponsor, Mozah Al-Missned, the wife of the Emir, livened up the peninsula in 2009.[108] Mauritania's democratization process encountered a setback with the 2008 coup d'état, but resumed after international pressure, whilst Sudan has experienced political instability and foreign intervention. International accusations of human rights abuses has been a characteristic not only of Sudan, but of all Arab countries.

Democracy in the Arab world is frustrated by illiteracy, poverty, corruption, social divisions, the socialization process and inadequate infrastructure. Changes are resisted by those who consider themselves part of the political establishment and infrastructure. They are worried that such changes could deprive them of their privileges and influence. People continue to be divided along tribal, sectarian and ideological lines. They are not united on the degree of political participation required. The facts that almost one-third of Arab people are illiterate and a significant number of them live under the poverty line or face economic hardship constitute other problems for the political process. A further drawback, as a result, is that most people lack political awareness. A large segment of Arab society, especially those in the lower social strata or with a tribal or rural background, is satisfied with the traditional way of political participation. They are not keen to change the method followed by the governments for a more democratic one. Lack of transparency and corruption constitute other obstacles facing the consolidation of real and effective democracy. People try to influence the voting behaviour of others through bribery or what commonly is known as 'buying votes'.[109] It is alleged that the ruling elite support, subsidize and lend special favours to candidates with similar party or political affiliations or tribal background during election campaigns in order to enhance the government position within parliament.[110]

Dependence on foreign powers for security represents a longstanding strategic option for Arab regimes' security that goes deep in history. Following the second Gulf crisis and the changing world order in the early 1990s, the United States became more committed to maintaining the status quo. The US presence in the area provided a security shield for existing Arab regimes. In the past, these regimes relied on the British and the French to secure their survival, whereas today the US is the guarantor of their destiny. A number of Arab countries concluded bilateral security agreements with the US, Britain and France, taking the region back to the colonial era. The security pacts concluded provide these regimes with a security umbrella, further distancing them from their people rather than helping to bring an evolutionary change towards democratization. The US and Western collusion with local strongmen has created the Arab exception – leaving the Arabs marooned in tyranny as waves of democracy broke over other parts of the world.[111] 'The United States, which is Saudi Arabia's main ally, and other Western countries rarely criticize the Gulf Arab state, which controls more than a fifth of global crude reserves and is a major holder of dollar assets as well as being a key trading nation.'[112] Consequently, the ruling elite in those countries have became more reluctant to give concessions and introduce democratic measures. Saudi Arabia and the UAE are the least receptive allies of the US, differing dramatically in their responses to Egypt and Bahrain. Arab countries used the American war on terror to eliminate their opposition with American blessings. Today, the Islamists, because of the US policy in the region, are the most alienated social group in Arab political life. It is argued that 'the West's morbid fear of political Islam has served to deny Arabs democracy in case they support Islamists'.[113] US Islamophobia was the reason that the US was initially hesitant to lend support to the Libyan Revolution despite Gaddafi's crimes against humanity. They are either banned from politics or face ruthless measures in violation of basic human rights. It is true that democracy must find its roots internally but it would be unforgivable if America's commitment to democratic principles in the region were to wane. It is argued that the US should encourage the development of democratic institutions and practices[114] because many of the crises experienced in the region were prompted by the absence of democracy and the existing authoritarian regimes in the area.[115] It is not possible to list every instance of this here, but the annual reports of human rights organizations like Amnesty International are full of condemnation for the Arab states' violations of basic human rights. Human Rights Watch accused Saudi Arabia of 'state systematic discrimination against the estimated 1.5m to 2m Shi'ites'.[116]

Separation of powers constitutes another principle absent from the Arab governing system. The executive power is headed by a president or a monarch or an emir. He is accountable to nobody, whether the people or any political institution. The supreme or high courts in Arab states are theoretically envisaged as having the power to interpret the constitutional articles, clauses and laws, settle any constitutional dispute or differences between the legislative and executive authorities, and confirm the constitutionality of government practices, including the right to review decisions taken by the government. Most of the constitutions of Arab countries emphasize the independence of the judiciary and the rule of law. However, a contemporary practice whereby such authority is delegated to the judiciary is in fact incompatible with contemporary Arab modes of governance.

The winds of change seem to have affected the people of the Arab world more than their governments. Since the early 1990s, people have talked about the necessity to reform the political systems to encourage more political liberalization. The governments' responses to public demands for political participation differed from one country to the other. Some Arab states embarked on parliamentary experiments. Kuwait, Jordan, Morocco, Algeria, Lebanon, Mauritania, Yemen and Iraq have successfully conducted competitive parliamentary elections. Jordan followed Morocco and embarked on opening up its political system by encouraging political participation, allowing a multi-party system and adopting elections for parliamentary membership. King Hussein of Jordan in 1989 introduced a 'managed democracy' form of government through the National Charter, whereby the Islamists won thirty-four out of eighty assembly seats. The success of the Islamists was alarming to the King and his Western allies. In response, he enacted new electoral laws to secure a majority in parliament of Bedouin loyalists and tribal grandees. As he grew ever more unpopular after the peace agreement with Israel in 1994, King Hussein decided to roll back his democratic reforms.[117] Other countries, like Oman, Qatar, Saudi Arabia and the UAE, adopted less radical initiatives and set up consultative bodies.[118] 'Saudi Arabia is an absolute monarchy without an elected parliament whose courts are run by clerics applying an austere version of mainstream Sunni Islam.'[119] However, none of the other Arab states could be viewed as democratic. Political parties are either banned or controlled and candidates for presidency, parliament, and the constitutional council are carefully scrutinized by the dominant party. People in most Arab countries are granted the right to elect their representatives or president from among those approved by the security forces. Lebanon, Iraq, Algeria and Mauritania hold free parliamentary elections. Iraq and Lebanon, though they are on the road to democracy, have democratic processes still governed by ethnic and sectarian narrow interests. On the other hand, both kingdoms surprisingly have appointed youngsters less than teenagers as crown princes who are likely to succeed to the throne anytime if something happened to the kings who happen to be their fathers.

Governments in Jordan are appointed by the monarch who uses appointments to the cabinet as a means to widen personal allegiance, as is illustrated in the frequent cabinet reshuffles whereby King Hussein had fifty-six premiers in forty-six years of his rule. Morocco seems to have accepted the rule of the game and appoints the leader of the majority winning party as a prime minister. Bashar Assad, in an interview, acknowledged that political reforms in Syria are not his number one priority. They come third, after political stability and economic reforms.[120] The re-election of the incumbent Algerian President Abdelaziz Bouteflika came about after the constitution was amended to give Bouteflika the right to stand for a third term and amid allegations of fraud. Mauritania's military junta, who led the coup, conceded to international pressure and held a presidential election in July 2009 which brought Wild Abdalaziz, the leader of the coup, back to power though the ballots. This reveals the nature of Arab politics and illustrates the argument that 'without the prospect of broad-based economic development, voters are likely to become disillusioned with politics and politicians and thus with democracy itself'.[121] It is argued that 'the forms of democracy found in the Arab countries were little more than make-believe and pageantry.'[122]

The changes going on in the Arab world since January 2011 are a sign of hope. The prospects for democracy in the Arab states, however, are not promising unless similar changes take place in Saudi Arabia and Syria.[123] Yet Arab countries, being part of the global village, are witnessing shortage in liquidity and most of their accumulated investments abroad have been severely hit by the world economic crunch. The decline in oil revenues due to the drastic drop in oil price, from almost $150 to just above $70 a barrel between May 2008 and August 2009, and the depreciation of the dollar that caused the devaluation of local currencies, coupled with the cost inflicted by the world economic recession, mean that some Arab states are expected to face low economic growth, high rates of unemployment, budget deficits and increased foreign debts. Consequently, to make up for its losses and to dominate the world oil market, Saudi Arabia increased its oil production to a record 12.5 million barrels a day. However, it pumps only 8.3 million barrels a day, keeping one-third of its capacity shut down.[124] Hence, the source of income that enabled the ruling elite to monopolize power and deny the people's right to power sharing is depleting, leaving no room for manœuvre. Eventually there will be a need to give in to public demands for political participation. Regional stability requires Arab governments to embark on real and effective political reforms, diversification of their economies and regional integration. 'As people's income rise and their horizon broaden, they are more likely to demand power sharing and the rule of law.'[125] Moreover, technology has infringed on state sovereignty and increased public political awareness. It has begun to transform the relationship between governments and the people in the region, strengthening the periphery at the expense of the centre. The local level is empowered while authority at the centre is undermined.[126]

Constitutional democracy, based on synthesizing Islam and democracy, could be seen as the only viable option for regional security and stability. Bernard Lewis argued that 'the idea of limited government is inherent and essential in Islam. The principle that the ruler is not above the law, but subject to the law is central to classical Islamic teaching on the state.'[127] A real and effective democracy in the Arab world requires the fulfilment of three concentric conditions: (1) the relationship between the ruling families and the people must be clearly defined; (2) the ruling families must acknowledge that democracy is an unalienable right of the people; (3) the democratic process has to be institutionalized.[128] The continuation of dualism within the Arab status quo or entering the stage of decay is not detrimental and reform is always possible since it depends on the political will. It is argued that the problem is not in the nature or the complexity of the Arab political condition, but is totally dependent on the presence of the political will to engage or disengage in the process of political reform.[129] The achievement of this goal is not feasible unless these countries undergo a social and political transformation, which the Tunisian and Egyptian revolutions and the uprisings in Yemen, Libya, Jordan, Bahrain and Syria have inspired. However, a reading of the current political developments reveals that, although democracy may not be realized within the coming decade, it is acquiring a significant importance in the Arab world's political life. H. L. Menken argued that 'the cure for the evils of democracy is more democracy'.[130] Thus, its realization becomes a matter of time.

4. Inter-Arab Politics

Inter- and intra-Arab states' relations have never been stable and political interactions have gone through different phases. but since the recent changes in a number of Arab countries, particularly Egypt, they now aspire to another phase. The nature of political interactions in the Arab regional orders differs from those in other regional orders. It is a dialectical relationship between official Arab political behaviour and that of their people, especially on issues of a pan-Arab nationalist nature, as manifested in the attitudes towards the Arab–Israeli conflict and the American invasion of Iraq.[131] 'The massacre in Gaza, during the Israeli invasion in December 2008, has further widened the gap between the Arab masses and their governments and pits the moderates against the hardliners in the Arab world.'[132] Islamist Hamas runs Gaza Strip and the Fateh group of Mahmoud Abbas controls the West Bank. The US and its allies back Abbas as the 'legitimate' leader in both territories and accuse Iran of pushing Hamas to continue resistance to Israel and drive hard terms for uniting the government, after it split amid street fighting in 2007.[133] Recep Tayyip Erdogan, the Turkish Prime Minister, in an interview, made it clear that his visit to the region showed that Arab governments were divided on the issue and some of them believed that Israel had the right to launch its war against Gaza, which he could not understand.[134] The UN Human Rights Council voted on Richard Goldstone's fact-finding report condemning Israeli atrocities on 16 October 2009 by 25 in favour to 6 against, with 11 abstaining.[135] At the time of writing, the report, which accuses both Israel and Hamas of war crimes and possible crimes against humanity, has been tabled until the council's spring session. The report was initially presented to the Human Rights Council in Geneva on 29 September 2009, urging the council and the international community as a whole to put an end to impunity for violations of international law in Israel and the Occupied Palestinian Territory. President Mahmoud Abbas agreed to defer a vote on the United Nations report on Israel's winter military offensive in Gaza. The deferment caused dissent throughout the Arab world, and has led to harsh criticism of Abbas's leadership.[136]

The unification of Yemen on 22 May 1990 brought the strife between the two Yemen to an end. However, social and political unrest continues to threaten Yemen's security and stability. In addition to the government war against al-Huwthyyn militia, Yemen has witnessed, in August 2009, social uprising in the southern part of the country, previously known as the People's Republic of Yemen. The uprising called for secession in protest against government policy of neglect. This ultimately led to a reallocation of resources for internal development on the one hand, and a reorientation of foreign policy undertakings on the other. A united Yemen would play a significant role in stabilizing or destabilizing the Peninsula subregion. Historically, relations between Saudi Arabia and both Yemens have been at odds. Saudi Arabia employed its oil income to circumscribe a Yemeni threat to its security. The Yemeni uprising against Saleh's regime and its likely democractic outcome would contribute positively to the inter-Arab relations on the one hand, and could become a destabilizing source to the Saudi kingdom on the other. The Saudis dedicated part of their foreign aid to both Yemens, used money as a means to bribe the Yemeni tribal leaders and create internal chaos, enacted legislative rules granting low-paid Yemeni labourers privileged migrant status, and froze their territorial problem through periodic renewal of the 1934 territorial treaty every twenty years. Analysts argue that 'the North Yemeni government's annual budget was provided by Saudi Arabia.'[137] The number of Yemenis living in Saudi Arabia, prior to the Gulf war, was around 1.5 to 2 million. The Saudis are displeased with the Yemeni unification because they consider it as part of their own backyard. The Saudi objection is based on the grounds that large sections of the border regions between Saudi Arabia and Yemen contain sizeable oil resources, a matter that had caused armed clashes between Saudi Arabia and both Yemens.[138] However, new Yemen proved to be more cooperative in its approach towards the settlement of its border dispute with the Kingdom, culminating in a bilateral agreement demarcating the national frontiers and bringing the prolonged dispute to a final end. The border agreement signed between Yemen and Saudi Arabia in Jeddah on 12 June 2000, coinciding with the visit of Yemeni President 'Ali 'Abdullah Salih to Saudi Arabia, defines the border between the two countries from the maritime boundary in the Red Sea to the intersection of the common border with the Omani border, specifying border points which are to be identified and marked by an international company using global positioning technology.[139] (See Map 1).

The Yemeni unification, on the other hand, means offsetting the balance of power within the Peninsula subregional system in favour of Yemen. A comparison of both countries' strength and weaknesses would reveal that new Yemen possesses a number of advantages vis-à-vis Saudi Arabia. The Republic of Yemen has a population that increased from 7 million in 1975 to 21 million in 2004, of which more than 99 per cent are nationals, with an annual growth rate of 3 per cent. On the other hand, Yemen is ranked among the twenty poorest countries worldwide, and has the highest population density on the Arabian Peninsula. Yemen's population is estimated to reach 43 million by 2035, hinting that such an increase means more poverty and development problems.[140] Saudi Arabia's population, on the other hand, almost quadrupled between 1974 and 2008 from 6.2 to 24 million people, of which almost 40 per cent to 50 per cent are expatriates. It is argued that three factors would strengthen the Yemeni government in any dispute with Saudi Arabia. First is the very strong sense of Yemeni nationalism. Second, the democratization process in Yemen is more advanced comparatively, enhancing the government position and conferring legitimacy on its external behaviour that would win it the internal support.[141] Third, the discovery of oil has given the Yemeni government an independent source of income. It would reduce Yemeni dependence on Saudi financial assistance and enable it to pursue an independent course of foreign policy. Riyadh continues to be nervous of Yemen's democratic experience, as evidenced by its reaction to the latter's parliamentary elections and pressure on oil companies not to explore in an area generally recognized as Yemen's side of the disputed border.[142]

The emergence of Yemen leaves the GCC states with two alternatives: either to engage it in subregional politics or isolate it. Isolating Yemen, however, would radicalize its foreign policy towards the GCC states. It could also retaliate by supporting internal opposition within the GCC states. It is argued that competing Arab countries seek to undermine the Saudi monarchy by supporting its internal opposition directly through Yemen.[143] This would prove to be an irrational policy. On the other hand, Yemen, through cooperation, could act as an effective stabilizing factor in regional stability. Accommodating Yemen in the subregional politics, hence, becomes a viable option for Arab states in the Gulf. Though Yemen could not be seen as a supplementary power, it could be incorporated as part of any future arrangement for Gulf subregional security. A quadruple security arrangement for maintaining the status quo in the Gulf represents an alternative option. It requires a six plus three (6+3) security equation arrangement that would include the GCC states plus Iran, Iraq and Yemen. The purpose of this arrangement is to create an equilibrium to act as a check and balance in subregional politics. It is also intended to make up for the Iranian demographic superiority to any of the Arab Gulf states by creating an Arab axis consisting of the subregional Arab states to contain any possible Iranian threat, on the one hand, and to alienate Yemen from cooperating with radical states or groups if one of them decided to advance its nationalist objectives at the expense of any of the GCC states, on the other hand.

Alliances within the Arab world are volatile and constantly changing. Inter-Arab relations are characterized by being fluid, shifting continuously from cooperation to conflict and vice versa. It is illustrated in the rise of new alliances and the disappearance of old ones in dealing with current issues. Prior to 1979, Saudi Arabia and the states of the lower Gulf cooperated with Iran to check the Ba'thist Iraqi government threat to their securities. Saudi Arabia and the Gulf emirates seized the opportunity of the Iran–Iraq rapprochement after the 1975 Alger Accord to manœuvre between the two regional powers to protect their national interests. Saudi Arabia, in particular, 'endeavored to enlist Iraq's support to frustrate the Shah's scheme to institutionalize his hegemonic inspirations through a Gulf collective defense pact, and to use Iran to check Iraq's aspirations to become the centre of the Arab countries of the Gulf'.[144] Competition for hegemony on the Arab side of the Gulf between Iraq and Saudi Arabia was, until the early 1990s, a longstanding issue.[145] For instance, the Saudis saw the National Arab Charter announced by Saddam Hussein, on 8 February 1980, as an indirect challenge to their influence in the Gulf and voiced their dissatisfaction with the Iraqi tendency. Saudi Arabia maintains that the Charter represents a condemnation of their connection with the US.[146] Further, the Iraqi press continued to criticize the Omani step of granting facilities to the American forces, despite the visit paid by the Omani Minister of State for Foreign Affairs to stop Iraq's press campaign against Oman.[147] Relations between Iraq under Saddam and the Gulf States further deteriorated during the second Gulf crisis.

The outbreak of the Iran–Iraq war paved the way for a leading Saudi role among the Arab countries within OPEC and OAPEC.[148] The Iran–Iraq war furnished the conservative Arab Gulf states with an opportunity for both checking the new Iranian threat and excluding Iraq from any regional security arrangement. On the one hand, the Arab states supported Iraq's war efforts politically and financially. Their contribution to the Iraqi war effort was estimated to be $200 billion. Saudi Arabia alone paid more than $25 billion.[149] Kuwait and Saudi Arabia allocated 300 thousand barrels of oil per day for Iraq to compensate for the decline in the latter's oil production due to the destruction of its oil installations. Saudi Arabia permitted the Iraqi construction of a pipeline to carry 1.5 million barrels a day of its oil to the Red Sea to avoid the Iranian blockade.[150] The former Secretary-General of the GCC, Abdullah Bishara, justified the GCC states' support to Iraq on the basis of maintaining the status quo in the region.[151] The GCC states collectively, on 21 May 1984, sent a letter to the President of the Security Council[152] calling on the council to shoulder the responsibilities envisioned for it under the UN Charter. They condemned Iran's provocative acts of aggression and warned against its recurrence. It is interesting to note, however, that the resolution adopted, on 1 June 1984, condemning the attacks and demanding that such attacks should cease forthwith, did not mention Iran by name.[153] The GCC countries pursued a dual policy towards Iran. They kept channels of communications open. 'The GCC states did not want to abandon all means of contact with Iran, a long-term insurance policy with their larger neighbour.'[154] The Saudi fear of Iranian retaliation against the GCC states' oil installations for the Iraqi bombardment of its oil installations led them to export petrochemical refined products to Iran to make up for its shortage.[155] Saudi Arabia had concluded a final agreement with the Iraqi government, during King Fahd's official visit to Baghdad in 1989, delineating the territorial boundaries between the two nations. Baghdad unilaterally nullified the agreement after the eruption of the second Gulf crisis. Fahd, during the Doha Summit Conference, was adamant and gave no hint of the possibility of 'any compromise with Baghdad on the territorial integrity of Kuwait or on political concessions that could be seen as a reward for an aggressor'.[156] The Saudis were ready to support a military campaign against Iraq that could seek to destroy Iraq's chemical weapons facilities and nuclear programme.

The Iran–Iraq, Iraq–Kuwait and Iraq–Saudi Arabia border disputes are by no means the only territorial problems in the area. The disintegration of the Saudi–Egyptian–Syrian alliance after years of cooperation on regional policy, manifested for the first time since the liberation of Kuwait, was over Lebanon. Political rivalry for hegemony in the Arab order among the regional powers, Egypt, Saudi Arabia and Syria, is constantly irritating, particularly to the less influential states.

The unsettled border dispute between Iraq and Kuwait and the increased oil production by both Kuwait and the UAE prompted the Iraqi government to adopt a hostile posture towards these states. Saddam Hussein, in the Revolutionary Day speech on 17 July 1990, blasted Kuwait and the UAE as stooges for America by keeping oil prices low.[157] Iraq exerted pressure on Kuwait by a mobilized armoured division mass on the latter's border. The alliance between Iraq and the GCC countries was short-lived. Kuwait's production of $2.5 billion worth of oil from the disputed al-Rumalia oil field was one of the Iraqi grievances in the Kuwaiti crisis, August 1990–March 1991, that revealed the extent of the territorial problems. The Iraqi–Kuwaiti territorial dispute is a longstanding one. Since the 1920s successive Iraqi governments have laid claims to Kuwait as part of Iraq. Though the Iraqis have consistently laid their claim on historical grounds, the geographical location of both countries plays the paramount role in shaping the foreign policy of both states towards each other. Iraq without Kuwaiti territorial concessions continues to be nearly a land-locked state. Its outlet to the Gulf is a 35-mile narrow corridor comprised of mostly shallow waters unsuitable for port construction.[158] As a result of the Iraqi threat to cut oil output, the Saudi government warned that it would not extend its protection to Kuwait in the face of Iraqi anger. However, the Iraqi invasion of Kuwait on 2 August forced the GCC countries to change their foreign policy orientations from an alliance with Iraq to an alliance against Iraq. Saudi Arabia was 'determined not to let Saddam Hussein dictate war or peace in the future'.[159]

The outcome of the Iraqi abortive attempt to annex Kuwait had adverse impacts on the GCC states' foreign policy orientations. On the domestic level, the crisis cost around $670 billion.[161] Each side lost approximately $240 billion and Kuwait had to use more than two-thirds of its reserves for the coming generations. War and the reconstruction reduced the government's estimated pre-war assets of $100 billion to around $15 billion, whilst Saudi foreign assets dropped from $215 billion in 1981 to about $50 billion, balanced by the national debt.[162] A further implication of the second Gulf crisis for the Arab states' foreign policies is the end of the effectiveness of oil as a strategic weapon in the hand of the oil-producing countries.[163] They had successfully used it thus in October 1973. Now they could not even manipulate their main source of income to influence the policies of the oil-importing countries in pursuance of their national interests. Moreover, one unintended consequence of the Gulf war was to centralize further the supply of oil. One-third of the oil produced by the thirteen nations of OPEC now comes from Saudi Arabia.[164] The war propelled Saudi Arabia into becoming the world's largest oil producer, jumping ahead of the USA.[165] The decline in oil prices due to the global economic crisis in 2009 has further weakened Arab countries' foreign policy undertakings.

The balance of power, as viewed by the political elites, is the determinant factor of inter-Arab relations. It is a balance between fragile and dependent powers uncertain of their future and hence it is destined to be continuously tense, competitive, jealous and fluctuating. It is capable of absorbing joint efforts as long as they do not change the status quo.[166] The absence of a balance of power among the Arab states inspired their policies towards both inter-Arab politics and the outside world. The Arab regional order does not adhere to the principle of equality among its members, as in the EU for example. Small Arab states feel insecure and instable in such a turbulent region.[167] Syria–Lebanon relations are another example of the nature of relations among Arab countries. The US, after the assassination of the Lebanese Prime Minister Rafiq al-Hariri, played a significant role in the escalating deterioration of relations between the two Arab neighbouring states. Distrust between the big brothers contributed to the creation of a great gap among the Arab states and forced the small countries, in their search for security, to look for alliances with outside powers, paving the way for foreign intervention in the region. The Lebanese political turmoil, the Kuwaiti predicament and the Qatari surge are clear cases in mind.

The European notion of a precisely demarcated border between nation-states which 'had a considerable effect on the very notion of the state and on the shared identity and allegiance of those who lived within its frontiers',[168] is again not applicable to the Arab world, whereby local citizen identity overlaps with the pan-Arab identity and in some cases with the religious identity of being a Muslim. In many cases Arabs adhere to the notion of Arabism, although the so-called 'new pragmatists' group emphasizes locality and holds a regionalist perception of a nation-state.

Relations between the big and small states in the inter-Arab politics is unhealthy and based on distrust and misperception. Big countries always push small countries to pursue policies to ensure their compliance with the mainstream of Arab politics. The relations between Syria and Lebanon, Iraq and Kuwait, Saudi Arabia and the other GCC states and Yemen, Egypt and Sudan and Algeria and Morocco are good illustrations of such unhealthy and suspicious conditions. Culturally, inter-Arab states' relations are always described in brotherly manner as *al-Ashaqiqa al-Arab* or *Ashaqiqa al-Kubra* (the big brother), especially when Saudi Arabia is mentioned in the media of the Gulf states. However, *Ashaqiqa*, in Arabic, also means a migraine. Thus, inter-Arab relations between big and small states are headaches for the small states. Territorial disputes are signs of the unhealthy and competitive nature of inter-Arab politics. In most cases relations are disturbed by territorial disputes. A mini war is brewing between Egypt and Sudan over the border triangle of Halayeb straddling the two countries, which Cairo and Khartoum claim to be rich in manganese, several minerals and oil.[169] Kuwait and Saudi Arabia continue to dispute ownership of Qaruh and Umm al Maradim islands.[170] The UAE and Saudi Arabia reached an agreement delineating their national borders on 21 August 1974. The two sides signed in Jeddah an agreement saying Riyadh will give up demands on al-Buraimi oases, while on the other side Abu Dhabi gave up Khour Al Adeed, a 25-kilometre-long coastal area separating Abu Dhabi and Qatar. Subsequently, Saudi Arabia recognized the UAE and the two countries exchanged diplomatic missions on ambassadorial level. The treaty was registered by Saudi Arabia on 9 September 1993. However, the UAE has yet to ratify the agreement.[171]

The UAE claims that the treaty has not been ratified by the Federal Supreme Council (FSC). The UAE argument, however, is negated on five grounds; first, the UAE is a federal state and the constitution gives full sovereignty to individual member emirates over their territories; second, each emirate has the right to conclude territorial agreements with neighbouring countries and give territorial concessions if it chooses to do so whilst the FSC has no power to reject; third, when Abu Dhabi signed the Jeddah agreement in August 1974 it did not ask for the FSC's approval prior to its conclusion; fourth, despite Abu Dhabi dissatisfaction with Saudi regional behaviour and its reservations on the agreement, the late UAE president and ex-ruler of Abu Dhabi Sheikh Zayed opted always for containment to prevent the deterioration of relations between the two GCC member states; fifth, the political row could not be viewed as a deliberate federal policy intended to weaken the Saudi negotiating position as much as a manifestation of the frustration on the part of some members of Abu Dhabi ruling family about the Saudi hegemonistic role in the Gulf subregion. Although UAE and Saudi officials denied that was a disagreement over the borders, Saudi Interior Minister Prince Nayef Ibn Abdalaziz Al-Saud announced, on 29 June 2005, that his country has officially lodged a protest to the United Arab Emirates and Qatar with regard to plans to build a causeway linking the two GCC member states, parts of which would go through Saudi regional waters.[172] The UAE on its part announced in mid-June 2005 that the Jeddah border agreement with Saudi Arabia of 1974 is not accepted any more. A senior UAE official commented on Prince Nayef's statement by saying: 'I don't have any problem with the old agreement. If KSA (the Kingdom of Saudi Arabia) took the land it is ok, just let us build this bridge.'[173] The UAE has 'insisted on full sovereignty over the territorial waters of the Khour Al Adeed', an area of dispute between the UAE and Saudi Arabia.[174] Some maps published in the UAE still reportedly show the country stretching as far westwards as Qatar.

The UAE publicly reopened the dispute in 2006, claiming some lost territories. The UAE territorial dispute has escalated since 2005, promoted competition between the UAE and Saudi Arabia over the permanent place of the GCC Central Bank and led the UAE, on 20 May 2009, to withdraw from the unified currency project. Saudi Arabia, on the other hand, in August 2009, revised its policy permitting UAE nationals to travel to Saudi Arabia by their national ID card because it carries the pre-1974 agreement UAE map. The UAE president, Sheikh Khalifa Ibn Zayed, in his effort to contain the political row between the countries,[175] manifested in media warfare and the exchange of bitter words,[176] issued his instruction to continue UAE policy of receiving Saudi nationals travelling to the UAE with their national ID.[177] He also was quick to condemn the attack on Prince Mohammed Ibn Nayef Ibn Abdalaziz, the Assistant Minister of Interior, and expressed solidarity with Saudi Arabia.[178]

The big Arab brothers put pressure on small Arab states to halt their democratic experiences in countries like Kuwait, Bahrain, Lebanon and Jordan, or to ensure their foreign policies are in line with contemporary Arab mainstream, like Syria and Sudan, breaching their independence and sovereignty, to keep them in line. Since the early 1990s, the influence of the big brothers has increased and the moderate perception of regional arrangements, especially towards security and the Arab–Israeli conflict, acquired significant importance in Arab politics. The approach pursued by the big states weakens regional integration and backfires by forcing the populations of those small states to lend their support to their governments, enhancing locality.[179] The absence of an acceptable mechanism for solving Arab states' differences, on the one hand, and the personification of the differences between states become differences among leaders,[180] on the other hand, have exacerbated the situation. Inter-Arab struggles fluctuate between escalation and de-escalation and this is because differences and disputes are mostly frozen, not brought to a final end. They are usually contained in a traditional mode, a 'brotherly manner', by treating the symptoms and not the causes, leaving the core of the problem unsettled.[181]

The Arab countries today are divided between two camps. The moderate camp includes Egypt, Saudi Arabia, Morocco, Jordan, Tunisia and other Gulf Cooperation Council (GCC) members who are practically allies of the US and view peace as a strategic option. The reluctant camp includes Syria, Libya and the Islamist resistant groups, Hezbollah, Hamas and the Islamic Jihad, supported by a non-Arab Middle Eastern country namely Iran, pursuing a more radical policy towards the Arab–Israeli conflict. The Arab order is fragmented and teetering. During the Israeli invasion of the Gaza Strip, the Arabs failed to stand up to their common enemy. Syria, Qatar, along with non-Arab regional power Iran, backed Hamas during the Israeli invasion of the Gaza Strip in late 2008, while Egypt and Saudi Arabia blamed Hamas for provoking Israel.[182] This further weakness of the Arab order rendered them impotent in the face of any future challenge.[183] Iran's relations with the Arab states demonstrate the complexity and multidimensional aspects of Arab–Persian interregional relationships. 'On the one hand, the connection includes cultural and social ties as well as active and substantial trading links. On the other hand, the relationship faces mutual distrust and misperception.'[184] Arab governments have struggled to respond to Iran's political clout since the US invasion of Iraq in 2003. Egypt and Saudi Arabia see Iran's hand behind the strength of Hezbollah in Lebanon and Hamas and Islamic resistant groups in the Palestinian territories, that refuse to renounce armed struggle in the historic Arab–Israeli conflict.[185] Arab countries maintain different attitudes towards Iran. Syria, Algeria, Iraq, Lebanon, Oman, Qatar, Libya and the Islamic Arab groups hold a cooperative perception towards Iran. Qatar, with ambitions to be a major regional power broker, has maintained close links with Iran, despite moderate axis pressures to keep its distance from a country they suspect of seeking to develop nuclear weapons which Tehran consistently denies.[186] Oman is another Arab Gulf state which enjoys good bilateral relations with Iran, manifested in exchange visits, including Sultan Qaboos's state visit to Tehran in August 2009. The moderates argue that Syria gave Iran a window of opportunity to extend its influence in the Arab world, stretching from Iraq to Lebanon and Palestine.[187] Saudi–Syrian relations entered a new phase of conflict from mid-2006. Tension exacerbated in 2007 culminated in media warfare for the first time. Egypt mediation success in containing the differences was short-lived. It paved the way for attendance by the Syrian President, Bashar Assad, at the 19th Arab summit held in Riyadh in March 2007, followed by a Syrian–Saudi summit meeting. However, in August 2007, Faroq al-Shar'a criticized the Saudi role in Arab politics and described it as becoming paralysed. He substantiated his claim by referring to the failure of the Makka Accord between the Palestinians and the Saudi absence from the security meeting held in Damascus by the neighbouring countries of Iraq. The Saudis replied by accusing Syria of spreading chaos and trouble in the region. The war of words continued until December 2007. Attitudes towards Lebanon were the main reason behind the two countries' differences. Saudi Arabia blamed al-Shar'a for the tension in inter-Arab relations. Al-Shar'a saw the convening of the Islamic Conference Organization summit (ICO) in Senegal on 13–14 March 2008 as intended to weaken the Arab summit scheduled for 29–30 March to be held in Damascus. Tension escalated and the Saudis and the Egyptian leaders opted not to attend the Damascus summit, being represented there by low-level delegations. The Saudis, at first, refused to hand over the summit presidency to Syria, but later on Arab states' mediation between the two belligerent parties succeeded in brokering a deal that ironed out the differences temporarily. Relations between Syria, on the one hand, and Saudi Arabia and Egypt, on the other, continue to be fragile. It was illustrated in the continuation of the media warfare. Both parties blamed each other for the recurrent fighting in Lebanon in May 2008, accusing the other of helping Lebanese war factions. The cold war between the two sides led Saudi Arabia and Egypt to accuse Syria of supporting Hezbollah and Hamas, which are accused by the Saudis and Egyptian of causing regional instability.[188] Conflicts in the Arab politics include Morocco–Algeria differences over the Western Sahara issue. The Saudi–Libyan differences, over perception of the American presence in the region, culminated in a verbal spat between Libyan leader Muammar Gaddafi and the Saudi monarch, then Crown Prince, during the extraordinary Arab summit held in Sharm al-Sheikh, Egypt in 2003, over who was responsible for making the Arab world an arena for American hegemony.[189] The Libyan leader Gaddafi boycotted the 19th summit conference held in Riyadh in March 2007. Saudi–Iraqi relations are at odds over the al-Maliki government. The Saudis declined to receive the Iraqi Prime Minister, Nouri al-Maliki, in April 2007, in protest at the way Sunni are treated in Iraq and due to the latter's special ties with Iran.[190] The rift between Arab states exploded spectacularly when the two camps tried to hold rival summits in January 2009. Saudi Arabia and Egypt refused to attend the Doha Extraordinary

Arab summit held in March intended to discuss the implication of the Israeli invasion of Gaza Strip in December 2008–January 2009, on the grounds that another Arab economic summit was scheduled to be held in Kuwait in the same month. The conference held in Doha failed to get the quorum necessary because of the big brothers' pressure on small states. Arab summit conferences reflect Arab divisions[191] and the nature of inter-Arab relations.

Relations between Syria and Iraq have never been cordial. Both countries, during the presidencies of Hafez Assad and Saddam Hussein, were competing over the leadership of Arab nationalist Ba'ath Party and the leadership of the Arab world. Competition between the two neighbouring states led Syria to ally itself with Iran during the Iraq–Iran war and both fought each other in Lebanon through supporting opposing factions. Finally, Syria took the side of the allied forces against Iraq during the Kuwaiti predicament. After the overthrow of Saddam Hussein, relations between the two neighbouring states witnessed a breakthrough in 2003. Despite American accusations that the Syrian government helped terrorists and granted custody to opposition groups, diplomatic relations on 21 November 2006 were restored after a break of nearly twenty years and embassies were reopened on 12 December 2009. A series of dignitaries' visits were exchanged between the two countries, including Jalal Talabani and Nouri al-Maliki and Walid al-Muallem, the Syrian foreign minister, to Baghdad. In the search to increase cooperation between them, Baghdad and Damascus signed in April 2009 a memorandum of understanding on the formation of the Supreme Council for strategic cooperation, in addition to the signing of nine memoranda of understanding and cooperation protocols, the most prominent in the areas of oil, trade and energy.[192] Efforts to upgrade bilateral relations between the two countries during Maliki's visit to Damascus culminated, on 19 August 2009, in the signing of economic and security agreements including an agreement to activate the issue of the Kirkuk-Banias oil and gas pipeline[193] and a security protocol to control the border and prevent infiltration of foreign fighters into Iraq. The talks also included a joint solution for the water issue, and the closure of the issue of financial receivables, as well as the examination of the conditions of Iraqis living in Syria. However, the restored relations were not strong enough to face the encountered challenges. Iraq accused Syria of being behind the explosions that rocked Baghdad on 26 August 2009[194] and the two countries recalled their ambassadors. Turkey, a regional power enjoying good relations with both countries, decided to use its good offices to mediate between Baghdad and Damascus. However, the fluid political situation and the strong competition among political parties in Iraq for influence, especially between those in favour of the 'state of law', rule of law, led by the Prime Minister Nouri al-Maliki and the regionalists led by the coalition between al Majlis al-A'ala li al-Thourah al-Islamiah represented by al-Hakim dynasty and the separatists Kurdish movement, forced Maliki to choose between two undesired policies. Maliki, aware of the consequences of the flexible and soft alliances in modern Iraq on the potential outcome of the forthcoming election, decided to side with militant Shi'ites, who do not want to see strong ties with Syria, against his wish for a better relations with neighbouring countries and to balance the relations with Iran through a new Iraqi–Syrian alliance. As a result, the dispute with Syria took a new course with Iraq rejecting the Turkish mediation and Bashar Assad describing the Iraqi allegations as unethical.[195] The Iraq tone of hostility further escalated, taking the matter to the UN Security Council and demanding an International Criminal Court be set up to investigate foreign involvement in support of terrorist groups.[196] However, Iraq's Presidential Council rejected Maliki's move to internationalize the issue. Jalal Talabani described Maliki's position as illegal. The Presidential Council called for the problem with neighbouring Syria to be contained. It called for dialogue with Syria to settle the pending issues through political and diplomatic means.[197] Iyad Samirai, the Speaker of the Iraqi Parliament, rebuffed the idea of internationalizing the issue and called for bilateral negotiations based on mutual respect and constructive engagement.[198] The Arab League, with Turkish mediation, seems to have succeeded in bringing the two countries together and the issue has been temporarily settled in 'brotherly manner'.[199] Relations between Arab countries are based on individual perception and narrow social and political interests rather than on realpolitik.

Despite the tensions between the Arab states relations on the surface are 'managed in a brotherly manner'. The Arab countries, with few exceptions, are keen to attend the annual summit conferences. Arab summits are usually fraught with tension, but follow a routine procedural pattern and methodology. They rarely take decisions of importance and have often showcased Arab division rather than unity. There are critical questions in play behind the scenes.[200] The Arabs have mismanaged their affairs due to the lack of an agreed method or a mechanism to settle their differences. However, inter-Arab relations have never reached a point where they cannot be mended, except for the relations with Iraq after the latter's occupation of Kuwait. Relations among Arab countries could easily reach a cold war status, but governments are restrained by the pan-Arab nationalist feelings held by their masses and always look for an exit from any dead-end. Differences are normally settled through mediations or initiatives from parties to avoid escalation of tensions.

On the road to reconciliation, Syrian–Jordanian relations witnessed a positive development, after three years of stalemate, on the visit paid by King Abdullah of Jordan on 18 November 2007 to Damascus. The visit culminated in the signing of twelve memoranda of understanding. Interpretations of the Jordanian move emphasize three reasons. First, a mediatory role convinced Syria to attend the Annapolis peace conference, conveying a message of assurances that the issue of the Golan Heights would be on the agenda. Second, it is argued that a deal between Israel and the Palestinians could be at Jordan's expense, becoming the substitute homeland for the Palestinians in diaspora. Third, water scarcity constituted another compelling factor for the visit, especially since it was a source of tension between the two neighbouring states.[201] However, the new light of hope in the two countries' relations was rapidly put out when Jordan decided to join Egypt and Saudi Arabia and send a low-level representative to the Arab summit conference in Damascus. However, the states' relations were energized again in March 2009 when Bashar Assad paid a short visit to Amman on his way back from Saudi Arabia, in an attempt to mend fences prior to the Doha summit conference. Syria also opted to strengthen ties with Arab Gulf countries and the countries of al-Maghreb al-Arabi. Bashar Assad paid state visits to Kuwait and the United Arab Emirates in June 2008 and to Libya on 10 July 2008. Egyptian President Hosni Mubarak opted not to attend the Doha summit conference because of bad feelings towards Qatar over Jazeera TV's critical programmes on Egypt. The US rapprochement with Syria promoted an easing of tension in inter-Arab relations between 'moderates', Saudi Arabia and Egypt, on the one hand, and the 'reluctant', namely Syria. Saudi Arabia, Egypt and Syria were keen to settle their differences before the Doha summit conference. The Syrian president on 4 March 2009 received Saud Al Faisal, Saudi Arabia's foreign minister, who conveyed an invitation from the Saudi monarch for the Syrian president to visit Riyadh.[202] The visit was intended to break the ice in the two countries' relations to iron out differences associated with the split in Arab position over regional issues. Bashar Assad flew to Riyadh in March 2009 to help mend fences. Riyadh saw a mini Arab summit, including the heads of Saudi Arabia, Syria, Egypt and Kuwait, on 11 March 2009 on the road to Arab reconciliation. The meeting called for the overcoming of Arab differences, a unified Arab policy on Palestine, and emphasized the importance of agreeing a mechanism for settling Arab differences.[203] Development in the Saudi–Syrian relations culminated on 7 October 2009 in King Abdullah's three-day state visit to Syria.[204] President al-Assad, in an interview, rightly pointed out that Arab diplomacy should be enhanced: 'we should meet whether we agree or disagree. The problem is not in the differences, because it is not possible to agree on everything, but in the principle of accepting the right to differ. Arab summit should convene to discuss the issues on which we disagree as well as those on which we agree.' Al-Assad denied that there is a conflict of interests, but only holding different views on the most appropriate way or method to deal with current issues.[205] Another positive development in inter-Arab relations was the Saudi–Qatari rapprochement which culminated in the Emir of Qatar's visit to Riyadh on 23 December 2007. The visit opened a new chapter in the two GCC members' relations. The most important new development was the visit by the Saudi Crown Prince to Doha on 10 March 2008 and the reinstatement of the Saudi ambassador to Qatar after six years of tension. In a further step, the two countries concluded in Jeddah on 6 July 2008 an agreement delineating their borders. They also decided to set up a policy coordination council headed by both Crown Princes.[206] Libya and Saudi Arabia appeared to have buried the hatchet at an Arab summit in Qatar on 30 March 2009 after a feud dating back to 2003 from an ugly public disagreement over US ties. Gaddafi is known for his quixotic behaviour at regional and international events. Gaddafi and King Abdullah held a separate meeting lasting around thirty minutes on the edge of the conference, billed by its organizer as a chance to heal the Arab spilt over relations with the US. The meeting came after Gaddafi appeared to attack the octogenarian Saudi monarch at the summit's opening session, but the intervention ended with a call for peace. Gaddafi said: 'For the sake of the Arab nation, I consider the personal problem between you and me to be over and I am prepared to visit you and receive a visit from you.'[207] The change of regime has brought Libya back into the Arab regional order and has helped rectify Libya's differences with other Arab countries. Saudi Arabia also, under American pressure, decided to send its ambassador to Baghdad, opening formal channels of communication. Relations between Syria and Lebanon have entered a new chapter with Syria sending an ambassador to Beirut for the first time in the two countries' history. The positive developments in the inter-Arab relations do not reveal that the Arabs have decided to set new solid foundations for their relations but confirm that Arab management of these are still carried out in the old-fashioned 'brotherly manner'. They continue to be based on distrust and misperception.

5. Conclusion

The study of the political process in this chapter sets out the following points:

1. Arab regimes lack any basis for political legitimacy, either democratic or Islamic, and are characterized by authority and leadership crises.
2. Measures adopted by some governments do not meet the aspirations of the masses for a share of power. People are not optimistic about a gradual and peaceful transition to a power-sharing form of government. The existing regimes 'think only of how to maintain power'.[208]
3. The absence of accountability, checks and balances, inevitably causes domestic and regional instability.
4. The fact that the Arab political systems are faced with lost political legitimacy enhances the argument that inter-Arab relations are unstable and will continue to fluctuate between cold war and détente until Egypt regains its role.
5. Western support for tyranny, autocracy and indulgence of corruption in the Arab world, far from securing regional stability, breeds extremism and failed states. Western support for oppressive Arab regimes has thwarted democratic attempts.[209]
6. Distrust and suspicion between Arab regimes add further complexity to the fragile situation prevailing in inter-Arab politics, promoting greater political instability in the region despite the changes in some Arab countries. The Arab world is expected to be divided on different grounds: the democratic and non-democratic political systems.
7. Arab states' foreign-policy-making is constrained by the political dynamics on both intra- and inter-Arab politics as part of the input process.

Chapter 2

The Socio-Economic Variables

1. Introduction

The Arab world has always been looked at as a monolithic region sharing religious, cultural, social, historical and linguistic similarities and faced by common threats. However, social heterogeneity and economic disparity are also present. Arab countries had different historical legacies, ranging from total annexations by the colonial powers, like Algeria and Palestine, to direct colonial rule, as were Egypt, Sudan, Iraq, Yemen, Syria, Morocco, Tunisia, Mauritania, Libya and Somalia, to indirect rule or protectorate as was the Gulf subregion. Saudi Arabia is the only Arab country without a colonial past.

The notion of the 'nation-state' is an alien concept to the Arab culture. The contemporary national borders of the Arab states were delineated by Western colonial powers. Most contemporary Arab countries either have short histories or were the by-products of the colonial 'divide and rule' policy. Contemporary Saudi Arabia, without a colonial history, was also formed with Western encouragement and support, especially by the British (see Chapter 9). Consequently, competition rather than cooperation among Arab states for hegemony prevailed in inter-Arab politics. The need for popular support or political legitimacy forced some localized socio-economic development initiatives, but these were hindered by the scarcity of economic resources at the individual level, leaving the Arab states without sustainable development and economically vulnerable.

The unfinished socio-economic development means that Arab states today continue to be part of the Third World. The structural fragility of Arab economies is clearly reflected in the HDI that includes per capita income, GDP, rate of economic growth, social inequality, standard of living, insufficient daily nutritional intake, life expectancy, poverty and hunger, illiteracy and female empowerment.

This chapter considers the hypothesis that the Arab states have failed to balance their abilities and objectives and consequently to achieve the dual objective of development and security. Sustained socio-economic development is achieved only when the human person becomes the core of such development, being both its means and end at the same time.[1] According to Islamic teachings freedom from hunger and fear is essential for humans' emancipation and development. The Qur'an says it is He 'Who provided them with food against hunger and with security against fear' (Q106.5). The UNDP definition of human security is commonly associated with freedom from fear and freedom from want. However, this chapter contends that human insecurity in the Arab world is not limited to those living in Iraq, Palestine or Somalia, but comprises all those who are deprived of their basic rights and needs in all Arab countries.

My analysis covers the most significant cultural, social and economic paradigms influencing the Arab states' foreign policy-making. It is only feasible for the Arab countries to achieve a sustainable socio-economic development through a collective approach. It includes promoting regional integration, enhancement of interdependent policies, mutual understanding, confidence building, settlement of contentious issues and regional cooperation.

2. The Cultural Variable

Social scientists have tried to understand the political changes sweeping the world. Alvin Toffler linked globalization to the technological revolution, while others, such as John Gilbert and Marshall McLuhan, have talked about the 'abundant society' and the 'global village'. Francis Fukuyama went even further by arguing that 'we may be witnessing the end of history', conjuring up the predominance of the Western economic and political model. Samuel Huntington points out that 'the end of the cold war has not ended conflicts but has rather given rise to new identities rooted in culture'.[2] He spoke of clashes between the Islamic/Confucian civilizations with the West or with each other and argued that the resurgence of Islam had been fuelled by population growth. 'Overall Muslims constituted perhaps 18 per cent of the world's population in 1980 and are likely to be over 20 per cent in 2000 and 30 per cent in 2025.'[3]

Cultural Alienation

At a time when traditional colonialism is in retreat, a new and just as intrusive and lethal kind, namely cultural dependence, has appeared on the scene. 'The cultural heritage, as one component of knowledge, should not be abandoned to become the undisputed arena of unexamined readings.'[4] The danger of cultural colonialism is that it controls people's minds and the way they think, destroys the national culture and its related values and civilization, and creates a new subculture in which the potential new elite, as well as new entrants into the political field, is reared. Cultural dependence occurs when local people are overly awed by foreign cultures, especially Western culture, entailing the diminishment of the local culture, and provoking crises of identity and belonging.[5] The question of national identity surfaces when Arabs must use foreign language, English in some parts or French in al-Maghrib al-Arabia, as a mean of communication in their home country. In the Gulf countries,[6] especially Dubai in the United Arab Emirates (UAE), people use English to communicate with foreign workers, almost in most sectors of the economy, and tourists. Children are exposed from their early days to foreign languages, literature, stories and legends and are forced to use English as a language of instruction. People in al Maghrib al-Arabia are in no better situation, the only difference the fact that French is substituted for English as a language of learning. Cultural dependence in the Arab countries can be seen in the spread of foreign schools, the establishment of branches of Western universities and the imposition of foreign control over the media (a phenomenon termed media dependence). Western or Eastern academic curricula are copied by Arab institutions, along with Northern academic and administrative rules and regulations, and the same testing and evaluation systems, even study subjects, despite Arab society's difference from those in the developed world. Cultural dependence may have other negative repercussions, such as feelings of estrangement/alienation that could lead to the emigration of scientists, as shown below. The contributions of Arab/Muslim culture to human knowledge is undeniable, however, given the lack of parity between the two sides, Arabs and Muslims in the present day and age seem to be more influenced by the dominant Western culture than the other way around. 'Power is a means to change or influence the behaviour of another person or group.'[7] Western influence has provoked divisions among intellectuals that have paralysed the Islamic renaissance, if not totally annihilated it. Western powers have effectively exploited the ailing condition of the Arab world to advance their interests through indirect but deliberate policies intended to weaken the local culture.

1. Beliefs are propagated and political organizations established in Arab and Muslim countries whose aim is to fulfil Western objectives. To this end, Western countries have encouraged religious and political sects and

contradictory political and intellectual currents. Iraq, Lebanon, Sudan and Algeria, among others, are a case in point. The organized ideological indoctrination campaign pursued by the colonial European powers through Christian missionaries in Syria and Lebanon and towards Christian minorities in different parts of the Arab world was intended to separate them from their historical and cultural context.[8]

2. National and ethnic identities are deliberately highlighted, as was evident in a letter addressed by British Colonial Secretary Ormsby-Gore (1936-1938) to Prime Minister Neville Chamberlain (May 1937-May 1940). In the letter, Ormsby-Gore says that British policy has always aimed at preventing Arab unity and Islamic solidarity from taking root, and that this was as it should be; he added that Britain had encouraged local identities in Sudan, Nigeria, Egypt and other Islamic countries since these were relatively less dangerous than Islamic unity. If we look at various developments in the Arab world today, we can still clearly see such policies unfolding in the West's support for the Kurds in Iraq, the Amazigh in Algeria, the Marionettes in Lebanon, the Copts in Egypt and the separatist movement in southern Sudan.

3. The European countries introduced secularism to the Arab world in order to foster a new Muslim generation that believes in Western ideologies and tenets. The importance of this policy lies in Morgenthau's description of political power as the state's ability to control the minds and actions of others, and in Edward Carr's belief that one kind of political power is the ability to control the thoughts and opinions of others.[9] The institute founded by Napoleon in Egypt was the first milestone on the road to promote secularism in the Arab world, being the first Western scientific establishment in the Arab world, in the modern era. Albert Hourani says that Napoleon's 1798 Egyptian campaign introduced new ideas to the Arab world, and marked the beginning of an intense acculturation process between East and West, during which the Arabs absorbed European culture.[10] Taha Hussein believed unequivocally that nineteenth-century educational curricula and programmes were developed on purely European bases, which led to 'our children being educated along European lines in primary and secondary school, as well as in higher education'.[11] On the other hand he also described Napoleon's invasion of Egypt in 1798 as 'blessed'.[12] Ikram al-Umar adds that when modern university curricula were first written in the Muslim world, there were no Muslim alternatives to social, economic and political sciences,

or to other fields of learning, and students were therefore taught Western tenets. Western scientific doctrines in these sensitive fields were inculcated as if they were irrefutable scientific facts.[13] The American Protestant Mission founded the American University of Beirut (AUB), previously known as the Syrian Protestant College. The phenomenon of opening branches of Western universities in Arab countries we are witnessing today, even if it is part of the inevitable globalization of university education, could not have taken place without the approval of the highest echelons of political power in the countries involved. 'The transfer of American academic expertise in light of the strategic considerations of the post 9/11 world involves the redesign of the new Arab generation's brain, a generation well known for its staunch enmity towards America's extreme reaction to anything remotely connected to these bloody events.'[14]

4. After the failure of the Crusades, the West used Christianization and Orientalism as weapons of choice, following a call by the Spanish priest Raymon Lull, a call further endorsed by Edwin Nils, in his book *Brief History of Christianisation*, and alluded to by Ernest Barker.[15] Lull called for the establishment of Islamic and Oriental Studies chairs at various European universities, thus introducing Orientalism, a move designed to provide a field of study for Western intellectuals. This serves Western interests and achieves their aims but at the same time it distorts Eastern thought, making a negative impact on Muslim students and fostering in them a permanent sense of inadequacy. The onset of Orientalism goes back to the Council of Vienna's decision in 1312 to establish professorial chairs in the Arabic, Greek, Hebrew and Syriac languages at a number of European universities. This move, according to Ahmad Sidqi al-Dajani (1985), contributed to the transfer of a number of specific ideas about Islamic culture to the West, and the transfer of Western ideas to the Muslim world. Orientalists compared Arab administration and sciences unfavourably with the Western model, underlining Western superiority in the process. At a time when Orientalism and Christianization had become two sides of the same coin, from the sixteenth century on, the Muslim world in general, and the Arab world in particular, fell under Western domination. The onset of direct Western colonialism, namely by the Dutch, Spanish and Portuguese, followed by the French and the British, led to the indirect, and mainly political and cultural, imperialism that the US today is exercising. The new secular thinking, which called for the separation of state and religion, was reinforced

by the claim that religion and Islam in particular is the explanation for Muslim underdevelopment.

In the twentieth century various non-homogeneous groups of Arab and Muslim intellectuals emerged, carrying with them new, diverse and often contradictory ideas that fall between Western secular liberalism and Marxist philosophy. Another new group, of pragmatists or realists, has devoted itself to defending the objectives, interests and policies of the United States in the Arab region, and to promoting the theories of the conservative American right, a group which Muhammad al-Sayyid Salyim calls 'the Arab Integrationists'. In its efforts to tighten its control over the Arab world under the overall umbrella of the 'war on terror', the United States urged friendly Arab governments to review, if not fundamentally change, their educational curricula. It also established new educational media outlets, such as the al-Hurrah television station and Sawa Radio, which broadcast exclusively to the Arab world. American films, programmes and advertising that promote American goods and products now occupy a large space in Arab media outlets and cinema theatres, influencing Arab public opinion and undermining Arab and Islamic identity.

Western and Westernized local authors have been mobilized to work under the banner of democracy, public freedom and human rights for the people of the Third World. They benefit from considerable financial and moral support through American-sponsored conferences and seminars, and politically from the pressure that the US brings to bear on Arab governments and from various interventions in the internal affairs of Arab states under the pretext of enforcing respect for human rights. The American administration has never shirked from intervening directly or indirectly in favour of individuals and groups whose interests happen to coincide with its own. Through such moves, it aims at further dividing, scattering and weakening a nation's grip on its achievements and material assets, in order to be able to gain control over them later. Huntington argues: 'the source of conflict between states from different cultures is the ability to impose one's own values, culture, and institution on another group as compared to that group's ability to do to you.'[16]

5. Foreign companies working in the fields of exploration, excavation, export and international marketing of natural resources have successfully monopolized Arab assets, while colonial European countries have succeeded in linking Third World economies to their own, and opening Arab markets

to Western products. They have also encouraged Arab investments in the West, working hard to attract Arab capital, which is often held hostage to the political whim of European and American leaders seeking to impose sanctions on this or that regime; examples are the American sanctions on Iran in 1979, Libya in 1986, Panama in 1988 and Iraq in 1990. As evidence, we could point to the events currently unfolding in Iraq, namely the fierce competition between Western companies, especially American, over Iraq's oil and other economic resources, with the aim of gaining special privileges that would allow them eventually to monopolize the country's oil wealth, and thus control its economy for decades to come.

6. The Europeans have encouraged minorities in Islamic countries to seize power, in the knowledge that once this is achieved they will need international allies to help them maintain their position. We may point, in this context, to Iraq and its Kurdish issue, Sudan and the problems in its southern and western (Darfur) regions, Egypt and the West's support for certain Coptic movements and, finally, to the Arab Maghreb and the Amazigh minority. On the other hand, and despite their calls for democratic empowerment and respect for human rights, a number of Western countries have assisted opportunistic groups in seizing power, and have not hesitated to support dictatorships following the emergence of pro-Western 'national' governments after independence has been achieved. Even though Western colonialism has shed its traditional garb, it has returned to us today in a new form, thanks to a series of inequitable agreements concluded with regional governments. Underlying these agreements is the readiness of European countries, especially those that were once the region's colonizers, to defend the security and stability of the newly emerging political regimes against any looming danger, whether internal or external. This is a natural outcome of the imbalance in a number of Arab states between abilities and objectives, and of the failure to achieve the dual objective of development and security. Some Arab countries have thus become overly dependent on various forms of foreign assistance, severely jeopardizing their independent decision-making processes and curtailing the scope they have for political manœuvre on international issues. 'Cultural identity defines the state's place in World politics.'[17] This is evidenced by the obvious retreat in international relations policy by some Arab countries, particularly Egypt and Saudi Arabia, after the American occupation of Iraq.

7. As indicated above, Western countries have taken advantage of their superiority in the fields of information technology, scientific development,

> and the communication revolution through modern media, to dominate the world, particularly, for the purposes of this study, the Arab world. They have tried, in the process, to weaken local cultures, led by a US that is trying to improve its image in the world.[18] Not only have branches of Western universities been established in Arab countries, but Arab universities have also incorporated Western culture into their own curricula, invited foreign professors to teach, and replaced Arabic with English as a language of instruction, under the pretext that it is the language of science and business. This has led to a marked neglect of the Arabic language and to imposing English on young students. Furthermore, rather than addressing the negative impact on the academic standard of Arab state university graduates, most of these universities and other higher education institutions,[19] conscious of the Arabic language's shortcomings, have done their best to use English as the main language for teaching and research. This linguistic reversal has taken place not only at the level of higher education but also at the basic state school level, with a number of Arab countries abandoning or radically amending their curricula to keep up with the culture of globalization. Despite the fact that constitutions in Arab countries stipulate that Arabic is the national language, many day-to-day business and formalities are now conducted in English, as if the secret behind the nation's backwardness lies in its language – the very language that dominated the world during the period of the Arab renaissance. It is relevant to note that neither Japan, Germany, France, South Korea, Malaysia nor China abandoned their language as a precondition for their scientific, technological and administrative advancement. Huntington argues that 'Chinese leaders celebrate Confucianism as the source of Chinese progress. They looked for legitimation in their common Chinese culture.'[20]

Further evidence of this Western campaign against the Arabic language is to be seen in the promotion of local dialects, with the emergence in the Arab world of a number of newsletters, daily newspapers and satellite stations that use only the local dialect. Attacks against the Arabic language began in Turkey under Mustafa Kemal Atatürk in the early twentieth century, when the Arabic alphabet was replaced by the Latin alphabet for the writing of Turkish, and continued in North Africa, where the French helped to revive the Amazigh language, and convert it into a written language, using the Latin alphabet. African countries, especially those whose languages use Arabic script, were made to believe that the Arabic alphabet was not appropriate for them, since it could not accommodate the full range of African sounds, and that they should therefore use the Latin alphabet. Now, the number of African languages that use the Arabic script has dropped from approximately seventy-five to less than ten, the last convert being Somalia, a member of the Arab League.[21]

A handful of Arab intellectuals, conscious of the need to spare the Arabs some of the problems arising from this linguistic duality in education and culture, are advocating the unification of the Arab nation's dialects and educational curricula, and calling for more attention to the classic Arabic language.[22] The identity issue becomes particularly intense in cleft countries that have sizeable groups of people from different civilizations.[23] In this context, the government of the United Arab Emirates, aware of the dangers entailed in having a multicultural citizenry, and of the importance of preserving the Arab identity, has a strategy aimed at the re-empowerment of the Arabic language,[24] but no concrete measures have yet been adopted. A symposium on language, identity and the Arab Gulf states held in Doha in February 2009 warned that the Arabic language is threatened in the Arab Gulf countries, affecting the very existence and identity of those countries.[25] Moreover it is argued that the political and ideological debate over the state of the Arabic language generally fails to address the heart of the subject, which is the state of educational institutions. It also ignores the state of language teaching and the competence of teachers and students in the fields of communication, expression and writing. For this reason, the debate tends towards the adoption of political positions based on emotion and incapable of visualizing the fate that awaits the Arabic language in the absence of a defined and publicly announced linguistic strategy.[26]

The Identity Crisis

In the second half of the twentieth century, the Arab world witnessed a tremendous scientific and cultural renaissance. Some Arab countries succeeded in eradicating illiteracy, and Arab culture spread and was recognized worldwide. In the overall picture, however, the first outcome of the unequal encounter between the East and the West was the emergence of many schisms and intellectual currents. Since the fall of the Ottoman Empire the Arab individual has plunged into an identity crisis.[27]

As a reaction two intellectual tendencies emerged within Arab society. One was to reject all that is Western, call for a return to traditional and pure Islam, and advocate a single-minded focus on Islam and its tenets. Followers of this tendency are known as salafis, not to be confused with the contemporary group of the same name. The other tendency was to believe that, if the Arab nation really wants to advance, it must take account of the course successfully charted by the West and learn the appropriate lessons. Followers of this line of thinking consider that Europe and the United States only started to advance when they adopted secular systems based on the separation of church and state, and that, if the Arabs want to achieve progress, they have no choice but to pursue this model. Hisham Sharabi says that the latter group, known as the 'Integrators', have moved from being 'borrowers' to 'embroiderer' of everything Western.[28] In the meantime, a third group has emerged in reaction to divisions within the Islamic nation, calling for the adoption of what is positive in both the Islamic and Western cultures, but without abandoning the Islamic heritage, and being eclectic as far as Western culture is concerned. Al-Dajani describes this group as 'inventive' and a movement of builders and workers (masons), not to be confused with the freemasons, due to their differences from the other two. Thus, rather than emerging in a reaction to Western culture, this third group is a movement by itself; and rather than copying and imitating, it thrives on invention. Al-Dajani believes that these three movements should not be described as 'religious', 'liberal' and 'progressive', respectively, since they all have elements in common.[29] Moreover, some positions with regard to this dilemma do not reflect an ideological struggle, such as a conflict over class interests, workers and labourers against landowners and capitalists. It reflects rather the dilemma of having to choose between the Western political, economic and cultural model, and the traditional local heritage as a genuine alternative that covers all aspects of modern life, and is better suited for Arab Muslim society. It is argued that 'all discussion of the repercussions of the knowledge society on Arab culture and identity overlook the fact that the knowledge society essentially requires rational economic management and relies on a social structure supported by a contemporary culture, as well as great capacities of intercommunication with the outside world'.[30] Others believe that the authenticity versus Westernization debate does not belong to the domain of either ideological choice or political decision-making, but is a theoretical dilemma. Muhammed Abid al-Jabiri does not believe that the Arabs are free today, or have ever had the freedom, to choose between adopting and rejecting the Western model, because the latter imposed itself on them at the beginning of Europe's colonial expansion eastwards, with all that expansion entailed. It involved, among other things, uneven commercial exchanges, interference in domestic affairs under the guise of protecting the rights of non-Muslim minorities, direct rule, economic hegemony and cultural and ideological control. The Western philosophy of democratic and cultural reform in Arab and Islamic countries rests on three basic tenets: establishing a society of knowledge and freedom, empowering women in order to gain public support for the American project and help it succeed[31] and entrenching the Western model in Arab countries and linking them to the European capitalist infrastructure.[32] Thus, because interaction between Islamic and Western cultures took place at a time when Western culture was stronger than Muslim culture, the West's influence on the Arabs was greater than the Arabs' influence on the West, and, despite a certain level of reciprocal exchange, the transfer of ideas and beliefs to a very important sector of Arab society accelerated, especially after Europe's powerful occupation of most Arab and Muslim territory. Moreover, Arab opinions differed regarding the very concept of nationhood: while some held onto the concepts of one Arab nation and Arab nationalism, others insisted on the concept of the 'nation-state', since nationhood rested more on an organic than on a cultural basis. The Arab world has witnessed the emergence of several, often contradictory, political currents or movements. In addition, in the early 1990s the new Western culture of globalization or 'Americanization', as some prefer to call it, emerged. Under the guise of promoting political and democratic reform and human rights, this new culture gave the coup de grâce to what was left of Arab Islamic identity. Bernard Lewis points out that there has been a recurring tendency, in time of emergency, for Muslims to look for their identity in religion. This created another cultural burden for the Arab individual, already torn between modernity and backwardness. Muslims, in massive numbers, are turning toward Islam as 'a source of identity, meaning, stability, legitimacy, development, power, and hope'.[33]

The Brain Drain

Islam urges people to learn and to seek knowledge; God said in the Qur'an: 'Teach Adam all the names' (Q2.31) and 'Teach people what they do not know' (Q96.5). The very first command God gave to the Prophet Muhammad, may God's blessings be upon Him, was 'Read' (Q96.1), and devoted an entire sura in the Qur'an, Surat al-Qalam: 'Nun, the pen and what men record' (Q68.1), to this topic. However, the situation now is very different. The standard of Arab universities has deteriorated over the years. Based on the international standard, only four Arab universities, King Saud University, the American University of Beirut, the UAE University and Cairo University, are ranked among the top

500 universities worldwide, according to Top University Ranking for 2009, occupying positions 247, 351, 374 and 400 respectively,[34] out of 152 accredited universities in the Arab world.

> The Arab region's expenditure on scientific research is one of the world's lowest in terms of GNP. Research and development institutions are weakly integrated with the cycle of production. The development returns of Arab scientific research are very weak and do not correspond to the magnitude of annual Arab expenditure on them, which tops $2 billion and which, in the period 2002–6, resulted in approximately 38.2 patents per year and 5,000 published scientific papers.[35]

The Muslim intellectual Zaghlul Raghib al-Najjar referred in a television interview to the fact that, in the West, the proportion of scientists to citizens is 4,300 per million, while in Egypt it is less that 190 per million. In the same vein, the percentage of scientists and engineers working in the field of research and development in Western Europe is 55.4 per cent, whereas it is less that 12.6 per cent in developing countries, of which the Arab world is part. Moreover, while the number of published research articles in all the Arab countries combined was 1,323 in 1976, in Israel alone there were 3,291. This means that the entire scientific output of the Arab nation was only 40 per cent of Israel's,[36] compounded by the fact that only 5 per cent of this Arab output is published in Arabic.[37] What are the reasons for this scientific decline in the Arab world? There are, of course, many and the most important of them may be summarized as follows:

1. The low level of spending on education and scientific research compared to government spending in other domains. At a time when 6–8 per cent of the budgets of advanced countries is allocated to scientific research and development, it does not exceed 2 per cent in the Arab countries.[38] Furthermore, while advanced countries allocate 2–4 per cent of GNP to scientific and technological research and to applying its output for development purposes, the corresponding figure drops to around 0.2 per cent in Arab countries.[39] The per capita share of spending on scientific research in the Arab world does not exceed US$2 per annum compared with between US$30 and US$100 in advanced countries.[40]

2. The emigration of scientists, more commonly known as the brain drain. I shall not analyse here the reasons behind the emigration of scientists from the Third World, including the Muslim and Arab worlds, northwards, since

it is a complicated issue that has several causes. Some of these are external and have to do with attractive opportunities and the possibility of a better quality of life, while others are internal and have to do with the hard life in the south, especially the political situation and lack of opportunities. There are also personal reasons that have to do with the scientist himself, his attachment to his nation, and whether he is ready to leave it.[41] It is important, however, to address the negative impact of this phenomenon on scientific progress in Muslim countries, given that the brain drain is one of the most serious economic and social problems facing the Arab world. Arab losses as a result of this phenomenon were in the range of US$11 billion in the 1970s,[42] and the Arab world's share of the total brain drain from the Third World is 31 per cent.[43] Moreover, Arab doctors and engineers constitute about 50 and 23 per cent, respectively, of the overall number of doctors and engineers who immigrate to the US, not to mention the ratio from the Muslim world as a whole. A full 50 per cent of all doctors, 23 per cent of engineers and 15 per cent of scientists in the Arab world leave for the West. An Arab League study found that no less than 450,000 highly capable scientists, doctors and engineers have emigrated from the Arab world,[44] of which around 200,000 went to the US, making up 6 per cent of all scientists in that country,[45] with the rest distributed throughout Europe, Canada and Australia. It is also worth mentioning that Arab doctors make up a significant percentage of all doctors in Britain.[46] Studies also show that 54 per cent of Arab students abroad do not return home after finishing their studies.[47] Saint-Simon said, in this context, that if a nation loses fifty of its richest citizens and business people, and another fifty of its international-level employees, the impact would not be as hard as losing fifty of its most talented scientists, and fifty of its greatest creative minds and artists. The nation would feel as if an important part of it had been amputated.[48] Another result of emigration is that, with 60 per cent of all Arab research projects undertaken outside the Arab world and three out of every five Arab researchers living abroad, most Arab scientific research output is published outside the Arab world.[49] Sources estimate the overall economic and social cost of the Arab scientists' migration at around US$200 billion per year.[50]

3. The Social Variable

Social underdevelopment is a consequence of the state's inability to improve its citizens' quality of life. This is reflected in the level of services, such as health and education, that it provides and in the extent to which relations between men and women, and the social status of women, has improved. The situation becomes even more complicated when we learn that the lion's share of GNP goes on military expenditure. Bias toward military overspending cannot be justified by the pretext of maintaining national security in the countries concerned, since overspending is liable to reduce the resources necessary for other important services, such as health and education. It might also lead to an increase in the power of the military as a domestic pressure group, to its interference in political affairs, and to the conversion of political regimes into military regimes. This development could pose a real threat to national security and stability by narrowing opportunities for internal political openness and development, at a time when the middle class is growing exponentially. Good governance systems and organizations concerned with human development issues, such as health and education, average life expectancy and the social status of women, among others, use recognized and objective scientific tools to measure development and underdevelopment. In the context of this review of social challenges facing the Arab world in the twenty-first century, I devote this section to social development issues by addressing some of the human development indicators.

Social Injustice

Social justice is measured by the extent of a government's commitment to policies that create prosperity. 'Any hope of the equitable social distribution of the results of development will disappear in the absence of a democratic climate that provides popular oversight and fights corruption.'[51] The recent uprisings revealed the degree of corruption in the Arab world, with Mubarak's assets in the US amounting to 31 billion dollars when 40 per cent of Egyptians are below the poverty line, Gaddafi's fortune estimated at 131 billion dollars and the case of Bin Ali no different. Relevant data indicate that most Arab countries spend undue amounts on military equipment at the expense of standards of health and education. Most Arab countries have health expenditures between 2.4 and 6 per cent of their GDP. The condition is further complicated by the fact that actual spending on health, which ranges from $25 per capita in Comoros all the way to $871 per capita in Bahrain, reflects clear intra-regional disparities.[52] Military spending in a number of Arab countries, such as the UAE, Oman and Syria, stands at 45.3 per cent, 43 per cent and 37.2 per cent of GNP respectively, more than a third of their total expenditure. Annual reports by some research organizations that monitor military developments showed an increase in Arab military spending at the expense of spending on other development domains. Some sources estimated the total amount spent on armaments by the Arab Gulf countries between 2000 and 2003 at around US$14,800 billion.[53] In 2006, Saudi Arabia, Egypt and the UAE were on the list of the ten highest weapons-importing counties in the world,[54] and in 2007, Saudi Arabia headed the regional list in terms of military spending.[55] Moreover, military spending in all Arab countries as a whole was well over what they spent on the health sector, which in 2002 stood at between 1 per cent in Yemen and Sudan, and 3.3 per cent in Saudi Arabia, Bahrain, Lebanon and Djibouti. However, Egypt, Syria, Tunisia, Jordan, Oman, Djibouti, Qatar and the UAE have reduced their scores on the Human Poverty Index by at least 25 per cent over the first decade of the twenty-first century. For the most part, progress was basic, with the exception of advance in per capita GDP, which has risen from $5,038 in 2001 to $7,760 in 2006 and to more than $8,000 in 2008. However, at the level of the Arab region, the significance of this improvement is reduced because of the great variation between the Arab states and the clear concentration of the increases in per capita GDP in the oil-exporting countries as opposed to others of the region.[56] According to the *Arab Knowledge Report*, despite the improvements in social welfare in the Arab states from the end of the 1990s until 2007, poverty in the Arab region is increasing. In 2005, the proportion of people living below the lowest national income poverty line in the Arab region reached approximately 18.4 per cent. The number of poor in the Arab countries for which data have been available exceeds the number of undernourished. It is argued that inhabitants living on less than $2 a day represent 60 per cent in Mauritania, 45 per cent in Yemen and 40 per cent in Egypt.[57] In the final analysis, figures confirm the fact that, several decades after independence, Arab countries are yet to achieve their national development and security objectives.

Life Expectancy at Birth

The life expectancy indicator is widely used to gauge how well the concept of the 'prosperity state' is being realized. Some use it as an alternative to per capita income to gauge the state's distributive ability across the social spectrum. Life expectancy at birth, which is an estimated figure that depends on the health care standard and infant mortality rates, reflects the wide disparities between advanced and developing countries. While the average life expectancy at birth in North America (US and Canada) is 82 years and in Europe 81 years, the average in Latin America does not exceed 62 years, in Asia 58 years and in Africa 46 years,[58] due to the high rate of infant mortality in that particular region, compared with that in advanced countries. In the Arab countries the average life expectancy rate does not exceed 74 years. Life expectancy in Kuwait, Qatar and the UAE is 74, 72 and 70 years, respectively. It is worth noting that in 2003 the average infant mortality rate was 48 per 1,000 births and for children under 5 61 per 1,000, compared with 9 and 10 respectively in advanced countries.[59] The reason for these disparities is due in large part to the low quality of health care afforded to citizens, as evidenced by the low numbers of physicians in the Third World, as well as in the Arab countries. Estimates put the average number of citizens per physician in advanced countries at 530, with 410 in Sweden, 460 in France, 500 in the US and 680 in Great Britain, whereas it is 640 in Lebanon, 620 in Libya and 760 in Egypt. Low life expectancy at birth affects the prosperity gauge, called Physical Quality of Life, used to differentiate between countries as far as health, education and other quality of life services provided by the state to its citizens are concerned.

Illiteracy

Illiteracy is another indicator measuring various countries' success in the field of human development. Arab countries are lagging behind many world countries quantitatively and qualitatively in education outcomes. This is due, among other factors, to limited spending on education. Despite the Arab region having spent 5 per cent of GDP and 20 per cent of government budgets on education over the past forty years, many of the structural aspects of weakness remain.[60] Whilst the average spending on education per capita in developing countries, including Arab countries, is US$14, in the US and Europe it is US$389 and US$166 respectively.[61] In a quick comparison between spending on education and the military, we see that in most Arab states military spending far exceeds spending on education, which does not exceed 6.5 per cent of GDP in Morocco, 6.4 per cent in Tunisia, 5.8 per cent in Oman and 4.8 per cent in Kuwait.[62] However, despite the marked increase in the rate of overall enrolment in primary schools from 34 million in 1993, to 42 million in 2000, a figure that could reach 57 million in 2025, registration in primary school officially stands at less than 75 per cent, which means that 25 per cent of Arab children do not go to school.[63] Almost 9 million children of elementary-school age are outside school, most of them in the countries that have not solved the illiteracy problem.[64] Sources state that 15 million do not attend secondary school and net secondary enrolment rates do not exceed the world average of

59 per cent,[65] whilst the industrially advanced states and those of Central Asia have achieved enrolment rates around 84 per cent.

Despite the success of a number of Arab countries in eradicating illiteracy, illiteracy rates in the Arab world are still higher than both the developed and the developing world averages. It is argued that around one-third of the adult population is unable to read and write, meaning that there are still some 60 million, almost 40 per cent of the adult population, illiterate people in the Arab countries. According to the Arab Organization for Education, Culture and Science (ALESCO), two-thirds of the overall number of illiterate Arabs are women between the ages of 15 and 45, who account for over 50 per cent of the population in some countries, such as Sudan, Morocco, Egypt, Mauritania, Yemen and the Comoros Islands.[66] If we compare these figures with those for other regions of the world, the severity of the problem becomes self-evident: the illiteracy rate in the US and Russia does not exceed 1 per cent, in Europe 3 per cent, while in Latin America, Asia and Africa rates stand at around 26 per cent, 33 per cent and 78 per cent respectively.[67] On the basis of official and semi-official indicators of illiteracy in some Arab countries, we can divide the Arab countries into several groups:

1. Illiteracy between 80 and 90 per cent, including Yemen, Saudi Arabia and Mauritania;
2. Illiteracy between 60 and 79 per cent, including Morocco and Libya;
3. Illiteracy between 50 and 59 per cent, including Syria, Iraq, Algeria and Tunisia;
4. Illiteracy below 25 per cent, including Qatar, the UAE and Jordan.

Female Empowerment

Despite the important role women play in society in general in the Arab world, they are still socially, culturally and politically restricted, and not free to participate efficiently in the development of their own societies. Moreover, though the winds of change that have been sweeping the world since the 1990s have added a new challenge, their impact on the Arab world have not produced the results that optimists among Arab intellectuals had hoped for, and the lot of women has been hardly affected. International calls to improve the status of women and the pressure brought to bear on Arab governments to introduce political reforms have had a very limited impact on women. Female empowerment compared with that of men in most Arab countries is quite low. For many leaders the issue of women's political rights has become a sort of democratic facade which they erect to ward off political criticism for their lack of democracy.[68] Thus, women in a number of Arab countries have occupied senior official posts, once the exclusive prerogative of men. Women became cabinet members, MPs, ambassadors and judges. Female participation in politics, formerly taboo, became a phenomenon, with Arab Maghreb states having the largest share of women membership in parliaments – recording a significant number of 165 MPs. Conservative GCC countries introduced new reforms on the road for women's participation in politics (see Table 2.1). Laws relevant to women's issues have been reviewed and amended to protect their right to education, work and travel.[69] However, the above developments, and various superficial reforms introduced into the Arab political order, failed to improve the status of women in either the labour-exporting or labour-importing countries.[70] The average presence of women in Arab economies is less than 50 per cent, except for Morocco where women make up 53 per cent of the workforce.[71] Women's participation in political life also differs according to each country's local civic culture, ranging from no participation at all to limited degrees of participation.

Up until 2005, the highest percentage of parliamentary seats occupied by women was 31.6 per cent (in Iraq), and ministerial positions held by women amounted to no more than 0.2 per cent of every cabinet reshuffle, also in Iraq.[72] Others point out that oil money and its use in consumption has added a new obstacle to women's social participation (see Figure 2).[73]

Political reforms have yielded positive impacts on the role of women in politics in the Arab world. Policies adopted do not acknowledge discrimination against women on the basis of gender, race, ethnicity or religion. They were, however, intended to give the impression of empowerment, thereby legitimizing nation-states, rather than actual or genuine reform for power sharing. It should be acknowledged that women are by no means globally empowered, so that the problems of Arab women are not overemphasized, or misconstrued.[74] Women in the Arab world make up 9.7 per cent in the Lower House, 7 per cent of the Upper House (Senate) composition and an average of 9.1 per cent in both Houses (see Table 2.2). The number of women in Arab parliaments in 2008 was 9.6 per cent lower than the world average ten years ago (12.2 per cent in 1998), and if the growth is maintained at the same level, it is very likely that Arab women will continue to consistently lag behind women in other parts of the world[75] (see Figure 2.2). However, statistics show that rapid increase is marked by severe contrasts, varying from 25.5 per cent in Iraq and 22.8 in Tunisia to 0–2 per cent in Saudi Arabia, Oman, Kuwait, Yemen, Egypt and Bahrain.[76]

Table 2.1. Female Empowerment in the Arab World (2009)

State	MG*	MP	Judges	Ambassadors
Algeria	2	35	137	4
Bahrain	2	10	1	2
Comoros	-	1	—	—
Djibouti	1		1	
Egypt	2	11	42	
Iraq	3	73	—	—
Lebanon	2	4	150	4
Libya	—	36		1
Jordan	4	14	48	3
Kuwait	1	4	—	1
Mauritania	3	17	—	2
Morocco	7	34	612	5
Oman	3	—	—	2
Palestine	2	17	2	1
Qatar	2	—	—	—
Saudi Arabia	1	6	—	—
Somalia	3	20	—	1
Sudan	2	2	76	2
Syria	2	30	170	8
Tunisia	1	43	509	5
UAE	4	9	3	2
Yemen	2	1	37	1

* members of governments

Table 2.2. Female Participation in Parliaments

Regional averages			
	Single House or Lower House	*Upper House or Senate*	*Both Houses combined*
Nordic countries	43.2 per cent	---	---

Americas	22.4 per cent	19.9 per cent	22 per cent
Europe - OSCE member countries including Nordic countries	21 per cent	19.4 per cent	20.7 per cent
Europe - OSCE member countries excluding Nordic countries	19.2 per cent	19.4 per cent	19.3 per cent
Asia	18.5 per cent	16.7 per cent	18.4 per cent
Sub-Saharan Africa	18.3 per cent	21 per cent	18.6 per cent
Pacific	13 per cent	32.6 per cent	15.2 per cent
Arab States	9.7 per cent	7 per cent	9.1 per cent

Regions are classified by descending order of the percentage of women in the Lower or single House

Source: http://www.ipu.org/wmn-e/world.htm

The low social status of women is most evident when the situation is considered from two different perspectives:

1. From the point of view of the level of women's participation in the labour force, despite the fact that there are over 150 million women in the Arab world, of whom 70 million are of working age, no more than 5 million are actually active in the labour market (not including those working in agriculture, the family home, as nannies or as roving salespersons). As evidence of women's low level of participation in the labour market, we might also point to the proportion of women in the total labour force: 9.6 per cent in Syria, 8 per cent in Morocco, 7 per cent in the UAE, 5.2 per cent in Kuwait, 4 per cent in Egypt, 2.7 per cent in Libya and 1.8 per cent in Algeria. In advanced countries, on the other hand, the ratio of women in the labour force is over 20 per cent of the total force: 46 per cent in Poland, 29 per cent in the US and 20.4 per cent in Greece.[77]
2. From the point of view of standards of education and levels of illiteracy, in Libya, for example, the illiteracy rate is 62.5 per cent among males and 95 per cent among females. The average number of university-educated Arab men is 5.75 times that of women, with the exception of certain Arab Gulf countries where the number of females in regular and higher education surpasses that of males by almost 2:1.[78] It is now incumbent upon Arab regimes to look after women's welfare, given that God Almighty has chosen to elevate women, as stated in Surat al-Nisa (Q4).

4. The Economic Variable

Economists agree that sustainable development is that which has a human person at its centre and main objective. A human person is no longer looked at as a commodity subject to the supply and demand variable or influenced by invisible market forces. The human person, from the late 1980s and the beginning of the 1990s, became the driving force behind development.[79] Thus, upon a quick reading of development indicators in the Arab world, one finds that the rankings of Arab countries in the human development report range between 40th for Qatar, the highest on the list, and 151st, for Yemen, the lowest, with Iraq and Somalia not included due to their particular circumstances.[80] On this basis, the researcher can state unequivocally that conditions in the Arab countries are not very different from those in other underdeveloped countries. Manifestations of underdevelopment are many and varied, but they may be briefly characterized as follows.[81]

1. It is difficult to differentiate or draw a line categorically between various forms of underdevelopment, especially political, economic and social underdevelopment, and the cultural and intellectual underdevelopment that links them together. Underdevelopment is a comprehensive condition, meaning that its dimensions are difficult to isolate and its components difficult to separate, and, to address it successfully, it is important to apply the best comprehensive model for development analyses.

2. Underdevelopment is a structural condition strongly associated with forces of production within society, and with the ensuing relationships with power and authority. This why underdevelopment is difficult to address, since any solution necessarily involves the re-examination of the entire social and class systems, as well as the redistribution of the state's resources.

3. It is difficult to apply a single yardstick to underdevelopment, for although it has several manifestations and dimensions, it cannot be accurately measured. There are also different levels of underdevelopment on the basis of which each country is categorized. For the purpose of categorization, various terms have been coined to indicate a given country's condition, such as 'advanced', 'developing' or 'in the process of development', where once they were all said to be 'underdeveloped'. It is important to study the various manifestations of underdevelopment in order to ensure the best means of achieving sustainable development and complementarity. However, due

to limitations of space I shall concentrate on the analysis of the economic underdevelopment condition prevailing in the Arab world, as I have already explored the cultural, intellectual and social underdevelopment variables.

Economic Development

Economic underdevelopment, instability and dependency on the outside world are not due to the lack of natural and human resources, but to the lack of the political will and to regional instability. Arab countries have failed to resolve the main dilemma between regime security and national development. They face a major challenge in the need to find job opportunities for their growing populations where the unemployment rate remains very high: in 2005 it varied from 46 per cent in Algeria to 6.3 per cent in the United Arab Emirates.[82] Sources estimated Egypt's rate of unemployment in the third quarter of 2009 at 9.2 per cent.[83] The situation is further exacerbated by the fact that they are plagued by corruption. The Arab states, over the last two decades, have remained weak and hidebound, without any notable change in terms of institutional performance. Available indicators make clear that the Arab states' weak performance in terms of governance indicators did not change greatly. According to Transparency International on corruption rating no Arab country is ranked among the top twenty-five least corrupt in the *Global Corruption Report* of 2009. Qatar, the UAE and Oman were among the leading world countries in combating corruption, but they are ranked 28, 35 and 41 respectively in this list (see Table 2.3).

Table 2.3. Corruption in the Arab Countries (2008)

Country	2008 CPI Score (a)	Surveys Used (b)	Confidence Range (c)	Rank
Qatar	6.5	4	5.7- 6.9	28
UAE	5.9	5	4.8- 6.8	35
Oman	5.5	5	4.5- 6.4	41
Bahrain	5.4	5	4.3- 5.9	43
Jordan	5.1	9	4- 6.2	47
Tunisia	4.4	6	3.5- 5.5	62
Kuwait	4.3	4	3.3- 5.2	65
Morocco	3.5	6	3- 4	80
S. Arabia	3.5	5	3- 3.9	80

Country	2008 CPI Score (a)	Surveys Used (b)	Confidence Range (c)	Rank
Algeria	3.2	6	2.9- 3.4	92
Djibouti	3	4	2.2- 3.3	102
Lebanon	3	4	2.2- 3.6	102
Egypt	2.8	6	2.4- 3.2	115
Mauritania	2.8	7	2.2- 3.7	115
Libya	2.6	5	2.2- 3	126
Comoros	2.5	3	1.9- 3	134
Yemen	2.3	5	1.9- 2.8	141
Syria	2.1	5	1.6- 2.4	147
Sudan	1.6	6	1.5- 1.7	173
Iraq	1.3	4	1.6	178
Somalia	1	4	0.5- 1.4	180
Palestine	N.a.	N.a.	N.a	N.a.

a '2008 CPI Score' relates to perceptions of the degree of corruption as seen by businesspeople and country analysts, and ranges between 10 (highly clean) and 0 (highly corrupt).

b 'Surveys used' refers to the number of surveys that assessed a country's performance. Overall, thirteen surveys and expert assessments were used, and at least three were required for a country to be included in the CPI.

c 'Confidence range' provides a range of possible values of the CPI score. This reflects how a country's score may vary, depending on the measurement precision. Nominally, with 5% probability the score is above this range and with another 5% it is below. Particularly when only a few sources are available, however, an unbiased estimate of the mean coverage probability is lower than the nominal value of 90%.

Source: *Global Corruption Report*, 2009, pp. 397–402.

Corruption is attributed to the absence of public enforcement in security regulations, transparency, lack of democracy, absence of accountability mechanisms and weak legislation to fight corruption. The other dilemma for the Arab states is the gap between the relatively high population growth and the growth rate of the economy. Basic economic indicators show that total Arab GDP is $1.47 trillion less than that of Italy, which was estimated to have a GDP of $2.3 trillion in 2008.[84] They are also characterized by declining per capita income from $5,282 in 2005 to $4,660 in 2007, with annual growth of 5.6 per cent and unemployment at 14 per cent in 2006.[85] There are many forms of economic underdevelopment in the Arab world, just as there are many economic yardsticks to gauge each condition. By looking at various statistical data, we are able to delineate the following:

1. Arab countries rely either on the extraction of raw materials or on agriculture as the main source of national income. This is determined according to each of the sectors' share of a country's gross national product (GNP), gross domestic product (GDP), or distribution of labour across the economic spectrum. Thus, only a few workers out of the total working population are employed in the industrial sector, while many more are employed in agriculture. Yet this sector's contribution to GNP does not exceed 3 per cent in Saudi Arabia, 20 per cent in Egypt and 4 per cent in Libya. This could be due to low productivity levels resulting from old production methods, the seasonal nature of agriculture and its dependence on rainfall and soil fertility, etc.[86] On the other hand, extraction-based industries have maintained their high importance; their contribution to GDP has increased, between 2004 and 2005, from 32.9 per cent to 38.8 per cent.[87]
2. Another economic challenge facing the Arab world is the rising level of unemployment; some sources estimate that 3 million young Arabs enter the job market annually, and that there were, in 2006, 14 million unemployed, i.e. 15 per cent of the total work force.[88] This figure is expected to reach 25 million in 2010, an annual increase of 5 per cent.[89] However, the challenge is even greater if we consider the youthful nature of Arab society, the improving standard of health care in a number of Arab countries, and the consequent fall in infant mortality rates. In 2003, 31.6 per cent of the population of 335 million were under 15 years of age, however, this figure is expected to drop to 28 per cent of 386 million in 2015.[90]
3. Arab countries, until 2009, had high rates of inflation (price rises). In 2007, in Iraq, for example, the rate of inflation stood at 37 per cent and at around 11.4 per cent in Yemen. A report by the International Monetary Fund estimated the rate of inflation at 9 per cent in the oil-exporting Arab Gulf states, because demand exceeded society's ability to produce goods and services to satisfy market needs. A report issued by the UAE Ministry for Economy and Planning blamed the high figures on rising fuel and real estate prices.[91]
4. In 2007, economic growth in most Arab countries showed tangible improvement thanks to the unprecedented rise in the price of crude oil and increased contributions from other economic sectors. In the UAE, the economy

grew by 8.5 per cent, in most other Arab countries by 6 per cent, and in the Arab Maghreb by 5 per cent. Some sources expected the upward trend to continue in 2008 to be between 6 and 7 per cent. However, due to the global economic crisis and the drop in the oil prices the rate of economic growth is actually expected to decline to between 2 and 4 per cent.

5. There are disparities in national per capita income: around 30 million Arabs live below the poverty line. The numbers of those living on $2 a day is higher than of those suffering hunger in Saudi Arabia, Kuwait, Egypt, Syria, Jordan, Lebanon, Morocco, Algeria, Sudan and Mauritania, whereas the ratio of poverty and hunger are approximately the same in Yemen.[92] The situation becomes more acute when it becomes clear that the daily income of nearly 60 million people is less than one US dollar a day. The Arab countries could be divided into three groups:

    a. Yemen, Mauritania, Palestine, Morocco, Egypt, Syria and Lebanon, where the per capita income is between US$1,300 and US$5,000 per annum;
    b. Tunisia, Libya, Algeria, Jordan and Bahrain, where the per capita income is between US$5,000 and US$9,900 per annum;
    c. The Gulf Cooperation Council countries, with a high per capita income of US$10,000 per annum.

Figures and statistics released by a number of regional financial institutions, such as the Arab Fund for Economic and Social Development, the Arab Monetary Fund, the UNDP and other relevant research organizations, indicate that in 2006 the total Arab public debt stood at US$800 billion, 44 per cent of which, i.e. US$350 billion, was the total external public debt. The average increase in external debt stood at between 8 and 10 per cent, and the ratio of public debt to GDP in Syria, for example, was 17.5 per cent. The fact that the Arab world is facing economic problems does not in any way mean that they do not have what it takes to move from underdevelopment to a more developed status. However, this would require better guidance and management of economic, human and technical resources, searching for new resources, separating political conflicts from economic cooperation, activating the role of national development institutions and reviewing public spending policies.

Inter-Arab Trade Relations

Inter-Arab trade relations have shown a steady increase over the last decade. However, data released in 2008 revealed that the increase of 16.7 per cent in the total value of inter-Arab trade in 2007 was less than the previous four years. The export indicator shows an increase of 12.7 per cent, amounting to US$64.8 billion, whilst the total value of imports was US$61.5 billion, with an increase of 20.6 per cent in the volume of inter-Arab trade in 2007 – less than 2006 which was recorded at 22.5 per cent (see Table 2.4). Mauritania was top of the inter-Arab trade balance sheet, followed by Libya, Lebanon, Iraq, Somalia and Algeria in exports, and by Yemen, Libya, Morocco and Iraq in imports.[93] Inter-Arab trade faces political, legal and logistic problems. The competitive nature of inter-Arab politics presents a major barrier to consolidating inter-Arab trade. New protection and subsidizing policies need to be introduced to facilitate inter-Arab trade, including the review of existing laws and regulations, setting up joint products with an emphasis on food security, prioritizing Arab products, facilitating trans-shipment, upgrading and enhancing the existing infrastructure and providing modern land, sea and air links.

Table 2.4. Inter-Arab Trade (2003–2007)

	Value (billion US$)					Percentage of annual change				
	2003	2004	2005	2006	2007**	2003	2004	2005	2006	2007*
Average Inter-Arab Trade	23.8	32.9	42.7	54.2	63.1	17.2	37.6	30.7	26.9	16.7
Exports	25.4	35.7	43.8	57.5	64.8	22.9	40.5	22.5	31.3	12.7
Imports	22.2	30	41.6	51	61.5	11.5	34.8	38.9	22.5	20.6

* Estimated figures.
Source: *Al-Taqrir al-Iqtissadi al-Arabi al-Muwahad,* 2008, p. 147.

Foreign Trade

Arab countries' foreign trade in 2007 grew with all major commercial partners, to different degrees. However, they continue to show a trade balance deficit whereby Arab states imports exceed their exports. International reports show that most Arab states have very low sovereignty in terms of food supply.[94]

China recorded the highest increase in the Arab exports among their trade partners, estimated at 23 per cent. The trend of the Arab trade shows that, in addition to the Arab markets, the EU, the US, Japan and China represent the main trade partners (see Figures 3 and 4). There has been a change in the mode and structure of foreign trade. The longstanding tendency of exclusive dependence on the West has been changed to a more balanced trade partnership. The conservative Arab states embarked on a new policy of diversification of sources through opening channels with China and other Asian countries. The new tendency was inspired by different factors including the entrance of new competitive actors to the world market, and the desire to reduce dependency on the West due to the latter's inconsistent and inconstant policy towards the region that was exacerbated by the credit crunch. It is estimated that the total losses for individuals, organizations and governments, including sovereign wealth funds, in the Arab region as a result of the global economic crisis are in the region of $2.5 trillion.[95] It is interesting to note, however, that the increase in the volume of Arab imports from China was 42.1 per cent in 2007, down from 63.3 per cent in 2006, with the increase of Arab imports from the EU and the US to 34.1 and 32.7 per cent respectively being more significant[96] (see Table 2.5).

Table 2.5. Trends of Arab Foreign Trade

	Exports					Imports				
	2003	2004	2005	2006	2007	2003	2004	2005	2006	2007
Arab states	8.2	8.7	7.7	8.5	8.3	10.7	10.8	12.4	13.3	12.1
EU	24.5	23.8	23.5	22.1	18.3	44.2	40.0	39.2	35.7	36.0
US	12.1	12.1	11.3	11.5	9.8	7.9	6.9	8.2	9.2	9.2
Asia	37.1	38.1	38.1	38.4	35.3	25.7	28.8	29.1	33.6	33.3
-Japan	14.1	13.5	13.8	13.7	11.4	6.0	5.1	4.8	5.6	5.5
-China	4.0	4.7	4.9	5.0	5.3	6.3	6.3	7.1	10.1	10.8
-Other Asians	19.0	19.9	19.4	19.7	18.6	13.4	17.3	17.2	17.9	17.0
Other World-Countries	18.1	17.3	19.3	19.5	28.3	11.5	13.5	11.0	8.2	9.4
Total	100	100	100	100	100	100	100	100	100	100

Source: *Taqrir al-Iqtissadi al-Arabi al-Muwahad*, 2008, p. 144.

Arab exports are dominated by crude oil and natural gas, making up 75.4 per cent of the total Arab exports in 2007 due to the unprecedented increase in the oil prices. Manufactured goods occupied the second position at 11.8 per cent, followed by machines and transport equipment at 4 per cent in the same year. Chemical by-products stood at 3.6 per cent, followed by food-processed commodities (2.2) and raw materials (2.1). Arab imports in 2007, on the other hand, were as follows: machines and transport equipments (38 per cent), a slight increase over 2006 in the volume of manufactured products (27.8 per cent), foods and drinks (12.7 per cent), chemical by-products (7.9 per cent). It is interesting to note that the share of fuel declined from 7 per cent in 2006 to 5.9 per cent in 2007, and the share of raw materials declined from 5 to 4.9 per cent in the same period.[97]

Oil and Gas

Arab countries have 50.3 per cent of the world oil reserves and 29.1 per cent of the world natural gas reserves. Official data show that 92.6 per cent of the confirmed Arab oil reserves are located in five Arab states: Saudi Arabia, Iraq, Kuwait, the UAE and Libya (with 39.5, 17.2, 15.2, 14.6 and 6.2 per cent respectively). Arab gas reserves increased in 2007 by 1.2 trillion cubic metres over 2006, to make 54.7 trillion cubic metres due to the new discoveries in Kuwait, Algeria and Egypt.[98] Qatar's new gas exploration almost doubled Arab gas reserves. Arab oil production saw a minor decline from 23.2 mbd in 2006 to 22.1 mbd, due to an OPEC decision to cut production by 500,000 barrels a day from the beginning of February 2007. However, despite the slight decrease in the volume of Arab oil production, the total contribution of the Arab oil production, including non-OPEC members Egypt, Sudan, Syria and Oman, was estimated at 25.8 per cent of the world oil production in 2007 (see Figure 5).

Arab members of OPEC alarmed the developed world when they used oil as a strategic weapon during the October 1973 war with Israel by implementing oil embargoes and initiating the 1973 oil crisis. Though oil is no longer a strategic weapon in the hands of the oil-producing countries Arab countries have been successful in using petrodollar diplomacy to play an influential role in world politics. OPEC's influence on the market has been widely criticized, since it became effective in determining the level of production and prices. Although largely political explanations for the timing and extent of the OPEC price increases are also valid, from OPEC's point of view these changes were triggered largely by previous unilateral changes in the world financial system and the ensuing period of high inflation in both the developed and developing world, so that OPEC countries were only 'staying even' by dramatically raising the price of oil. On the other hand and despite the influential role they have acquired, Arab countries are influenced by their membership in the international and regional specialized organizations, OPEC and OAPEC, and the invisible forces of the international markets as well. OPEC's ability to control the price of oil has diminished somewhat since then, due to the subsequent discovery and development of large oil reserves in Alaska, the North Sea, Canada, the Gulf of Mexico, the opening up of Russia, and market modernization. OPEC nations still account for two-thirds of the world's oil reserves, and, as of April 2009, 33.3 per cent of the world's oil production, affording them considerable control over the global market.[99] The confirmed OAPEC reserves account for 59 per cent of world reserves. OAPEC said in its October 2007 bulletin that the volume of confirmed OAPEC oil reserves is 665.2 billion barrels (see Table 2.6), while their geological oil reserves are 2,420 billion barrels.[100]

Table 2.6. Proven Arab Oil Reserves

Rank	Country	Reserves (billions of barrels)	Rank	Country	Reserves (billions of barrels)
1	Saudi Arabia	262.3	9	Algeria	12.7
3	Iraq	115	11	Oman	5.5
4	Kuwait	101	12	Sudan	5
5	UAE	97.8	13	Egypt	3.7
6	Libya	41.5	14	Yemen	3
8	Qatar	15.2	15	Syria	2.5

Source: US Department of Energy, *Oil & Gas Journal*; 2007 figures. http://middleeast.about.com/od/oilenergy/a/me080207d.htm

Simultaneously, the Arab share of natural gas production in 2006 was estimated at 13.1 per cent of the world gas production, in comparison to 12.7 per cent in 2005.[101] Fifteen Arab states are producing gas for the world markets. Qatar, Algeria, Saudi Arabia, UAE, Egypt, Oman and Kuwait are today the main gas producers in the Arab world, with total production of 329.1 billion cubic metres. Qatar's gas reserves and production have increased significantly in the last decade, with it becoming the third largest gas reservoir at 25.8 trillion cubic metres, followed by Saudi Arabia, the UAE, Algeria, Iraq, Egypt, Kuwait and Libya[102] (see Table 2.7). Qatar production was estimated at 59.8 billion cubic metres in 2007. It is investing heavily in this sector to meet its earlier commitment to produce 77 billion cubic metres by 2012.

Table 2.7. Proven Arab Gas Reserves

STATE	TRILLION CUBIC METRES	WORLD RANK	STATE	BILLION CUBIC METRES	WORLD RANK
Qatar	25.8	3	Oman	795	26
Saudi Arabia	6.6	4	Yemen	459	33
UAE	5.8	5	Syria	240	42
Algeria	4.4	8	Bahrain	88.3	55
Iraq	3.2	10	Sudan	86.6	57
Egypt	1.6	19	Tunisia	74.7	59
Kuwait	1.5	21	Jordan	6.6	84
Libya	1.4	22	Morocco	1.6	93

Source: *CIA World Factbook* as of 1 Jan. 2009.

5. Conclusion

The above analyses reveal that the performance of the Arab countries in socio-economic development is unsatisfactory – despite the fact that the Arab world holds huge oil and gas reserves, a large skilled and unskilled labour force, a vast area and abundant natural resources. Arab states continue to rely on the outside world to secure their domestic needs and are economically vulnerable. The human development annual reports reveal through the analyses of the different socio-economic variables that they lag far behind the developed countries in almost all aspects. The under-representation of women in Arab parliaments is often related to cultural constraints, but also associated with the level of human development and the absence of a real and effective democratization process in most Arab countries. Corruption constitutes another factor hindering the process of development in the Arab countries. Unfortunately, policies adopted by the contemporary Arab governments have widened the gap between the governing and the governed, consolidated the patriarchal culture, enhanced social, religious, ethnic and sectarian cleavages and class division, increased the gap between the haves and have-nots in Arab societies, inspired corruption, intensified inter-Arab competition, emphasized the disintegrative factors in Arab politics, promoted cultural and economic dependency and alienated the intelligentsia. Arab development is compromised by 'legal loopholes, overseen and regulated by coercive institutions, and based on the citizen's forfeiture of personal freedoms in exchange for a limited form of personal and social security'.[103] Arab states' economies are fragile and all are part of the Third World. Social human developments fall short of achieving their objectives. Total Arab GDP is less than one European country and only seven Arab countries are ranked as part of the high human development group, namely the GCC countries plus Libya. The rest, according to the human development index (HDI), with the exception of Palestine, Iraq, and Somalia, torn by civil war, internal chaos and occupation, are ranked as having medium human development. Arab states in general rank low on the political empowerment of women. Legal, institutional frameworks, traditional and cultural obstacles play major roles in hindering the advancement of Arab women.[104]

Chapter 3

The Changing World Order

1. Introduction

The changes in the Soviet Union, instigated by Mikhail Gorbachev from 1985, that led to its final dismemberment and the outcome of the second Gulf crisis have inspired vigorous changes in the international order. Many spectators and analysts have talked about the birth of a 'new world order'. Though they differed on the structure and nature of the 'new world order', they have agreed that it would have different features to the previous one. Such changes, they have argued, would have significant impacts on world politics and relations among nations.

The purpose of this chapter is to examine the impacts of the changing world order on the Arab world. Since the conclusion of two European peace treaties on 15 May and 24 October 1648 introduced state sovereignty and national boundaries, the world order has witnessed continuous changes. It has moved from multi-polar to uni-polar to multi-polar to bi-polar to uni-polar and is currently developing as a result of the credit crunch towards a multi-polar system with new features based on what could be called glocalization. Simultaneously, the world has moved from localization to globalization to glocalization. Here I assume that the international variable weight in the foreign policy-making of the less developed countries exceeds by far their inputs into world developments. The Arab countries as part of the international community are by no mean immune from being affected by international changes. In fact, being part of the developing world, they are possibly more influenced by the changes in the international system than the developed countries. This, however, does not negate the idea that the Arabs' inputs into the changes, particularly those that took place in the early 1990s and led to the birth of a uni-polar international system, were significant. This chapter considers the hypothesis that, although the Arabs played a significant role in bringing about such changes, their impacts on the Arab world were minimal. It uses an analytical approach to investigate and comprehend the effects of such changes on the foreign policy dynamics of the Arab states. The chapter deals with the changing world order: a bi-polar system, a uni-polar system, a multi-polar system, followed by a conclusion. It investigates the impacts of the world order, since 1945, on the Arab states' interactions with the outside world, emphasizing the international context as well as their impacts on intra- and inter-Arab politics. The analysis seeks to understand the role of the international variable as a determining factor in the foreign policy-making of the Arab countries.

2. The International Order

Sweeping changes on the international scene that brought an end to the cold war era have helped the United States to impose its hegemony on the world at the lowest possible cost to itself.[1] These international changes have had significant and deeply negative repercussions for the international order in general, and the Arab regional order; in particular, there have been repeated calls to replace the Arab regimes with a new Middle Eastern order,[2] or a 'Greater Middle East'.[3] The negative repercussions on the Arab world may be summarized as follows.

First, the Arabs were greatly affected by the changes in the Soviet Union after 1985 as a result of the reforms brought about by Gorbachev's Perestroika, Glasnost, and the new thinking in foreign relations. In his meeting with Jimmy Carter in July 1987, Gorbachev said that the Soviet Union had adjusted its policy in the Middle East and now conceded that America had vital interests in the region. He also said that the Soviet Union would not attempt to destabilize these interests, but rather looked forward to receiving treatment in kind from the United States. Although on the surface these policies reflect a certain détente in relations between the two major powers, they contain the seeds of the Soviet Union's abandonment of its support for the Arabs in their struggle against Israel, on the one hand, and its own readiness to change its policy towards that state, on the other. This new Soviet policy opened the floodgates to Soviet Jewish immigration to occupied Palestine, the most important such wave being in 2002 when around two million people left the former Soviet Union for Palestine, hugely affecting the demographic balance. By 2005, the Palestinian Arabs were on course to make up around two-thirds of the overall population of the Occupied Territories by 2025. Despite the fall in the number of Jewish immigrants to occupied Palestine in 2007, their lowest level in twenty years (6,445 of 15,663 immigrants were from the former Soviet Union, the rest being from Ethiopia (3,607), the USA (2,957), and France (2,654)),[4] Soviet Jewish immigration affected the demographic picture and lengthened the Palestinians' struggle. The increased number of Jews in Palestine intensified competition in the Palestinian job market, leading to deterioration in the Arab population's economic situation and encouraging Palestinian Arab migration outside the Occupied Territories. It also reinforced the military dimension of the conflict by increasing the Zionist government's ability to raise the number of military recruits and reservists.

If we view the relationship between the Arabs and Israel as a zero-sum game, i.e. any gain for Israel is a loss for the Arabs, then the growing relationship between Israel and the Soviet Union, as well as with the Eastern European countries, reduces the relations between the Arabs and those countries. Moreover, and as the result of the improvement in relations between Israel and the Soviet Union, the latter reduced both the size of its military fleet and the level of its military activities in the Mediterranean, off the shores of Palestine. The transformation of Soviet policies towards the region also meant that it had abandoned its allies. The Soviets did not adhere to the treaty they had signed with Iraq in 1975, thus allowing the United States to pass several resolutions against that country in the UN Security Council during the Gulf crisis, including Resolution 678, which sanctioned the use of all available means to expel Iraq from Kuwait. The Soviet Union's abandonment of its allies also forced South Yemen to accept unity with North Yemen, against its will.

Soviet policy in the Middle East changed from one of military strategy, upholding the principle of the balance of power between the Arabs and Israel and commitment to supplying its Arab allies with military equipment, to a policy of peaceful coexistence and upholding the principle of a balance of interests between the two sides. On that basis, the Soviets imposed new restrictions on the export of weapons to the Arab countries, particularly to Syria, which depended entirely on weapon supplies from the Soviet Union. In 1987, during a visit by President Assad to Moscow, the Soviets asked Syria to pay 50 per cent of the cost of the weapons they purchased prior to their shipment, with the rest paid by installments, over a ten-year period, at 2 per cent interest. They called upon the Palestine Liberation Organization (PLO) to change its policies and attitude towards Israel in order for it to be accepted as party to any settlement. The inevitable outcome of this shift was an increase in American influence in the region, and the concomitant shrinkage of the Soviet role. The final breakdown of the Soviet Union cast a long shadow over the Middle East and culminated in long-term changes. According to Shimon Peres, the Arabs had no source of weapons and less political support: The old antagonistic Soviet Union that once supported the Arabs against Israel is now gone, replaced by a democratic Russia that supports the peace process.[4a]

Second, the emergence of a new unilateral world order robbed the Arab states of the room for manœuvre they had enjoyed under the polarized world of the cold war. The United States, Israel's main ally, thus became the controller of all interactions that took place in the world, allowing it to be both the enemy and the judge in the Middle East peace process. It is worth noting here that, in a speech delivered at the Arab Gulf Cooperation Council meeting, held in Oman on 24 February 1990, the former Iraqi President, Saddam Hussein, had warned against American hegemony in the Gulf, and against increasing Jewish migration from the Soviet Union to Palestine. He called upon the Arab countries to withdraw their funds from the West and reinvest them in the Soviet Union, in order to re-establish the balance within the world order, and maintain the margin of manœuvre in a manner that best served Arab national interests.

The United States sought to promote its interests in the world in general, and to achieve its aims in the Arab world in particular, those being to ensure Israel's security, to guarantee American access to oil and to combat Islamic fundamentalism. To achieve these objectives, it pursued several parallel policies, such as flexing its military muscles by deploying its navy in the Indian Ocean, establishing military bases, including Diego Garcia in the Indian Ocean and others in nearby Arab allied countries, and using raw military force, as in the second Gulf crisis. It provided material and military assistance to its allies in the region, signed security agreements, sold them weapons, and made sure they remained dependent on the United States through economic and trade relations. It promoted first its Greater Middle East Project, and then the Larger Middle East Project, the precursor of the American empire of which the occupation of Iraq is the cornerstone. The aim behind expanding the traditional Middle East region to include Central Asia is Washington's desire to impose its hegemony on the world's major sources of oil, given that by 2010 the US will have to import around 70 per cent of its energy requirements.[5] Despite all these policies, the American government realized that the Middle East would remain the most unstable region in the world if peace between the Arabs and Israel were not achieved. This explains why the Bush administration seized the opportunity afforded by the Arabs' weakness and division after the second Gulf crisis and used its new clout to promote its own interests. It sought to relieve itself of the financial and military burden that its commitment to Israel entailed, in order to turn its attention to internal economic, social and educational problems. It also sought to distance itself from the widespread perception of its dual policy by accepting the principle of land for peace. It was within this context that the US, together with the Soviet Union, sponsored both the Madrid Middle East Peace Conference at the end of October 1991 and, more recently, the Annapolis Conference of November 2007. However, its position as the sole leader of the new world order, and the heavy influence of the conservative right-wing ideology promoted by George Bush Senior, Dick Cheney and Donald Rumsfeld triumvirate, turned the United States' attention to the 'war on terror', leaving the political arena to other countries, including Russia and China. In the meantime, it tried to establish order at home and to work at building its economic and military power in order to compete for oil, the backbone of the world economy. Africa became an arena of American–Chinese rivalry, especially in light of the advantages China had gained in that continent. Not only had a number of Chinese companies succeeded in obtaining various oil concessions in Africa, but China was also investing heavily in the continent and increasing its external trade balance. China, alongside Russia, also strongly opposed America's plans to position a missile defence shield in Poland and the Czech Republic, a move Russia threatened to respond to. Bearing in mind Russia's role in the Iranian nuclear programme, this would be bound to contribute to an American retreat, and reinforce the possibility of the world reverting to a multi-polar system in the next decade.[6]

Third, the ramifications of the Gulf crisis contributed to the success of the Bush initiative. The most important of these ramifications was the alliance forged between a number of Arab countries and the United States, and the ensuing change in the attitude of these states towards Israel. Several factors helped make this success easier, such as the Palestine Liberation Organization's support for Iraq, and the imbalance of power resulting from the retreat of Soviet influence and increase of American influence in the region. Not only had the Arabs lost their room for manœuvre, but the imbalance of power resulting from the destruction of Iraq's military might, the neutralization of those Arab countries that could potentially have opposed peace, the international embargo on Iraq, and the crises the United States created in Libya and Sudan, also tipped the balance in favour of Israel. Moreover, the second Gulf crisis destroyed what was left of Arab nationalism and strengthened the regional state concept in the Arab world, and the Arabs thus became more open than ever to endorsing a peace initiative. Some Arab countries were no longer embarrassed to cross the red lines that had once existed, and were now competing to establish contact with Israel. The Gulf war overturned in its wake the Arab consensus over Israel and set the stage for other ominous divisions. The Arabs entered the negotiations in a state of total weakness, and unable to surmount two major shocks: the downfall of the Soviet Union and the second Gulf war. Ghassan Salameh believes that the Arabs turned to peaceful negotiations for the following reasons:

1. America's success, over the past two decades, in entrenching the position of Arab incapacity versus Israeli intransigence;
2. America's stunning success in the cold war, with the Middle East helping speed up a resolution in favour of the West;
3. America's readiness to intervene directly in the region.

3. The Impacts of a Bi-Polar Order on the Arabs

The international system since 1945 had been dominated by the power struggle between the two supreme powers, the US and the Soviet Union, in what was then described as a bi-polar system. The world was divided into two camps and relations between the two superpowers fluctuated from cold war to détente to cold war. Consequently, the world witnessed a proliferation of nuclear weapons, an arms race and instability, the emergence of military alliances and nationalist and civil wars.

The changes within the Soviet Union left the Arab world to face its destiny without its strategic ally. Gorbachev's new foreign policy undertakings reflected the change in the Soviet attitudes towards political developments in the Middle East. The democratization process opened the door for the Jews to seek exit visas to Israel, offsetting the demographic balance in Palestine and leading to the establishment of more settlements in the 'Arab occupied land', the West Bank and Gaza, hindering the peace process.[7] The developments in Eastern Europe paved the way for the restoration of diplomatic relations and the exchange of dignitary visits between the East European states and Israel. On the subregional level, the former USSR changed its policy towards Iraq and South Yemen. Both countries had to suffer as a result of the new Soviet policy. Iraq saw itself as facing the US almighty power alone, while the socialist party ruling the Peoples Democratic Republic of Yemen (PDRY) decided to end its hostility to North Yemen and to unite into one state.[8] As a result of the changes in the world order, particularly the decline of the Soviet's world influence, three positive developments took place in the Arab world: Yemeni unity, the independence of Eretria, and the introduction of democratic measures in some of the Arab countries.

The attitude towards the Arab–Israeli conflict was one of the Soviet Union foreign policy undertakings that had to be adjusted to meet the US conditions for rapprochement.[9] The US had set out four conditions that can be summarized thus: the freezing of Soviet military support for Syria, pressuring Syria not to think of waging war against Israel, commitment to ensure the restoration of diplomatic relations with Israel and the changing of the Soviet emigration laws.[10]

The United States played an important role in encouraging Gorbachev to change the Soviet emigration laws as a sign of goodwill. President George Bush Senior, in a speech delivered at Texas A&M University on 12 May 1989, declared the USA willingness to open the way extending the 'most favored nation' trade status to the Soviet Union on condition that Moscow codified its emigration laws in accordance with 'international standard'.[11] The US–Soviet Trade and Economic Council (USTEC), a private group aiming at promoting US–USSR trade relations, called for an end to the link between United States trade relations with the USSR and the latter's policies on human rights and Jewish emigration.[12] President George W. Bush, on 2 June 1991, waived the 'Jackson-Vank trade' restrictions on the Soviet Union for another year[13] because of liberalized emigration policies.[14]

The constraints placed on Jews desiring to migrate from the Soviet Union to places other than Israel was another policy adopted by the former USSR with the encouragement of the US. In the past, most of the Jews who left the Soviet Union went either to the United States or to Western Europe;[15] only less than 10 per cent went to Israel.[16] In an attempt to divert Soviet Jewish emigrants from coming to the United States and to force the majority to go to Israel, the then US President, George Bush Senior, issued a decree limiting the annual US entry visas for Jews to 40,000 – less than Harry Truman did in 1948 when he limited the number to 70,000. Moreover, the Zionist organizations sent a delegation, in February 1990, headed by Edger Brungman, the President of the Jewish Hungarian leadership, to facilitate Soviet Jewish migrants and to ensure that their departure from Budapest would be only to Tel Aviv.[17] Consequently, the percentage of Jewish emigrants to Palestine increased by 41 per cent in the period from 1985 to 1990.[18]

The Zionist Movement played a significant role in utilizing the new situation in the Soviet Union in two contradictory ways. The first was its bullying of the US administration, through the American-Zionist lobby, to pressure Moscow to change its emigration policy. The second was putting more pressure on Gorbachev, through their cooperation with militant Marxists inside the

Soviet Union,[19] in order to extract more concessions to facilitate the Soviet Jewish emigration to Palestine. This was revealed by the chairman of the Zionist Movement in the Soviet Union, in August 1989, when he said: 'the central goal of the Zionist Movement in the Soviet Union is to play a prefatory role for the emigration to Israel.'[20] The Zionist Movement in the USSR, out of fear that the end of the cold war and the beginning of détente might detract from the importance of Israel in US strategy, also worked on creating problems for Gorbachevism with the intention of destroying it if possible.[21]

The Arabs, however, were the prime losers of Gorbachev's new thinking. The demographic factor in the conflict was influenced by the exodus of Soviet Jews to Palestine. It inspired a shift in the Soviet policy towards the Arab world from a balance of power to a balance of interests between the Arabs and Israel, it prompted a change in the Soviet attitude towards the new US role in the Middle East, and led to the Soviet abandonment of their traditional allies in the Middle East. The changes in the Soviet policy towards the Middle East are manifestations of the effects of the changing world order on the Arab world. At the same time, Soviet Jewish emigration is looked upon in Israel as its saviour. Yitzhak Shamir, the Israeli Prime Minister, described the influx of Soviet Jewish emigrants as 'a miracle like the other miracles that always saved the Jewish people'.[22] The world Zionist Movement has always looked to the demographic factor as the first line of struggle for the survival of the Jewish nation. Moreover, Israel has escaped the Arab policy of containment initiated since the 1960s. This is reflected in the restoration of political, economic, social and diplomatic ties with the East European countries. The official visit by the Polish president to Tel Aviv, on 20 May 1991, is an example of such development. The Soviet Union ended its conditions for the restoration of formal political ties with Israel and agreed in advance to take part in an international peace conference under UN auspices.[23] In a major step towards the restoration of full diplomatic ties, both parties, in December 1990, upgraded their representative offices, in both Moscow and Tel Aviv, to consul-general.[24] The exchange of dignitary visits was another aspect of improvements in the relations between the two sides. Most important of all, however, was the unofficial visit paid by the Soviet Foreign Minister, Bessmertnykh, to Tel Aviv in May 1991 and his cordial talks with the Prime Minister Shamir.

The importance of the demographic factor in the Zionist strategy is illustrated in the following. First, a special immigration department was set up by the Jewish Agency and known as the Absorption Department. Second, Israel allocated a ministerial post for immigration in its successive governments, since its proclamation in May 1948, known as the Ministry of Absorption. Third, a law enacted in 1950 granted every Jew who migrates to Israel the right to be naturalized immediately.[25] Fourth, in reaction to the success of some of the Soviet and East European Jewish emigrants in obtaining entry visas to the United States, the Israeli government, in February 1990, authorized the legal committee working for the department responsible for the reception of the Soviet and East European Jewish emigrants to draft a law 'forbidding the opposite emigration' from Israel before completing five years of residence in Israel. The emigration of Soviet Jews to Palestine has negative impacts on the future prospects of peace in the Middle East. The large numbers of emigrants led the Israeli government to embark on setting up new settlements in the Arab occupied land, especially the West Bank. Such settlements would be used as one of the justifications for Israel not withdrawing from the West Bank, and especially Jerusalem, as part of a peace deal. The issue of emigration also enhanced the right-wing parties and fundamentalists, both in Israel and abroad, who oppose the idea of land for peace and call for security for peace. Moreover, some of the newcomers would join the Israeli armed forces, promoting the Israeli military capabilities that would enhance the Israeli militant tendency and increase the threat of instability in the region. They also compete with the Palestinians, living in the occupied land, for job opportunities, causing more Palestinian emigration. Statistics reveal that 35,000 Palestinians left for Jordan and did not come back, during 1988 and 1989. This fulfils Israel's ambitions since it is pursuing a policy that 'Jordan is Palestine' as the 'substitute homeland' and has set up a political committee to execute that policy.[26] The improvement of relations between the USSR and Israel and the Soviet–American rapprochement led to a drastic reduction in the Soviet naval force presence and activities in the Mediterranean Sea, to the degree that the remaining force is only symbolic.[27]

The Soviet Union has changed its Middle Eastern policy to peaceful coexistence between the Arab states and Israel[28] and the internationalization of the problem. As a result, the Soviet Union, in September 1986, proposed setting up a preparatory committee under the auspices of the UN Security Council to prepare for an international peace conference on the Middle East, and demanded that the state of Palestine become part of the world political map beside Israel. In a further development, the Soviets refused to supply Syria with the required military equipment before paying 50 per cent of the total value in advance, with interest payable on the rest.[29] The USSR also asked the Palestinian Liberation Organization (PLO) to change its policies towards Israel in order to be accepted as a party to any peaceful settlement.[30] American recognition was then to be given of the Soviet role in a peaceful settlement, something acknowledged by President Bush Sr at the Helsinki Summit Conference, in September 1990.[31]

Yet the impacts of the changes in the Soviet Union on the Arab–Israeli conflict could be seen as not totally negative. The talk about the unbalanced demographic status did not take into consideration four things: the Palestinians in diaspora representing around 50 per cent of the Palestinian population, the Arab and Muslim population since the question of Palestine is looked at in the Arab and Muslim worlds as a pan-Arab and pan-Islamic issue, the opposite Jewish emigration from Israel and the fact that waves of Soviet Jewish emigration are not new in the history of Palestine. It is interesting to note that in 1979 alone more than 51,000 Soviet Jews had migrated to Palestine.[32]

Soviet Jewish emigrants do not constitute a real obstacle for peace if they are not settled in the lands occupied by Israel in 1967.[33] Others argue that, even if some settlements were set up in these lands, such settlements do not threaten the peace process, and though they would be used as a bargaining card, they can either be removed or the borders can be adjusted,[34] as happened when Israel decided to withdraw from the Gaza Strip. Simultaneously, the Soviet Jewish emigrants would have an adverse impact on Israel's stagnant economy. They would cause inflation and a higher rate of unemployment. The rate of unemployment in the occupied Palestinian territories reached 28.4 per cent in 2007[35] and was estimated at 7.8 per cent in Israel in 2008.[36] The Israeli government would need 60,000 extra job opportunities annually to absorb the new Soviet Jewish emigrants.[37] The Soviet Union's declining power in world politics prompted the new Soviet policy. It was bullied by the US to support the American proposal of a peace conference under the auspices of the 'superpowers', leading to direct negotiations between the Arab states and Israel. The Soviets, however, were hesitant to accept the American initiative, preferring an international conference under the auspices of the United Nations. The Soviet endorsement of a peaceful settlement for the Arab–Israeli conflict does not represent a fundamental change in Soviet policy. Such policy has been pursued by the Soviets since 1967. The change, however, is in the ways and methods of approaching the problem. Moreover, the Arab states, including the PLO, have accepted the idea of exchanging land for peace in the Faze initiative in 1982 and the Saudi King Abdullah's initiative that was endorsed at the Arab Summit held in Beirut in May 2001 and became another Arab peace initiative, but was rejected by the Israelis. Thus, the changes in the Soviet's attitudes should not be looked on as taking sides. The continuation of instability in the region is not in the interests of the USSR since the Middle East occupies a geopolitical importance in the

Soviet strategy. The Soviet Union had no intention of sacrificing its vital national interest in the Arab and Muslim states. The relations between the two sides are interdependent. They represent a market for Soviet products and an important source of raw materials and energy supply for the Soviet Union, since it is a potential oil buyer. Above all, however, the Arab and Muslim states constitute a bulwark of security for the former Soviet Union. The conditions laid down by the USSR to meet the Syrian military request represented 'Moscow's need for hard currency'.[38] Accordingly, the formal contacts between the USSR and Israel might enhance the peace dialogue since the achievement of peace depends exclusively on Israeli goodwill.

The Soviet–American rapprochement has given the Arab states much less room to manœuvre. Sources believe that the United States' stand on Israel would change in the future. This analysis is based on the belief that the Soviet–American rapprochement would end the superpowers' rivalry in the Middle East, at least in the short run, ending the Israeli strategic importance in American Middle Eastern policy. George Bush Senior's acceptance of the idea of an international peace conference and the exchange of land for peace to settle the Middle East problem is used to substantiate the above argument.[39] The United States, out of its desire to achieve a permanent stability in the Middle East, especially after the Kuwaiti predicament, to secure its vital interests, would eventually pressure Israel to give concessions in the pursuance of peace. This was clear in the shuttle diplomacy carried by James Baker, the American Secretary of State, and the statements he made during his visit to Israel in March 1991. It is also believed that the developments in the United States' relations with the East European states and the American desire to utilize the new situation to its interest would inspire the reallocation of its foreign aid accordingly. Such policy would ultimately affect Israel. Senator Robert Dole, in an article published in January 1991, called for the revision of the US foreign aid policy, estimated at $11.8 billion annually, reducing the amount allocated to the main beneficiaries: Israel $3 billion, Egypt $2.1 billion, Philippines $6.1 million, Turkey $6.1 million and Pakistan $5.4 million. He added that the cuts should be redistributed among small states and especially the East European countries to assist them in fulfilling their people's aspirations.[40]

The foreign policy orientations of the Soviet Union and the East European countries shifted from a pro-Arab stand to a more cooperative approach towards Israel. The growing cooperation between the great powers ultimately affected 'the military and strategic balance in the Middle East'[41] and the political support the Soviet unequivocally lent to the Arab countries in the UN Security Council.

As a result, Saddam Hussein, the President of Iraq, at the Arab Cooperation Council Summit Conference, on 24 February 1990, held in Amman, warned against an American dominance in the Gulf, and the influx of Jewish emigrants to Israel as Soviet world power waned. He suggested that Arabs withdraw their assets from the West and reinvest them in the Soviet Union.[42] Saddam Hussein had to pay a dire price for his warning. The cost included his life and the occupation of Iraq.

The outcome of the Iraqi miscalculated adventure against Kuwait led the GCC countries, since the second Gulf crisis, to gravitate more overtly towards the US. For the first time, a public military alliance of American–GCC states was initiated. The Saudi government invited the American forces onto their territory. On 7 August 1991, President George W. Bush ordered the deployment of US military aircraft and troops in Saudi Arabia to defend it against any potential Iraqi incursion. On 19 August, Bahrain and the UAE permitted the deployment of Arab and 'friendly' forces on their soil.[43] US allies pledged a total of $54 billion to offset the costs of the US military operation. Saudi Arabia, Kuwait and the UAE contributed $36,991 billion[44] to offset US costs of Operation Desert Storm. Saudi Arabia changed its attitude towards the American presence in the Gulf and became openly supportive of 'having US forces remain in the Gulf for two to three years as the backbone of regional security forces'.[45] According to Howard Geller, the executive director of the American Efficient Economy, 'it is hard to imagine right now the Saudi doing anything that would hurt the United States'.[46] Daniel Yergin, an oil historian, described the US–Saudi relations by saying: 'what we had before was a special relationship', but 'now we have a more special relationship'.[47] Further the Emirates have changed its policy from being more or less anti-American[48] to becoming part of the American Middle East strategy. The UAE was reported to be negotiating plans with Washington to establish a small regional headquarters for the US Central Command in its capital. It would oversee any future US military operation in the Middle East.[49] This, however, was denied by an informed military source.[50] The US Secretary of Defense, Dick Cheney, upon concluding his tour of the GCC states, announced that the GCC countries accepted the American proposal for regional security, adding that some of its articles will remain secret.[51] It is interesting, however, to note that all GCC states, with exception of the UAE, have concluded bilateral security agreements. Bush's administration argued that a comprehensive programme of well-conceived arms sales by the US to GCC states would contribute to their stability to defend themselves collectively by promoting standardization and interoperability.[52]

The crisis has presented the Arab Gulf states with a new security dilemma. On the one hand, it exposed the unreliability of the Iraqi Ba'thist government. On the other hand, the crisis has upset the balance of power in the Gulf subregion, leaving Iran as the most powerful country in the area. Apprehension about the new Iranian policy redoubled with Iran's annexation of the whole island of Abu Musa in August 1992. Consequently, fears have been raised about Iran's other ambitions in the area. It has been noted that Iran has revived an old claim to Bahrain. This argument is substantiated by the fact that Iran's oil reserves will not last more than three decades and by such a move Iran could claim sovereignty over the oil fields and oil reserves within the twelve-mile zone constituting the islands' territorial waters. Such apprehension is enhanced by the Iranian military build-up. Iran is spending $2 billion annually to fill its arsenal with modern weapons in a determined effort to become the dominant power in the Gulf.[53]

One of the major changes revealed by the Iraqi invasion of Kuwait was the upsetting of the balance of power between the Arabs and Israel and the changing attitude of the GCC states towards the Arab–Israeli conflict. The disarming of Iraqi strategic weapons while Israel continues to possess up to 300 nuclear warheads is one of the negative outcomes of the 'new world order' on the Arab world. The PLO alliance with Iraq during the crisis inspired a shift in most of the GCC states' foreign policies to a more lenient attitude towards Israel. The GCC states froze their foreign aid to the PLO while they relaxed their economic boycott rules against Israel. The GCC states, due to American pressure manifested in Baker's shuttle diplomacy, agreed to be represented as an observer at the American-sponsored peace conference on the Arab–Israeli conflict. Saudi Arabia, upon Baker's visit on 20 July 1991, advocated the American idea for stopping the Arab boycott of Israel if the latter commits to stop building new settlements in the Arab occupied land. They have also taken part in multilateral talks.

Since the second Gulf crisis, the US became the primary arms supplier to the GCC countries, particularly Saudi Arabia and Kuwait. The US adopted a comprehensive approach to strengthening the defence capability of its Arab allies. A cornerstone of this strategy was to strengthen defence ties between the US and the GCC countries. The crisis allowed the US president to waive the Congressionally imposed cap on deliveries of F-15 aircrafts to Saudi Arabia. In late August 1990, George W. Bush ordered the transfer of an additional twenty-four F-15 aircrafts (models C and D), together with AIM-9L Sidewinder and AIM-7F Sparrow missiles. Bush also waived the Congressional bans in legislation on sales of 200 Stinger anti-aircraft missiles and fifty Stinger launchers, the sales of 105mm depleted uranium and anti-tank shells for M-60 tanks and 150 M-60A-3 tanks. The estimated value of the emergency arms package was $2.231 billion.[54] The US commitment to enhance the GCC states' defence capability is a presumptive indication of the US concern for GCC–US political and military ties. Continuing US arms transfers to the GCC states, however, could undermine the credibility of the US calls for restraint on the part of arms suppliers to the Middle East.[55]

The outcomes of the Gorbachev 'new thinking' policy were the frequent summit conferences between the leaders of the two 'superpowers', the collapse of the Warsaw Pact, the conclusion of a number of agreements on disarmament between the USSR and the US, the positive developments in Soviet-Sino relations and Soviet–Japanese relations, the final dissolution of the Soviet Union and the emergence of new democratic Russia, the enhancement of the Russian role in world affairs, the 'rethinking' in US foreign policy as a direct result of the global recession, the election of Barack Obama as president and finally the more active role played by the UN. This was clearly illustrated in the unofficial and official meetings held by the delegations of the five permanent members of the UN Security Council to coordinate their attitudes and adopt policies towards global issues. Examples include the decisions taken with respect to the United Nations Peace Keeping Force in Namibia, the attitude towards the Iran–Iraq war culminating in the adoption of resolution 598,[56] the international stand on the Kuwaiti crisis (August 1990–March 1991), the Bosnia and Kosovo issues, the North Korea Nuclear Programme, and the international cooperation to contain the Iranian nuclear programme. The developments in world affairs were the ultimate by-product of the wind of changes that swept the world from the beginning of the 1990s. The major world powers have adopted a more lenient approach towards each other and pursued compatible policies on certain issues but generally in parallel.

4. The Effects of a Uni-Polar Order on the Arabs

The second Gulf crisis and the final disintegration of the Soviet Empire left the US as the key actor in world politics. In other words, the world order became a uni-polar system. US officials spoke of a benevolent hegemony whereby the US assumed the role of being 'the policeman of the world'. After the end of the cold war, the US forces and defence expenditures were reduced, but, in reality, its percentage in comparison with world defence expenditures has increased on its becoming the only superpower. During the cold war, the

US was first among equals, primum inter pares, and was a leader for different alliances, obliged to consult and reach a compromise with its allies, but since the change in world order it has chosen to act unilaterally.[57] The US military establishment is 2.5 times bigger than those of Russia, China, Iran, Cuba, North Korea, Iraq, Libya, Syria and Sudan, possessing 30,000 tons of chemical weapons. The US defence budget increased from $260 billion in the mid-1990s to $329 billion in 2002 and $460 billion in 2005 – almost half of world defence expenditure. The US strategy was based on the idea that the twenty-first century will be an American century, adamantly refusing any participatory role to any other power in administering world affairs. President Barack Obama, admitting to US mistakes in his speech to the NATO summit, said US–European relations had been allowed to 'drift', hitting out at anti-European feeling in the US and 'insidious' anti-American feeling in the continent. He added: 'in America, there is a failure to appreciate Europe's leading role in the world; instead of celebrating your dynamic union and seeking to partner with you to meet common challenges, there have been times where America showed arrogance.'[58] Na'om Chomsky, argues that the US is perceived by most of world nations as a terrorist state. A BBC survey showed that '60 per cent of the sample used in 11 countries has negative attitudes towards the former US President George W. Bush. They also viewed the US as more dangerous and likely to become a member of the axis of evil.'[59] Others argue that, despite the US public foreign policy objectives of democratization, respect for human rights and free trade, the underlining objective is to ensure US domination of world affairs in pursuance of its national interests. The US justifies its intervention in world affairs as defending democracy, freedom and human rights, whereas it always ends by securing new markets for US products.[60] The US seems to be selfish, unethical and not trustworthy, as illustrated in its unequivocal support to totalitarian regimes like the Shah in Iran before the revolution in 1979, Marcos of the Philippines and Suharto of Indonesia. The US wars on Afghanistan and Iraq reveal US willingness to use force as the appropriate means to ensure and promote its national interests. Harold Pinter, a famous drama writer, said: 'the US used a sustained, methodological and barbaric unjustified excessive force all over the world under the pretext of benevolent hegemony. The US intervened 134 times in 111 years in the period between 1890 and 2001. It has manipulated the international law, bullying, ignoring and exploiting the UN. It is the most dangerous power the world ever witnessed. It is a rogue state equipped with giant economic and military power.'[61] The US world policy centres on the adoption of a new military dictum: the right to the first strike whenever threats to its national interests are perceived.[62] The US defence initiatives like the Strategic Defense Initiative (SDI) and the anti-Missile Defense (NMD) are clear manifestation of US objectives. Moreover, it is worth mentioning here that the military industrial sector represents a major source of national income and provides an important number of jobs. The volume of military products in international trade in 1999 accounted for US$52 billion, with the US share estimated at 65 per cent.[63] The US Defense Department emphasis, as revealed in the 'Defense Planning Guide', is that the US should be poised to act unilaterally when collective action cannot be orchestrated. The US administration, under George W. Bush and with the help of the right-wing conservatives, adopted a more vigorous approach towards world issues than did his predecessors. The US foreign policy during the eight years of George W. Bush witnessed a shift of strategic emphasis from the former administration of Bill Clinton. The US policy towards events in the former Yugoslavia could be seen as a manifestation of the cooperative approach in the US. Though the US would have preferred a limited military action, it saw the endorsement of its Western allies as a prerequisite for such action. The US initiative, due to the refusal of its Western allies, was frozen. The Clinton administration also decided to pull out its forces from Somalia and to request multinational forces under UN auspices to take over. The American unilateral campaign against both Iraq in June 1993 and General 'Adaid in Somalia in July 1993 prompted resentment from other members of the coalition. Italy was the first member to talk about a possible withdrawal from Somalia. However, the 11 September 2001 predicament inspired a fundamental change in US foreign policy. George W. Bush, hostage to the right-wing conservatives, became more obsessed by insecurity scenarios and the probability of another attack on the American mainland launched by 'Islamic terrorist groups' led by bin Laden. Bush not only abandoned the cooperative approach adopted by his predecessor but went to the extreme of classifying the world into two groups: either with the US or with the terrorists. The US began to initiate unilateral policies. It is almost an open-ended list and would be unpractical to mention them all here. However, the list, in brief, starts with the Taliban and al-Qaeda in Afghanistan, the axis of evil (Iraq, Iran and North Korea), the rogue state, the ousting of Saddam Hussein from power in Iraq, the North Korea nuclear programme, the Iranian nuclear programme, and using democratization and human rights as variables determining US foreign policy towards its adversaries, including China and Russia. After the collapse of the Soviet Union, China came to be portrayed, in American strategy, as the potential rival who needs to be monitored and controlled. This explains the US's vague and contradictory signals towards China. On the one hand, the US encourages trade and investment relations with China. Moreover, the US in its petition to win China's support to impose sanctions against Iran opened the way for China to access Latin American oil and bilateral cooperation.[64] On the other hand, the US concentrated its military establishment and strategic planning on China.[65] In a further development the US initiated an anti-missile defence initiative in Eastern Europe, provoking Russian outrage and triggering a new cold war. President Barack Obama, in his petition to remedy the legacy of his predecessor George W. Bush, opted for a new course in US–Russian bilateral relations. Obama met the Russian President Dmitri Medvedev on 1 April 2009 in London. The meeting was a fresh start between the two countries. The two leaders expressed their desire for better and constructive relations aimed at restoring normality and agreed to arms-control talks in order to cut weapons' stockpiles and prevent the spread of nuclear weapons to Iran and North Korea. The two sides hoped for a new arms-control pact in July, when President Obama visited Moscow, replacing START Agreement before it expired in December 2009.[66] START was signed in 1991 between former US President George H. Bush and the then Soviet President Mikhail Gorbachev and called for a 30 per cent reduction in strategic weapon stockpiles. Analysts argue that the US, since the September 11 attacks, has become the irresponsible superpower in its international behaviour. They describe the US foreign conduct as a 'rogue state' becoming more 'out of control or irrational and vindictive'.[67]

The Middle East occupies a strategic importance for the US foreign policy. It is characterized as volatile region presenting different kinds of challenges to the US foreign policy-making apparatus. Analysts argue that not 'rogue states' but states with unprecedented demographic growth are likely to be the biggest challenge to the American position in the region in the twenty-first century.[68] According to the UN Population Division, Muslims in 2008 represented 23.6 per cent of world population estimated at 1.52 billion, expected to increase to more than 30 per cent in 2025. On the one hand, demographic challenge constitutes a further destabilizing factor. Currently the Arabs are about 300 million and more than 40 per cent are under the age of 15. Though it could be argued that a young and dynamic population can be economic and political asset, they present economic challenges and GDP would have to increase by 6–7 per cent per annum to accommodate the new entrants into the labour force over the coming decades.[69] The population of the high income states represent only 10 per cent of the total Arab population, with 52 per cent of GDP and only 6 per cent of the cultivated lands.[70] On the other hand, world oil consumption is expected to increase from 77.8 million barrels a day (mbd) in 1995 to 104.6 mbd in 2015. Moreover, after 11 September 2001, the US began to retrieve Richard Nixon's dictum of the so-called 'Islamic threat'. The George W. Bush administration did not miss any opportunity to emphasize that threats to US national interests emanate from the Muslim world.[71]

For the above reasons, the US pursued a consistent policy of carrot and stick with the regional countries, intended to maintain its national interests. The US developed good ties with Saddam's Iraq during the Iran–Iraq war. The US support took different forms: political, economic, military and technical. On 25 July 1990, Saddam Hussein met with the US Ambassador April Glaspie who assured him of President George H. Bush's intention to improve relations between the two countries. She reiterated the US position of non-interference in Arabs' internal conflict such as Iraq's border dispute with Kuwait.[72] After the Iraqi invasion of Kuwait, on 2 August 1990, the US was first to rally international forces to evict Iraq from Kuwait. The neo-conservatives in George W. Bush administration's were not happy with the end result of the international coalition mission and decided to send American forces to Baghdad to bring a final end to the former US ally Saddam Hussein in 2003. The US invasions of both Afghanistan and Iraq failed to bring security and stability to either country.

The US is at odds with Iran on a range of issues, including Tehran's Nuclear Programme, which Washington says is aimed at building bombs, although Iran denies the charge.[73] Iran has come under UN sanctions for refusing to suspend sensitive uranium enrichment. It is also accused of funnelling arms to military anti-Israel groups Hezbollah and Hamas. President Mahmoud Ahmadinejad has stirred outrage by expressing doubt about the Holocaust. Analysts argue that the use of the military option is not practical. Brzezinski, the former American National Security Adviser, and Secretary of Defense Robert Gates were clear in their opinion, when asked in a press conference on 19 July 2004, by saying that 'an air strike would not be effective and could imply an adverse effect on US interests'. An Israeli air strike would also be extremely difficult because of the distance, nature, widely dispersed, multiplicity, locations and fortification of these targets.[74] The US policy that seeks to influence Iran with penalties but without incentive has failed. 'Washington has been unable to induce change by the Iranian government in three areas of key concern to the US policy makers; sponsoring terrorism; acquiring missiles and nuclear capability; and opposing the Arab–Israeli peace process.'[75] On the other hand, despite the strained relations between the two countries, the US did not hesitate to ask for Iran's help in its war on Iraq and Afghanistan. Iran lent its indirect logistic support to the US in its war on Iraq: closing its national border, allowing American fighters to cross Iranian air space, not protesting against American missiles mistakenly fired on Iranian soil and supporting the ousting of Saddam Hussein.[76] President Obama, making a sharp break from the previous administration, said in his speech to the Iranians for their New Year (Nowruz) on 25 March 2009 that he expects 'steady progress' in resolving disputes with Iran and urged an end to three decades of animosity.[77] Moreover, Iran, upon the US invitation, took part in the international conference on Afghanistan held in The Hague on 31 March 2009. Iran's participation in the conference is widely seen as a result of the recent rapprochement by the Obama administration. Hillary Clinton, US Secretary of State, said her country and Iran had agreed to keep in touch after her special representative for Afghanistan and Pakistan, Richard Holbrooke, had a 'brief and cordial' exchange with Mehdi Akhundzadeh, Iranian Deputy Foreign Minister, on the sidelines of the conference.[78] However, analysts argue that the 'success of US re-engagement will partly depend on how far Iran is able to reassure Israel about its security concerns. Only then will some US hardliners in Congress be satisfied. No Iranian official has argued for direct Iranian involvement in the Arab–Israeli conflict, but the regime's rhetoric has at times seemed to suggest such involvement'.[79] Mahmoud Ahmadinejad, on 20 April 2009 in a speech to the UN conference on anti-racism, accused Israel of being the most cruel and racist regime in the world. He added that the West was using the Holocaust as a 'pretext' for aggression against Palestinians, prompting European diplomats to walk out. Comments could also further strain efforts to improve relations with the United States, Israel's top ally. Iran has been mostly lukewarm to overtures from President Obama, but recently Ahmadinejad said the Islamic Republic was ready for a new relationship with Washington.[80] The US still wants to engage in direct talks with Iran.[81] President Ahmadinejad, on the other hand, in a significant move softened his language and accepted the US initiative for a 'two states'[82] solution for the Arab–Israeli conflict – a fundamental development in Iran's position.

Support for democracy is not an absolute imperative that takes precedence over competing goals.[83] Non-Westerners do not hesitate to point out the gaps between Western principles and Western practice. Hypocrisy and double standards are the price of universalist pretensions. Democracy is promoted but not if it brings Islamic fundamentalists (Algeria and Palestine are cases in point) to power; non-proliferation is preached for Iran and Iraq, but not for Israel; free trade is the elixir of economic growth, but not with Saudi Arabia;

aggression against oil-owning Kuwait is repulsed with massive forces, but not so aggression against oil-less Bosnia.[84] The former Malaysian Prime Minister, Mahathir Mohammed, in a speech to the non-aligned nations in February 1993, said that the US is not fighting a war on terror, but in fact a war for hegemony. He referred to the US policies towards the Muslim world and particularly towards the Arab–Israeli conflict. He condemned the US double standard and stressed the US's unjustified and oppressive policy against other nationalities.[85] When the US calls for a strict international position on the Iranian Nuclear Programme but turns a blind eye to the Israeli nuclear installations, it makes it easier for Iran to argue at home and regionally that it is being bullied while being in compliance with the international treaties, while Israel, a non-signatory to the Non-Proliferation Treaty of 1968, is let off much more lightly.[86] The Americans perceive Israel as a friend and an ally and Palestine is the Promised Land.[87] Israel receives 40 per cent of the total US foreign aid estimated at US$3.5 billion, giving every Israeli US$500 dollars annually.[88]

Moreover, over the last sixty years, the US remained the most faithful strategic partner for Israel, providing it with the necessary security shield, giving to Israel the most advanced strategic arms and financial support. In the period 1978 to 1987, the US voted thirty-eight times against the General Assembly resolutions on Israel lawlessness and violations of international law.[89] In the aftermath of the cold war, Israel has been forced to reshape its policy toward the US. The role Israel assumed in the Middle East vis-à-vis the Soviet Union is no longer valid. Thus Israel has attempted to carve out a new security niche focusing on Central Asia and the Caucasus. The new policy was intended to take advantage of US support in the Central Asian republics. Israel was seen by the newly independent republics as a gateway to the West, particularly the US. Israel began to sell itself as a new pro-American pillar against Islamic fundamentalism.[90] On the other hand, after 11 September 2001, the Americans began to look on Israel's conflict with the Palestinians as similar to their war on terror and against al-Qaeda.[91] It is argued that 'the Middle East will almost certainly develop a growing ability to resist the inclusions of others and even to punish those who try, but it will have very little ability to project its power onto or over others'.[92]

The US policy towards the UN has been a one-way road. On the one hand, successive US administrations used the UN to confer legitimacy on its international role as the leading power. On the other hand, the US has been the first to block the UN from playing its universal role to maintain international peace and security. Washington has found itself – often alone, sometimes joined by one or two countries – standing in opposition to 152 General Assembly resolutions, during the period 1978–2004, aimed at furthering human rights, peace, nuclear disarmament, economic, justice and other progressive causes.[93] The International Court of Justice in 1986 indicted the US for using illegal military force. The US also vetoed a Security Council resolution calling on all states to adhere and abide by international law.[94] Ronald Reagan, ex-US president, commented on the UN disapproval of the US invasion of Grenada in 1983 by saying, 'one hundred nations in the UN have not agreed with us on just about everything that's come before them where we are involved, and it didn't upset my breakfast at all'.[95] Mary Robinson, the former President of Ireland and UN High Commissioner for Human Rights, was very critical of US violations of human rights.[96] The US is the only country which refused to ratify the UN Charter on children's rights. The UN Economic and Social Council, for the first time since it was set up in 1946, voted in a secret ballot to expel the US in May 2001 from the committee on human rights. The US, despite being the biggest source of carbon dioxide gas emissions and a participant in the past thirty years of negotiations aiming at reducing the danger of fossil fuel emissions contributing to global warming, has resisted the application of any quantitative measures until further studies are done. The US participated in the Earth summit held in Rio de Janeiro, Brazil, 3–14 June 1992, and agreed to its protocol to work on limiting the fossil fuel emissions, but insisted on keeping the objective quotas out of the agreement. The George W. Bush administration refused to sign the Kyoto agreement on global warming.[97] The treaty is intended to achieve 'stabilization of green houses gas concentrations in the atmosphere at a level that would prevent dangerous anthropogenic interference with the climate system'. The EU committed itself to cut CO_2 by 20–30 per cent by the year 2020.[98] By 2008, 183 countries had ratified the protocol, which was initially adopted for use on 11 December 1997 in Kyoto, Japan, and which entered into force on 16 February 2005.[99] A new conference on climate change was held for two weeks in Copenhagen, Denmark, in December 2009 to renew the protocol to protect the environment, introducing a 30 per cent clean coal energy as a new global target by the year 2020.[100] On 19 December an accord had been reached that has significant elements, but that is not legally binding. 'The key points of the accord include the objective to keep the maximum temperature rise to below 2 degrees Celsius; the commitment to list developed country emission reduction targets and mitigation action by developing countries for 2020; USD 30 billion short-term funding for immediate action till 2012 and USD 100 billion annually by 2020 in long-term financing, as well as mechanisms to support technology transfer and forestry.'[101]

Analysts argue that the world is becoming more multi-polar. Richard Haass argues that the post-cold war international community will be build on four foundations: using less military force to resolve disputes, reducing the number of weapons of mass destruction, accepting a limited doctrine of humanitarian intervention and economic openness.[102] Huntington argues that governments have in considerable measure lost the ability to control the flow of money in and out of their countries and are having increasing difficulty controlling the flows of ideas, technologies, goods and people.[103] Barack Obama, who based his presidential campaign on the desire to change, pursued from his first days in office a policy not only to review but to change US foreign policy orientation. Obama, faced with the hard economic effects of the global economic crisis and aware of the difficult time ahead of him, became more inclined to fulfil his promises. Samuel Huntington argues that power is shifting from the long predominant West to non-Western civilizations. Global politics has become multi-polar and multi-civilizational.[104] The new constraints have promoted the need for new thinking in US foreign policy. The Obama administration is putting more emphasis on world consensus, bilateral consultations with the allies, cooperation with China and Russia, a new approach towards the Muslim world, accommodating the national aspirations of the developing countries, enhancing engagement policy over isolation, abandoning his predecessor's classifications of axis of evil or rogue states, and acting through the UN on issues of world concern. Obama's new world order carries with it new ideas of cooperation and coordination. Most of the hallmarks of the George W. Bush foreign policy are over. The old conservative idea of 'America exceptionalism' which placed the US on a plane above the rest of the world as a unique beacon of democracy and financial might has been rejected. Almost at every step, President Barack Obama has made clear that the US is but one actor in a global community. Talks of American economic supremacy have been replaced by a call from Obama for more growth in the developing countries. Claims for American military supremacy have been replaced by a heavy emphasis on cooperation and diplomatic hard labour.[105] The world political and economic developments enhance the argument that the world is shifting from a uni-polar to a multi-polar system. 'US superiority will not last. As power diffuses around the world, America's position relative to others will inevitably erode.'[106]

Analysts have differed on how to explain the scope and nature of the 'new world order'. Some believed that the new world order would witness a transfer from a bi-polar to a multi-polar system.[107] Others argued for a uni-polar system. Brzezinski argued that the absence of the Soviet Union means that the United

States was the sole superpower with international responsibilities. Europe, at the best, would be an economic power and its emphasis on Eastern Europe would slightly delay its integration and unity.[108]

Commentators argue that, though the 'new world order' has not yet been totally shaped,[109] it would witness fundamental changes in the principles of international behaviour and conduct. The 'new world order' would be characterized by less ideological struggle and proliferation of alliances in East–West relations. The world would witness a decline in the role of ideologies in influencing relations among nations. The attitudes and policies of states would be empty of ideological militancy.[110] This is clear, today, in the development of relations between the US and China, despite the latter's resistance to adopting liberal democratic measures. On the other hand, it is also argued that it would be more democratic based on what has taken place in the former Soviet Union and the East European countries. Integration is seen as a third characteristic of the perceived new order. The basis for this assumption is the developments in the international arena like the proposed European unity, Russian–Western rapprochement and the talk about 'a common European home', the increasing cooperation among the permanent members of the Security Council, integration among the Latin American states, and the greater coordination of policies between Southeast Asian states.

5. The Changing World Order

The world is changing shape today, due to effects of the global economic crisis. Gordon Brown, the British Prime Minister at the time, said in 2009 that a new world order was emerging out of the global economic crisis.[111] The IMF expects a drop in the global economic growth from 3.4 per cent in 2008 to ½ per cent in 2009 with growth picking up to 3 per cent in 2010.[112]

The US economy was still the largest in the world with a GDP at $14.29 trillion in 2008, but because of the global economic crisis the budget deficit for the first half of the fiscal year 2009–10 was $2 trillion[113] with $12 trillion in debts[114] and growth was expected to witness a sharp decline from 1.3 per cent in 2008[115] to 0.1 per cent in 2009, whereas the EU economic growth would decline from 2.6 per cent in 2007 to 0.2 per cent during the same period.[116] Britain's economy, despite optimistic readings that the worst of the recession was over,[117] would shrink by 3.5 per cent in 2009. The budget deficit for fiscal year 2008–9 amounted to £175 billion[118] and is expected to climb to £190 billion for the fiscal year 2010–11, a record in cash terms, with the employers' organization the CBI expecting unemployment to peak at 10.3 per cent in the second quarter of

2010.[119] Data released show that the Spanish economy was expected to shrink by 3 per cent and the Irish by 7 per cent in 2009, and the rate of unemployment in Britain would reach 9 per cent in 2009 whereas the Spanish would hit 19 per cent by 2010. The US budget for the fiscal year which began on 1 October 2008 includes US$711 billion for the military – $541 billion for the Pentagon and the nuclear weapons-related activities of the Department of Energy, and, according to Robert Gates, at least $170 billion for ongoing military operations in Iraq and Afghanistan. The United States is far and away the global leader in military spending (see Figure 6). It spends more than the next forty-five highest spending countries in the world combined, accounting for 48 per cent of the world's total military spending. The United States spends on its military 5.8 times more than China, 10.2 times more than Russia, and 98.6 times more than Iran.[120]

The world today is at a crossroads, witnessing a retreat from the ideas that inspired international relations prior to the beginning of the global economic crisis. Fukuyama's theory about the end of history has proved to be wrong and he has himself backed down from it. The European countries, the US and Japan – great advocates of globalization – have retreated towards localization through their protectionist policies: subsidizing the agricultural sector, bailing out national companies, giving priorities to national products, allocating resources to encourage innovative local businesses, setting up policies with greater incentives to attract foreign investment and being less keen to advocate foreign intervention. At the same time, the world has become a small village due to the technological revolution which infringes the sovereignty of the state, the environmental constraints from the climate change, the universality of good governance, the importance of world peace to national interests, the role of the multinational corporations and the fact that the world has become more economically interdependent. Countries have no alternative but to act globally. Contemporary nation-states are faced with a dilemma between attending to local needs and global demands. The new world order would be characterized by glocalization whereby countries would adhere more to the notion of the nation-state giving more priority to domestic politics and pursuing a foreign policy based on the principle of cost-benefit rather than zero-sum-game theory, becoming internationally more cooperative, giving the international organizations a greater role to play and being less inclined to use force in foreign policy. Canada in June 2009 expressed concern over US protectionist policies. China allocated US$542 billion to a stimulus policy and faced an international fuss over guidance for government bodies to source domestically when possible. The World Bank on 18 June 2009 said that massive stimulus should keep China's economic growth at a respectable rate in the years 2009–10, but a robust recovery is unlikely, given global weakness and soft non-government investment. The American Chamber of Commerce in China said in a statement that any protectionist policies emanating from Beijing or Washington could prove 'extremely detrimental' to decades of progress on promoting greater openness.[121]

The changing nature of the international order will ultimately have an impact on North–South relations. It is argued that 'the ability of the North to use its technological advantage to dominate the South is, in fact, declining. The South will become increasingly assertive and the North progressively constrained.'[122] The 'new world order' would be a multi-polar system with the US, Germany, Japan, Russia and China playing the role of the full-fledged actors. Figures on cash reserves show new rich countries replacing old ones (see Table 3.1). It is argued that China, India and Brazil will become major actors in the new world order because the US needs their cooperation to overcome its financial and economic crisis.[123] This is clearly illustrated in the unofficial regular meetings held by the delegations of the five permanent members of the UN Security Council to iron out differences, coordinate their attitudes and adopt similar policies before the official meetings of the Security Council are held. Examples of this are the decisions taken with respect to the United Nations Peace-Keeping Force in Namibia, the attitude towards the Iran–Iraq war and the adoption of resolution 598,[124] the international stand on the Kuwaiti crisis and the new international approach towards the Middle East peace process on the one hand, and the stalemate in the Bosnian crisis, the challenges confronting the coalition following the second Gulf crisis and the attitude towards the Iranian nuclear programme on the other.

Table 3.1. Cash Reserves in Contemporary World Order (2009) (billions US$)

Country	Amount of Reserves
China	2000
Russia	407
India	220
Brasil	155
US	60
Britain	42

Source: Dr Martin Williams, a seminar on Globalisation vs Localisation, London Management Council, 21 April 2009, *Jazeera*, 15 Nov. 2009.

Despite the dismemberment of the USSR, Russia today is pursuing a policy to regain its international status. Russia has a total armed forces of 988,100 plus deterrent forces estimated at 149,000 and reserves of about 20 million[125] and defence expenditure at 3.9 per cent of its GDP, estimated in 2008 at US$2.22 trillion (see Table 3.2). Data shows that Russia, with a population of 140 million people and a military power of around 1.4 million, and despite its financial losses due to the credit crunch – foreign debts represent one-third of the GDP – today is second among the richest countries of the world, with $407 billion in cash reserves (see Table 3.1). The state component of foreign debt has declined, but commercial short-term debt to foreigners has risen strongly. These positive trends began to reverse in the second half of 2008. The global economic crisis affected Russia's banking system, which faced liquidity problems. Moscow responded quickly in early October 2008, initiating a rescue plan of over US$200 billion designed to increase liquidity in the financial sector.[126]

Russia has become more inclined to pursue foreign policies similar to those of the last Soviet administrations. Russia in its early years adopted a conciliatory pattern in relations with the West. It was argued that such a pattern was likely to continue as long as Russia was in need of the Western funds and technology.[127] This was clearly illustrated in the evolution of the Russia position on the issue of Yugoslavia. The Russians decided to abstain on the resolution adopted by the Security Council on 23 April 1993 freezing Yugoslavia's membership of the UN. They also put pressure on the Belgrade government to accept the Vance–Owen peace plan and to terminate its support for the Bosnian-Serb self-styled government. Finally, the Russians, on 16 May 1993, endorsed the peace plan and called on the international community to begin implementing it, regardless of the outcome of the referendum.[128] At the same time, they threatened to veto any Security Council decision to lift the arms embargo imposed on the Muslims of Bosnia or to use force to repel the Serb aggression. The Security Council failed to reach an agreement, in its meeting on 22 March 2006, regarding the Iranian nuclear programme, due to Russian and Chinese opposition to the British proposal. Russia and China want to give more time to diplomacy to convince Iran to give up voluntarily its activities related to the production of highly refined uranium enrichment. Uranium enrichment is used to make fuel for nuclear reactors, but a highly refined level is needed to produce the core of an atomic weapon. The Russian Foreign Minister, Sergei Lavrov, said on 21 March 2009 that 'there was no proof that Iran is trying to develop a nuclear weapon' and urged the West to respect and reach out to the Iran.[129] For the same reason, the Security Council on 5 April 2009 failed to reach a decision on the North Korean launch of a long-range missile. The Russians and the Chinese called for a further investigation to see whether or not the North Koreans had violated previous UN resolutions. Russia and China called on all parties concerned to refrain from any movement that could escalate the tension. China, sharing 1400 kilometres of its border with North Korea, has the latter as part of China's back yard. Since North Korea is ruled by a socialist regime China has become a guarantor of North Korea's survival, allocating more than a third of its foreign aid to support the North Korean economy. For these reasons, China plays a detrimental role in any US potential move towards North Korea.[130] On the other hand, China voted, on 14 October 2006, in favour of Security Council resolution 1718 proposed by the US, in reaction to the first North Korean nuclear experiment, imposing political, economic and military sanctions against North Korea. Chinese diplomacy succeeded on 31 October 2006 in reaching an agreement between the US and North Korea to resume multilateral talks, culminating in 2008 in North Korea abandoning its nuclear project and dismantling its installations for US assistance.

China enjoys all features and advantages that should enable it to become a superpower. It possesses a large population of 1.33 billion; the second largest economy in the world after the US with a GDP estimated in 2008 at US$7.8 trillion, replacing Japan, and a growth rate at 9.8 per cent, with the largest liquidity reserve estimated at $2 trillion,[131] exceeding the total reserves of the richest five countries in the world (see Table 3.1); advanced technology; active military manpower of around 2.27 million plus strategic mission forces of 100,000 and reserves estimated at 600,000,[132] with defence expenditure equalling 4.3 per cent of the total GDP,[133] equipped with advanced conventional and non-conventional weaponry machines (see Table 3.2); a high educational standard; and a permanent seat in the Security Council. China pursues open relations with the world of nations and enjoys the ability to influence a significant number of Third World countries. Analysts argue that China is expected to become a superpower by the end of the first quarter of the twenty-first century. China is working on assuring Asian countries of peaceful coexistence, to avoid forcing them to look for realignment with the US.[134] The US today is challenged with a trade balance deficit with China estimated at $85 billion, increasing US dependency on China.[135] Moreover, China has huge reserves in US dollars, becoming second only to the US and investing US$1 trillion in American government bonds. The Chinese Premier, Wen Jiabao, expressed concern on 14 March 2009 about China's investment in US government debt. He said: 'we have lent a huge amount of money to the US. Of course we are concerned about the safety of our assets. To be honest I am definitely a little worried.'[136] Moreover, Germany, Japan, India and Brazil, due to their economic achievements, are likely to acquire a permanent status in the Security Council, which would substantiate the argument that the world system is shifting from a uni-polar to a multi-polar system.

Table 3.2. Defence Expenditures of World Leading Powers (billions US$)

Country	Military Spending	World Ranking
United States*	711.0	1
China	121.9	2
Russia	70.0	3
United Kingdom	55.4	4
France	54.0	5
Japan	41.1	6
Germany	37.8	7
Italy	30.6	8
Spain	14.4	15
Netherlands	9.9	18
Greece	7.3	21
Poland	6.2	25
Sweden	5.8	26
Belgium	4.4	30
Denmark	3.9	33
Portugal	3.1	41
Finland	2.8	43
Austria	2.6	44
Czech Republic	2.5	46
Romania	2.3	47
Hungary	1.3	56
Ireland	1.1	57
Total EU	245.4	n/a
Total World (not all countries shown)	1,472.7	n/a

* The figure for the US is the budget request for Fiscal Year 2009 and includes $170 billion for ongoing military operations in Iraq and Afghanistan, as well as funding for DOE nuclear weapons activities. All other figures are projections based on 2006,

the last year for which accurate data is available. All countries that spent over one billion per year are listed.
Sources: International Institute for Strategic Studies, *The Military Balance 2008*.

Despite the line by the US Defense Department, as portrayed by the conservative right wing, that the US should be poised to act unilaterally when collective action cannot be orchestrated, and the George W. Bush world adventures in the period 2000–8, the current Democrat US administration is less inclined to use force in foreign policy. Barack Obama, burdened with the most severe economic recession since the 1930s, is more reluctant to act unilaterally. The Obama administration is pursuing a more compromising foreign policy, putting more emphasis on world consensus through bilateral consultations with its allies and major powers including Russia and China, and acting through the UN. During his visit to Europe, President Obama emphasized his new policy of partnership, not of mentor, with his NATO allies. Obama, also, spoke in Prague on 5 April 2009, of a world free of nuclear weapon. He added that the US, being the only nuclear power to have used such weapon of mass destruction, holds an ethical responsibility to pursue a world without nuclear weapons.[137] President Obama's fast-paced trip to Europe, Turkey and Iraq, started to fulfil Obama's campaign pledge of reinvigorating America's international alliances, which were left ragged by foreign policy rows with allies of the George W. Bush administration.[138] The US foreign policy is going through re-engineering and a new thinking is currently in place. The new US administration realizes that they cannot continue to act unilaterally in world politics. The George W. Bush administration had decided to place interceptor missiles in Poland and sophisticated radar in the Czech Republic – a system designed to shoot down long-range missiles. Scuttling this missile defence shield helped smooth relations between the US and Russia.[139] Russia was outraged at the notion of missiles being pointed in its direction from a region that was firmly in the Soviet orbit just twenty years ago. President Barack Obama's new administration offered, initially, to review the policy and on 17 September 2009 announced that it would scrap the Bush-era plan.[140] This was hailed by President Dmitry Medvedev as a 'responsible move'. In return, Russia decided to give up plans to deploy missiles in Kilingrad near Poland.[141] The Americans are hoping to win Russian support in putting more pressure on Iran to abandon its nuclear option. For the same reason, the US offered to let China have open access to Latin American oil.

In the new world order era, the Middle East remains strategically vital to the US national interest. The US, argues George McGovern, has a continuing national interest in preventing any hostile power from dominating the region; in maintaining access to the region's oil at a reasonable prices and to the region's strategic waterways; in supporting and helping to defend friendly countries; in promoting regional stability through the resolution of conflict; and in promoting human rights, economic opportunity and political self determination.[142] A further important element is the security and stability of Israel as another determining factor of the US foreign policy towards the Middle East. The change that Barack Obama talked about during his campaign includes a new thinking in the US foreign policy towards the Middle East. He dedicated part of his inaugural speech to extend a hand of peace to the Muslim world on the basis of mutual respect and recognition of mutual interests. Obama in a speech on 6 April 2009 to the Turkish Parliament spoke of partnership with the Muslim world and said that 'the US is not and never will be at war with Islam'.[143] He added that US ties with the Muslim world could not be simply defined by opposition to terrorism. The speech was intended to mend frayed relations with key strategic allies.[144] Obama initiated a major shift from his predecessor George W. Bush in dealing with Middle Eastern issues. He emphasized the US support for the Middle East peace process and promised to play a more effective role to bring about the two-states solution. The new US position was reiterated by the US Secretary of State Hillary Clinton on her first visit to the region in February 2009 and President Obama upon his visit to Turkey. George Mitchell was chosen by Obama to be the new US special envoy to mediate between Israel and the Palestinians.

Another positive sign in the new US Middle Eastern strategy is the American rapprochement with Syria. A senior US delegation paid an official visit to Syria. Jeffrey Feltman, acting assistant Secretary of State for Near East, and Dan Shapiro of the White House's National Security Council, on 7 March 2009, held high-level talks in Syria, the first senior US officials to visit Syria since 2005.[145] Feltman's visit came upon the instruction of the US President, Barack Obama, and the US Secretary of State Hillary Clinton, to start a dialogue with Syria as part of Obama's new policy based on dialogue and diplomacy.[146] Relations between Syria and the US deteriorated during the George W. Bush administration after the assassination of the former Lebanese Prime Minister, Rafiq al-Hariri, in February 2005. Washington withdrew its ambassador to Syria and stepped up sanctions against Damascus. US President Barack Obama has made moves to talk to Syria, but Secretary of State, Hillary Clinton, during her first visit to Ankara, said no decision had been made on returning an ambassador. President Bashar Assad of Syria, in a press interview with a Japanese newspaper, welcomed the new US administration's move and expressed his intention to cooperate and engage in a dialogue for peace in the region.[147] Analysts argue that the new policy was inspired partly by the new American approach towards Iran. It is intended to weaken the Iranian position on its nuclear programme by containing Iran's allies through constructive engagement. The US is opting to enlist Syria to influence Hezbollah, through accommodating it in Lebanese politics, and to weaken Hamas to accept the American two-states initiative for Middle East peace. Another significant development is the announcement of the new US administration to withdraw its forces from Iraq by the year 2011.

The US, aware of the overlapping interests and realizing the importance of the role that Iran can play to achieve peace and security in the region, has adopted a constructive engagement policy towards Iran. Iran is a major player in the Middle East and Central Asia. Iran seeks stable borders and has sought influence in surrounding Central Asian states based on economic interests rather than promoting radical Islam. In Afghanistan, both the US and Iran deplore the Taliban excesses and want a multi-ethnic, multi-party coalition.[148] Iraq is another area of similar convergence where the US is looking for Iran's help to create a safe exit for US forces without affecting Iraq's stability and territorial integrity. Engaging Iran also would help to bring about regional stability in the Gulf and promote cooperative interactions between the Arab states and Iran; it would reduce its sense of exclusion, eliminating the threat to the supply of the free world oil, neutralize Iran's position on the Arab–Israel peace process and block Iran's support to Hamas and Hezbollah. Hillary Clinton made the new administration's first public overtures towards Iran by inviting Tehran to the forthcoming conference on Afghanistan by the end of March 2009.[149] Analysts argue 'a strategy of engagement could substitute disclosure for denial. As mutual confidence is established and dialogue resumed, restraints on Iranian WMD potentials will appear both less arbitrary and less urgent.'[150]

In a major shift from the policy of George W. Bush, who branded Iran part of an 'axis of evil' and spearheaded a drive to isolate it, Obama offered a 'new beginning' of diplomatic engagement between the two old foes without any preconditions.[151] He spoke of extending an olive branch to Tehran if it 'unclenches its fist'. Obama said in his video message released to mark the Iranian New Year: 'The US wants the Islamic Republic of Iran to take its rightful place in the community of nations.' He added 'that place cannot be reached through terror or arms, but rather through peaceful actions that demonstrate the true greatness of the Iranian people and civilization.' However, Khamenei, the supreme leader in Iran who has the final say on all matters of state, commented that 'they give the slogan of change but in practice no change is seen'. He spoke of 'oppressive sanctions' imposed on Iran, Iranian assets frozen in the US and Washington's backing of Israel. He added: 'you change, our behaviour will change'.[152] In a further development representing the change in the US policy towards the Muslim world, President Obama and his Vice President Joe Biden conceded that they would engage in dialogue with the Taliban.[153] Kai Eide, UN Special Envoy to Afghanistan, told France's *Le Monde* on 21 March 2009 that 'reconciliation is an essential element. But it is important to talk to the people who count.' He added that a 'fragmented approach to the insurgency will not work. You need to be ambitious and include all Taliban movement.'[154] Obama met NATO leaders on 3 April 2009, to outline his policy review for Afghanistan, having earlier said that it would contain an exit strategy and greater emphasis on economic development.

6. Conclusion

The preceding analysis of the changing world order shows that the Arabs have been affected negatively and positively. Arab states became subject to regional threats and the need for support to compensate for their inherent weakness prompted closer cooperation between the moderate Arab countries and the US and deprived some of them of an independent foreign policy. It is interesting, however, to observe recent developments in the US–Arab states relations. Some Arab countries, particularly the reluctant camp, chose to disassociate themselves from US regional and international policies. In fact some moderate Arab countries opted for a similar course in foreign policy. The UAE government for example has repeatedly assured the Iranians that the US would not be permitted to use its territory against Iran, nor is it looking for US military support to regain sovereignty over the disputed islands. The UAE's stand on the issue is based on peaceful settlement through bilateral negotiation or arbitration. The Arab states were divided as usual regarding the unilateral US attack in September 1996 against Iraqi military bases in the south as well as the extension of the no-fly zone. In a further attempt to distance their policy from that of the US, some Arab countries voted against Taiwan membership in the United Nations. In February 1998 most of the GCC countries refused in February 1998 to grant permission to US forces to use their facilities to launch air strikes against Iraq.

At the same time, the Arabs have been important players in international developments. Their importance stems from their geostrategic location, their economic resources – nearly half of the world oil reserves – and their prolonged conflict with Israel, the US's most strategic ally in the region. For all of the above factors, the Arab world occupies a top priority in the foreign policy agenda of the main international actors. On the one hand, the Arabs have lost a strategic ally, namely the Soviet Union, leaving them more vulnerable to US pressures with respect to the peace negotiations with Israel, controlling arms sale to the region, curbing the Arabs' power through its campaign against Iraq, upsetting the regional balance of power to the advantage of non-Arab powers in the region (Israel, Iran and Turkey) and pursuing a double-standard foreign policy on democracy and human rights values. On the other hand, the changing world order has prompted positive developments in the Arab world of great significance, namely Yemeni unity, the adoption of some democratic measures in some of the Arab states like Iraq, Yemen, Jordan, Morocco and Kuwait, and introduction of greater political participation in some other Arab countries like Bahrain, Oman and Sudan. The regional developments have affected the Arab states' foreign policy-making, as we will see in Chapter 4.

Chapter 4

The Regional Variable: Unstable Region

1. Introduction

Since the early 1990s, instability and political tensions among local and regional states have been the main characteristics of the Arab regional order. The Arab states have been divided into two main camps: the moderates, Egypt, Saudi Arabia, Morocco, Jordan and the other Gulf Co-operation Council (GCC) members, and the reluctant, Syria, Libya, Sudan and the Islamic resistant groups Hamas, al-Jihad al-Islami and Hezbollah (supported by Iran, a non-Arab state). Other Arab countries are more inclined towards the moderate camp. Qatar, a conservative US ally, maintains good relations with Iran, a US foe, and seeks to play a regional mediatory role between the two camps. Contemporary Arab countries in their need for security and regional stability have been forced to initiate foreign policies that compensate for their inherited weaknesses and to search for an ally in the global system.[1] On the regional level, the Arab countries are lagging behind their neighbours in almost all aspects of power. For this reason, states in the moderate camp have transcended their conflicting national interests in favour of cooperation and coordination that culminated in the formation of an axis. Political stability in the Arab regional order is invariably tied to economic prosperity and the Middle East peace process. This requires the Arab states to move from a status of conflict to that of economic cooperation and integration. Equally important is the role played by the international actors in the Arab regional order that could contribute positively or negatively to regional stability. The increasing US role in the area since the Kuwaiti predicament is considered in this chapter as a destabilizing rather than a stabilizing factor.

This chapter investigates the regional context, concentrating on regional political developments and their impact on regional security, stability and interactions. It is intended also to examine the effects of the changing world order and the increasing US involvement in Middle Eastern affairs. It highlights regional order, the Turkish engagement, the Iranian challenge and the Arab–Israeli conflict. I argue that regional stability depends on non-interference, mutual understanding, confidence building, settlement of contentious issues and regional cooperation.

2. The Regional Order

A regional order compromises a designated geographical area that includes three or more countries, not including a superpower, with intensified political interactions among its members. The Arab world represents a regional order consisting of more unifying factors than any other contemporary regional order: the language, culture and the national identity.[2] Others have argued that the designated area of the Arab order includes all Arab states from Mauritania to the Gulf. Members are interlinked with geography and similarities in linguistic, cultural, historical and social variables.[3] Throughout history the Arabs have constituted a distinguished homogeneous unified identity and faced common threats and challenges, from Western colonialism to the Arab–Israeli conflict and foreign powers' intervention and hegemony. The political system in the period from between the caliphates to the Fatimid state was close to a federal system: the central government dealt with the religious, judicial, financial, war and peace and foreign affairs, and other responsibilities were delegated to the local/regional governments.[4] In the eighteenth and nineteenth centuries, many Islamic regions fell under the tutelage of European imperial powers. After the First World War, the remnants of the Ottoman Empire were parcelled out as European protectorates. Since 1924, there has been no major widely accepted claim to the caliphate. Analysts define the Arab regional order as a framework for a specified nation, namely the Arab nation, spreading over the designated geographical area of the world named the Arab homeland.[5] Arab nationalism since the nineteenth century represented the principal force behind the political parties and the ideological struggle against colonialism.[6] Common culture encourages cooperation among states, crystallizing in the emergence of a regional grouping among countries, especially in the economic field.[7]

The Middle East differs from much of the rest of the world in terms of security issues. It is a cauldron of discontent. Total expenditure on inter- and intra-regional conflicts in the last six decades amounts to US$3 trillion and the Middle East annual military expenditure equals US$1.2 trillion, equivalent to 5 per cent of the total world expenditure.[8] Despite the multiplicity of political wills and the priority of state security, the key issues remain external threats[9] and the efforts to secure adequate resources.[10] Despite the material differences – small or large, poor or rich, large or small population, social, ethnic, religious and localization tendencies between the Arab countries – relations among them are controlled by a perception of pan-Arabism. Consequently, the national interest approach falls short of interpreting inter-Arab relations or the political behaviour of the Arab states towards each other.[11] It is argued that 'any regional event that had the potential for stoking the embers of Arab nationalism posed a direct challenge to the legitimacy of several Arab regimes, impelling leaders to make policy choices that damaged prospects for regional integration'.[12] Unless the Arab countries recognize the challenges facing them, the future of the Arab regional order is bleak. Instability comes not from any genetic tendency towards violence, but from social, cultural and political pressures. The objective of any regional system is to speak with a common voice and to play an effective role as a group of countries, with the tendency towards gradual total integration. Unfortunately, in the Arab regional order, disagreement and lack of consensus limit the principal regional organization, the Arab League.[13] In terms of culture, language, labour mobility and investors' perceptions, the Arab order constitutes a neighbourhood. Important differences between countries, however, persist.[14] According to Arend Lijphart there are four prerequisites for regional stability and integration:[15]

1. Awareness of the dangers inherent in fragmented systems;
2. Commitment to system maintenance;
3. Ability to transcend subcultural cleavages;
4. Ability to forge appropriate solutions that can meet the demands of other partners.

Ghassan Salama summarizes the features of the Arab regional order in the following:

1. The international variable shaping the Arab regional order is not the same.
2. There is political fluidity, since any state can move from one group to the other, to become smaller or bigger, in the face of major developments.
3. There is no one variable or criterion, wealth, population or area, which could support the justification for any Arab countriy to go alone.[16]
4. Most of the Arab states are in state of crisis.

5. Political borders of every Arab country were drawn by the colonial powers. This has made the issue of national borders continuously irritating for most of the Arab political systems.
6. Contemporary political systems lack political legitimacy.
7. Arab countries are dependent on foreign powers.
8. Arab states are undemocratic and lack regional equality.

Regionalism involves consensus and capacity on a regional scale and not the assertion of dominance by a single actor over its neighbours.[17] Absence of leadership forced the Arab regional order to become multi-polar and stimulated competition for leadership.[18] The power vacuum left after Gamal Abdel Nasser's death encouraged other prominent Arab countries to compete for the post.[19] The Arab order is faced with many obstacles, namely: divided into twenty-two countries promoted conflicting national interests that culminated in unilateral peace agreements with Israel, border clashes or incursions like the Iraqi–Kuwaiti crisis, weak infrastructure due to severe domestic problems and the absence of internal social integration (for example, Iraq, Lebanon, Algeria and Sudan), water crisis and food insecurity (see Chapters 7 and 8), lack of political reform (see Chapter 1), and foreign dependency.[20] Egypt opted for a unilateral peace with Israel, culminating in Anwar Sadat's historical trip to Jerusalem and the signing of the Camp David peace treaty in 1979, and led to Egypt's expulsion from the Arab League. It caused Egypt's isolation and exacerbated inter-Arab frictions. Egypt, after being readmitted to the Arab League in 1989, decided to move from regional isolation to become a facilitator, playing a compromising role in accordance with the existing balance of power to achieve a low level of solidarity. The decline in the Arab order led other Arab countries to pursue policies that were taboo a few decades back. The Palestinian Liberation Organization and Jordan followed Egypt, whereas countries like Mauritania,[21] Morocco, Tunisia, Oman and Qatar opted for diplomatic and commercial ties with Israel. The changes in Egypt and Tunisia towards democratization and the uprisings in Yemen, Libya, Jordan and Syria have now led to a new era of Arab reawakening and a revival of the Arab regional order.

The Arab regional order faces domestic and external challenges.[22] There are risks of coups d'état, as happened in Omdurman, Sudan, in May 2008, and social and political unrest culminated in labour strikes and protests against economic hardship seen in the high rate of unemployment, inflation and the adverse effects of the global economic crisis, particularly in Egypt and Syria. A further domestic challenge is the struggle between the state and the people over reforms and democratic changes. Social cleavages on ethnic, tribal, religious and sectarian bases represent a further disintegrative factor. The external challenges are multiple, ranging from the American occupation of Iraq, the Iranian challenge, the Turkish involvement, the Arab–Israeli conflict, the call for a Greater Middle East and the cold war in inter-Arab relations.

The Arab regional order, as a result, is in a state of cold war among its main actors, with each party trying to deny the other's hegemony and dictate regional interactions,[23] as illustrated in the arms race in the region (see Table 4.1). This not only explains the diversity in the Arab states' attitudes towards regional developments, such as the Iraq–Iran war 1980–8, the American invasion of Iraq in 2003, the Israeli attack on southern Lebanon in 2006 and the Israeli invasion of the Gaza Strip in December 2008 and January 2009, but has fuelled regional inter-Arab struggles. It is often argued that the Lebanese civil war was a manœuvre by which conservative moderate states in the region, particularly Egypt and Saudi Arabia, sought to deny influence to the radical progressive states, namely Syria, Iraq, Algeria and Libya, while both sets of states armed the various Lebanese militias and political parties.[24] Arab countries did not hesitate to mobilize or actually use force as a mean to settle their territorial disputes with each other. Iraq decided on 2 August 1990 to occupy Kuwait to bring a final end to its prolonged differences with Kuwait. The Iraqi invasion of Kuwait and the American invasion of Iraq in 2003 created huge rifts in the Arab regional order.

Developing countries, including the Middle East region, rely on exporting raw materials and depend on Western sources for data and information. The absence of accurate data and the lack of transparency forced Arab investors to look to foreign markets for their investments. This contributed to the decline in the GDP, a low economic growth rate, increasing foreign debts and more dependency on the foreign markets. The Arabs lost around US$2.5 trillion because of the credit crunch. The rapidly changing world balance of the 1990s and new developments stemming from the acceleration of economic globalization have forced the regional states to re-evaluate and reshape their foreign policy strategies.[25] Furthermore, the volume of economic and trade relations among the Arab states is relatively low.[26] 'The Middle East remains one of the few areas of the world where the struggle over resources – oil and water – continues and where, therefore, war still plays. Both oil and water will become increasingly pressing issues in the Middle East in the coming decades.'[27] Oil, being a depleted resource, is unlikely to continue as a determining factor of the region's economic performance. 'Petroleum can no longer provide sufficient resources for sustained regional development.'[28]

Table 4.1. Middle East Military Expenditures (2007) (billions US$)

Country	Military Spending (Billions of $)*	World Ranking
Turkey	11.6	16
Israel	11.0	17
Iran	7.2	22
Saudi Arabia	29.5	9
United Arab Emirates	9.5	19
Egypt	4.3	31
Kuwait	3.5	36
Oman	3.3	38
Algeria	3.1	42
Qatar	2.3	48
Morocco	2.2	50
Jordan	1.1	58
Total Arab	58.8	n/a
Total Middle East	88.6	n/a

* Figures are projections based on 2006, the last year for which accurate data are available. All countries that spent over one billion per year are listed.

Sources: International Institute for Strategic Studies, *The Military Balance 2008*.

After the second Gulf crisis, the Arab regional order was further weakened and witnessed fresh calls for a new Middle Eastern regional structure. A larger Middle East extends from Mauritania to Afghanistan and would include Israel, Turkey, Iran and Pakistan. The proposed region has been a longstanding Israeli national objective. Shimon Peres, in his book on the Middle East, talked thoroughly about Israel's role in the new regional order. Israel in the 1950s sought to create a 'periphery strategy', setting up an alliance consisting of Turkey, Ethiopia, Iran and Israel. The strategy failed after the fall of the Shah in Iran in February 1979.[29] The integration of Israel in its regional context has been a longstanding US objective as the only chance of achieving a lasting peace and stability in the region. Israel, since the Camp David peace treaty, has become an important actor and major player in inter-Arab politics. Israel also plays a significant role in the domestic politics of regional states like Lebanon, Jordan and Egypt, and is a determining factor in inter- and intra-Arab political struggles, especially Syrian–Lebanese relations and Egyptian policy towards Arab affairs.[30] It is argued that foreign powers have no interest in maintaining a strong and stable Arab order and this is clearly manifested in their regional policy which insists on dealing with the Arab countries on an individual basis and not as a bloc.[31] The Western policy towards the region since 1991 has been to discard the Arab League as a regional organization in dealing with Arab affairs because it does not fit with its objective of restructuring the region. They pursue a policy encouraging subregional cooperation, bilateral or trilateral cooperation, and the integration of Israel into any inter- or intra-regional or subregional project with the US or the EU countries. Examples of this are the conference on the Middle East and North Africa held in Morocco in 1994, the Middle Eastern–European cooperation and the Middle East federation. The EU has negotiated separately with Tunisia, Morocco and Jordan. The dualism in the EU foreign policy towards regional orders is clear: refusing to deal with the Arab countries as a bloc through the Arab League while accepting in 1996 to cooperate with the Association of Southeast Nations (ASEAN) and later with the premier trading bloc Mercosur[32] of Latin America.[33] The European Union has favoured the strengthening of Mercosur and supported its initiatives, notably through the inter-institutional agreement to provide technical and institutional support for its newly created structures. In 1995, the EU and Mercosur signed an Interregional Framework Cooperation Agreement, which came into force in 1999. The latest political dialogue meeting took place in Buenos Aires on 25 April 2008.[34]

The Iranian Challenge

Iran today constitutes a significant regional power, with a population of 66.5 million and population growth at 2 per cent. The Iranian social composition is a mosaic of different religious and ethnic groups. Islam is the religion of 99 per cent of people (Shi'ite 84 per cent and Sunni 15 per cent), with the remaining 1 per cent belonging to other religious groups. On the ethnic level Iran is more divided, with Persians making only 51 per cent, Azeri 24 per cent, Turkmen 15 per cent, Kurds 7 per cent, Arabs 4 per cent and the remaining 4 per cent being other nationalities.[35] Economic indicators reveal that the estimated GDP in 2008 was around US$842 billion, with the economic growth rate at 6.2 per cent; however, foreign debt was estimated at US$21.8 billion and the inflation rate was at 23.6 per cent.[36] It is the fourth biggest oil-producing country, and fifth in the world in terms of oil reserves, with 138.4 billion barrels, and the second in world gas reserves, estimated at 26.8 trillion cubic metres. High oil prices in recent years allowed Iran to greatly increase its export earnings and amass over $70 billion in foreign exchange reserves. Iran is faced with economic stringency that could lead moderates away from an opening with the West since it continues to suffer from double-digit unemployment and inflation. Underemployment among Iran's educated youth has convinced many to seek jobs overseas, resulting in a significant 'brain drain'.[37] Iran needs to generate jobs at the rate of at least 700,000 per annum to cut its unemployment rate. Iran's society is economically unequally divided, with 30 per cent of the wealthy people controlling 80 per cent of GNP.[38] 'A weaker, impoverished Iran is not necessarily more pliable or less dangerous.'[39]

Arab relations with Iran are influenced by a multiplicity of factors, most important of which are the Iranian regional behaviour and ambitions, the US interventionist policy in the region, the Arab–Israeli conflict, sectarianism/nationalism, lack of regime accountability on the Arab side and public opinion. The determinants of Iranian foreign policy run from its religious posture to its security dilemma.[40] They are complex and have never been stable. Michel Foucher argues that 'the gulf has become the Persian Gulf because of the strong and historical influence of Iran, especially during the time of the Shah when he found the support from the American strategy supporting him to achieve regional security as the police man of the Gulf, in the protection of oil'.[41] According to Nabil Khalifa, 'the dispute between Arabs and Iranians is not simply over the name of the Gulf, it reflects a political conflict and nationalistic dimension. The strategy in summary is based on who controls the Gulf, the waters, islands, oil, the strategic position, and its wealth.'[42] They moved from cooptation at the time of the Shah's regime to belligerency during the Iraq–Iran war to détente during the time of the Rafsanjani and Khatimi presidencies to cold war in the period of Ahmadinejad presidency. The Saudi–Iranian alliance – part of the American 'Twin Pillar' policy during the reign of the Shah – collapsed with the success of the revolution in February 1979 and shifted to a Saudi–Iraqi alliance orchestrated to frustrate the objectives of revolutionary Iran. It is argued that Iranian regional behaviour and its initiatives for regional security caused it to become part of the security dilemma and not part of the solution. On the one hand, Iran's security is threatened as a result of regional political developments and foreign intervention. On the other hand, Iran's regional behaviour constitutes a threat to regional security.[43] Arab states, with exception of Syria, Libya and Oman, then supported the Iraqi war efforts against Iran. However, the ad hoc alliance was shortlived due to the latter's invasion of Kuwait.

Since the fall of the Shah, Saudi Arabia and the Gulf States have shared a common apprehension of the new Iranian government.[44] Revolutionary Iran showed continuity with its monarchial predecessor in its claim to be the region's paramount power.[45] Anwar Gargash argues that, despite the great shift from a monarchic to a revolutionary republican system, Iran's goals in the region have neither shifted nor changed.[46] The new Iranian government posed a threat of a different nature to the Arab Gulf States. It places more emphasis on Shi'ite communities sprinkled throughout the region.[47] It is alleged that Shi'ite disturbances have been orchestrated from Tehran.[48] Members of Shi'ite communities in the GCC countries were active during the Iran–Iraq war in supporting Iran by collecting donations, arranging arms deals for Iran, and acting as a third party or a broker to overcome the US-led arms embargo imposed against Iran. It is argued that 'Iran's foreign policy is not minimalist and continues to be bellicose; it is animated by general and diffuse ambition, and it is reactive and opportunistic.'[49] There is a persistent element of ambiguity about the foreign policy objectives of the revolutionary government. This emanates from the dualism within the revolution, 'a dual strategy to have both things both ways – to plausibly deny the extreme, while exploiting it'.[50] The advent of the revolution confronted the Arab Gulf States with a threefold problem: it transferred Iran from a strategic shield to a potential threat; it placed these states between two mutually hostile regimes; and it constituted an immediate threat to the freedom of navigation in the Gulf.[51] Should Iran carry out its threat to close the Straits of Hormuz it would affect all the GCC states to various degrees. It has also challenged the Saudi Islamic legitimacy. Other equally distressing activities and policies include:[52] (1) Iran's continued occupation of the islands of Abu Musa and the Greater and Lesser Tunbs; (2) ongoing Iranian programmes to develop a conventional military arsenal and to acquire weapons of mass destruction (WMD), including its continued ambition to acquire nuclear capability; (3) Iranian sponsorship of extremist groups and covert operations around the world; (4) Iran's active role in attempting to destabilize Arab Gulf governments; (5) Iran's attempt to dominate the region as the sole hegemonic power. The total length of the Gulf coast is about 3,300 kilometres, with Iran's share being about one-third only. Arabs live on the both sides of the Gulf; on the western side we find the Gulf Cooperation Council's members and Iraq, but on the eastern side we find Ahwaz and Linga – that are actually called the Arabistan region by Iranians themselves, because the people who live there are Arabs. [53]

The end of the Iraq–Iran war, Iraq's encroachment of Kuwait and the new thinking in Iran's foreign policy played a significant role in Iran's rapprochement and succeeded in restoring its strong ties with its Arab neighbours. However, the political vacuum created by the American occupation of Iraq in 2003 led to a complete standstill and cleavages among Arab countries. Oil boom in the years following the American invasion until the global economic crisis equipped Iran with a huge amount of cash flow, enabling it to embark on money diplomacy in order to fill the regional power vacuum and mark an Iranian era in Middle Eastern affairs.[54] However, the problem with Iran since the success of the revolution is not the diffusion of power, but the multiplicity of decision-making circles. Most Arab countries are critical of the Iranian pattern of behaviour attempting to influence the region. They accuse Iran of intervening in the affairs of Arab countries – Iraq, Lebanon, Palestine, Bahrain, Saudi Arabia, Kuwait, Yemen, Egypt and Morocco. It is accused of lending financial and political support to non-state actors, namely the Shiʿite minorities, and trying to spread Shiʿism in other countries. The Yemeni government accused Iran of supporting the Huwthi rebellious group. Morocco decided, in March 2009, to sever diplomatic ties with Iran on the ground that it was attempting to spread Shiʿism which contradicts the Sunni doctrine of that state. The cold war in Arab–Iran relations led countries like Saudi Arabia, Egypt, Jordan and Bahrain to criticize Hezbollah's operation kidnapping two Israeli soldiers, describing it as an 'irresponsible, endangering Arab interests'.[55] The UAE, despite strong trade relations, is the only GCC member to retain territorial disputes with Iran, due to the latter's occupation of the three disputed islands, Abu Musa and the Greater and Lesser Tunbs, since November 1971. Territorial problems continue to be the main contentious issue hindering political developments in the Gulf subregion. 'Iraq's lack of a maritime boundary with Iran prompts jurisdiction disputes beyond the mouth of the Shatt al Arab in the Arabian Gulf; Iran and UAE dispute Tunb Islands and Abu Musa Island, which are occupied by Iran; Iran stands alone among littoral states in insisting upon a division of the Caspian Sea into five equal sectors.'[56] However, Syria has repeatedly reiterated its position on Iran as a strong ally to the Arab causes. Bashar Assad said: 'any neighbouring country would have an influence whither positive or negative, but in any case relations with neighbouring countries should be strong despite the differences that might sometimes occur.' He added that Syria, through its good relations with both the UAE and Iran, 'could use its good offices to assist in settling the dispute between them or the differences between Iran and the Arab countries'.[57]

The US military presence in the Gulf encourages further political rivalries among the Gulf States. On the one hand, the GCC states look at the American military presence as a protective shield and an insurance policy against any possible new Iranian adventure designed to take advantage of their inherited weakness. They view Iranian regional policies as the main reason for the American presence. On the other hand, Iran sees the American presence in the region as part of a containment policy that represents a direct threat to its sovereignty and territorial integrity. The US policy that seeks to influence Iran with penalties but without incentives has failed. Washington has been unable to induce change by the Iranian government in three areas of key concerns to US policy-makers: 'sponsoring terrorism, acquiring missiles and nuclear capability, and opposing the Arab–Israel peace process'.[58] However, US and Western pressure and the Arabs' changing attitude towards the Arab–Israeli conflict inspired a change of position to accept the US two-states solution initiative.[59] It can be argued that US involvement prevents the setting of the terms for inter- and intra-regional consultation. It contributes to widening the gaps between the Arab states rather than helping to bridge them, instigating an arms race, border disputes, different foreign policy undertaking, and greater internal political resentment.

Political turmoil engulfed the region with the eruption of the second Gulf crisis and promoted new developments in the Arab states' relations with Iran. Statements issued after the meetings of the GCC Council of Ministers, in 1991 and 1992, reflected the desire of the GCC states to improve relations with Tehran.[60] During the Kuwait GCC summit conference in December 1991, they reaffirmed their desire to cooperate with Iran on regional security issues. The Iranian Foreign Minister, Ali-Akbar Velayati, visited the Gulf States and met the GCC countries' foreign ministers collectively in New York. Ties with the UAE, until August 1992, and Oman remained amicable. The Iranian embassy in Riyadh was reopened shortly after the restoration of Kuwaiti sovereignty. The visit by Saudi Foreign Minister, Saudi al-Feisal, to Tehran in May 1991 set a seal on improved relations. In further developments, a senior economic delegation visited Saudi Arabia and Kuwait, in February 1992, to strengthen economic ties between Iran and the two GCC countries.[61] However, development of relations between the two sides encountered setbacks due to Arab concerns over increasing Iranian regional intervention. Obama's rollback policy to engage Iran could open a new chapter for relations between Iran and moderate Arab countries. Hence, the coming years could witness a re-emergence of the Iranian–Saudi axis for Gulf security.

Despite their own increasing arms expenditure (see Table 4.1), the GCC states view the Iranian military build-up and its policy to acquire nuclear capability with great suspicion. Iranian military production increased by 64 per cent in

1986. Iran's defence budget for 1998 was US$5.8 billion, up from US$4.7 billion in 1997 – an increase of some 23 per cent. Official figures show that Iran's defence spending has almost tripled since 1993.[62] Iran pursued a policy to make up for its losses in its war with Iraq of an estimated 40–60 per cent of its military arsenal.[63] It is argued that Iran possesses a biological arsenal of around 400 chemical tons, and low-, middle- and long-range missiles capable of travelling 250 to 10,000 kilometres.[64] The Iranian government adopted a fifteen-year military build-up programme with an emphasis on air defence. It increased its armed forces personnel from 350,000 to 520,000 in 2002, plus 125,000 for the revolutionary guard and reserves estimated at 350,000.[65] Iran in 2007 spent $7.2 billion on military expenditure to fill its arsenal with modern weapons in a determined effort to become the dominant power in the Gulf (see Table 4.1). In the period 1988–1994, Iran spent around $31.3 billion on armaments. Iran's indigenous conventional-weapon programmes include 122mm and 155mm self-propelled artillery built under Russian licence. Iran also produces Russian-designed T-72 main battle tanks (MBTs) and BMP-derivative Boragh armoured personnel carriers (MPCs) under Russian licence based on a 1988/1989 agreement.[66] The arms-package deal with Russia included 200 fighting aircraft, 500 tanks, three submarines, carrying sophisticated sonar systems, specialized mine-laying equipment and up to twenty-four mines each, with 1,000 pounds of explosive, and kilo class diesel-powered patrol boats armed with eighteen torpedoes.[67] The deal included a large quantity of MIG-29S, Sukoi-24s, Su-22s, missiles, and tanks, armoured personnel carriers and artillery.[68]

The US views the Iranian armaments as an attempt to control the Straits of Hormuz and a threat to disrupt the free flow of oil to the West. During a Gulf States visit in December 1996, a former US Defense Secretary expressed his country's concern regarding the Iranian military build-up that exceeds its defensive need.[69] The US has adopted a policy of containment in an attempt to force a change in the Iranian external behaviour. George W. Bush's policy towards Iran lacked the support needed from the closest US allies and the international community. Europe's preference for critical dialogue with Iran is based on a number of vital interests. European transactions with Iran[70] exacerbate the differences between the US and Europe.[71] Russia and China, because of the US policy towards Iran, have made strong bids to restore and expand their involvement in the Gulf subregion through their opening policies towards Iran.[72] The American policy has forced Iran to look elsewhere and pursue a policy of rearmament. Such a policy created an environment of suspicion in Gulf relations and prevented the setting of terms for regional security. Iran's regional policy, until the election of President Khatimi, was conditioned by the US.

In light of Iraq's uncertain future and Iran's strong regional position, Iran's potential role in regional politics has acquired new importance.[73] The feeling in the Arab world, particularly among the small states of the Gulf, is that with the defeat of Iraq followed by its US occupation in 2003, the Iranians were trying to see how far they could push their luck as the new dominant regional power. The change of the regime in Iran apparently has not changed its self-appointed role as the 'police man of the Gulf'. The Iranian posture towards the region has not been consistent. It speaks of regional cooperation and a non-interference policy, but constantly pursues provocative steps. The Pentagon believes that Iran is receiving radar testing devices, navigation and avionics equipment, oscilloscopes, logic analysers, fibre optic cables, digital switches, high speed computers, remote sensors, and jet engines, all of which have dual military use.[74] 'Many security studies analysts have noted Iran's military resurgence with alarm, and scholars list in substantial details specific Iranian military acquisitions of recent years.'[75] The significance of the Iranian rearmament lies in the fact that it ordered equipment designed to take control of the waterway, 'such as Kirov-class submarines and long-range Soviet planes designed to attach aircraft carriers'.[76] Such a project would enable the Islamic republic to[77] (1) secure its position as the regional superpower of the Gulf; (2) gain leverage over the US – believing it can follow the North Korean example – by trading nuclear capability for economic support; and (3) use its power to blackmail neighbouring Arab states into increasing oil quotas and participating in foreign investment opportunities in Iran.

Consequently, Iran pursued provocative policies towards the littoral Arab states – taking sides in the Saudi–Qatari border dispute, the encroachment of Abu Musa Island, giving overt and covert support to the Shi'ite militants in the area, infringing Iraqi sovereignty by overflying Iraqi inland, bombing Mujaheddi Khalq bases[78] and supporting Shi'ite groups, and announcing a 12-mile zone as its territorial water without declaring their point of start. They perform military manœuvres, test different kinds of missiles with different ranges, carry out suspicious nuclear projects, defy Arab consensus on regional issues and reject Gulf States security arrangements. Iran has also repeatedly echoed claims infringing Bahrain sovereignty as an Iranian province. Bahrain's Foreign Minister Khalid bin Ahmed al-Khalifa, after meeting with his counterparts of Turkey and Russia, confirmed on 19 February 2009 that his country had suspended negotiations with Iran on a natural gas import deal, due to Iranian officials' recent claims of Bahrain as a province of Iran: 'We will never accept distortion of historical facts about the history of the Kingdom of Bahrain.'[79] Moreover, Iran continues to occupy Arab islands historically belonging to the UAE.[80] The Iranian attitude towards Bahraini Shi'ites' uprising in March 2011 was seen by GCC countries as an alarming threat and led them to dispatch Jazeera shield to maintain security on the island, which was criticized by the Iranian leader.

The Territorial Disputes

The most contentious issues hindering the development of relations among the states of the Gulf are the territorial problems. The first Iranian encroachment of Arab land was in 1925 when Iran annexed all the Arab territory making al-Ahwaz, confiscating all Arab properties there, silencing the opposition and pursuing an ethnic cleansing policy against its Arab population.

Another contentious territorial problem is the Iranian–Iraqi territorial dispute over Shat al-Arab which was settled in the Alger Agreement in 1975 and later on was nullified by Saddam Hussein on the eve of the Iran–Iraq War in September 1980.

The third Iranian territorial dispute with neighbouring Arab countries is the Iranian occupation on 30 November 1971 of three Arab Gulf islands: Abu Musa and Greater and Lesser Tunb, at the mouth of the Gulf. Although Iran's violation of the Memorandum of Understanding concluded in late 1971 between the Shah of Iran and then ruler of Sharjah started in early 1980s, the crisis erupted in August 1992. Iranian police turned back a passenger ferry with 110 Arab schoolteachers and their families on board returning to the island after their summer vacation, demanding Iranian entry visas.[81] During the Iran–Iraq war from 1983, Iran placed surface-to-air missiles in the Gulf islands. Further, Iran has used Abu Musa as a base for speedboat attacks on shipping and oil installations.[82] Following Iran's encroachment of Abu Musa, fears have been raised about Tehran's other ambitions in the area. 'The very size and weight of Iran will keep alive fears of a constant ambition to exercise Iranian hegemony in the Gulf.'[83] On 16 November 1996, the Iranian navy commander, Ali Shamakhani, acknowledged that Iran placed missiles batteries on the disputed three islands.[84] It is also believed that Iran will use Abu Musa as a base for the three submarines obtained from Russia to command the entrance of the Gulf. It is argued that Abu Musa may only be the beginning. Iran has revived an old claim to Bahrain. Iran continues to pursue a policy of military intimidation of GCC countries to achieve economic objectives. This argument is substantiated by the fact that Iran's proven reserves amount to about 9 per cent of the world's oil reserves and 15 per cent of world's proven gas reserves.[85] By such encroachment, Iran could claim sovereignty over the oil fields and oil reserves within the 12-mile zone constituting the islands' territorial waters.[86] Iran has also initiated a $1.7 billion development programme on the Iranian side of an oil and gas field that is predominantly under Qatari territorial water. In a further provocative step, it was announced that a branch of one of the Iranian universities would be opened in Abu Musa.[87] The Iranian military build-up enhances such apprehension.

The unsettled border disputes create an environment of continued political tension and encourage a continued arms race in the region. This is illustrated in the increasing defence budgets in the Gulf States (see Table 4.1). Boosted by imports of advanced weaponry, Gulf defence spending in the first decade of the twenty-first century remains high.[88] The US, despite its earlier commitment to freeze military shipments to the Middle East as a whole, achieved the largest share of the increase in arms sales in the 2000s to the Gulf States, followed by France, Russia and China.[89] The American policy of arming its Gulf allies encourages the use of force in foreign policy, prompting greater regional instability.

The Iranian Nuclear Programme

The Iranian nuclear programme constitutes another controversial issue between Iran and the Arab countries. It is the most contentious issue in Iran's relations with the outside world. The nuclear programme was launched in the 1950s with the help of the United States as part of the Atoms for Peace programme. The Shah decided to construct twenty-three nuclear reactors with a production capacity that reaches 1300 megawatt for some reactors. French and German companies were pioneers in helping Iran achieve its goals. Siemens, a German company, had completed half of the project at Bushehr when the revolution erupted in Iran.[90] The new Iranian government temporarily disbanded elements of the programme, and then revived it with less Western assistance.[91] The Iranians had learnt of Arab weakness and inability to challenge the Iranian ambitions from past Israeli experience[92] and from their eight years of war with Iraq. Iran, a member of the Non-Proliferation Treaty (NPT) since 1970, contends that its nuclear programme is for peaceful power-generation purposes to produce 20 per cent of its electricity and to help free up oil and gas resources for export, thus generating additional hard-currency revenues. Iran has consistently denied any intention of developing WMD, describing them as immoral and illegal. Sources maintain that Bushehr plant is for peaceful use whereas the Natanz plant has dual function, but there are not enough plants for unconventional weapons to be produced and Iran needs five more years to do so.[93] The US countered that Iran did not possess sufficient natural reserves of nuclear fuel, meaning that it would be dependent on costly imports to sustain a nuclear power programme. It is argued that no area of US–Iran relations is more fraught than the dispute over WMD. The US thinks that Iran's pattern of procurement suggests an intention to develop WMD in all categories.[94] On 23 February 1998, the US State Department reaffirmed US opposition to the fulfilment of Iran's nuclear programme, arguing that nuclear reactors were expensive, unnecessary and could be used for military purposes.

US opposition to Russia finishing the construction of Bushehr rested on three main issues. First, weapons grade plutonium could be extracted from the reactor, allowing the Iranians to construct nuclear weapons. Secondl, the US feared that the Russians and the Iranians were using Bushehr as a cover for the transfer of other sensitive technology that would normally be prohibited. Finally, the knowledge gained by Iranian scientists working at Bushehr could further Iran's nuclear weapons programme.[95] Despite Iran's denials, diplomats said investigations showed Tehran had had full possession of enrichment know-how for two decades, after acquiring the information from the black-market network of Pakistani nuclear scientist Abdul Qadeer Khan. The *Washington Post* quoted a Pakistani official as saying that the programme originated at a secret meeting in Dubai, as early as 1987, between Iranian officials and Mr Khan's associates.[96] The officials said Tehran, which was then at war with Iraq, bought centrifuges and an enrichment starter kit but also used the meeting as a guide before purchasing more expensive items elsewhere. The transfer of Pakistani nuclear technology began in 1989. The International Atomic Energy Agency (IAEA) reportedly had evidence that Pakistani assistance continued as late as 1996.[97] Iran, faced with Western sanctions, bypassed them by concluding bilateral agreements with Russia to finish what the Germans had started in Bushehr. Iran was a signatory to the NPT, though it had not ratified two additional protocols to the IAEA's Program 93 + 2, which was designed to prevent states from developing nuclear weapons covertly, despite IAEA inspections, as Iraq was able to do prior to the Gulf war. Iran maintained that it would not ratify 93 + 2 due to it being denied civilian nuclear technology for Bushehr, despite its positive record with the IAEA.[98] The conclusion in 2005 of an agreement in which Russia will supply Iran with nuclear fuel for a 1,000 megawatt light-water nuclear power reactor marks the latest step in a decade-long controversy. In 1995, Russia agreed to finish the Bushehr reactor project expected to be operational in 2009, which is widely reported to be worth about $800 million.[99]

To date, Iran has invested around $6 billion in nuclear power.[100] Sources reveal that Iran is cooperating in this field with countries like Russia, China, North

Korea, Pakistan, Argentina and Brazil. In February 2003 Mohammed El Baradei, the IAEA's director general, went to Iran to meet with nuclear officials. During the visit, Iran confirmed that it was building a heavy-water production plant in Arak and officially declared the two uranium enrichment plants it was building in Natanz, which El Baradei visited. In June 2003, the IAEA criticized Iran for hiding nuclear facilities and called on the country to sign an additional protocol to the NPT, putting its nuclear programme under greater scrutiny.[101] The CIA confirmed reports that Iran was seeking to acquire nuclear capability. The Israeli intelligence service AMMAN, in its report to the prime minister in March 1995, alleged that Iran would possess a nuclear weapon in less than three years, despite the argument that Iran was not in a position to finance a large nuclear project similar to Iraq because of the difficulty in acquiring the necessary technology and the nation's lack of sufficient scientists, experts and technicians.[102] Western intelligence sources further revealed that Iran would soon test a nuclear weapon.[103] The IAEA inspectors visiting Iran in August 2003 discovered traces of enriched uranium in Natanz[104] and visited the new reactor near Qum in October 2009. According to Hans Friedrich Meyer, the IAEA spokesman, Tehran's nuclear programme was destined only for peaceful purposes. In a further step, Iran and China concluded a nuclear energy cooperation agreement, in September 1992, under which Peking would provide a Qinshan-1-type 300 megawatt pressurized water reactor.[105] According to official reports in Tehran, in 2006 and 2007 the Islamic Republic also initialled agreements with China to build twenty nuclear power stations in Iran. The first of these stations is already under construction at Dar-Khuwayn, in the oil-rich province of Khuzestan, close to the Iraqi border.[106] Iran has boasted about running 7,000 uranium centrifuges, which can have dual uses both civilian and military. President Ahmadinejad inaugurated on 9 April 2009 the country's first nuclear fuel production complex near Isfahan in central Iran. He announced that Iran had mastered the final stage of nuclear fuel production, with the manufacturing of uranium pellets and rods for use in Iran's Arak heavy-water reactor. Iran as a result proved that its nuclear fuel cycle has been completed.[107] However, Iran's programme is still in its infancy with capabilities of LEU at 3.5 per cent not even ready for fuel plates. Iran needs to acquire the capability to reach 20 per cent to reach its peaceful objective, let alone going for an atomic bomb which requires uranium to be refined at 90 per cent purity.[108] Hillary Clinton denied that the latest development would have an adverse effect on President Obama's policy towards Iran.

In times of crisis, parties try to secure their national interests with the maximum return and least cost. Neither the US nor Iran want to refer to the military option. Iran's objectives are to avoid regime change, any American or Israeli air strike against its nuclear installation and further international isolation. The US does not want to use force against Iran while having more than 140,000 American troops in Iraq, still militarily engaged in Afghanistan and encountering the pressures of the global economic crisis. It was reported in 2008 that the US had prevented Israel from going alone and launching an air strike against Iran's nuclear installations. Mohammed El Baradei in May 2009 warned Israel not to play with fire. Hillary Clinton, on her visit to Ankara in March 2009, said that the US would seek Turkey's help for Obama's plan to engage Iran.[109] Iranian and American officials have held in Moscow their first talks about ending the war in Afghanistan, amid signs that President Obama's efforts to thaw relations with Tehran are paying off. The Russian initiative brought together Patrick Moon, the US diplomat in charge of south and central Asia, and Mehdi Akhundzadeh, Iran's deputy foreign minister, as well as a British diplomat who was acting as a mediator.[110] US special envoy Richard Holbrooke said that he had chatted briefly with Iran's foreign minister at a Pakistan donors' conference in Tokyo, another milestone on the road to a possible thaw.[111] The US also decided to take part in the team negotiating with Iran to bring about a peaceful solution to the crisis. The US joined Russia, China, France, Germany and Britain in asking EU foreign political chief Javier Solana to find a diplomatic solution to Iran's disputed nuclear programme. Iran, for its part, has welcomed Obama's initiative. It said it would review an offer of talks on its nuclear programme from the US and five other world powers.[112] The 6+1 meeting to discuss the issue in October 2009 was described as 'good'.[113] The Iranian Foreign Minister, Manouchehr Mottaki, was quoted by Japanese *Yomiuri* newspaper saying: 'Iran could respond to US efforts to engage Tehran; if Washington turns the new tenor of its words into reality, we can also be change on our side.' He added: 'we are studying the comment of the US government precisely and with respect'.[114] On the other hand, Mottaki reiterated that Iran insists on its right to acquire nuclear facilities for peaceful use.[115] The Iranians' multiple cycles of decision-making have been giving conflicting signals. Ahmadinejad in September 2009 offered the olive branch by accepted the idea of a third-party provider of uranium enrichment for the Iranian nuclear reactors. To ease international tension over Iran's nuclear programme, the UN nuclear watchdog presented a draft deal to Iran and three big powers at the Vienna conference suggesting that 1.2 tons of Iran's known 1.5 ton LEU stockpile be sent to Russia for further processing then shipped on to France for conversion into fuel plates to provide Iran with fuel for a nuclear medicine facility.[116] Both Washington and Tehran welcomed the proposal, but voiced scepticism. A senior Iranian MP rejected the idea, and a US administration spokesman reaffirmed US policy of denial, threatening to use all means to stop the Iranian nuclear programme.[117] Iran formally responded to the UN draft nuclear deal on 29 October 2009, proposing major amendments that could sink the plan, including sending its LEU abroad in stages instead of all at once. Another demand is to import fuel for the reactors from foreign suppliers at the same time that it is sending its own material out.[118] Tehran is keeping harsher sanctions at bay by not rejecting the proposal outright. The Iranian hesitancy to accept the IAEA proposal was due to its reluctance to give up its LEU stockpiles without securing further shipment of nuclear fuel to its reactors and to its distrust of France right-wing President Sarkozy. In an attempt to alleviate Iranian worries, Turkey proposed participating in the processing of the Iranian LEU.[119] However, Iran, being sceptical and distrustful of the Western powers, refused the IAEA proposal asking for Western commitment to provide Iran with the necessary fuel for its reactors. The IAEA angered Iran on 27 November when it censured Tehran for secretly building a second uranium enrichment plant in a mountain bunker near Qum. The Iranian government responded with defiance. It announced that it would build ten new uranium enrichment plants, further aggravating tensions between Iran and major powers over Iranian nuclear activities.[120]

The Iranian nuclear programme remains a source of contention. It is hindering the development of the US–Iran relations and moderate Arab states' relations with Iran, further complicating the prospect of regional security and stability on the other hand. The outline deal, along with a fresh UN inspector trip to a hitherto covert Iranian enrichment site, were the first fruits of Obama's outreach policy towards Iran that led to new dialogue of 6+1 to defuse confrontation and ultimately a risk of Israeli attack.

Perspectives on Gulf Security

The issue of the Gulf security is a multifarious one. Gulf security has been a major concern for the GCC states, Iran, Iraq and the West, particularly the US. The perspective on Gulf security, however, has never been the same for all parties concerned. The GCC countries themselves, until the second Gulf crisis, were never united on their perception of threats to their security. Before the Iranian revolution, they accepted the US perception and relied on the US 'Twin Pillar' doctrine for security. The collapse of the Shah's regime and the outbreak of the Iran–Iraq war brought new security dilemmas.

Apprehension over the Iranian revolution, in the 1980s, inspired greater cooperation with Iraq and led the Arab Gulf States to accept the Saudi perception of external and internal threats. The formation of the GCC as an umbrella for cooperation and coordination of defence and security among member states was seen at that time as a means to fill the power vacuum and maintain the status quo. However, the Kuwaiti predicament further complicated the GCC states' security dilemma. On the one hand, it exposed the unreliability of the Iraqi Ba'athist government. On the other hand, the crisis upset the balance of power in the Gulf subregion, presenting Iran as the most powerful country in the area.

On the subregional level, the GCC states face a triple security problem: Iran, Iraq and Yemen. Maintaining warm bilateral relations with the three subregional states is the appropriate option. Iran's perspective on Gulf security centres on the idea that it is the responsibility of the littoral states. The Iranian authority believes that there are three states of significant importance for any Gulf security arrangement: Iran, Iraq and Saudi Arabia. Thus, any arrangement that does not coincide with this perspective would not be feasible or acceptable to Iran and this in turn explains Iran's opposition to the Damascus Accord.[121] In November 1996, Iran's defence minister, Ali Shamakhani, called for a joint strategy to maintain regional security and stability and to consider any act of aggression against any of the Gulf States an aggression against all, to be deterred collectively.'[122]

Fears of a regional threat continue for both the GCC states and the US. Despite the Iran–Iraq war and the second Gulf crisis, Iran has been rebuilding its forces by acquiring amphibious assault craft, as we have seen earlier, and is allegedly seeking a nuclear weapons capability. The US policy towards the GCC countries centres on maintaining the status quo. The US proposed several steps to promote stability in the Gulf subregion:

1. Improve the GCC states' overall defensive capabilities and accelerate the integration of their plans and programmes for the defence of their territory.
2. Strengthen US military ties with the GCC states.
3. Maintain a limited military presence in the peninsula.
4. Work with the GCC states to develop a greater role for regional and extra-regional powers such as Egypt, Syria, the UK and France.

A basic element in a post-war security structure is likely to be an improved and expanded GCC force, probably incorporating contingents from Egypt and Syria, to serve as a partial deterrent against future aggression, conceivably from Iran. Although the US would like to continue to be the most privileged ally of the GCC states, it wants the Damascus Accord to be put into effect to ensure regional stability without direct US involvement. However, some GCC countries do not see the Damascus Accord as more than a platform providing for bilateral consultation and limited cooperation that might take place among any group of friendly states. Therefore, in the continued absence of active Egyptian and Syrian participation, the viability of the US security strategy in the coming years will still remain open to question. The US concluded bilateral agreements with the Arab Gulf states obtaining formal arrangement, logistical support and bases for its forces and equipment. The US developed a multi-tiered approach to the problem of Gulf security. In April 1993, the assistant-secretary of state, David Mack, in his speech to the US–GCC Business Conference, outlined the US strategy in the Gulf:

> We encourage both regional security co-operation and collective defense arrangements within the GCC. We have engaged in bilateral security activities with the individual Gulf States and have excellent working arrangements with all of them. Further, we sell arms to Gulf States to satisfy their legitimate defense needs. And we have had a naval presence, now significantly enhanced, in the Gulf continuously since 1949.

The Clinton administration proposed a further policy to maintain regional security in the Gulf. This policy, which could be called the Clinton doctrine, was one of containment of both Iran and Iraq, followed by the Dilmato policy towards Iran intended to squeeze the Iranian economy. Such a policy seems to be impractical in an unstable world. The success of the policy of containment initiated against the former Soviet Union, if it did succeed, was due to Soviet domestic factors. It is true, however, that the Soviets, because of the cold war, had to reallocate their resources and to invest heavily in the military establishment at the expense of political, economic and social development. But to see this as the only or even the major factor leading to the collapse of the Soviet Union is merely an oversimplification of the Soviet predicament. Today, world economic recession, the increasing importance of oil in world politics, the desire for hard currency by the newly independent former Soviet republics, the absence of an effective world government, and the post-war situation of both Iran and Iraq all suggested that this US policy would not be effective. The lack of leadership shown by the Clinton administration enhanced the argument.

US foreign policy shifted from paying lip service to the notion of collective security to putting more emphasis on it.

The establishment of diplomatic relations between the GCC states and Russia paved the way for greater Russian involvement in maintaining the status quo. In 1992, the Russian foreign minister, during his tour of the six GCC states, expressed his country's appreciation of the establishment of relations between the two sides and its willingness to cooperate with the GCC countries in the field of security. In May 1993, Kuwait decided to conclude a security pact with Russia. American policy towards Iran forced the latter to look north, expanding the role of Russia in the Gulf subregion. Iran's perspective on Gulf security is based on its perception of foreign threats to Iranian security, hence it calls for a regional arrangement that excludes foreign powers and the conclusion of a non-intervention pact between the states of the Gulf. It is argued on the Arab side that Iran's security initiatives are not intended to be cooperative as much as to be defensive. It is intended to substitute the international defence pacts concluded by the conservative Arab Gulf countries with foreign powers with a regional one. Iran is looking to form an anti-Western alliance which de facto is not acceptable to the other Gulf countries.[123]

Some analysts argue that a foreign power, such as the US, should act as the supplementary power to enhance the GCC states' ability to secure their stability. An offshore US presence and access to local bases has been bilaterally arranged. Others argue that a more prominent role by Arab states such as Yemen, Jordan, Egypt, Syria and the rehabilitated Iraq would be an alternative to total dependence on the West. The absence of a stable regional balance of power necessitates the integration of Yemen within the subregional system to enhance the GCC states' ability to manœuvre. Although Yemen could not be seen as a supplementary power, it could be part of any future arrangement for subregional security. Despite the cool relations in inter-Gulf politics, a fourfold security arrangement for maintaining the status quo remains a viable alternative option. It requires a six plus three (6+3) equation for security that would include the GCC states plus Iran, Iraq and Yemen.[124] The purpose of this arrangement would be to create equilibrium of power in subregional politics. It is also intended to offset Iran's numerical superiority over any of the Arab Gulf States by creating an Arab axis of the subregional Arab states to contain any possible Iranian threat, on the one hand, and, on the other hand, to contain Yemen as part of the security equation if any party decides to advance its national interests at the expense of any of the GCC members. The proposal here is not to minimize the Arab role in Gulf security arrangements; but to adopt an arrangement based on three concentric circles: the Gulf circle, the Arab circle and the international circle. Gulf security and Arab security are interdependent.

3. The Turkish Engagement

Turkey's geopolitical position places it in one of the most unstable, uncertain and unpredictable regions of the world. Its concern stems from neighbouring countries, namely Russia, Greece, Israel, Iran, Syria and Iraq.[125] 'The collapse of the Soviet Union has created a window of opportunity for Turkey. The emergence of the newly independent states in Central Asia has caused a radical shift in Turkey's foreign policy.'[126] Its location in the regional context of the Arab world presents a challenge of different nature to Arab governments. The challenge emanates from the fact that Turkey today is an influential regional power and is not necessarily negative if Arab states understand the rules of the game in contemporary world politics. Modern Turkey was found from the Anatolian remnants of the defeated Ottoman Empire in accordance with the two peace Treaties of Lausanne signed on 15 May and 24 October 1923.[127] Mustafa Kemal Atatürk declared Turkey a republic.[128] It joined the UN in 1945, becoming a member of the North Atlantic Treaty Organization in 1952, associate member of the European Community in 1964 and currently is pushing hard, with US support, to join the EU. However, despite the fact that Turkey started talks for accession in 2005, some EU members are adamantly refusing to extend membership to Turkey for no reason other than that Turkey is a Muslim state, 99.8 per cent, presumably to keep the EU as an exclusive club for Christian countries. This argument is substantiated by the fact that EU membership has been extended to less developed countries of Eastern Europe in a very short period. Samuel Huntington argued that 'the European countries do not want a Muslim state, Turkey, in the EU and are not happy having another Muslim country, Bosnia, on the European continent'.[129]

Turkish political life during the past few decades has been characterized by political instability. Democracy has been fractured by intermittent military coups, in 1960, 1971, 1980 and 1997, which in each case eventually resulted in a return of political power to civilians. The approach of the AKP, with an Islamist background, in dealing with the secularist forces in the country, particularly the military junta, on many domestic issues including the veil has been versatile. The AKP pursued a policy of containment rather than confrontation in managing the crisis, allied itself with the parties with which it shared similar perspectives on the issue, used the EU as an example, and made use of the military commanders' engagement in their war against Kurdish separatists.[130] However, the secular forces are not happy with AKP policies, looking at them as a revisionist and deviating from the Kemalist doctrine. They have attempted repeatedly to overthrow the AKP government, not through coup d'état but through the use of the judiciary; their last attempt was in March 2008, but the Supreme Court decision came short of what they had hoped for. Turkey's modern experience is a clear example that Islam and democracy are compatible, negating some Western rhetoric associating Islam with terrorism. US Secretary of State, Hillary Clinton, held up Turkey on 7 March 2009 as proof that 'democracy, modernity and Islam can coexist'.[131] President Obama's choice to visit Turkey in April 2009 and deliver a historical speech marking the beginning of a new approach in the US policy towards the Muslim world illustrates the importance of Turkey in the American strategy. He pledged a 'new way forward' with the Islamic world.

Another threat to Turkey's political and economic development emanates from the ongoing Kurdish separatist movement. In 1984, the Kurdistan Workers' Party (PKK) began a separatist insurgency, causing political, economic and social unrest. The Turkish government pursued a dual policy in dealing with the Kurdish problem internally. Turkey voiced its opposition to Syria's hosting of the PKK guerrillas and claimed that they operated against Turkey from Syrian territory.[132] The Turkish accusation that Syria was giving refuge to the PKK's leader Abdullah Ugylan was elevated in 1998 as both countries accused each other of massing troops along their common border. After the capture of the group's leader in 1999, the insurgents largely withdrew from Turkey, mainly to northern Iraq. In 2004, the People's Congress of Kurdistan (KGK) announced an end to its ceasefire and attacks attributed to the KGK increased, particularly against Kurdish rebels inside Iraq. Turkey, after the accession to power of the AKP, adopted a series of political and economic reforms to enhance democratization and develop the socio-economic infrastructure[133] in the Kurdish region. On the domestic level a more relaxed policy was adopted towards the Kurds, who represent 20 per cent of the population, delegating autonomous regional authority, conceding to their cultural demands, integrating them in the political structure of the country and embarking on economic development in their region in an attempt to drain the insurgency out. The policy was based on peaceful means, with the recognition of Kurdish right for self-identity to preserve their language, culture and history as part of the multicultural Turkish identity. Though it was argued that Ankara foreign policy can be described as cautious, passive and adhering to the status quo[134] it is actually proactive and positive. Fighting the insurgency not only required the use of force and the allocation of resources, but an active regional foreign policy to neutralize foreign support to the Kurdish cause, culminating in a new chapter in Turkish relations with Arab countries, especially Syria and Iraq, and strengthening ties with Iran and Israel. Turkey's exports to the Middle Eastern countries in 1997 represented 10.5 per cent of the total Turkish exports whereas its imports from there were 8.05 per cent of its total imports.[135]

Turkey is a regional power, with a population of 76.8 million people stretching over a total area of 780.5 square kilometres, and a Euro-Asian country connecting the East with the West. It has armed forces larger than any of the Middle Eastern countries, estimated in 2003 at 514,850 with reserves of 378,700. Its military expenditure in 2005 was estimated at 5.3 per cent of GDP.[136] It has MBT 4205 M-48, M-60 and Leopard, SAM 108 Stinger, Helicopters 37 attack AH-1W/P, SPT 50 S-70A and Falcon 600, submarine 13, principal surface combatants 19, patrol and coastal combatants 49 and Min Warfare 24, 480 combatants' aircraft and missiles including Sparrow, Sidewinders and Maverick.[137] Turkey is ranked 16 in the world in terms of defence expenditure, estimated in 2007 at $11.6 billion (see Table 4.1). Turkey's dynamic economy is a complex mix of modern industry and commerce, along with a traditional agriculture sector that still accounts for more than 35 per cent of employment. Turgut Ozal, as Prime Minister and later President December 1983–April 1993, transformed the economy of Turkey by paving the way for the privatization of many state enterprises. Turkey since 2002, with the accession to power of the AKP, has achieved remarkable success in the economic field. GDP during the period 2002–8 increased from $300 billion to $729.4 billion, at an annual growth rate of 6.8 per cent, causing per capita improvement from $3,300 to $11,900.[138] The IMF report in 2008 showed a significant increase in Turkey's volume of exports from $30 billion to $130 billion over the previous five years.[139] Economic development embarked on by the AKP succeeded in diversifying the economy. Other sectors, notably the automotive and electronics industries, are rising in importance within Turkey's exports. Despite the strong economic gains from 2002–7, which were largely due to renewed investor interest in emerging markets, IMF backing and tighter fiscal policy, the economy in 2008, due to the global economic crisis, shrank to 3.5 per cent growth from 5 per cent in 2005; inflation was about 10.2 per cent and the unemployment rate was at 7.9 per cent in the same year. It is still burdened by a high current account deficit and high external debt estimated at around $294 billion. The Turkish economy may be faced with more negative economic indicators in 2009 as a result of the global economic slowdown.[140]

Arab-Turkish Relations

The historical variable continues to play a significant role in shaping the Arab–Turkish relations. The Ottoman Empire,[141] on the one hand, refused to give concessions to the Zionist movement for establishing a Jewish homeland in Palestine.[142] Ottoman reforms contributed to the development of the infrastructure, introducting industrialization, initiating a modern educational system, adopting modern constitutions, reforming of the tax system and upgrading services. However, the reforms adopted by the Ottoman Empire in the nineteenth century were incomplete. They promoted Westernization and led eventually to the beginning of the colonial era in the Middle East, particularly the Arab world, in accordance with the Sykes–Picot agreement of 1916.[143] The declining power of the central government in Istanbul led to political chaos, disintegration of the empire, greater foreign involvement and economic and social underdevelopment. The Ottomans today are blamed by part of the Arab intelligentsia for the backwardness of the Arab world.

One enduring legacy is the Turkish dismay at the Arabs for joining the anti-Turkish alliance during the First World War. The region was also influenced by the French revolution calls for equality, freedom, brotherhood, democratization, liberalization, the nationalist identity and social justice. Such developments contributed positively to Arab renaissance and the introduction of different political ideologies into the Arab world.[144] European political values inspired the birth of modern political movements in the Arab world. The price the Arabs had to pay for the collapse of the Ottoman Empire was dire. The Arab countries became Western colonies, Palestine was lost for the foundation of the Jewish state by the Zionist movement with the support of the Western colonial powers[145] and contemporary national borders were drawn by the colonial powers. Modern Turkey has chosen to disassociate itself from the Ottoman legacy, looking to the West for a better future. However, the links between the Arabs and modern Turkey remain strong enough for the development of better relations. They are bound by common historical, cultural and social ties.

Turkey–Arab relations, until the beginning of the twenty-first century, were characterized by distrust and discontinuity, dominated by contentious issues including: border disputes due to Turkish annexation of Hatay province in 1939, claims to the Mosul province, the Kurdish separatists' issue, water (see Chapter

7), and Turkey's strategic alliance with Israel. Prime Minister Adnan Menderes spearheaded the Baghdad Pact of 1955, tried to subvert the Syrian regime in 1957 and repeatedly threatened to intervene in Iraq.[146] Syria had longstanding claims to Hatay province and opposed the southeast Anatolia Project which, according to Syria, sharply reduced its water supply (see Chapter 7). During the Gulf war in 1991 Turkey opted to align itself with the coalition. Turgut Ozal shut down the pipeline transferring Iraqi oil through Turkish territory, allowed the coalition planes to launch missions from bases in Turkey, massed troops along Iraqi borders and negotiated with foreign powers. Najmel Din Erbakan toed the line, allowing US planes in Turkey to continue flying over Iraq.[147]

Turkey is a predominantly Sunni Muslim state, sharing not only history but a religious doctrine that could be mobilized to balance Iran's sectarian position in the region with the Arabs. This illustrates why the GCC countries referred to Turkey during the Bahraini 2011 uprising, to benefit from its good relations with Iran to prevent and escalation of the crisis. Turkey has also engaged on a new foreign policy, distancing itself from the US through promoting relations with Russia. The two countries agreed on the transfer of Russian gas through Turkey to Europe[148] and the increase in the trade volume that reached US$40 billion in 2008. Turkey has enhanced ties with Iran, as illustrated in the exchange of visits by senior officialss and the increase in the volume of trade (to $7 billion and expected to increase to $20 billion by the year 2012),[149] and refused to take part in the annual 'Anatollia Eagle manœuvres', with the US and Israel, in protest against Israeli atrocities in the occupied Palestinian territory. Despite Turkish–Iranian rapprochement, Turkey and the Arab countries share concerns over Iran's regional policy.

Turkey has other issues of concern in its policy towards Iran:

1. Turkish ambitions in Azerbaijan threatens Iran's very existence since a quarter to a third of Iran's populations are Azeri Turks, which made Iran tilt in favour of Armenians in the Nagorno-Karabakh conflict and sometimes coordinate with Russia to reduce Turkey's influence in Baku.
2. Turkish involvement in northern Iraq threatens Iranian interests in the region since the latter is building up its own proxies in Iraqi Kurdistan.[150]
3. There are ideological and sectarian differences.
4. Financial and strategic rewards at stake in the oil exports from the Caspian Sea. Oil began to flow through the Baku-Tbilisi-Seyhan pipeline in May 2006, marking a major milestone that will bring up to 1 million barrels per day from the Caspian to market.

Arab–Turkish differences include the water issue, Turkey's repeated military incursion into northern Iraq, Turkish intervention on behalf of the two million Turkomans minority in Iraq and the ambiguity in the Turkish role in the 6 September 2007 Israeli air assault on a suspected nuclear reactor in the early stages of construction.[151]

Differences between Iran and Turkey did not prevent the development of relations. Najmel Din Erbakan embarked on an open policy, paying an official visit to Tehran in which he concluded on 12 August 1996 a deal of $23 billion to buy natural gas from Iran.[152] Prime Minister Recep Tayyip Erdogan followed a similar course. Erdogan, in a press interview, said that Turkey works with all parties in the region despite their differences and pursues a policy based on respect for mutual interests. He added that Iran plays a positive regional role but because of mistrust it is misperceived.[153] Arabs are suspicious of the non-Arab regional states. They perceive neighbouring countries, Turkey, Iran and Israel, as constituting a potential threat to Arab security, but at the same time they could likely be perceived as possible allies[154] (see Table 4.1). Arab countries could play off the non-Arab regional states against each other, but such policy would inevitably fail. Therefore, the Arabs have to choose between alienating Turkey and engaging it in the regional affairs. The importance of Turkey lies not only in the fact that it is a regional neighbouring state, sharing a long history of interactions with the Arab world, and representing a bulwark for regional security, but it is also a major actor in world politics.

The election of the AKP in 2003 brought with it important changes to Turkey's foreign policy. Erdogan initiated a compromise approach in Turkey's regional foreign policy. Arab countries received favoured attention among the new Turkish political elite. Erdogan believes that Turkey had a historical role in the area and has a responsibility towards it.[155] The new approach towards the neighbouring Middle Eastern countries culminated in the development of relations between Turkey and Saudi Arabia, Egypt, Syria, Iraq, the GCC states and Iran. The Saudi monarch paid two state visits to Ankara in fifteen months. It has also embarked on a cooperative policy with Egypt, ending decades of suspicion, regional competition and mutual distrust. Turkey has also concluded political and cultural agreements with the Arab League.[156] Relations between Turkey and the GCC states witnessed further development after 2003, with an emphasis on economic cooperation. Relations between the two sides are determined by socio-economic and political factors. Turkey, on the one hand, needs to import 90 per cent of its domestic oil consumption, to encourage foreign investment to make up for the shortage of cash flow and to open new markets for its manufactured goods. The GCC countries, on the other hand, could make use of Turkey to balance Iranian regional influence, and desire to make use of Turkey's geographical location as an outlet to both Europe and Central Asia as a new investment opportunity and a potential source for fresh water. The new development of relations culminated in GCC countries investing \$4 billion in 2007, with a possible increase to \$20 billion in the coming few years.[157] Statistics reveal that 16 per cent of Turkish foreign trade in 2007 was with the Arab world and total Arab investments in Turkey are estimated at US\$36 billion.[158]

Syria and Turkey decided to manage their differences through bilateral engagement. They exchanged visits of senior level dignitaries. Bashar Assad paid a landmark official visit to Turkey on 6 January 2004 aimed at improving ties between the once hostile neighbours. The visit effectively helped develop bilateral relations in all fields. The development of relations between the two sides since 1998 led to an increase in trade relations from \$800 million to \$1.2 billion in 2007 and Turkey refused to take part in the American isolationist policy against Syria.[159] Erdogan visited Syria on 23 December 2004 and this was viewed as a turning point in their relations, culminating in setting up a free trade zone between the two countries. Ahmed Necdet Zesar, then president of Turkey, paid a state visit to Damascus on 16 April 2005. Assad paid his second official visit to Turkey on 16 October 2007. Erdogan argued that the two countries' decision to put emphasis on issues that both countries agree upon, with the intention of diffusing differences until they are overcome and eventually brought to a final settlement, was the principle behind the strength of relations. Bashar Assad of Syria saw no problem in a neighbouring country trying to influence regional contemporary issues, whether positively or negatively. He added that relations between neighbouring countries should always be positive despite the differences that might occur.[160]

Relations between Turkey on the one hand and Syria and Iraq on the other, in 2009, saw important developments including an exchange of visits by top officials, opening the Turkish–Syrian border, the easing of travel regulations including visa requirements, joint military manœuvres, and greater Turkish attention to the water problem. President Abdullah Gul paid an official visit to Damascus in May 2009, whilst Bashar Assad paid his visit to Turkey in October 2009. Gul made the first state visit to Iraq by a Turkish president to Baghdad in thirty-three years.[161] Turkey also received senior Iraqi officials, who went on to be both the Iraqi president and the premier. The two countries also agreed on general principles to overcome the differences in their relations, mainly the Kurdish problem and managing the flow of water from Turkey to Iraq.

The Palestinian question began to occupy significant importance in determining Turkish foreign policy towards Israel. Turkey assumed a mediating role in the Arab–Israeli conflict. It hosted the Syrian–Israeli indirect talks and sponsored a series of meetings between the Palestinians and Israeli presidents. Relations between Turkey and Israel, which have close diplomatic and military ties, have been strained after Turkish and Israeli officials' remarks following the Jewish state's 2008–9 twenty-two-day offensive in Gaza. Political developments in the Palestinian territories has inspired a cautious shift in Turkish regional policies and a coolness in Turkish–Israeli relations, with Turkey adopting several positive stances towards neighbouring Arab states, such as its stance towards the military cooperation with Israel and the al-Aqsa Intifada. In October 2009, Turkey called off scheduled joint military manœuvres with Israel, refusing to allow Israeli jets use of its airspace. And for the first time, Turkish official TV aired a Turkish film showing episodes of Israeli atrocities against the Palestinians. This provoked an Israeli reaction, calling the Turkish ambassador in protest. Turkish official TV continued to show the film, but with some censorship.[162] Turkey did not hesitate to side with the reactions of its people towards the uprisings in Tunisia, Egypt, Yemen, Libya, Bahrain and Syria, reiterating its position of non-interference and calling on existing Arab regimes to accept their peoples' legitimate demands.

Turkey–Israel Connections

Arab foreign ministers met on 12 March 2001 and expressed their great concern over the continuing Turkish–Israeli military cooperation, calling on Turkey to reconsider this cooperation which constitutes a grave threat to Arab national security and the region as a whole.[163] Turkey has always been well aware of Israel's position in the American regional strategy. Israel, for its part, has been sympathetic towards Turkey due to the historically tolerant attitudes of the Ottoman Empire towards the Jews after the Spanish inquisition. Both countries are secularist democratic non-Arab countries on the periphery of the Arab world.[164] Turkey believed that developing relations with Israel, which date back to 1951 when Turkey recognized to the Israel state, would increase its leverage in regard both to Israel and its adversaries. Ties were limited in the past to diplomatic representation without cooperation or official visits, with periods of stagnation and tension. However, the reaching of the Washington Agreement between Palestinians and Israelis,[165] and the declaration to establish a Palestinian state and Turkish recognition of it, led to the renewal of Turkish–Israeli ties and the upgrading of diplomatic representation to the level of ambassadorship. Turkey took advantage of the window of opportunity created by the accelerating Arab–Israeli peace process to enter into highly significant military cooperation with Israel.[166] The possible transfer of Russian S-300 missiles to Greek Cyprus forces led Turkey and Israel to develop new security initiatives.[167] The Islamist government of hardliner Najmel Din Erbakan upheld Turkey's military accord with Israel[168] and did not hesitate to conclude a series of agreements with Tel Aviv in 1996 despite Arab criticism. In the first half of 1997 several agreements relating to military cooperation were added to the previous one.[169]

The importance of Turkey for Israel's regional strategy lies in the fact that it is a Muslim secular state with an influential role in the contemporary politics of the Muslim world. Erdogan's government pursued a two-track regional policy separating the Turkish–Israeli relations from Turkish–Arab relations, however, with some overlap when it came to the peace process or the brutal Israeli policy against the Palestinians. Turkey also enjoys good relations with the former Muslim Soviet republics and Iran. It is a NATO member and has good bilateral relations with the US and is looking to join the EU. The shifting world balance drew Turkey, Israel and the US closer under the same interests in the region.[170]

Turkey and Israel exchanged a series of visits by senior dignitaries and concluded bilateral cooperative agreements. The visit by Israeli President Ezer Weizman to Ankara and the visit of Turkish Prime Minister Tansu Çiller to Israel culminated in the development of ties between the two countries. Turkey plays a role in limiting Islamist militancy, has extensive borders with Syria and Iraq, from which Israel can benefit to put pressure on these countries, a huge market for Israeli products and finally it is a major source of tourism, especially as Turkish pilgrims visit religious sites in Jerusalem. The volume of trade between the two states reached $2 billion in 2007, with Israeli exports to Turkey tripling since 1997 and imports estimated at $1.7 billion. The number of Israeli tourists to Turkey is estimated to be 360,000 annually, spending over $600 million.[171] From the outset in 1992, the Israeli–Turkish military alliance has consistently been directed against Syria. A 1993 Memorandum of Understanding led to the creation of Israeli–Turkish 'joint committees' to handle regional threats. Under the terms of the memorandum, Turkey and Israel agreed 'to cooperate in gathering intelligence on Syria, Iran and Iraq and to meet regularly to share assessments pertaining to terrorism and these countries' military capabilities'.[172] The first military dialogue between the two sides started in 1996, prompting tension in relations between Turkey and the Arab states,[173] and culminated in the conclusion of military agreements including the updating of F4 and F5 jet fighters and M-60 tanks. A significant turnaround in Turkish foreign policy occurred in the immediate wake of the cold war, which contributed to redefining the Turkey–Israel relationship. Initially forged under the helm of Prime Minister Tansu Çiller, the Israeli–Turkish military pact is characterized by the landmark 1994 Security and Secrecy Agreement (SSA). This strategic realignment of Turkey with Israel was part of Washington's post-cold war agenda in the Middle East, which was also supported by US covert intelligence operations. In 1997, Mrs Çiller was accused of having been recruited by the CIA and 'of accepting money from foreign governments [the US] to work against Turkey's national interests'.[174]

Turkish–Israeli ties, since the accession to power of the AKP, witnessed few setbacks. Relations between the two countries entered a new phase of tension as a result of the Israeli policy towards the Palestinians.[175] The AKP government accused Israel of being a 'terrorist state'.[176] The Turkish's army leadership cancelled the visit of the Israeli army chief Shaoul Mofaz to Turkey in October 2000 and two other important visits to Israel that were due to be held by the commander of the Turkish naval forces and the commander of the Turkish air force in November and December 2000, in response to the prevailing circumstances of a recent Islamic summit held in Doha and the continued killings and repression committed by the Israeli occupation army against the Palestinians in the occupied Palestinian territories.[177] Ehud Barak's official visit to Ankara on 12 February 2008 was intended to ease the tension in relations, emphasize Turkey's role as Israel's strategic ally, enlist Turkey against Iran, invite Turkey to play a mediatory role with Syria, mediate between Israel and Hamas to ensure the release of the captured Israel solider Shalit, and preserve and develop the bilateral economic ties. However, Barak's visit failed to enlist Turkey against Iran and Hamas. Erdogan criticized the Israeli regional policies and called for a freeze in military operations against the occupied Arab lands and the lifting of the Israeli blockade against Gaza; he reiterated the Turkish position on a Middle East nuclear free zone. Turkey refused to grant Israel permission to use its territory to launch an attack against Iranian nuclear installations. Barak also failed to reach an agreement with Turkey on new military projects.[178] Ehud Olmert, Israeli former premier, paid an official visit to Ankara, in December 2008. The visit was intended to discuss the future of the peace talks between Israel and Syria after the breakthrough in the indirect talks between the two foes facilitated by Turkey's mediatory role. Turkey offered to mediate between Israel and Hamas over a captive Israeli soldier. Erdogan revealed in an interview that a deal was proposed to Olmert during his visit to Ankara that would lead to the release of the Israeli soldier, Shalit, in return for Israel's release of Palestinian prisoners. Olmert promised to consult with Israeli officials, but he never replied to the Turkish proposal and Israel invaded Gaza – which represents a 'disrespect for Turkey', Erdogan added.[179] The Turkish facilitator role in the indirect Israeli–Syrian talks was frozen and the negotiations were suspended as a result of the Israeli assaults on Gaza.

The developments in Palestine caused a drift in Turkish–Israeli relations. Turkey sought rapprochement with Israel to have an effect on any settlement to the Arab–Israeli conflict. The AKP government, though maintaining its official ties with Israel and adhering to agreements concluded between the two sides, embarked on developing its relations with the Palestinian authority and particularly with Hamas. It condemned the Israeli repeated assaults on the Palestinian territory. The Turkish government took a strong stand against the Israeli twenty-two-day war on the Gaza Strip in December 2008–January 2009. Erdogan withdrew from the Dofus World Economic Forum in 2009 in protest at not been allowed enough time to comment on Shimon Peres's speech justifying the Israeli self-declared war on Gaza. In his speech to the Turkish Parliament on 5 January 2009, Erdogan called on Ehud Barak and Tzipi Livni not to use their aggression against Gaza as election propaganda. He then spoke to the Jewish people saying that 'when your ancestors faced oppression and deportation it was us who gave them refuge and help. I am talking here as a leader to the grandsons of the Ottoman Empire, not a leader of another country. Israel cannot be excused for what it is doing in Gaza. The Palestinian cause is Turkey's humanitarian cause and we cannot remain silent towards what is going on.'[180] Despite the new Turkish position, Erdogan said that 'emotions should have no place in politics and hence severing ties with Israel is currently not the appropriate option. Such thing needs a time frame based on the development and a decision like this needs to be thoroughly reviewed.'[181]

4. The Israeli Threat

Despite the recent peace agreements between some Arab countries and Israel, the Arab–Israeli conflict continues to be destabilizing. It is argued that the 'Arab–Israeli conflict has weighed heavily on the region as a whole and provided a rallying for extremists of all kind'.[182] Israel's nuclear arsenal presents today the most challenging issue for Middle Eastern security. For the first time in the history of Israel, the Arabs won a majority vote on 18 September

2009 at the IAEA annual conference calling on Israel to join the NPT and to open up its nuclear installations for international inspection.[183] Furthermore, Israel's regional alliances with neighbouring countries represent a threat to Arab national security.[184] The linkage between Arab national security and the Palestinian question has multiple dimensions. On the one hand, there is the Israeli threat to the vital Arab oil, economic and military installations. On the other hand, there is the fear that a deadlock on the Palestinian issue could cause Palestinian movements to take subversive action against Arab regimes.[185] It is argued that 'Israeli security strategy does not exclude any Arab country' (see Chapter 6). Israel did not hesitate to launch an air attack against Iraqi nuclear installations on 7 June 1981, to send its jet fighters in September 2007 to destroy a Syrian site suspected of being a nuclear power plant or to fly over Egypt to bomb a Sudanese convoy, in January 2009, suspected of carrying ammunition allegedly sent by Iran to Palestinian resistance groups. Israeli security strategy also includes the 'moderate' Arab states, namely Egypt and Saudi Arabia, 'in the second of three concentric circles of countries to which it must extend its strategic attention.'[186] Israeli fears that the Saudi arms build-up could end up in unfriendly hands caused them to frequently overfly the area (Tabuk in 1977–8), occasionally dropping empty fuel tanks on the runway to demonstrate their capabilities.[187] The Israeli threat, on 26 March 1988, to launch a pre-emptive air strike against the Saudi Silkworm missiles[188] caused the Saudi monarch to declare, on 8 April, that 'the missiles do not carry nuclear warheads and they will not be used against Israel'.[189] With American advice, Saudi Arabia decided on 26 April 1988 to join the Nuclear Non-Proliferation Treaty of 1968 (NPT), to ease Israeli anger.[190]

The second Gulf crisis caused a change in the attitudes of the Arab countries towards the Arab–Israeli conflict. Both the stance of the PLO and the American role in restoring Kuwaiti sovereignty inspired the change. It was manifested in their acceptance of the American Middle East peace initiative. They attended the Madrid Peace Conference in October 1991 and participated in multilateral peace talks (see Chapter 6). Relations between moderate Arab countries and the PLO became strained, with some Arab states opted for freezing their annual financial assistance. In an attempt to enlist PLO support in the ninth round of bilateral peace talks held in Washington in April 1993, the moderate Arab countries promised to resume financial assistance to the PLO. This act was intended to woo the Palestinians back to the peace process and to enhance the Palestinian moderate tendency.[191] Some Arab countries including the GCC states began to relax their boycott imposed on Israel. Kuwait was the first to remove the names of the American companies associated with Israel from the boycott list. The Arab League, in 1994, condemned the Gulf Cooperation Council's decision to end the secondary and tertiary trade embargo against Israel, insisting that only the Council of the Arab League could make such a policy change, and member states could not act independently on such matters. After the Kuwaiti liberation most of the minesweepers were brought from Israel through Germany.

The US is seen by many as taking the side of Israel in the Arab–Israeli conflict. Accused in the Arab world of operating with a double standard, US policy towards the Middle East is argued to be distorted by the influence of the strong pro-Israel lobby.[192] 'Europeans blame the US for making Israel its primary interest in the Middle East raising serious Arab concerns about US even-handedness.'[193] President Obama's new policy has failed to bring any concrete breakthrough. George Mitchell, the US Middle East peace envoy, did not manage in September 2009 to push the Israelis to accept a one-year freeze on the settlements and work out resumption of a new round of the Palestinian–Israeli negotiations.[194] The scenario anticipated in the case of failure in the peace process would be a radicalization of Arab politics through the Islamist tendency currently seeping through the region. Analysts argue that it could lead to 'geometric progression' through a unity between the Islamist and the residual pan-Arab nationalists in one front against their political regimes. Regional stability is strongly connected to the progress achieved in the Middle East peace process. No Arab country would be immune from political turmoil if such a scenario materialized, inflicting greater regional instability.

5. Conclusion

The above analysis of the regional political dynamics reveals that Arab countries' foreign policy-making is constrained by the fact that they exist in an unstable region. The Arab regional order has been weakened by multiple factors including distrust and mismanagement of inter-Arab differences, the Israeli threat, the Iranian challenge, Turkey's regional ambitions and the dependence on the US for security. Developments following the second Gulf crisis in August 1990 contributed in shaping the outcome of world political developments and have played a major role in Arab countries' foreign policy undertakings. On the one hand, it enhanced the US position, marking the beginning of a uni-polar world order. On the other hand, almost all Arab states gravitated more towards the US. This culminated in the public alignment between most Arab states and the

US in its war against terrorism. Inter-regional relations have not been stable and the Arab world has been divided into two camps, the 'moderate' and the reluctant. Turkey and Iran could play a positive role in regional cooperation and integration, provided that confidence building takes place, namely the settlement of territorial disputes, the water issue, the Iranian nuclear programme and regional security arrangements.

The outcome of the Middle East peace process would ultimately affect the foreign policy orientations of Arab states. The success of the peace talks would mean that the conflict for moderate Arab governments is essentially over.[195] Yet success of the peace talks does not mean simply reaching a peace accord, but normalization of relations, in all fields – political, economic, and cultural – between Israel and the Arab world. In other words, accepting Israel as part of the Middle East region is not an easy task. It would mean a change in perception for both Arabs and fundamentalist Jews.[196] Simultaneously, the process of normalization might stimulate political discontent among two social forces, the Islamists and the residual pan-Arab nationalists, which would lead ultimately to radicalizing Arab politics and could cause the demise of existing political regimes, bringing the peace agreement to a standstill and possibly revoking it. Despite the possibility of peaceful settlement, a taboo would continue to exist, namely the Israel nuclear capability. It could be argued, however, that the Israel nuclear capability would act as a deterrent force to preserve Israel security and territorial integrity. On the other hand, maintaining Israeli military superiority would fuel a further arms race in the region (see Table 4.1) that would justify the radicals' opposition to the peace accord. Arab states' foreign policies towards the peace process is one of the macro-level case studies to which Part Two of this book is dedicated.

Chapter 5

The Arab–Israeli Conflict

1. Introduction

The Arab–Israeli conflict did not begin on 15 May 1948; in fact the conflict between the two sides goes back to the Basle Conference, the First Zionist Congress held on 29 August 1897 by the modern Zionist movement in cooperation with the Western imperial powers, who clearly lent their unconditional support to Jewish migration to Palestine. However, clashes between the Arabs and Jewish settlers did not reach a climax until the end of 1935 and the beginning of 1936. The Zionist movement was able to use a number of methods, most prominently terrorism, the building of military force and encouraging Jewish migration to Palestine, buying land and using diplomatic activity on the international level, in order to gain the support of foreign countries for its claim to Palestine. At the time, the majority of the pan-Arab nation was subject to Western colonialism and living in a state of direct subordination to the West as well as a state of backwardness, military weakness and divisions. Britain and the US's unconditional support to the Zionist movement to succeed in taking Palestine by force is seen as part of plots hatched by colonial powers against the Arab world. The colonial powers saw in the Zionist movement a faithful ally that they could rely on to control the Arab nation. This chapter argues that the international variable, especially since the second Gulf crisis, has played a predominant factor in shaping the foreign policy undertakings towards the Arab–Israeli conflict.

The Arab states' perception of a peaceful settlement with Israel is based on the achievement of the inalienable rights of the Palestinian people for self-determination and the establishment of an independent Palestinian state on the land occupied by Israel in the six-day war of June 1967. The Arabs hold the view that peace cannot be achieved without the active involvement of international actors, namely the United Nations, the US, the EU, Russia and the main parties to the conflict, including the PLO in its capacity as the sole legitimate representative of the Palestinian people. Israeli holds a different perception, based on the exchange of security for peace that can be achieved only through direct bilateral negotiation with the different Arab parties to the conflict. However, Israel holds the view that peace cannot be achieved without a strong military power to preserve Israel's security. Yitzhak Shamir said, 'Peace is linked to strength; strength gives peace a chance.'[1] It holds the view that the international role should be limited to giving support to whatever settlement is reached.

Regardless of the differences of opinion regarding the objectives behind Western support for the Zionist movement and then Israel, the Arab–Israeli conflict no longer only threatens the security of the Arabs; it also poses a serious threat to the world's peace and security. This chapter is dedicated to the international variable in the conflict as part of the input process in the dynamics of the Arab states' foreign policy-making which led eventually to a fundamental change in the Arab states' foreign policies towards Israel and the peace process. It analyses and covers briefly the history of the international role in the conflict, the Soviet/Russian roles, US policies, the European position, developing countries' attitudes and policies and finally the role of the United Nations.

2. Overview

Summer 1990 marked the beginning of a transformation in the Arab–Israeli conflict from military confrontation to peace as a strategic Arab option. The shifting balance in favour of Israel brought with it fragile peace agreements. Up until the present, all peace treaties and negotiations between the two parties, from the Madrid Conference in 1991 to Annapolis in November 2007, were the natural outcome of fallout of the second Gulf war. This period also witnessed major transformations in international relations, the most important of which was the collapse of the Eastern bloc and the dismantling of the Soviet empire. An important factor was the growing Islamic resurgence, which interestingly enough threatened Israeli security not the Arab states,[2] but also posed a direct challenge to the legitimacy of Arab regimes.

Iraq's downfall, as the result of the second Gulf crisis, had a considerable impact on the ensuing balance of power between the Arabs and Israel, weakening the Arabs' military capability at a time when Israel was succeeding in preserving its own. Moreover, when the PLO sensed the Arabs' lack of seriousness in demanding the return of Israeli-occupied lands, it eventually lost all hope in Arab regimes and their leaderships. Consequently, it entered into direct talks with Israel with the hope of obtaining some concessions before it was too late. The fact that there were divisions among Arab allies of the United States, while others proved incapable of withstanding American pressure, further contributed to the success of the negotiations. The peace treaty between Israel, the PLO and Jordan would not have taken place had it not been for the above-mentioned international and regional transformations. However, the conclusion of a peace treaty between Israel and the Arabs does signify a shift from a culture of conflict to one of peace – normalization of relations between the two sides is a difficult if not impossible proposition. Menahem Begin, in his book *The Revolt: The Story of the Irgun* (1951), said that there would be no peace for the people or for the land of Israel and no peace for the Arabs, or for the land of the Arabs. He said that the Jews would continue to fight to liberate their nation and lands from Arab subjugation and that war would continue, even if the Arabs signed a peace treaty with Israel. The peace experiment between Egypt and Israel reflects this, since despite it being three decades since the signature of the Camp David agreement there is yet to be peace between the two sides. Moreover, reports out of Jordan and Palestine say that forces opposed to peace, especially the Islamists, reject the notion of normalization and are working hard to foil the peace agreements between their respective countries and Israel.[3] We could refer here to Hamas's refusal to engage in direct negotiations with Israel, even when it was at the helm of the Palestine National Authority's government. It continued its military activities by repeatedly attacking Israeli targets, which not only resulted in the death of some of its leaders, most prominent among whom were Shaykh Ahmad Yassin and Rantisi, but also in a confrontation with the Fateh movement, which still upholds the Oslo Accords. Hamas subsequently rebelled against the authority of President Mahmoud Abbas and stood in opposition to the Arab initiative, which it considered even worse than Oslo.[4] It also rejected the Annapolis resolutions, despite wider Arab participation, seen by some as a move to further isolate Hamas, both regionally and internationally,[5] as evidenced by the financial assistance granted to Mahmoud Abbas by the Paris Donor Conference of December 2007.

Linguistically, peace means the opposite of war; however, a more precise meaning of the term would be the stability of power within a legitimate framework in which good governance and the rule of law prevail. In this context, a regime is considered legitimate when the codes of conduct that obtain are respected by all. With regard to the Arab–Israeli conflict, real peace will not prevail as long as attempts at finding a settlement ignore the conflict's roots and main causes;[6] this means that any settlement imposed by force without resolving the core issues is just a short respite in the ongoing conflict. A political settlement is the total or partial coordination between the objectives of parties to the conflict, based on the existing balance of power at the time of signature. A settlement then therefore reflects the real power of each of the signatories rather than their vital interests, which is what differentiates it from a genuine peace process.

Within the same context, but on a different level, on 19 August 1995, a number of Muslim 'Ulama and imams, religious interpreters and professors of Islamic Shari'ah in Jordan, issued a religious decree banning, both religiously and legally, the sale of real estate owned by Muslims in the Greater Syria region to Jews. It is obvious, if one looks objectively at the path that the Arab–Zionist conflict has followed, that opposition to reconciliation with Israel will increase, auguring in turn a stronger fundamentalist current and a coalition with the residual pan-Arab nationalism. This will undoubtedly impose a new *de facto* situation on the Arab states, which could eventually lead to their granting secret financial assistance to rejectionist movements. It could also, on the one hand, reinforce the possibility of a rift between the United States and its Arab allies in the medium term and, on the other, bring about political changes in the region, including in Israel and a number of Arab states.

Some sources believe that yet another scenario could eventually intervene and greatly complicate matters: certain modes of behaviour could cause powerful Palestinian political forces, opposed either to the agreement itself or to the way it would be implemented, to emerge, causing further Palestinian internal instability, if not civil war.[7] The same could happen on the Israeli side, if the fundamentalist right wing in Israel succeeds in convincing the country's elite that their government had made concessions against Israel's best interest, especially if there is progress on the Syrian–Israeli track. It is worth mentioning here that Orthodox movements within Israel, including Agadot Yisrael, coalesced against the peace treaty, as evidenced by the categorical vote against the Palestinian–Israeli agreement in the Knesset, in September 1993, and the abstention of Shas Party members. On 6 October 1995, after a stormy fifteen-hour debate, the Knesset agreed by a small majority of 61 to 59 to expand the self-rule area in the West Bank despite the opposition of a number of Labour Party members. The murder of former Israeli Prime Minister Yitzhak Rabin by a Jewish extremist, on 4 November 1995, is a clear example of internal Israeli divisions regarding the peace process in the Middle East. Others include the demonstrations in both Gaza and the West Bank, as well as in Israel itself, against the Annapolis Conference of November 2007, which ended without a peace agreement, despite the importance that the United States and its Arab allies, including the Palestine Liberation Organization, had attached to it. The most important result of the conference was a decision to continue negotiations between the Israelis and

Palestinians, and a session did actually take place on 14 December 2007, with the aim of reaching a permanent status agreement without the intervention of a third party. The conference's final document did not mention any of the core issues and focused instead on the road map. Palestinian demands regarding Jerusalem, the settlements, the refugees and an independent state were set aside; as was Israel's demand to become a national home for the Jews.[8]

Any peace agreement between Israel and the Arabs is bound to be fragile and vulnerable to collapse at any time. Moreover, even though the Arab–Israeli conflict could be contained, it 'will remain ongoing' as long as there are still many unresolved issues that could impede progress towards peace, namely Israel's nuclear weapons[9] and the issues of water, the refugees, the settlements and Jerusalem. The water issue is gaining importance since both sides have suffered from a dire shortage since 2000, estimated at 800 million cubic metres in Israel, and 30 billion cubic metres on the Arab side, with these figures expected to reach 2,500 million cubic metres and 260 billion cubic metres respectively in 2030 (see Chapter 7). The issue of Jerusalem is another major obstacle on the road towards a permanent peace between the Arabs and Israel. Given its religious significance to both sides, the importance of Jerusalem is in its moral value rather than as an object of negotiations. The fact that neither side is able to give up or negotiate over Jerusalem is another impediment to the shift from a culture of conflict to one of peace. In addition, Israel's possession of nuclear weapons, which Israeli Prime Minister Ehud Olmert acknowledged for the first time in an interview on German television in 2007, reflects the lack of parity in any peace negotiations, and dooms them to producing only temporary settlements, since the regional scales will continue to be tipped in favour of Israel.

There are also differences of opinion between the Arabs and Israel regarding 'the Jewish character of Israel', a notion that President Bush supported at Annapolis.[10] Not only does this issue raise many questions regarding the Palestinian refugees' right of return, but it also puts into question the fate of around 1.5 million 'Arab Israelis'. Although most observers agree that the most intransigent issue in any negotiations, whether bilateral or multilateral, is that of the refugees, it is the settlements, which have been the object of discussion and disagreement between the two sides over many decades, that are now the main impediment to reaching a peaceful resolution.[11] This issue was the main obstacle in all Israel's negotiations with the Arabs, i.e. the PLO, Jordan and Syria, and will continue to be the main obstacle on the path towards genuine peace (see Chapter 6). It is worth mentioning here that, at the end of his first meeting with President Abbas after Annapolis, Prime Minister Olmert refused to freeze settlement activity, as the Palestinian President had requested during their meeting in Jerusalem.[12]

3. The Impacts of the International Role on the Conflict[13]

In reality, the Arab–Israeli conflict is mainly an ideological conflict because, in essence, it is a conflict between civilizations: the Islamic civilization on one hand and the Western, Jewish-Christian, civilization on the other.[14] The Zionist movement, and its Western allies, hide behind other factors and reasons. Nevertheless, the civilization factor cannot be ignored, even if its impacts and implications differ from one time to another, in relation to other compelling factors predominantly affecting the Arab–Israeli conflict.[15]

The alliance between Zionism and Western colonialism is considered a proof of the enmity that European states have towards Islam. Napoleon Bonaparte, during his invasion of Egypt and Palestine, was the first to call upon the Jews to migrate to Palestine and establish a homeland. A number of prominent politicians encouraged Jews to do the same, such as Lord Palmerston, Lord Shaftesbury, Benjamin Disraeli, Joseph Chamberlain, Winston Churchill, Arthur Balfour and Harry S. Truman, who adopted the Zionist ideology based on founding a state for the Jews. In the early 1860s Jewish scholars and writers began to call for work towards returning to Palestine and colonizing it. Among those were Zvi Hirsch Kalischer, Leon Pinsker and Theodor Herzl, the latter of whom succeeded in bringing the Jews of the world together at the Basle conference held in Switzerland in 1897 and called for the establishing of the Zionist state. Zionist ideas were presented and well received by the colonial powers of that period. It was clear that the goals of both sides were compatible in their stance towards Islam. Lawrence Brown, one of the West's military commanders during the crusade on the Middle East, said, 'Islam is the only obstacle to European colonialism,'[16] whilst Prime Minister Shimon Peres said in 1979 that it was not possible to achieve peace in the Middle East 'as long as Islam was drawing its sword and we cannot guarantee our future until Islam sheathes its sword forever'.[17] The Zionist ideology began to present itself in response to the policy of British colonialism. Britain pursued a programme based on Jewish migration and settlement in Palestine. Later, the United States of America became involved through the Truman–Brandeis alliance to complete the process of putting a Zionist state on the world map.[18]

The Zionist movement relies heavily on the myths of 'God's chosen people' and 'the divine promise', 'from the Nile to the Euphrates, your land, O Israel' and 'a historical right'. The Zionist movement translated these concepts into a mixture of religious fanaticism, chauvinism, racism and aggressive exploitation justified by the Torah and Talmud. This movement claimed a right to establish a state in Palestine displacing its natives and pursuing a policy of ethnic cleansing. Palestinians who chose to stay in their homeland despite Israeli barbaric measures have become second-class citizens.

To achieve the goals of the Zionist movement, and as a result of British and Zionist efforts, the numbers of Jews migrating to Palestine increased whilst the number of Palestinians refugees multiplied. Fears of the Palestinian increased and led to a revolt against the Jewish influx. Clashes between the Arabs and the Zionist militia started as early as 1910. The unbalanced confrontation left a considerable number of Arabs dead, tortured, imprisoned and expelled for refusing to evacuate their homes and hand their land over to the Jews. Arab efforts to resist Zionist plans proved to be in vain due to the Western unequivocal support. The Palestinians, over the last sixty years, have been victimized for no reason and their case can no longer be ignored.[19]

4. The Soviet/Russian Role

The Soviet Union's position shifted from being among the first countries to recognize the Zionist entity in May 1948 to being a strong supporter of the Arabs from the early 1950s. The immediate Soviet recognition of Israel could be attributed to three main factors:

1. A key role was played by the Zionist movement, as the Jews were the most prominent leaders in the Bolshevik movement and Communist revolution in Russia.[20]
2. The Soviet Union, at that point in history, did not have any sphere of influence in the Middle East and was encircled by the US policy of containment. As one of the world's superpowers, it strove to win over influential areas in the world and appreciated the geopolitical significance of the Middle East. The Soviets hoped that it could use Israel in its power struggle with Western capitalism, which was dominating most parts of the Arab world at that time.
3. The Soviet Union was relying a great deal on the Jews who migrated from the Soviet Union and East European countries, which adhered to the Marxist ideology, hoping that Israel could become a Communist state.

> As a result, the Soviet Union, as a Marxist state, committed to – or burdened itself with – the vanguard mission of defending communist regimes worldwide, believing that establishing ties would be the first step on the path of consolidating ties between the two sides.

Israel opting for a Western mode of government caused great disappointment to the Soviet Union, especially after Israel chose to ally itself with Western countries. However, the Soviet Union maintained its diplomatic ties with the Zionist entity and at the same time it sought to pursue a policy of wait and see. The golden opportunity for the Soviet Union was the 23 July 1953 Revolution in Egypt. The political developments that followed the success of the revolution represented the turning point in Soviet–Egyptian relations in general and in the positions of the Soviet Union towards the Arab–Israeli conflict in particular.

Until 1967, the Soviet Union adopted a dual policy towards the Arab world. On one hand, the Soviet Union maintained its diplomatic ties with Israel and, on the other, it became the main arms-exporting country to Arab states. For example, sources indicated that Egypt received heavy arms from the Soviet Union in 1955 worth US$650 million;[21] moreover, Soviet financial aid to Egypt between 1958 and 1965 amounted to roughly US$831 million,[22] representing another element of Soviet support to friendly Arab countries. In addition, the Soviet Union became the United Arab Republic's main trade partner, as exports to the United Arab Republic increased from approximately US$40 million in 1958 to US$135 million in 1967 and imports from the United Arab Republic to the Soviet Union amounted to roughly US$141 million in the same period; the volume of trade between the two countries reached approximately US$500 million in 1970.[23]

During the trilateral attack on Egypt in 1956, by Britain, France and Israel, the Soviet Union took the side of Egypt and showed a firm supportive position despite a large part of its military forces being stationed overseas. In November 1956 Soviet Premier Nikolai Bulganin sent a letter in protest against Britain, France and Israel, calling for an immediate cessation of hostilities and warning that the Soviet Union would intervene strongly to support Egypt if the invading powers chose not to withdraw their forces immediately.[24]

The Soviet Union, however, did not take a similar stand against the Israeli assault on Arab countries during the six-day war in June 1967. The Soviet position was sceptical and dual; on the one hand, the Soviet statement was strong and positive in the interests of the Arabs; on the other hand, it showed the Soviet hesitance to deliver the required military assistance to its Arab allies. The Soviet

Union, however, unhappy with Israel's reluctance, decided on 8 June to send its planes with supplies of arms to Egypt and Syria. They also decided on 10 June to sever diplomatic relations with Israel. The Soviet Premier Leonid Brezhnev, in a meeting with the Iraqi President Abdul Rahman Arif and the Algerian President Houari Boumediene, stated that the Arabs had been compensated with large amounts of weapons transferred over 445 plane journeys and by 15 ships and that 48 tonnes of military artillery had also been sent.[25] Some reports indicated that Cairo received ten Soviet TU-16 jets with long-range bombers.[26] In June 1968, President of Egypt Gamal Abdel Nasser confirmed that the United Arab Republic received large quantities of weapons from the Soviet Union, including armoured cars and jets and some electronic equipment; moreover it was given MiG-12 fighter and defence jets.[27] On 30 September 1968, *The Times* reported that the United Arab Republic received large quantities of military aid from the Soviet Union, compensating for its losses in the June war and that the first instalment included 500 armoured cars and 600 MiG jets and hundreds of machine guns.[28] *The Daily Telegraph* estimated that the amount of military aid provided by the Soviet Union to Egypt since the June war in 1967 stood at US$1600 million.[29] The United Arab Republic's Minister of Defence, Mohammed Fawzi, revealed in a statement on 17 November 1979 that the Soviet Union provided the United Arab Republic with modern advanced weapons that it had never had in its possession before.

The Soviet Union, on the other hand, pursued a policy aiming at internationalizing the Middle East crisis. On 13 June 1967 it called for an emergency session to be held by the UN's General Assembly to eliminate the Israeli aggression against the Arab states and called for the withdrawal of Israeli forces to their positions before 5 June.[30] When representing his country at the emergency General Assembly meeting between 16 and 26 June, Premier Alexei Kosygin met US President Lyndon B. Johnson on 23–25 June in Glassboro, New Jersey, in the United States. In a communiqué issued after his discussions with Johnson, the Soviet Premier said that the main issue in the Middle East was the immediate withdrawal of the Israeli forces, which carried out the attack against the Arab states,[31] to the pre-war borders in accordance with the truce. The Soviet Union strived to contain any possible US manœuvre and presented a plan to the Security Council during a session on 20 November 1967, based on the Latin American proposal and in which there was a paragraph calling for limiting the arms shipment to the regional countries, which is what the United States was calling for. The objective behind what the Soviet Union initiative was to push for a more constructive US engagement to reach a peaceful settlement. The Soviet manœuvre succeeded in getting the other permanent members of the Security Council to agree to the British proposal, which called for the complete withdrawal of the Israeli forces from the territories occupied since the beginning of the war on 5 June. The British plan received the acceptance of some Arab parties and the Soviet Union as well. During a session that was held on 22 November 1967, there was a unanimous vote for the resolution known as Resolution 242. It is worth mentioning here that, following his visit to Moscow, the Algerian President Houari Boumediene along with the Iraqi President Abdul Rahman Arif criticized the Soviet position, saying: 'they want us to agree to the UN resolution to transfer the responsibility of the entire issue from the shoulders of the Soviets to the international community.' President Abdel Nasser used Arab states close to the Soviet Union to pressure the Soviets. The Soviet leadership, however, insisted on internationalizing the conflict and adhering to the peace process and called for the necessity of a unified Arab position despite the different orientations of the Arab countries that would prevent enough time for military build-up.

Abdel Nasser attributed the lack of success of the Iraqi and Algerian presidents' mission to convince Moscow to meet the Arab military demands to Algeria's special relations with China and the Soviet Union's position towards these ties. It is worth mentioning here that, during his meeting with Gamal Abdel Nasser in June 1967, the Chairman of the Presidium of the Supreme Soviet of the USSR, Nikolai Podgorny, asked Abdel Nasser to intervene to stop China's accusations that the Soviet Union was conspiring with the United States and Israel against the Arabs.[32] Soviet sources believed that the reason for the Soviet Union's hesitation towards the Arab–Israeli conflict was, as Brezhnev had pointed out once, during his meeting with the Algerian and Iraqi presidents, that 'we suffered humiliation too because we have linked our reputation to yours. We have found our most advanced jets, tanks and rockets in the US research centres just as if we had decided to send our tanks to "West" Germany.'[33] Abdel Nasser summarized the changes in the Soviet position, during the Khartoum Arab Summit meeting in 1968, by saying: 'The international position currently is entirely different from that of 1956. In that year, America and the Soviet Union agreed to stand against the tripartite offence whilst now in 1967, they have agreed to Israel's right to exist and the two have agreed to put an end to the state of war as well.'[34]

Despite the Soviet Union's hesitation about supporting its Arab allies militarily, the supply of Soviet weapons did not stop with the death of the Egyptian President Gamal Abdel Nasser, although this was less than what

Egypt had actually sought. Reports stated that, in 1971, Egypt acquired 600 MiG-16 jets, 600 MiG-17 and MiG-15 jets, and 160 Sukhoi-5 jets in addition to 360 SAM 2 missiles and 160 SAM 3 missiles from the Soviet Union.[35] The Israeli air raids on Egypt, at the end of 1970, and the inability of the Egyptian aerial defence force to combat them, left Egypt vulnerable and unable to set up the SAM 2 and SAM 3 missiles in the areas preassigned for them around Cairo and Alexandria. As a result Egypt sought to obtain MiG-23 bombers and modern Soviet armoured vehicles, but the Soviets failed to respond promptly. Moreover, the modern military weapons and apparatus would be under the complete supervision and management of Soviet military technicians, causing further delay. Some sources believed that the Soviet's hesitation to provide Egypt with sophisticated offensive and defensive weapons was behind Sadat's historical decision, in July 1972, to expel Soviet experts.[36] President Anwar Sadat said in a statement on 13 October 1972 that the expelling of Soviet military advisers was due to the fact that they had become a heavy burden on Egypt after the Soviet leaders had stated that they were against the continuation of the conflict in the Middle East.[37]

In spite of the sharp tension in Soviet–Egyptian ties in 1972, relations improved once again and in 1973 the Soviet Union increased military aid to Egypt. The Soviet Union supported its Arab allies during the October war in 1973. Reports indicated that 400 military technicians were dispatched to Egypt and the Soviets approved the delivery of SAM 2 missiles to Egypt.[38] In addition the Soviet Union engaged in active diplomacy through the Security Council and blamed Israel for failing to adhere to the ceasefire.[39] Mohammed Hassanain Haykal has indicated that 90 per cent of the weapons that the Arabs used during the October war came from the Soviet Union.[40]

The ups and downs of Soviet–Egyptian relations did not prevent the Soviet Union from consolidating its relations with a number of Arab states, especially those such as Syria, Libya and Iraq to which it was connected by amity treaties. They adhered to their policy of supporting legitimate Arabs' rights, calling for Israeli withdrawal from the occupied territories since the June 1967 war, the right of the Palestinian refugees to return home and to the self-determination and the establishment of an independent Palestinian state. Moreover, the Soviet Union maintained excellent ties with the Palestinian Liberation Organization (PLO) as it considered it the sole legitimate representative of the Palestinian people.

When Mikhail Gorbachev came to power, the Soviet Union adopted active diplomacy towards the Middle East and presented a series of proposals:

1. In April 1986, the Soviet Union announced that it would practise all its navigational rights in the air and the free seas in the Mediterranean and denounced the Americans' attack on Libya.
2. In September 1986, the Soviet Union suggested setting up a preparatory committee in the framework of the Security Council in order to prepare for holding an international conference for peace in the Middle East and called for the Arab state of Palestine to be part of the world's political map side by side with Israel.[41]

Even if the two points were not directly related to the Arab–Israeli conflict, the underlying principles were to emphasize the role of the Soviet Union as a superpower and a main party in any agreement because its aim was to establish security and stability in the Middle East in general. Moreover, its condemnation of the American attack on Libya is confirmation of the Soviet Union's determination to maintain its excellent ties with its Arab friends. In addition, the Soviet Union looked on the issue of security and stability in the Middle East as indivisible, and saw the Arab–Israeli conflict as the main obstacle to stability in the region. It also maintained that the peaceful settlement to the conflict was a longstanding goal of the Soviet Union in the region. We can attribute this to the following.

1. The Soviet Union's desire to alleviate the tension with the United States, both of them being allies to parties in the Middle East conflict. This was made clear in Gorbachev's statement on 2 July 1987, during his meeting with former US President Jimmy Carter in Moscow, when he said that the Soviet Union had come to realize that 'Washington and the West have interests in the Middle East and that it does not intend to abuse [these interests] because that is unattainable'.[42]
2. Reaching a peaceful settlement to the Arab–Israeli conflict, even costing the Arabs some of their legitimate rights, would consolidate the Soviet machine in the Arab world at the expense of the United States, and this was one of the Soviet Union's short-term objectives, if we consider US–Soviet rivalry one of the main limitations of Soviet foreign policy.
3. Reaching a peaceful settlement involves ensuring the right of Israel to exist, in order to alleviate Israeli pressure on the Soviet Union exercised through the Zionist lobby in Moscow on the one hand and the Israeli connection in determining US–Soviet relations on the other hand.

Beginning in 1993, however, Russian policy towards the Middle East became more assertive in selected areas. On the one hand, 937,000 Jews poured into Israel after the collapse of the Soviet Union, but migration patterns remained fairly stable, with 60,000 to 80,000 new arrivals each year, dropping in 2001 to about 43,000, after the start of the Intifada, the Palestinian uprising. However, thousands of Russian Jews, estimated at 75,000, who immigrated to Israel, decided to return to Russia, some of them soured by the Jewish state's anaemic economy, limited job opportunities and dangerous security environment. At the same time, statistics show that immigration to Israel in 2003 dropped to a fifteen-year low of 23,200, which Israeli officials blamed not only on the economic downturn and continuing violence, but also on the smaller reservoir of Jews in the former Soviet republics to draw from, and a decrease in the flight from persecution by Jews around the world.[43] On the other hand, in December 1994, Russia signed a trade agreement with Egypt with the stated purpose of restoring Egypt's Soviet-era position as the most important trade partner in the Middle East. At a low level compared to the Soviet era, Russia, in the early 1990s, began arms sales to Kuwait, the United Arab Emirates, Algeria, Egypt and Syria.[44] President Putin called for the renewal of contacts with the countries with which Russia maintained long friendly relations and invested a lot of material and intellectual resources. The Arab countries constitute a large part of those countries. In general, the positions of Russia and the majority of Arab countries on key issues of development of the political situation in the region coincide.

In July 1999, a few months before Vladimir Putin succeeded President Boris Yeltsin as president of Russia, Hafiz Assad of Syria paid his last state visit to Moscow. Nevertheless, relations between the two sides were clouded by differences over Syria's $13 billion debt to the former Soviet Union. Russia virtually froze cooperation with Damascus pending a resolution of the debt issues. Efforts to improve relations culminated in the exchange of visits of senior dignitaries in the period 2000–2005. Benjamin Netanyahu paid an official visit to Moscow on 1 March 1997 to express concern regarding Russia's technical and military cooperation with Syria, arguing that it would threaten regional stability.[45]

Russian–Syrian differences over how to resolve the Arab–Israeli conflict were clear in the decision by Syria and Lebanon to boycott a February 2000 Moscow meeting of the Multilateral Steering Group for Middle East Peace. It was also evident in March 2002, when Russia along with thirteen other members of the UN Security Council (UNSC) voted in favour of Resolution 1397 calling for the coexistence of an Israeli and a Palestinian state, while Syria (a non-permanent member of the UNSC) abstained on the measure. In addition, although Russia did vote in favour of a UNSC resolution proposed by Syria and Sudan (which the United States vetoed) calling upon Israel not to expel Palestinian leader Yasser Arafat from the occupied territories, Russian Deputy Foreign Minister Yury Fedotov indicated Moscow's lack of enthusiasm for the measure, saying that 'the vote should not have been rushed'. What these instances indicate is that Moscow has been unwilling to support Syria's harder line on the Arab–Israeli issue, while Damascus has not been willing to moderate its position in order to align itself more closely with Russia.[46]

The government of Vladimir Putin intensified Russia's involvement in the region. Relations improved dramatically after the Syrian President Bashar Assad met with Russian President Vladimir Putin in Moscow in January 2005. Russia decided to soften its position and agreed to write off 73 per cent of Syria's $13 billion debt and to let the rest of the loan be repaid on favourable terms. Russia and Syria have signed an agreement that could pave the way for a major weapons deal. The agreement was concluded in Moscow on 25 January 2005. Officials said Assad and Vladimir Putin signed an accord that would enable Russia to resume major arms sales and upgrades for Syria's military. 'The two countries agree to pursue traditional cooperation in the military-technical sphere in keeping with their mutual interests and international obligations.'[47] Russia also agreed to sell an advanced Strelets air defence missile system to Syria despite both American and Israeli objections.[48] The two sides have also agreed on a joint oil and gas project to be carried out in Syria.

Russian diplomats encouraged Arab participation in the Arab–Israeli peace talks that began in 1992, and Russians participated in talks between Israel and the PLO on the issue of PLO self-rule in Israeli-occupied territories. Among other reasons, Russia supported the peace process as a mean of reducing the threat of the spread of Islamic fundamentalism.[49] Vladimir Putin, during a visit to Madrid in September 2006, reiterated that Russia did not consider Hamas a terrorist organization, and urged the global community to work with a Hamas-led Palestinian government.[50] Russia–Hamas talks began on 3 March 2006, when Russian Foreign Minister Sergei Lavrov met with Hamas leader Khaled Meshaal to discuss the future of the peace process in the Israeli–Palestinian conflict after Hamas became the majority party of the Palestinian National Authority Legislative Council. During the talks Lavrov called on Hamas to comply with the earlier commitments signed by the PLO, and reiterated Russia's position, but Hamas refused. The prospect of giving legitimacy to Hamas has angered some Israeli officials.[51] Russian–Israeli relations, by contrast, became very close under both Putin and Israeli Prime Minister Ariel Sharon. 'Putin has sought to maintain close ties to Israel. While this has not been easy, he has been relatively successful at this delicate balancing act.'[52] The dissolution of the Soviet Union left Russia the successor engaged with managing its own affairs and unable to pursue a competitive policy with the US in world affairs. Russia with the other major world powers decided to support the US policy in managing the Arab–Israeli conflict.

Russia as a member of the Quartet committee on the Middle East, which comprises the UN, European Union, Russia and United States, acted collectively through the UNSC to bring an immediate end to the devastating Israeli offensive against the Gaza Strip in December 2008/January 2009. Russia attended the Quartet meeting in Trieste, Italy, on 26 June 2009 as part of the ongoing efforts to promote peace in the Middle East which was attended by UN Secretary-General Ban Ki-Moon and other members of the Quartet.[53] It called on Israel to freeze all settlement activity and lift its blockade of the Gaza strip. The Quartet underscored that the only viable solution to the Israeli–Palestinian conflict is the two independent states solution.[54]

5. United States Policies

The United States' support to Israel surpassed that given by Britain. It was the first country to recognize Israel's independence, consistent with a 1922 Congressional resolution backing the League of Nations mandate for a Jewish homeland in Palestine.[55] On a number of occasions, US President Harry Truman intervened to help the Zionist leadership achieve its goals in Palestine, as the British government was pressured to allow more Jews to migrate to Palestine and to support the Partition Plan in 1947. The US sought to collect money from the imports and exports bank on 15 June 1949, amounting to US$130 million, to meet the demands of the Jewish Agency. When it became clear that the Arab states were mobilizing their forces to intervene in Palestine in 1948 before the establishment of the State of Israel was declared, the US Secretary of State recalled Arab diplomats in Washington and accused them of being hostile, warned them that there would be punishments and informed them of America's serious concern about any possible raid against 'Jewish Palestine'.[56]

Truman and a group of Zionist historians were the embodiment of American non-Jewish Zionism on the political level. There are differences of opinions regarding the reasons for Truman's unconditional support to the Zionist objectives. Some argued that he was an opportunist who caved in to Zionist pressure whilst others believed that his position was based on humanitarian reasons because of the suffering and persecution suffered by the Jews under the Nazi oppression. Regardless of the motives behind the US support, some leaders of the Zionist movement such as Gideon Raphael believed that the US diplomatic acknowledgement that approved of Israel helped to put the new state on the political world map.[57]

The US, from the early 1970s, used the UN organs to demonstrate its full support for Israeli policy. It did not cast its first veto until 1972, on a Syrian–Lebanese complaint against Israel. From 1967 to 1972, the US supported or abstained on twenty-four resolutions, most critical of Israel. From 1973 to 2000, the Security Council adopted approximately ninety resolutions on the Middle East, again, most critical of Israel. The US vetoed a total of thirty-three resolutions and, hence, supported the Council's criticism of Israel by voting or by abstaining roughly two-thirds of the time.[58] US support of Israel was not limited only to the political acknowledgement; it surpassed this and they became allies. US support to Israel took other forms. The financial support to Israel reached over $24 billion between 1948 and 1982, around $16 billion of which was military aid.[59] In the history of the Arab–Israeli conflict, the United States has never denounced Israel's repeated unilateral attacks on Arab states and the Palestinian territories, including the December 2008/January 2009 offensive on the Gaza Strip, with the exception of its position against the tripartite attack in 1956. Analysts believed that this was not because it believed that Egypt's position was just or out of fear of its interests in Egypt. The US was not consulted prior to the invasion by Britain, France and Israel and wanted to put an end to the ailing British and French powers in the Middle East. The US Secretary of State John Foster Dulles did not completely rule out the military option for the Suez issue. John G. Stoessinger believes that the US position stemmed from the pride of President Eisenhower and Dulles and their desire to restore their dignity after they felt they had been duped by their allies. Furthermore, the American side was observing events in Hungary where developments were working in favour of the United States, and relations between the Soviet Union and its allies in Eastern Europe were entering a new phase which Dulles referred to as a 'miracle'. If the US had taken the side of its Western allies it would have cost it its moral credibility.[60] Dulles noted: 'it is no less than tragic, when we are at the point of winning an immense and long-hoped-for victory over Soviet colonialism in Eastern Europe, we should be forced to choose between following the footsteps of the Anglo-French colonialism in Asia and Africa and splitting our course away from their course.'[61] Therefore the US position was not merely a defence of Arab rights and cannot be considered a change in America's position towards Israel as US military support to Israel continued. In 1963, the administration of John F. Kennedy agreed to sell the bases of five Hawk missiles, to the value of US$21.5 million. In the financial year of 1965–6 President Lyndon Johnson's administration gave Israel 650 M48 tanks and 48 adapted Skyhawk fighter jets and electronic communication equipment with artillery.[62] The agreements that were signed by the two parties on 19 May 1966, in particular that the US would provide Israel with A4 Skyhawks and Sherman tanks, are thought to be the first to focus on American shipments of weapons since the inception of the state of Israel.[63]

The United States took the side of Israel during the 1967 and 1973 wars. During the six-day war of June 1967, the US pledged that it would intervene to support Israel if the balance of power was seen to be tipping in the favour of the Arabs. However, that did not happen because Israel was able to secure a clear victory. After a ceasefire was agreed, the US worked to compensate Israel for its losses, and took a defensive position towards Israel in the UN, most notably in the Security Council. Furthermore, the United States also set up a communications aerial in order to support Israel in the Ramadan/October 1973 war. Israel would not have been able to make up for its own losses itself, which were estimated at $8 billion (valued according to the prices of 1973) if it weren't for the foreign financial aid it received, especially from the US, which gave Israel no less than $3 billion. Following the October 1973 war the Nixon administration sent a US airlift of weapons and supplies to Israel. Starting on 14 October 1973 US Air Force 'Operation Nickel Grass' flew resupply missions to Israel for a full month. As a direct result of the Yom Kippur war, the US quadrupled its foreign aid to Israel, and replaced France as Israel's largest arms supplier.[64] The US financial aid then was approximately $2 billion per annum[65] until it reached $3 billion per annum after the Camp David Accord, divided into $1.2 billion in economic assistance and $1.8 billion in military aid. In exchange for Israel's signing the Camp David Accords, the US pledged to sell Israel the weapons that it wanted in 1978 and to shoulder much of the burden of Israel's new 'security bulwark', which was estimated at roughly $5 billion dollars, $2.3 billion of which was paid by the US in 1979.[66]

The US depended on Israel to implement its Middle East security strategy in order to block the Soviet Union and to subjugate the Middle Eastern countries to American control. Successive US administrations since Truman, who adopted the containment policy based on the idea of establishing military alliances between the US and the West on the one hand and the states that surrounded the Soviet Union (Atlantic alliance, Baghdad alliance, Southeast

Asia alliance) on the other, saw Israel as their most viable ally. The containment policy lasted until Nixon was sworn to the Oval Office. He initiated a new doctrine of relying on regional states to implement America's policies to protect Western interests. The Nixon administration's support to Israel did not prevent the rise of differences between them over the Israeli nuclear programme which cast a shadow over talks between Richard Nixon and Golda Meir. It is alleged that 'there is circumstantial evidence that some fissionable material available for Israel's weapons development was illegally obtained from the US about 1965'. Kissinger noted: 'this is one programme on which the Israelis have persistently deceived us' and 'may even stolen from us'.[67] Avner Cohen argued that 'there was then enough evidence to indicate that the President (Nixon) and the Prime Minister (Golda Meir) had reached a secret understanding on at least one issue: Israel would keep its nuclear devices out of sight and not test them, and the US would tolerate the situation and not press Israel to sign the NPT'.[68]

It has been argued that Israel became the main means for the US to achieve its goals in the Middle East, proving its value in the five wars against the Arabs.[69] On 30 November 1981, Israel's Defence Minister Sharon and the US Defense Secretary Weinberger signed in Washington a memorandum of understanding on strategic cooperation.[70] The alliance between the two sides culminated in the signing of a strategic cooperation agreement at the end of November 1983. The scope of the accord was extended to cover the Gulf sub-region. The agreement came about after the Lebanon war which affirmed Israel's role as a regional military power and inspired a US policy to increase and enhance Israel military power. Article 9 of the agreement, reached between Yitzhak Shamir and Ronald Reagan, pledged the following:

1. To extend financial support to fund Israel's security needs until after 1985 and transferring all military aid that the United States provided to Israel as a donation, which reached US$1.4 billion between 1984 and 1985. It also promised to increase financial aid from $910 million to $1.4 billion in the financial year of 1985.
2. To provide industrial military support to Israel. Israel was allowed to use $550 million of military financial aid to develop production of Israel Lavi jets; it also paved the way for American arms dealers to buy Israeli weapons worth $200 million.[71]

The close partnership between the US and Israel has yielded leading military technologies such as the Arrow anti-ballistic missile defence system that is currently deployed in Israel. Jointly developed by the two allies, the Arrow is among the world's most sophisticated missile shields.[72]

The close cooperation between the United States and Israel can not be interpreted only from the perspective of US national interests because the Arab states represent a huge potential market for US investment, products, commodities and services, surpassed only by the purchasing power of the Jews, both in Israel and the entire world. It is expected that whilst the number of Arabs will reach more than 395 million by the year 2015, the number of Jews in the world will not exceed 15 million by the same year. The Arab states possess strategic and vital resources, most importantly oil, and constitute an important market for American products. The Arab states enjoy geostrategic importance as they control a number of straits and are located close to the former Soviet Union.[73] US–Israeli cooperation 'fundamentally goes back to the increasing role of Zionism in US politics since 1956'.[74] The Zionist movement was able to manipulate and pressure US Congress to stop the Maverick missiles deal with Saudi Arabia on 11 June 1987.

Israel's cooperation with the Zionist lobby in the US is aimed at maintaining excellent ties between the US and Israel and preventing any Arab regime or party from representing a potential alternative to Israel to act on America's behalf. The US Public/General Accountancy Office issued a report on 24 June 1983 saying that the sales of US weapons to any Arab state were met most of the time with sales to Israel or an increase in the amount of military aid to compensate it, on the 'basis of its security needs'. The report indicated that the selling of AWACS jets and the improvements to the F-15 jets to Saudi Arabia also led to an increase in military aid to Israel estimated at $400 million – Israel received fifteen F-15 and F-16 jets in 1978 in return for agreeing to allow the US to sell to Saudi Arabia sixty F-15 jets and Egypt fifty F-15 jets in the same year.[75] A similar approach was adopted in 2007 to allow the $20 billion arms deal with the Gulf States.

The role of the Zionist lobby in the United States did not end with the establishment of Israel; it is still apparent in its influence on elections in the US and in the keenness of successive US candidates to reiterate their commitment to preserving Israel's security and stability. The Zionist lobby acts vigorously to influence any development in the US–Arab states relations, especially those related to weapons sales or the peace process. The US Senate agreed to a resolution to prohibit selling to Saudi Arabia sixty sophisticated F-15 jets but agreed to sell to it sixty old F-16 jets. The US government had announced its intention to sell twelve F-15 jets to Saudi Arabia in a deal worth $500 million; however, the Zionist lobby objected to this as a threat to Israel's security.[76] On the other hand, Israel received the first instalment of a deal including thirty-four F-16 DI jets, which were the most sophisticated at that time, and three jets of this kind touched down on 22 December 1987 at one of the air bases in occupied Palestine.[77] On 16 October 1986 the US Congress also agreed to grant Israel a donation of $3 billion.[78] Furthermore, on 17 February 1987, US President Ronald Reagan signed legislation giving Israel the privileges of a NATO member state. despite it not being one.[79] Israel was the first country to sign a free trade agreement with the US, which resulted in a quintupling of trade between the two countries. The US–Israel Free Trade Agreement (FTA) has served as a model for other trade agreements, including the October 2000 FTA between the US and Jordan.[80] The US did not hesitate to block international initiatives or moves to bring the Arab–Israeli conflict to a final settlement. This was evident in its use of, or threat to use, the veto power at the Security Council to block any criticism of Israel's oppressive and discriminatory practices against the Palestinians in the occupied territories.[81]

In the period of the US–Soviet cold war, a series of peace proposals to the settlements of the Arab–Israeli conflict was one of the main tools to win over the support of some parties and to maintain their own interests. The international arena witnessed many proposals and counter-proposals from the Soviet Union and the United States towards a peaceful settlement of the Arab–Israeli conflict. On 20 June 1967, the United States presented a proposal to the General Assembly to counter a Soviet proposal. What distinguished the US proposal was its rejection of the idea of unconditional Israeli withdrawal. It called for the holding of direct negotiations between the Arabs and Israel. The most prominent features of the proposal were as follows:

1. The conflicting parties must agree to cease all hostilities against each other.
2. The concerned parties must decide that their goal is to seek permanent and ongoing peace negotiation in the Middle East.
3. The conflicting parties must see that this goal can be achieved only through arrangements that have been negotiated with the help of a suitable third party based on the following:
    a. Mutual recognition of political independence and regional sovereignty of all states in the region;

b. Freedom of navigation of waterways;

c. A just solution to the refugees' problem;

d. Limiting and registering weapons shipment to the region and limiting it;

e. Recognizing the rights of all states to sovereignty and the right to peaceful coexistence.

4. The US calls on the international community and the UNSC to continue monitoring regional developments.[82]

In this proposal, it is noticeable that the US has completely ignored the Palestinian national right to self-determination and to establish an independent state. Moreover, the US proposal treats the Palestinian problem as that of refugees, not as a nation that has been displaced and driven out of its land. It is also clear that the proposal was aimed to guarantee Israel's right to exist as an independent state on Palestinian land as well as its right to use the waterways under Arab control. Furthermore, the US proposal overlooked the issue of Jerusalem.

The US decision after the second Gulf crisis to open direct talks with the PLO, call for the Madrid International Conference, and host rounds of peace talks does not represent a fundamental shift in US foreign policy since the move is handicapped by the influence of the Zionist lobby in the US. The US perception of the conflict does not disagree with that of the Israeli government. The US policy towards Middle East peace after the second Gulf crisis and the acceptance of an International Peace Conference did not prevent the US from channelling the outcomes to suit its national interests as the only superpower. Israel's objectives in the post-cold war era are: to solve its border conflict and form a security belt within the peace process; to conclude the process of regional integration and recognition as a legitimate and equal state; to gain diplomatic flexibility in manipulating the inter-state conflicts of Middle Eastern countries; to exploit the resources of the region and introduce multi-country projects with the support of the international Jewish community; to open up Asia and then to develop its diplomatic and economic relations with more southern states; to create a sphere of influence in the Greater Middle East; to have an influential global presence.[83] The US mediatory role is not impartial and always takes the side of Israel. The two-states solution initiative adopted by George W. Bush signals the first fundamental change but due to the September 11 attacks on the US, Bush Junior became hostage to right-wing fundamentalists and his war on terror. Bush's eight years in the White House failed to produce any concrete solution to the conflict. Barack Obama, who was voted in as US President on a drive for change, embarked on a series of procedures to pursue a more independent course of foreign policy towards the conflict (see Chapter 6).

6. European Union Policies

The Western European countries from the 1960s came to hold mixed views towards the Arab–Israeli conflict. On the one hand, Charles de Gaulle of France on 27 November 1967 condemned Israel's six-day war for its subsequent occupation of Arab territories in Jordan, Syria and Egypt, and subjugation of local populations. De Gaulle's words would prove keenly prophetic as he predicted that Israel could not carry out a long-term occupation 'without oppression, repression, expulsions and resistance, which Israel, in its turn, calls terrorism'.[84] France since De Gaulle has disassociated itself from the US policy towards the Middle East and particularly on issues related to the Arab–Israeli conflict. On the other hand, countries like the Netherlands in particular have pursued a supportive stand towards Israel. Other European countries adopted a more neutral position. As a result of the complexity of Western European interests in the Arab world, some countries worked towards separating their policies towards the Arab–Israeli conflict from that of the US. France prompted other members of the European Economic Community (EEC) to adopt a positive policy towards the conflict. France's efforts paid off as a secret statement was issued in May 1971 by the second meeting of European foreign ministers – the first attempt by the EEC to adopt a joint position towards the Arab–Israeli conflict, in which European states called for:

1. Israeli withdrawal from all territories that it occupied in 1967 with possible minor modifications;
2. Preserving regional security and stability of every country in the region, by establishing demilitarized zones where UN-affiliated troops are stationed;
3. Internationalization of Jerusalem;
4. Solving the problem of the Palestinian refugees, either by adhering to their right to return or by compensating them under the auspices of an international commission.[85]

The European communiqué did not call for a peaceful settlement to the conflict. However, the European need for 60 per cent of the world's oil consumption and the effects of the Arab decision to carry out an oil embargo during the October 1973 war against those countries supporting Israel in the war led the EEC member states to issue another statement, the Brussels Declaration, on 6 November 1973 in which it called for the Israeli withdrawal in line with the 22 October 1973 ceasefire, just as Egypt was demanding.[86] The EEC expressed its willingness to take part in the peace process, acknowledged the importance of international guarantees and suggested having demilitarized zones. Israel objected to the statement and considered it foreign intervention at a very critical time. However, it did accept the European role in the peace process and acknowledged the fundamental importance of international assurances, which Israel has previously denied, along with the legitimate rights of the Palestinian people.[87]

As a result of the bilateral role played by the Arab states in pressuring the European countries to take a clearer stand in the Arab–Israeli conflict, the EEC, which held an important summit in London in June 1977, issued a communiqué that read: 'The nine member states of the EEC believe that there cannot be a solution to the Arab–Israeli conflict unless the Palestinian people can translate their legitimate rights for national identity through the establishment of a homeland.' This was considered a shift within the EEC attitude, from a refugee problem to a political problem, emphasizing the importance of national identity which should be translated into a homeland.[88] The EU has a strong record in support of the Palestinian cause. The EU financial contribution in the period 1994 to 1999 amounted to €6.1 billion. This represented 60 per cent of international financial assistance, in addition to the €100 million annual contribution to the United Nations Relief and Works Agency (UNRWA).[89]

Despite the Arab-European dialogue being over by the end of 1978, Arab states continued to pressure Western European countries to take a clear stand regarding the Palestinian rights to self-determination and to establish an independent Palestinian state. As a result of the fact that the EEC became aware of the importance of preserving its ties with the Arab world, it released another statement known as the Venice Declaration on 13 June 1980:[90]

1. The heads of state and government and the ministers of foreign affairs held a comprehensive exchange of views on all aspects of the present situation in the Middle East, including the state of negotiations resulting from the agreements signed between Egypt and Israel in March 1979. They agreed that growing tensions affecting this region constitute a serious danger and

render a comprehensive solution to the Israeli–Arab conflict more necessary and pressing than ever.

2. The nine member states of the European Community consider that the traditional ties and common interests which link Europe to the Middle East oblige them to play a special role and now require them to work in a more concrete way towards peace.

3. In this regard, the nine countries of the community base themselves on (UN) Security Council resolutions 242 and 338 and the positions which they have expressed on several occasions, notably in their declarations of 29 June 1977, 10 September 1970, 26 March and 18 June 1979, as well as in the speech made on their behalf on 25 September 1979 by the Irish minister of foreign affairs at the 34th UN General Assembly.

4. On the bases thus set out, the time has come to promote the recognition and implementation of the two principles universally accepted by the international community: the right to existence and to security of all the states in the region, including Israel, and justice for all the peoples, which implies the recognition of the legitimate rights of the Palestinian people.

5. All of the countries in the area are entitled to live in peace within secure, recognized and guaranteed borders. The necessary guarantees for a peace settlement should be provided by the UN by a decision of the Security Council and, if necessary, on the basis of other mutually agreed procedures. The nine declare that they are prepared to participate within the framework of a comprehensive settlement in a system of concrete and binding international guarantees, including (guarantees) on the ground.

6. A just solution must finally be found to the Palestinian problem, which is not simply one of refugees. The Palestinian people, which are conscious of existing as such, must be placed in a position, by an appropriate process defined within the framework of the comprehensive peace settlement, to exercise fully its right to self-determination.

7. The achievement of these objectives requires the involvement and support of all the parties concerned in the peace settlement which the nine are endeavouring to promote in keeping with the principles formulated in the declaration referred to above. These principles apply to all the parties concerned, and thus to the Palestinian people, and to the PLO, which will have to be associated with the negotiations.

8. The nine recognize the special importance of the role played by the question of Jerusalem for all the parties concerned. The nine stress that they will not accept any unilateral initiative designed to change the status of Jerusalem and that any agreement on the city's status should guarantee freedom of access for everyone to the holy places.
9. The nine stress the need for Israel to put an end to the territorial occupation which it has maintained since the conflict of 1967, as it has done for part of Sinai. They are deeply convinced that the Israeli settlements constitute a serious obstacle to the peace process in the Middle East. The nine consider that these settlements, as well as modifications in population and property in the occupied Arab territories, are illegal under international law.
10. Concerned as they are to put an end to violence, the nine consider that only the renunciation of force or the threatened use of force by all the parties can create a climate of confidence in the area, and constitute a basic element for a comprehensive settlement of the conflict in the Middle East.
11. The nine have decided to make the necessary contacts with all the parties concerned. The objective of these contacts would be to ascertain the position of the various parties with respect to the principles set out in this declaration and in the light of the results of this consultation process to determine the form which such an initiative on their part could take.

The EU member states have gradually shifted their attitudes and policies towards the Arab–Israeli conflict. They began to take a positive standpoint with respect to the Arab–Israeli conflict, shifting towards the position of the former Soviet Union and Arab states in calling for an international conference on the Middle East to find a peaceful and comprehensive solution to the conflict. On a visit to Algeria on 23 March 1988, German Foreign Minister Hans Dietrich Genscher said that his country and the member states of the EU supported the idea of holding an international conference on the issue of the Middle East and that the Palestinian problem was the core issue. This standpoint differs from the longstanding US position, until 1991, which supported Israel in calling for direct negotiations between it and the Arab states involved in the conflict. The European standpoint also differs from the US in its view of the PLO, and the right of the Palestinian nation for self-determination and the establishment of an independent homeland. This difference between the United States and its European allies can be attributed to the political culture of the European states and their realization of the importance to preserve historical and economic links with the Arab world. On 10 March 1988, the European Parliament condemned the oppressive practices carried out by the Israeli forces in the occupied territories and expressed its solidarity with families of the victims and with the Palestinians of the region, 'who are living in conditions that cannot be tolerated'. The EEC voted on a resolution that condemned 'torture practices, tyrannical arrests and operations of expulsion'. It highlighted the need to hold an international conference on the Middle East with the PLO taking part. On 9 March 1988, the European Parliament, with a significant majority, had also rejected giving 'the green light to the free trade and financial agreements reached with Israel' by the European Economic Community. Israel announced that it was shocked and disappointed with the European parliament's rejection of the three agreements. The then Israeli Minister of Agriculture said, 'It is strange that the European parliament is mixing politics and economic issues.' Claude Cheysson, the EEC's Commissioner, said, 'The entire world should acknowledge the fact that the Palestinian people chose the PLO to represent it; just as the Israelis have the right to their state in which they live, the Palestinians have a right to an independent Palestinian state.' It is argued that the roadmap peace proposal advocated by the US was initially a European initiative introduced during the German Foreign Minister's visit in July 2001 to Israel.[91] During the Marseille conference 16–17 November 2000, the European ministers reaffirmed their adherence to the achievement of a just and comprehensive peace in the Middle East on the bases of international legitimacy, resolutions 242, 338 and 425 and the Madrid Conference.[92] The EU opposed the construction of the Israeli Wall separation fence, and collectively voted for the freeze in its construction. On 28 October 2002 the Commission approved €29 million in support of Palestinian reform efforts and in response to the deteriorating situation on the ground.[93] The European ministers reiterated the EU commitment in their Munich conference on 7 February 2004. The twenty-five-member EU Council of Ministers at the end of the meeting in Brussels on 30 January 2006 stated that it would not yet be halting its financial aid to a Hamas-led Palestinian government, giving more time to the winner of Palestinian elections to renounce violence and recognize Israel.[94] The EU released in February 2006 financial aid to the Palestinians to avert a looming crisis.[95] The EU member states in 2006 made a political decision to halt high-level discussions until Hamas renounced violence and accepted the right of Israel to exist. Hamas is also listed on the EU's register of terrorist groups, putting a legal block on financial assistance.[96] But the European Union has resumed direct financial aid to the Palestinian government of Palestinian Authority Chairman Mahmoud Abbas of Fateh.[97] The EU urged Israel to halt its unilateral aggression against the Gaza Strip in December 2008/January 2009. EU foreign policy chief Javier Solana said the Israeli attacks were 'inflicting an unacceptable toll on Palestinian civilians and will only worsen the humanitarian crisis as well as complicate the search for a peaceful solution'.[98]

7. The Attitudes and Policies of the Developing Countries

The Zionist movement looks at the developing countries as the future for the young Israeli generations, according to Levi Eshkol. This goal was further reaffirmed by David Ben Gurion: 'The economic future of Israel and its international situation depends on its links that Israel is working towards establishing with Africa and Asia.'[99] The Arabs with the leadership of Nasser's Egypt succeeded in containing Israel, forcing it out of any Third World collective or joint projects. Zionists were disappointed that Israel wasn't made a member of the Non-Aligned Movement after the Bandung conference in April 1955. As a result, Israel's diplomacy towards the developing world was intensified. Senior Israeli officials embarked on visits to many Asian and African countries. Israeli Prime Minister Moshe Sharett visited Burma, the Philippines, Japan, Hong Kong, Singapore, Malaysia, Ceylon, India, Nepal, Thailand, Laos and Cambodia between September and December 1956. Between January and February 1962 Golda Meir also visited Japan, the Philippines, Hong Kong, Thailand, Burma and Cambodia. In March 1957 the then Foreign Minister Abba Eban visited Thailand, Burma, Singapore, Cambodia and the Philippines. As for Israeli–Chinese ties, despite Israel's *de jure* recognition of the People's Republic of China on 9 January 1950 and attempts to establish diplomatic ties, especially in the period before 1955, there was no progress. The Chinese attitude was shaped by many factors including the eruption of the Korea war, the West's continued support of Taiwan as the only legal representative of the Chinese people, fear of US domination of the Middle East and the Soviet influence. China had 'initially regarded Israel as a country which had gained independence from the clutches of western colonialism after a bitter national liberation war'.[100] However, it took sides in favour of the Arab position. It allowed the PLO to open an office in Peking in 1965 and provided it with weapons as well as military training for some of its members. After the Cultural Revolution bilateral relations with Israel began to thaw. Development of relations was very slow but there was a rapid growth in unofficial exchanges between China and Israel. There was cooperation in science and technology, specifically in agriculture, irrigation, chemicals, medicine, aeronautics, military and other high-tech fields. Diplomatic relations were not established until 1991.

It is argued that 'the problem was the continued hostility between Israel and the Arab world despite the peace treaty between Egypt and Israel'.[101]

Chinese–Israeli relations witnessed new positive developments from the 1980s and were strengthened in the 1990s. The two sides exchanged visits by senior dignitaries, signed bilateral agreements and embarked on military cooperation, including the sale of Israeli advanced military equipment despite US objections. In 1990, the office of the China International Travel Service in Tel Aviv and the liaison office of the Israeli Academy of Sciences and Humanities in Beijing were set up, marking a significant breakthrough towards normalizing bilateral relations. In 1991, staffers of these offices changed their business passports to diplomatic passports, both offices started to issue visas and the volume of contacts increased. On 25 January 1992 China and Israel raised their diplomatic relations to ambassadorial level.[102]

The new developments in Chinese–Israeli relations came about for different reasons, including domestic changes in the Chinese political system and the new leadership's perception of world politics in general and the Middle East in particular, the collapse of the Soviet Union, the Chinese desire to strengthen its ties with the US and the potential role Israel could play in this, the outcome of the second Gulf crisis and changes in the contemporary world order, the increase in the number of countries that have diplomatic relations with Israel and the unlikeliness of Arab retaliation due to the changing political climate in the Arab world and the dominance of moderate Arab states who have no objection to the development of Chinese–Israeli relations, the start of the peace process, the Chinese desire to acquire American technology from Israel to modernize its military capability, and China's desire to accommodate Israel to weaken the Indian–Israeli axis.

In spite of the fact that India officially recognized Israel in 1950, its strong historic ties with the Arab world prevented it from establishing diplomatic ties with Israel. India's Nehruvian policies kept India and Israel politically apart for over forty years. Indian–Israeli relations are determined by multiple factors. In the era of Gamal Abdel Nasser, Egypt–India relations played a prominent role in distancing India from Israel. Moreover, India's desire to join the Non-Aligned Movement, which would require the approval and support of the Arab states, pushed the Indian government to strive towards supporting the legitimate rights of Arabs and to take sides against the Israeli settlements policy and Israel's repeated aggression, atrocities and ethnic cleansing against the Palestinians. A further factor that shaped India's policy towards the conflict was its fear of antagonizing its Muslim minority, which made up 12 per cent of the entire population. However, the collapse of the Soviet Union and increasing concerns over the rise of Islamic extremism in the Indian subcontinent convinced India to change its position. On 29 January 1992, full diplomatic ties between the two were established and since then bilateral relations have grown steadily, despite Indian attempts to keep this flourishing relationship out of public view.[103] During the tenure of the Hindu nationalist Bhartiya Janata Party (BJP) between 1998 and 2004, relations between India and Israel blossomed. Ariel Sharon in 2003 made the first ever visit by a ruling Israeli prime minister to India. Relations have continued since the Indian National Congress (INC) came to power in 2004. By 2008, bilateral trade between India and Israel exceeded US$4 billion and Israel was India's second-largest military supplier after Russia. By 2008, India had bought more than US$5 billion worth of Israeli equipment since 2002. In addition, Israel is training Indian military units and discussing an arrangement to give Indian commandos instruction in counter-terrorist tactics and urban warfare. There is also growing space cooperation between the two. In February 2008, the Indian Space Research Organization (ISRO) launched an Israeli spy satellite to monitor the activities of Iran. The Indian Secretary of Defence Vijay Singh paid a visit in November 2008 to Israel. He discussed security-related purchases, including three Phalcon aircraft radar systems, manufactured by Israel Aerospace Industries, as well as missiles, helicopters, maintenance, equipment and unmanned aerial vehicles.[104] It was expected that Israel would overtake Russia as the largest arms supplier to India, which it did in 2009.[105]

The Indian attitude was inspired by other factors including the absence of Arab objections, the conclusion of peace treaties between Israel and Egypt, Jordan and the PLO, the nuclear power acquired by India's rival Pakistan, India's desire to improve relations with the US through the manipulation of the US–Israel special relations, India's desire to modernize its military capabilities through cooperation with the Israeli military establishment, Indian political rivalry with China, India's fight against terrorism using Israeli expertise and the exchange of intelligence and secret information about Islamic fundamentalist groups.

On the other hand, despite the diplomatic success that Israel achieved during the 1980s and 1990s, today Israel has had few breakthroughs, apart from China, India and some Asian countries (Burma, Japan and the Philippines). Israel's efforts towards Central Asian countries are promising as the country aims to create a sphere of influence there.[106] However, most of the developing countries maintain a pro-Arab/Palestinian stand. Israel failed to enlist the support of the Asian countries in the General Assembly of the UN and failed to acquire membership to the UN Council of Human Rights. Moreover, Israeli attempts to establish diplomatic relations with most of the Islamic countries – Indonesia, Malaysia, Bangladesh, Pakistan and Afghanistan – proved to be in vain.

Africa is another part of the developing world where Israel has sought to acquire an influential place. Israel's African policy seems to have been more successful and it managed to gain a foothold in some African countries like Ethiopia, Ghana, Uganda and Tanzania. It adopted a more defensive policy towards Africa after its application for membership of the Non-Aligned Movement in 1955 was overwhelmingly rejected. The Zionist movement showed a particular interest in Africa as early as the late nineteenth century. This was clear in the statements made by a number of Israeli leaders. Theodor Herzl said, 'I am not ashamed to say, though I may expose myself to ridicule for saying so, that once I have witnessed the redemption of my people, the Jews, I wish also to assist in the redemption of the Africans.'[107] After the state of Israel was established, Herzl's vision of the outside world influenced Israeli foreign policy-making and Africa became one of Israel's main targets. In this regard, former Israeli Prime Minister Sharett said, 'Africa, in our view, is an important sphere and we do not want to start a vacuum there after its countries achieve independence because to have this vacuum filled by an unfriendly force is considered a setback for us.'[108]

Israel's interest in Africa was crystallized in the establishment of a specialized apparatus to monitor and develop relations between Israel and Africa. The Israeli government formed a number of specialized departments, including the African Department at the Foreign Ministry, the Economic and the International Cooperation Department and the Media and Culture Department, and it established a special agency to monitor the Zionist activities in Africa. For example, there is a department within the Ministry of Defence whose duty is to monitor Zionist military activity and another in the Ministry of Agriculture intended to monitor Zionist agricultural activity. Israel did not overlook the cultural aspect as it encouraged its universities to open different schools and departments to study the culture, languages and the political, economic and social conditions in Africa.

After the 1973 war the twenty Latin American countries began to show greater interest in the Arab–Israeli conflict. Israeli concerns with Latin American states centre around political, economic and demographic factors. Confronted with various economic and financial repercussions of the Arab oil embargo and the rise of the Palestinian problem, 'the Latin American countries have for the first time been forced to replace a non-committal approach by one involving serious decision-making'.[109] The accession to power by the socialist parties in many Latin American countries led some of them to gravitate more towards supporting the Arab position in the conflict. Venezuela adopted the strongest reaction to the Gaza offensive by any country with ties to Israel.[110] On 6 January 2009 Venezuela decided to break off its diplomatic relations with Israel in protest and informed its ambassador in writing that he and his diplomatic staff were persona non grata and must leave Venezuela within seventy-two hours. President Hugo Chavez called the Israeli attacks on Gaza a Palestinian 'holocaust'.[111]

Israel's interests in developing countries can be summarized in the following points:

1. To win over public opinion in those countries and to enlist as much support as possible from these countries in the international conferences and assemblies.
2. To break up the isolation imposed by the Arab states on Israel in the developing world, especially during the era of Gamal Abdel Nasser. This goal was clear in Abba Eban's statement following his tour of Africa in 1979 when he said: 'We will work towards flying Israel's flag in hundreds of capitals and we will work towards creating an international presence for Israel in all continents of the world.'[112]
3. Realizing a strategic security doctrine for Israel which aims at threatening the social and nutritional security of Arab states that depend on the water of the Nile, increasing its own influence in Ethiopia, for example; securing safe passage at the mouths of the Red Sea that lead to Israel; influencing the economies of Arab states by exporting its products to compete in the African markets and encouraging African countries to cultivate resources that they usually import from Arab countries.
4. Consolidating the importance of Israel to Western countries, most prominently the United States, in its capacity as a strategic ally, in implementing its colonialist and monopolistic plans in the developing countries.
5. To ensure open formal communication channels with the Jewish communities living in Africa that according to Golda Meir 'will determine, to a large extent, the ties between Israel and the countries in which these communities live'.[113]
6. To break up the Islamic solidarity with the developing countries, manifested in the Non-Aligned Movement and in the financial and political

support that the Islamic states usually allocate to aid the less fortunate countries. Israel's objective is to lessen the support for Palestinian legitimate rights for self-determination in the developing world and to weaken the collective approach in the international organizations, most prominently the United Nations.

7. To open up the vast markets of the developing countries to Israeli manufactured goods and products.

8. The Role of the United Nations

The main objective of the United Nations, as envisaged in the Charter, is to secure world peace and stability. The Arab–Israeli conflict presents a serious challenge to this goal. Despite the reservations voiced by both parties on the impartiality of the UN, it could be safely argued that the UN has dedicated part of its mission to bring the warring parties to an agreement that would secure the national interests of both parties. The UN involvement in the conflict goes back to the UN Partition Plan on 26 November 1947, as the General Assembly issued a resolution that stated the following:

1. The Mandate for Palestine shall terminate as soon as possible but in any case no later than 1 August 1948.
2. The British armed forces shall be progressively withdrawn from Palestine.
3. Independent Arab and Jewish States and the Special International Regime for the City of Jerusalem shall come into existence in Palestine two months after the evacuation of the British armed forces.
4. The period between the adoption by the General Assembly of its recommendations on the question of Palestine and the establishment of the independent Arab and Jewish states shall be a transitional period.

On 29 November 1947 the UN Resolution 181 was issued, calling for the partition of Palestine. The resolution was seen by the Arabs as unfair, giving 5,700 square miles of Palestinian land to the Jews despite the fact that they did not make up more than a third of the population whilst giving the Arabs 4,300 square miles. The resolution allocated the fertile and coastal area of Palestine to the Jews. It also stated that Jerusalem would be an international city.

After the state of Israel was established and the Arab–Israeli conflict entered a new phase, Count Folke Bernadotte was appointed as the international mediator to spare no effort in improving relations between the Jews and the Arabs and achieving a peaceful settlement to the conflict. His proposal included the following points:

1. Shifting from a ceasefire to achieving a permanent truce, or peace, between the Jews and the Arabs.
2. The City of Jerusalem will be placed under the control of the UN.
3. An international commission from the UN will be given the duty of demarcating the frontiers between the Arabs and the Jews.
4. An international commission will solve the problem of the refugees so that the refugees will have the choice to return or receive compensation.
5. The UN will call for forming an international follow-up and reconciliatory committee to reach a peaceful settlement.

Despite the assassination of Count Bernadotte, the UN General Assembly on 1 December 1948 issued another resolution, number 194, which called for the following:

1. To establish a Conciliation Commission consisting of three member states of the United Nations to assume the functions given to the United Nations Mediator or carry out the specific functions and such additional functions and directives as may be given to it by the General Assembly or by the Security Council; and to develop good ties between Israel, the Palestinians and the Arab states.
2. To place the City of Jerusalem, in accordance with the Partition Plan, under the control of the United Nations.
3. To resolve the refugees' problem through giving them the right to choose between the return to their homes and live in peace, or accept compensation that should be paid for the property of those choosing not to return and for loss of or damage to the property, under principles of international law.

The UN Chief Mediator Ralph Bunche, who succeeded Count Bernadotte, was able to achieve an armistice agreement between Egypt and Israel, which led to the convening of the Rhodes Conference. In the framework of this conference, indirect negotiations between the Arabs and Israel were held for the first time, which led on 3 April 1949 to the signing of armistice agreements between Egypt, Lebanon, Syria and Jordan on the one hand and Israel on the other.[114]

As a result of the June 1967 war, the UN Security Council issued Resolutions 233, 234, 235 and 236 that called on the warring parties to agree to a ceasefire and to hold peaceful negotiations to settle the existing conflict between them. On 22 November 1967, the Security Council issued Resolution 242 in which it expressed its continuing concern regarding the grave situation in the Middle East. It

1. Affirms that the fulfilment of the Charter requires the establishment of a just and lasting peace in the Middle East which should include the application of the following principles:
    a. Withdrawal of Israeli armed forces from territories occupied in the recent conflict;
    b. Termination of all claims or states of belligerency and respect for and acknowledgement of the sovereignty, territorial integrity and political independence of every state in the region and their right to live in peace within secure and recognized boundaries free from threats or acts of force.
2. Affirms further the necessity:
    a. For guaranteeing freedom of navigation through international waterways in the area;
    b. For achieving a just settlement of the refugees' problem;
    c. For guaranteeing the territorial inviolability and political independence of every state in the region through measures including the establishment of demilitarized zones.
3. Requests the Secretary General to designate a Special Representative to proceed to the Middle East to establish and maintain contacts with the states concerned in order to promote agreement and assist efforts to achieve a peaceful and accepted settlement in accordance with the provisions and principles in this resolution.
4. Requests the Secretary General to report to the Security Council on the progress of the efforts of the Special Representative as soon as possible.

A new representative, Dr Gunnar Yaring, was appointed as a mediator two days after the resolution was issued, but the international efforts failed. Syria rejected the resolution and refused to receive Yaring.[115] The PLO, Algeria, and Iraq also rejected UN Resolution 242 whilst Egypt and Jordan accepted it. However, the UN continued to play a role through its different agencies concerned with the issue.

After the October 1973 war erupted, the US and the Soviet Union contacted one another and presented a joint proposal to the Security Council calling for the warring parties to cease all fire. All members of the Security Council, with the exception of China, which abstained from voting, agreed to the US–Soviet resolution proposal on 22 October 1973. It came to be known as Resolution 338. It [116]

1. Calls upon all parties to the present fighting to cease all firing and terminate all military activity immediately, no later than 12 hours after the moment of the adoption of this decision, in the position they now occupy;
2. Calls upon the parties concerned to start immediately after the cease-fire the implementation of Security Council resolution 242 (1967) in all of its parts;
3. Decides that, immediately and concurrently with the cease-fire, negotiations shall start between the parties concerned under appropriate auspices aimed at establishing a just and durable peace in the Middle East.

Egypt, Syria, Jordan and Israel approved Resolution 338 and pledged to respect it. However, Israel did not adhere to it in practice as it mobilized its forces and attacked Egyptian territories, which led to the issuing of Security Council Resolution 339, which came to affirm Resolution 338 (for more details see Chapter 6).

9. Conclusion

The study reveals that the international variable has been significant in the development of the Arab–Israeli conflict. It played a determining factor in changing the Arab states' attitudes and policies towards the conflict. It acquired importance after the June 1967 war. However, the conflict became more internationalized with the October 1973 war after the Arabs decided to use oil as a strategic weapon. The Arab oil embargo inspired a clear shift in the foreign policy undertakings of many world countries, including the European countries, Japan and the Latin American states. The cold war between the superpowers led to greater polarization of the conflict, with each power taking sides in supporting the warring parties. The US and the Soviet Union hold different perspectives on peace in the Middle East, with different interests and alliances with the conflicting parties. For example, whilst the former Soviet Union called for holding an international conference in which all parties would participate, including the PLO and Israel as well as the United Nations, the United States called for direct negotiations between Israel and the Arab parties. It excluded the PLO and requested that there be a Palestinian delegation as part of one of the Arab delegations like Jordan.

The second Gulf crisis and the decline of the Soviet Union inspired tremendous changes in the contemporary world order. These prompted the world powers to show greater interest in the settlement of the conflict through the peace process, culminating in the convention of the first international peace conference held in Madrid and the conclusion of the Oslo Pact between the Israelis and the Palestinians, and another peace accord between Israel and Jordan with US sponsorship. The Madrid International Peace Conference initiated a number of multinational committees to iron out the differences between the warring parties. A Quartet Committee, consisting of the UN, the US, the EU and Russia, has been set up and the US presented a number of proposals for a peaceful settlement of the conflict, including the roadmap and finally the two-states solution initiative.

The changes of regimes in some Arab countries, particularly Egypt, would have an effect on the balance of power between the Arab states and Israel. Democractic governments accountable to the people would have no option but to pursue a more independent course of foreign policy representative of the peoples' aspirations. A democratic government would transfer the Egyptian foreign policy from a conservative orientation dependent on the US to a more independent course with Arab issues at its centre. Egypt regaining its central role in Arab politics would be more supportive for the Palestinian cause and would play a more active role in the Middle East peace process on the basis of land for peace and the two-states solution based on the UN 242 and 338 resolutions. Egypt was quick to warn Israel during the March 2011 incident not to escalate its aggression against Gaza.

Part Two

THE OUTPUT: CASE STUDIES

Chapter 6

Arab States' Policies towards the Middle East Peace Process

1. Introduction

The Middle East acquired importance in world politics with the foundation of the state of Israel. International calls for peace go back to 1929 in the early days of the Palestinian dispossession of their homeland. However, the peace process, in the early 1990s, after the eruption of the second Gulf crisis with the Iraqi invasion of Kuwait, witnessed a breakthrough with the Palestinians and Israelis concluding a transitional peace accord and the signing of the Jordanian–Israeli peace treaty. The ongoing Syrian–Israeli peace negotiation, though facing some setbacks, is a success in itself.

This chapter suggests that the conclusion of peace accords between the two parties is no more than a temporary settlement. They will amount to nothing more than agreements for shaping future interactions, political, economic or security, between Israel and the Arab states, but will not signify permanent peace in the region. The conflict is based on religious, traditional, historical and ideological struggle. Peace requires the transfer from conflict culture to peace culture. Nevertheless, the peace process represents a fundamental change in the Arab states' foreign policies. The purpose of this chapter is to analyse and investigate the different variables that led to changes in both Arabs and Israeli perspectives and to examine the durability of the ongoing peace accords.

This chapter focuses mainly on the dynamics of the peace process, leaving the other variables of the conflict to be discussed elsewhere in the book. It relies on analytical and inductive[1] approaches in order to understand the reality of unbalanced negotiation between the Arabs and Israel and the future of negotiations in the region.

2. The Peace Initiatives

The Palestinians, choosing the path of resistance, manipulated all means at their disposal, whether military or political, including suicide attacks, hijacking, homemade light ammunitions, Arab support, linkage politics, international platforms and the mass media, to make their case known. They have succeeded in rallying not only Arab or Muslim, but world public opinion behind their cause. The revolution in information technology helped the Palestinians to enlist worldwide support, resulting in more pressure on world governments to bring about a peaceful settlement. For different reasons, the Palestinian question began to acquire importance on the regional and international levels. Consequently, domestic pressure culminated in the introduction of a number of regional and international peace initiatives to end the Arab–Israeli conflict. The most important of these initiatives include the following.

Arab Peace Initiatives

Arab initiatives were based on the philosophy that there will never be a just and permanent peace[2] in the Middle East unless the Palestinians are given the right to self-determination and an independent Palestinian state has been established in accordance with UN Resolutions 242 and 338. A number of Arab states have put forward proposals to bring about a peaceful settlement[3] to the Arab–Israeli conflict. Tunisian President al-Habib Bourguiba presented two peace initiatives, on 21 April 1965 and in July 1973. The most important article of the first initiative was that Israel must return a third of the land that it had occupied since May 1948 so that an Arab Palestinian state could be established. In the second initiative, Bourguiba suggested that Israel accept the idea of partition for Palestine in accordance with UN Resolution 181 issued in 1947 to establish a Palestinian state along with the Israeli state. In 1972, King Hussein of Jordan presented the idea of a united Arab kingdom that would encompass the West and the East Banks.[4] The Jordanian initiative, however, did not address the Palestinian right to self-determination and considered Palestinian territories as part of the united Arab kingdom. This led to Palestinian rejection of the initiative.

The Arab Summit conference held in Morocco on 6 September 1982 adopted the Fez Initiative, also known as the King Fahd Initiative, and later as the Saudi Initiative, backed by the Gulf Cooperation Council member states. The most important articles of this initiative included:

1. Israeli withdrawal from all lands occupied in the June 1967 war including Jerusalem, and the dismantling of Israeli settlements in these lands.
2. The establishment of an independent Palestinian state with Jerusalem as its capital.

All Arab states participating in the Fez Summit, including the PLO faction, accepted the Saudi Initiative. Israel, however, rejected the initiative, arguing that it was aimed at the gradual destruction of the Israeli state. Arab initiatives centred on the exchange of land for peace solution. Saudi Arabia seeking to play a regional coordinating role and to moderate the Arab position in the conflict introduced through King Abdullah, then Crown Prince, a new peace initiative to the Beirut Summit on 13 February 2002. The Saudi initiative won the approval of all Arab states and was reconfirmed during the Riyadh Summit in 2007. In their efforts for peace, the Arab states accepted the idea of an international peace conference on the Middle East that would give all parties in the conflict, including the PLO, the right to participate. The Doha Summit held 30–31 March 2009 reiterated Arab commitment to peaceful settlement with Israel on the principle of a land-for-peace deal that sees the establishment of a Palestinian state, but the peace offer will not last forever. In light of the surge in the 2009 election of the Israeli right it is less likely to accept a compromise with the Palestinians. With a new US administration in place, the Arabs want to look responsible and put the onus on Israelis to act on peace – or risk looking like the bad guys if they do not. US President Middle East envoy, George Mitchell, called on 17 April 2009 for an Arab peace initiative to be part of a planned US drive for a two-state solution.[5] President Obama's Middle East peace initiative, based on two-states solution, is not acceptable to the right-wing Israeli government.

All initiatives failed because Israel opposed the principle of the right to self-determination for the Palestinian people, despite all initiatives acknowledging Israel's right to exist whether explicitly or implicitly. There was always some kind of opposition to every initiative, whether from the Arab or the Jewish side. The Arab perception of peace as a strategic viable option represents a fundamental shift in the Arab position towards Israel.

Israeli Peace Initiatives

Israel on the other hand, which is adamant about not accepting the two-states solution and consistently refuses to withdraw from all the territories occupied in 1967, proposed a number of initiatives, each one more dictatorial than the last. Israel's peace initiatives centre on the principle of self-government, whilst attending to the security- and defence-related needs of Israeli authorities. On 8 October 1968, Abba Eban presented a peace plan to the United Nations. Eban explained that Israel's aim was to reach a certain position whereby holy sites would be given their international status by reaching suitable agreements with the concerned parties. In 1977, Menahem Begin's initiative was clearly harsher with regards to Jerusalem, considering it the capital of the Israeli state.

It is clear from reading the Israeli initiatives that Israel completely rejects the idea of an independent Palestinian state. In addition, it denied the right to belong to Palestine and called for Palestinians to have either Jordanian or Israeli citizenship. Despite Israel pledging that the Palestinians would enjoy equality in ownership and elections in the same way as Jewish Israelis, the reality on the ground contradicted this thesis; the Israelis practised discrimination and inequality against Jews of different ethnicities such as Ethiopian, Indian and Arab Jews, so what would the situation be like for Arabs who obtained Israeli citizenship? The Israeli initiatives were intended to present an obstacle to the peace process because they were biased in favour of Israel without giving anything of any value to the Palestinians.

Analysis of the Arab and Israeli initiatives reveal the differences in orientations and approaches of the two parties on how to achieve peace. On the one hand, it was apparent that the Arab initiatives were limited to the territories occupied by Israel in 1967 and accepting in principle the idea of a two-states solution. On the other hand, Israeli initiatives focused on direct negotiations between the Zionist entity and individual Arab states and the exchange of peace for security. However, all initiatives encountered domestic opposition on the regional level in both Arab states and Israel.

Successive Israeli governments have showed no flexibility in dealing with the Arabs in the peace process. Yitzhak Rabin was the first Israeli prime minister to engage in direct peace negotiations with Palestinians in 1993 and to conclude the Oslo Peace Accord. Rabin was assassinated by Israeli fundamentalists to prevent further concessions to the Palestinians, and the Oslo peace process failed to reach a final peaceful settlement to the Middle East problem. Israel accelerated its illegal annexation of East Jerusalem through municipal and security policies that discriminated against Palestinian residents. Moreover, the number of settlements has more than tripled and Israel has constructed a defensive concrete security fence annexing more of the Arab lands. It did not hesitate to invade Palestinian territories repeatedly, for example, with the twenty-two-day invasion of the Gaza Strip, in December 2008–January 2009, which left more than 1,300 people dead. After this, two Arab states, Mauritania and Qatar, decided to freeze relations with Israel.[6] The UN Human Rights Council special envoy to the occupied territories, Richard Paul, described the Israeli invasion, in his report on 30 March 2009, as a crime against humanity and the Palestinian resistance as self-defence and legitimate.[7]

At the same time, newly elected Prime Minister Benjamin Netanyahu, in his inaugural address to the Knesset on 31 March 2009, pledged to make every effort possible to achieve peace with Israel's neighbours and the Arab world. He said that he wanted to focus on shoring up the Palestinian economy rather than on territorial issues that have blocked progress in negotiations that are currently frozen. Netanyahu said: 'we are talking about a dramatic, painful and heart-wrenching compromise, but one that is necessary'. However, he shied away from a direct commitment to the establishment of a Palestinian state alongside Israel. The new Israeli Foreign Minister, Avigdor Lieberman, went further by saying that Israel is not bound to conduct negotiations on a final settlement with the Palestinians, as agreed at a 2007 conference in Annapolis, adding that the Israeli Knesset had never adopted Annapolis. 'We will go exactly according to the roadmap.'[8] Lieberman sees the realization of comprehensive peace with Palestinians as unrealistic. He believes that issues like Jerusalem and the right to return for Palestinian refugees could not be compromised on or accepted by the Israelis.[9] Palestinian officials have said peacemaking stands no chance without an explicit Israeli commitment to statehood. Ehud Olmert, the former Israeli Prime Minister, urged Netanyahu to endorse clearly the creation of a state in the West Bank and the Gaza Strip: 'Two states for two people. There is no alternative. They are trying to be too clever about it.'

Washington vowed to pursue the peace process vigorously. President Obama reiterated his administration's commitment; he said that peace efforts with a Netanyahu-led government were not getting any 'easier', but they were 'just as necessary'. He added: 'it is critical for us to advance a two-state solution where Israelis and Palestinians can live side by side in their own states with peace and security.'[10] Obama and Netanyahu differed publicly on the issue during the latter's visit to Washington in May 2009.

Other initiatives were presented by the United States of America, the United Nations, Europe and the former Soviet Union. I will briefly address the most important US- and the UN-sponsored initiatives due to their importance in the peace process between the Arabs and the Israelis at present.

UN Peace Initiatives

The UN has tried to reach a peaceful settlement to the Arab–Israeli conflict through a number of UN resolutions. In November 1947 the General Assembly voted on Resolution 181 partitioning Palestine into two states, Jewish and Arab. The resolution was unfair, giving the Jews 56.47 per cent of Palestinian land when they only owned 5.6 per cent of the land, and the Arabs were given 43.53 per cent[11]. On 15 September 1948, Count Folke Bernadotte presented a proposal for the Arab–Israeli conflict in which he called for the return of Negev to the Arab state as well as the Arab state's inclusion of Jerusalem. In April/May 1949, the Lausanne Treaty was signed under the auspices of the UN Conciliation Commission for Palestine. A map of Palestine delineated according to the General Assembly's Resolution 181 agreement was attached to the agreement (see Chapter 5).

In the period 1951–2, the issue appeared on the General Assembly's agenda as the 'UNRWA Annual Report of the Director from Palestine'. In 1974, after the Ramadan war of 1973 and the use of oil as a strategic weapon for the first time, the Palestinian question regained a new prominent status. Israel's attack on Arab states in June 1967, extending its occupation to new Arab lands, led the Security Council to issue Resolution 242, calling on Israel to withdraw from lands occupied in the six-day war. The Security Council, after the outbreak of the October war in 1973, called for warring factions to cease all fire and reiterated its position through Resolution 338 calling on Israel to withdraw from all lands occupied in 1967. Egypt, Syria, Jordan and Israel all agreed to the resolution and promised to respect it, but Israel failed to adhere to it in practice as it mobilized its forces and attacked Egyptian territories. The Security Council responded by issuing Resolution 339 to reaffirm Resolution 338[12] and Resolution 425 calling on Israel to evacuate southern Lebanon. In a further development, the Security Council, on 16 December 2008, passed Resolution 1450 by fourteen members, with Libya abstaining, calling for a more active role for the Council. Although it represented a change in the approach of US policy towards the Middle East peace process by accepting an international involvement through the United Nations, it did not reaffirm the international community's commitment to enforcing previous international Resolutions 242 or 338, nor did it endorse the Arab peace initiative. The resolution did not deal with the Jewish settlements in the 1967 occupied territories and gave no time frame for the establishment of the Palestinian state. It is argued that the resolution was intended to clean up the record of George W. Bush administration in its last days in office and was intended to force the parties involved, including the new US administration, to pursue the peace process on the basis of the Annapolis understanding.[13] In a further development, the UN Secretary General Ban Ki-Moon visited the Gaza Strip to witness the destruction and devastation caused by the twenty-two-day Israeli invasion in December 2008 and January 2009. The UN appointed Richard Goldstone as head of the fact-finding committee in the Gaza Strip.[14]

The preceding analysis reveals that Western influence left the UN peace initiatives paralysed and biased in favour of Israel. Perhaps the biggest weakness of these UN initiatives is, on the one hand, the lack of the Palestinian participation. On the other hand, achieving a sustainable peace requires action and not words. Moreover, another negative aspect in the UN initiatives is that they deal with the Palestinian question on the basis of achieving a fair settlement to the refugee problem, forgetting that the core of the conflict is land occupation and dispossession of the indigenous population.

As for other efforts that were exerted for a peaceful settlement to the issue, the United States played a predominant role. It presented a number of initiatives, the most important of which was the initiative of President George H. Bush, which culminated in the Madrid Conference for Peace followed by the Oslo Accords and the Jordanian–Israeli Agreement, the two-states solution and US sponsorship of Syrian–Israeli negotiations.

US Peace Initiatives

The US strategy in the Middle East revolves around the necessity to achieve peace and to integrate Israel in a Middle Eastern regional security system. Israel's security occupies top priority for American foreign policy and has been the main channel to gaining political and economic support from Israeli lobbies in the US.[15] The Arab–Israeli conflict constitutes one of the most important aspects of US foreign policy in the Middle East. Successive American governments presented a number of projects for peaceful settlement in the Middle East. On 20 January 1967, the US presented a peace project to the General Assembly, rejecting the unconditional Israeli withdrawal, and called for direct negotiations to be held between Arab states and Israel. President Richard Nixon in September 1969, after his meeting with the Israeli premier Golda Meir, described the situation by saying 'the problems in the Middle East go back centuries. They are not susceptible to easy solution. We do not expect them to be susceptible to instant diplomacy.'[16] On the other hand, the United States, as a mediator, played a significant role in concluding the Camp David

Accords in 1979. The most important outcomes of the Camp David Accords were the neutralizing of Egypt in the conflict and the remote possibility of an Arab coalition launching a unilateral war against Israel, let alone an individual Arab state declaring war against Israel.[17] 'After the hostilities between Egypt and Israel came to an end, in accordance with the Camp David Accords, the balance of military power shifted in favour of Israel's interest.'[18] Ronald Reagan, after becoming US president, introduced, on 2 September 1982, a new peace initiative for the Arab–Israeli conflict:

1. The United States would not support the establishment of an independent Palestinian state in the West Bank and the Gaza Strip.
2. The United States would not support Israeli sovereignty or permanent control over the West Bank and the Gaza Strip.
3. The United States calls for an autonomy rule and self-governing by the Palestinians of the West Bank and Gaza in association with Jordan.
4. The United States remains convinced that Jerusalem must remain undivided, but its final status should be decided through negotiations.
5. America's commitment to the security of Israel is ironclad. The United States will oppose any proposal from any party and at any point in the negotiating process that threatens Israel's security.

However, none of the concerned parties accepted the Reagan Plan, including Israel; it was also criticized by Moscow Radio which warned against the encroachment of the legitimate rights of the Palestinian nation. It is worth mentioning that the Reagan initiative did not differ in essence from the Israeli initiatives. On the one hand, it rejected the idea of an independent Palestinian state and, on the other hand, it did not make any mention of the status of Jerusalem. In spirit and essence it was clearly biased towards Israel.

Reagan's initiative was not the first US proposal not to have been implemented. Since the 1967 war, American involvement in the Middle East produced a series of peace initiatives that were intended to block any international consensus against Israel and to delegitimize Palestinian resistance. One example of this was the plan presented by US Secretary of State, George Schultz, which did not offer the Palestinians much more than self-government, and repeated the calls that were made by the Camp David Accords for bilateral talks to be held to determine the issue of sovereignty in the West Bank. Moreover, the initiative did not attempt to find a permanent settlement to the conflict but to achieve other goals, the most important of which were:

1. To suppress the Palestinian Intifada and to stop it from spreading to the region and therefore maintaining the status quo in accordance with American interests.
2. To be in agreement with the demands of American public opinion and the requirements of American policy.
3. To enhance US hegemony of the Middle East.

None of the main parties of the conflict took the initiative seriously, neither the Arab states, even those who enjoyed friendly ties with the US, nor the Palestinians nor the Israeli 'aggressors'. Jordan, for example, realized that any temporary settlement proposing self-government instead of the right to self-determination would be a settlement destined to fail, especially after the Intifada. The Israeli Prime Minister, Yitzhak Shamir, who rejected any settlement based on the principle of land for peace, declared that the only acceptable part of the plan was Schultz's signature.

The Schultz initiative was not the last, US Presidents George H. Bush, Bill Clinton, George W. Bush and Barack Obama have all had their inputs and put forward peace plans to bring the Middle East crisis to a final end. President George H. Bush proposed an international peace conference. President Bill Clinton opted to support a more active US role in the Middle East peace process. The Clinton administration, however, was faced with a broad agenda and a number of difficult challenges, as well as a serious risk to the future of the region and American interests there. Bill Clinton was keen to seize the opportunity and stated:

> We cannot impose a solution on the Middle East. Only the leaders of the region can do. There is an awesome responsibility. Those who oppose the process, who seek to subvert it through violence and intimidation, will find no tolerance here for their methods. But those who are willing to make peace will find, in me and my administration, a full partner. This is an historic moment. It can slip away all too easily. But if we seize the opportunity, we can begin now to construct a peaceful Middle East for future generations.'[19]

In his policies, Clinton focused on the need for bilateral negotiations between Israel and the Arab factions, without having to resort to direct intervention unless it was needed to save the negotiations from collapsing. George W. Bush, despite his unconditional support for Israel and being influenced by his neoconservative aids and his campaign on what he called the 'war on terror' in retaliation for the 9/11 attack on the US, sponsored in 2003 the 'Roadmap' as an international peace plan under which Israel bound itself to the principle of a Palestinian state. The plan calls on Israel and the Palestinian to take a series of steps, among them a freeze on Jewish settlement activity in the occupied West Bank and an end to violence, eventually leading to a final peace deal.[20] In a further step on 29 August 2007, in a letter to Saudi Crown Prince Abdullah, George W. Bush was the first to talk about a two-states initiative.[21] The US, in 2007, hosted a peace conference at Annapolis, Maryland, that relaunched peace negotiations on the basis of the roadmap. The harsh tone reflected the increasing isolation of Hamas, with the Arab states, including Syria, a patron of Hamas, having chosen to participate in the Annapolis meeting.[22] The conference ended with no peace deal and spoke of the necessity to continue bilateral negotiations between the Palestinians and Israel to reach an agreement on the final status on the basis of the roadmap plan. The conference avoided the discussion of the most sensitive issues, namely, Jerusalem, the Jewish settlements, the right to return for the Palestinian refugees in accordance with Security Council Resolution 195, and the establishment of the independent Palestinian state, but reaffirmed that Israel is the national homeland for the Jews.[23] Dozens of rounds of talks between the two sides have produced little visible progress. Eight years in the White House were not enough for George W. Bush to fulfil his objectives and to put his initiative in place to end sixty years of struggle and to achieve regional peace and security. President Barack Obama appointed, from his first day in office, Senator George Mitchell as US special envoy to the region. Obama said the step signalled that 'we are going to be serious from day one in trying to move the parties towards two-states solutions'.[24] Hillary Clinton, the US Secretary of State, during her visit to Ankara in March 2009, said her visit 'had focused on Turkey's role in the Middle East peacemaking, particularly in mediating between Syria and Israel'.[25]

The above analyses of US peace initiatives reveal that US policies centred on preserving Israel's security, even if they were not presented as such. It is a clear manifestation of the US–Israel strategic alliance and US double standard policy in the Middle East. Washington acknowledges that the only way to reach a sustained peace in the Middle East would be through linking US aid to Israel to Israeli withdrawal from the 1967 occupied Arab lands and dismantling all Israeli settlements in these territories apart from those agreed upon in bilateral agreements.[26] Richard Paul, the UN Human Rights special envoy to the occupied territories, said that the US should use its $3 billion in annual aid to Israel to pressure the latter to concede to the international community demands to reach a sustained peaceful settlement to the conflict.[27]

As already noted, the United States played an important role in pressuring the Gorbachev government to change migration laws in the Soviet Union. In his speech at Texas A&M University on 12 May 1989, President Bush expressed his country's willingness to give the Soviet Union the 'most-favored-nation' trade status on the condition that Moscow changed its migration laws to be in accordance with international norms.[28] Even though the Soviet Union was not given this status, on 2 June 1991, President Bush froze trade restrictions imposed on the Soviet Union through the Jackson–Vanik amendment[29] for another year so that the Soviet Union would relax migration policies.[30]

The Soviet Peace Initiatives

Some of the most important proposals by the Soviet Union for a peaceful settlement in the Middle East included the project it presented to the United Nations on 19 June 1967 and the Brezhnev initiative which was announced at the Twenty-Sixth Communist Party conference. In June 1967 the Soviet Union presented a peaceful settlement proposal to the UN General Assembly that called for:

1. Stopping Israeli aggression and withdrawing from occupied Arab territories.
2. Immediate and unconditional Israeli withdrawal from the lands it occupied during the six-day war in accordance with the delineated borders of the truce.
3. Israel entirely repairing all the damage it caused to the citizens of the three Arab countries that it attacked.
4. The Security Council pledging to take effective and immediate measures to eliminate the effects of Israel's occupation.

The Brezhnev initiative called for an international conference to be attended by all parties involved in the conflict, including the PLO and Israel, as well as the Soviet Union, the United States, some western countries and the United Nations. The Soviet proposal suggested:

1. Calling for holding an international peace conference to be attended by all parties including the PLO.
2. Israeli withdrawal from all territories occupied in 1967.
3. Emphasizing the Palestinian right to self-determination and the establishment of an independent state on its own land.
4. Guaranteeing security and sovereignty to the regional states and their right to peaceful coexistence.
5. Cooperation between the US and the Soviet Union and western states and whoever wants to contribute to guaranteeing permanent, just and lasting peace in the Middle East.[31]

The Brezhnev plan was met with different reactions from the conflicting parties. Israel rejected it and some Arab states supported it, especially Syria and the PLO, whilst others were hesitant.

The Soviet policies towards the Middle East shifted away from a military strategy, the principle of a balance of power between the Arabs and Israel. It became an advocate of a policy of peaceful coexistence and the principle of a balance of interests between the two sides. Accordingly, the Soviet Union imposed new restrictions on weapons exports to Arab states, particularly Syria, which relied on the Soviets for armaments. It did not hesitate to call on the PLO to change its position and policies towards Israel to be accepted in any future settlement.[32] The inevitable result of these shifts was an increase in American influence in the region while Soviet influence dwindled.[33] The collapse of the Soviet Union had a huge impact on the Middle East and led to long-term changes whereby the Arabs, as Shimon Peres stated, no longer had a source for arms and the political support they received declined.[34] 'The Soviet Union enemy that supports Israel's Arab enemies is gone and has been replaced by a democratic Russia that supports the peace processes.'[35]

3. Peace Negotiations

International and regional developments since August 1990 formed a turning point in the Arab–Israeli conflict. Peace agreements and negotiations between the Arabs and Israel, launched since the Madrid Peace Conference in 1991, were considered a natural outcome of the overwhelming impact the second Gulf crisis had upon the region. The talks also clearly reflected the important changes that took place within the realm of international relations – most notably the collapse of the Eastern bloc and the disintegration of the Soviet empire.[36] In addition, Islamic resurgence pushed both the Arabs and Israel to opt for peace instead of military confrontation as it began to pose a threat to Arab governments' legitimacy and Israel's existence in the region. It is embodied in the Hamas and the Islamic Jihad movements in Palestine and Islamic resistance, represented by Hezbollah, in South Lebanon. The domestic situation in America and the global economic crisis forced the US to review its global policies, including the Middle East. The US could no longer afford to continue endlessly being the guarantor of Israel. For this reason, the US sought to protect Israel from Arab threats and guarantee its stability through peaceful settlement and normalization of relations with its Arab neighbours. This would provide Israeli security at the least cost since it would no longer require direct US intervention.

The collapse of Iraq brought by the American invasion in 2003 left the region's balance of power in favour of Israel. Arab military power had weakened whilst Israel maintained its overwhelming conventional and non-conventional forces. The PLO, who took the side of Iraq during the second Gulf crisis, felt that the Arabs were not serious in their calls for regaining the occupied territories. The ultimate conclusion of the PLO was that it was left with no choice but to enter into direct negotiations with Israel, hoping to achieve some concessions before it was too late. The Arab states, divided between those who chose to ally themselves with the US and states unable to confront US pressure, helped to channel the negotiations properly and to push them to reach a successful end. Therefore, concluding peace agreements between Israel and the PLO and Jordan would not have been possible had it not been for previous international and regional changes.

First, the Arabs became more affected by the changes in the Soviet Union engineered by Mikhail Gorbachev. During his meeting with Jimmy Carter in July 1987,[37] Gorbachev stated that the Soviet Union had abandoned its foreign policies towards the Middle East and had begun to accept America's vital interests in the region as a reality. He added that the Soviet Union would refrain from destabilizing those interests and hoped in retrospect to occupy a similar position in the US Middle Eastern strategy. Externally, this policy reflected a détente between the two superpowers; however, internally it reflected the Soviet Union's abandonment of its supportive policy of the Arabs and prepared for a change in Soviet policy towards Israel. The new Soviet policy culminated in immigration of more than 1.2 million people to Israel. It was estimated that, by 2025, the Arabs in Palestine would make up two-thirds of the population. The migration of Soviet Jews to Israel froze the effect that demographic trends had on the conflict for a longer period. On one hand, the number of Jews in Palestine increased, forcing more competition in the labour market between Palestine workers and the newcomers, causing further economic hardship for the Arabs. On the other hand, the new wave of migrants forced more Palestinians to leave the occupied territories. Moreover, Soviet migration helped to consolidate the military; the Zionist government was able to increase its number of soldiers and reserves at the same time.

Second, the emergence of a uni-polar international order, as already discussed, caused the Arabs to lose the ability to manœuvre as they had during the cold war. The United States, Israel's main ally, dominated interaction in the international system, and bullied its allies and adversaries through its stick and carrot policy. Therefore, it was both enemy and referee with regards to the peace process in the Middle East. America's regional objectives can be summarized as: ensuring Israel security, guaranteeing the free flow of oil and fighting Islamic ideology.

In order to achieve these goals the United States followed a number of policies. It flexed its muscles through the existence of its military fleets in the Indian Ocean and established a number of military bases such as the US military base in Diego Garcia in the Indian Ocean and in a number of US-allied Arab states including Qatar. It used force, just as it did during the Gulf crisis; it provided military and financial aid, reached security agreements and sold weapons to the allied states. The US strengthened the dependency of these countries upon it through economic and trade relations, particularly Egypt. Despite the multiplicity of policies, the US realized that the Middle East would be one of the most destabilized regions in the world as long as there was no peace between the Arabs and Israel. Bush Senior's administration sought to exploit the weaknesses and divisions among the Arab states (following the second Gulf crisis) and to invest in its own increased influence. The US sought to strengthen itself internationally by pursuing its national interests without having to continuously shoulder the burden of financial and military expenses. Moreover, it absolved itself of the belief that it followed double standards and it accepted land for peace. The George H. Bush initiative led to the Madrid Conference for Peace in the Middle East in October 1991. The Bush Junior peace initiative was the first American initiative to acknowledge the idea of a two-state solution. President Obama showed an interest from his early days in office in bringing about a peaceful settlement on the basis of a two-state solution.

Third, the Gulf crisis had several other implications that helped George H. Bush's initiative to be realized, most prominently that a number of Arab states allied with the United States changed their position towards Israel. It contributed to the alienation of PLO as a result of its decision to side with Iraq after it occupied Kuwait and an imbalance of power in the region occurred as a result of the Soviet Union's dwindling influence, the increase of American influence, the loss of Arab marginal manœuvring, and the shift in Israel's favour after the destruction of Iraqi forces led to neutralizing Arab states opposed to the unbalanced peace process after Iraq began to suffer from the international blockade. Moreover, the United States fabricated new international crises with Arab rejectionist countries such as Libya and Sudan. Similarly, the Iraqi invasion of Kuwait destroyed the concept of pan-Arabism and strengthened the idea of state interests as a priority over pan-Arab interests, forcing the Arabs to become more inclined to accept a peace initiative than ever before. A number of Arab governments became less reluctant to cross the cultural red lines establishing formal contacts with Israel. The first Gulf war caused further inter-Arab cleavage. 'Arab unity, the strongest bond shaping the Arabs attitude towards the Arab–Israeli conflict, became paralysed and could no longer carry out its role, paving the way for numerous dangerous divisions among Arab states.'[38] Regional developments show that the Arabs became more divided, with the conservative axis consisting of Egypt, Saudi Arabia, Morocco and Jordan opting to ally with the US against the reluctant axis including Syria, Libya, Sudan and suspicious Qatar backed by Iran, a non-Arab regional power.

Arab parties to the peace negotiations joined the peace process rounds in a complete state of chaos as they had experienced two great historical shocks: the collapse of the Soviet Union and the Iraqi invasion of Kuwait. Ghassan Salama attributed the resort to peace negotiations to the following reasons:[39]

1. The American success for the first time in two decades in consolidating the equation of Arab absence of ability and Israeli absence of willingness.
2. America's astonishing victory in the cold war. The Middle East contributed to speeding up the West's decisive victory.
3. America's readiness to intervene directly in the Middle East.

4. Peace Agreements

The peace negotiations launched since the Madrid Conference have opened the road for Israel to conclude peace agreements with the PLO and another one with Jordan while carrying out indirect peace talks with Syria.

The Egyptian–Israeli Peace Treaty

Egypt and Israel chose to sign a peace treaty in 1979 with American sponsorship. The first peace agreement between Israel and any Arab country signed by Egypt was known as the Camp David Agreement. Since the signing, the treaty was faced with opposition from both sides, Arabs as well as Jews. Two members of Israeli Prime Minister Menahem Begin's cabinet and the Egyptian Foreign Minister, Ismail Fahmi, resigned in protest at the signing of the Accords. In addition the two countries continue to witness ongoing internal discontent and opposition to the Accords. Anwar Sadat, the Egyptian President who signed on Egypt's behalf, paid with his life for supporting it. President Hosni Mubarak, despite his twenty-eight years in office, has so far refused to pay a visit to Israel. However, though severely and repeatedly strained, the deal has come to be taken for granted as a linchpin of the fragile Middle East order. On the other hand, thirty years after signing a peace treaty, Egypt and Israel are only frosty friends. The peace treaty has always had its critics. Nowadays sceptics on both sides are no longer seen as marginal or fanatics. The hawkish right-wing Israeli government of Benjamin Netanyahu includes Avigdor Lieberman as its foreign minister. He holds public anti-Egyptian views. Inside Egypt, opponents have mounted a surprisingly effective campaign to challenge the countries' main commercial agreement signed in 2005. It committed Egypt to export natural gas to Israel. Critics have won court rulings in their favour. Analysts believe that neither Israelis nor Egyptians desire a return to war, but 'as Egypt's regime may be nearing a change at the helm and Israel lose hope of ever gaining acceptance in the Arab world, the cold peace between them may drift towards something more like a cold war'.[40] Despite claims from the Military Supreme Council of Egypt, in power since the success of the January 2011 revolution, to adhere to all regional and international agreements including the Camp David Accord, this does not mean that a new Egypt would be more Arab-oriented.

The Palestinian–Israeli Peace Accord

The PLO and Israel, on 13 September 1993, signed a peace accord in Washington considered the beginning of the success of American efforts in achieving peace in the Middle East. It was officially called the Declaration of Principles. It outlined the general framework of upcoming agreements between the two sides and the timetable for implementing them. The agreement started with two letters of mutual recognition between the two sides. The agreement divides Palestine into four regions:[41]

1. The territories occupied since 1948 (currently the state of Israel according to international law). The agreement completely ignores these territories

and does not allude to the conditions of the Palestinians here or to the right of refugees who migrated from this area to return.

2. Greater Jerusalem that Israel seized in the June 1967 war and the sphere of its municipality that has continuously been expanded from that time. The agreement excluded this topic and left it to be decided at the negotiations for a final settlement. Israeli officials confirmed that the unification of the city that took place in 1967 was not up for negotiation regardless of the PLO leadership's proposals. This has been reiterated by all Israeli PMs ever since.
3. The Gaza Strip and Jericho would witness immediate Israeli withdrawal and become self-governing for five years until a final permanent settlement, on the future of the Palestinians, is reached.
4. The remaining parts of the West Bank could be classified as partially self-governing. The agreement reads that the settlements issue in the West Bank was not discussed and no restrictions have been imposed on settlements' expansion. On 24 September 1995, an agreement was reached regarding delegation of authorities in these areas. They witnessed a redeployment of occupying Israeli forces and the handing over of civil authorities – education, health, tourism, taxes and social affairs – to the Palestinian authority.

The agreement culminated in Israeli recognition of the PLO as the sole legitimate representative of the Palestinian people. However, the Declaration of Principles and the agreement on expanding self-government did not mention, in their articles or supplements, that Israel had accepted the idea of land for peace, leading eventually to the establishment of an independent Palestinian state. Moreover, the agreement handed over border security in the self-governing area to Israel as well as the security of the main roads. It gave the Israeli forces the right to intervene in the area when necessary.[42] The readings of the agreement's articles and supplements demonstrate its weakness and absurdity and the real gains that Israel achieved due to the imbalance of power between the conflicting parties. Apart from that, the seventh clause of the fifth supplement of the Declaration of Principles states that military withdrawal would not prevent Israel from exercising its authority and carrying out its responsibilities in fields transferred to the Palestinians. Furthermore, important and sensitive matters of mutual importance for both sides were delayed for future negotiations. They included: the status of Jerusalem, the refugees issue, the settlements, borders and security arrangements, ties and cooperation, and cooperation with neighbouring countries. The fifth supplement of the Declaration of Principles alludes to the continuation of guaranteeing Israel the responsibility for external and internal security and law and order. The Israeli military and civilians maintained a free hand to use all roads in Gaza and Jericho. It is argued that surrendering Gaza and Jericho was not a loss for Israel; on the contrary, it showed Israel's motives for withdrawing from Gaza and Jericho, as they present Israel with serious challenges and problems. According to Peres,[43]

> We do not have the means to rescue Gaza from its difficult conditions: overpopulation, poverty, and refugees, and we don't have any self-interest in running the life of Gaza's people or being responsible for preserving law and order in its crowded, dirty streets. Our control of Gaza was a continuous, great error and I regretted that we established settlements there.

Shimon Peres added that he assured Rabin that 'the concept of Gaza firstly will completely serve Israel's interests, as the majority of the Israelis wanted to leave the Gaza Strip which is overcrowded and plagued by violence'.[44]

Despite local, regional and international praise for the agreement that expanded the Palestinian self-rule to include 31 per cent of the occupied West Bank area, and regardless of the compromise being reached regarding the city of Hebron and the postponement of the issues of the Sanctuary of Abraham and the Old City, the agreement fell short, being in favour of Israel instead of being a real step towards the anticipated establishment of a Palestinian state. The Palestinian Authority today controls no more than half the actual Palestinian land designated by the UN as the occupied Arab land in June 1967. The proposed Palestinian state would be divided into two detached parts and the West Bank would have no outlet to the sea. Through the agreement, Israel had achieved real gains, especially through the letter of recognition that was sent by Yasser Arafat, on 9 September 1983, to Yitzhak Rabin before the agreement was concluded. The letter stated that the PLO officially recognized Israel's right to exist in peace and within secured borders, that the PLO accepted Security Council Resolutions 242 and 338 and would adhere to the peace process and desist from terrorist acts, and pledged to prevent violence and punish the offenders. The letter further stated that the PLO would revoke fundamental clauses of the Palestinian National Charter that denied Israel's right to exist and other contradictory clauses as well as commitments in the charter that are considered 'ineffective and dated'.[45] It is, however, worth mentioning here that the Palestinian National Council never met to approve the agreement. A thorough reading of the agreement demonstrates that:

1. The agreement took place outside the framework of the Palestinian constitution. It was not presented to the legislative bodies in the Palestinian National Council and the Palestinian Central Council and it did not obtain consensus within the executive committee, which did not have the authority to decide. Rather, it was a secret agreement that crystallized outside the context of negotiations.

2. The agreement 'will redefine the Palestinian Cause' by transforming it from a nationalist and pan-Arab issue into a mere political issue regarding a minority that has rights and demands.

3. The fourth and fifth articles indicate that the Palestinian self-governing authority will encompass the West Bank and Gaza Strip except with respect to issues that would be negotiated in the future and these are: the status of Jerusalem, refugees, settlements, the borders and security arrangements, ties and cooperation with neighbouring countries and other issues that concern both parties. This agreement will raise questions over the fate of these issues.

4. The series of Palestinian–Israeli agreements that began with the Gaza–Jericho Agreement was not confined to the Arab nationalism of Arab generations whose main requirement was to eliminate settlements, which represented the direct antitheses of the Arab Renaissance. In reality, the PLO gave itself more liberty in dealing with the Palestinian issue and even though it had a clear nationalist dimension, it was one of the rights of the pan-Arab nation that has a wide religious and cultural depth transcending narrow national framework.

5. It was clear that, through secret negotiations and unilateral agreements, Israel was aiming to divide the Arabs, negotiating as one front, from one another and to dismantle the Arab cause by transforming it into individual conflicts and this is exactly what happened. The indications of this are clear in the lack of coordination among Arab negotiating teams, the weakening of their negotiation position and the sowing of seeds of discord between Arab parties themselves who often have conflicting interests, as demonstrated by the Palestinian reactions to the Jordanian–Israeli agreement which gave Jordan some religious rights in Jerusalem.

Therefore, a bilateral peaceful settlement was reached between an occupying state and a nation striving for self-determination, the practice of its legal rights and the exercise of sovereignty over its national territories. The fragile agreement, intended to end the Middle East conflict in a way that would not only ensure Israel's security, but launch the new Middle East Project[46] that had begun to be implemented,[47] paved the way for another, the Jordanian–Israeli Agreement.

The Jordanian–Israeli Peace Treaty

After the PLO signed a peace agreement with Israel came a window of opportunity for Jordan to pursue a unilateral course of peace talks with Israel. Jordan, for its own reasons, came to realize that it had no other option but to do the same. After it supported Iraq's invasion of Kuwait, Jordan wanted to regain America's support.[48] It also intended to obtain financial aid in order to pay off its debts and to stimulate the stagnant economy that had been declining since the Gulf war. In addition, it sought to secure its western borders with Israel and relieve itself of the irritating fears that Jordan would become the substitute homeland for the Palestinians. The fate of the Palestinian refugees was an issue that was excluded from the Palestinian–Israeli agreement, and could cause an imbalance in the demographic trends of Jordan. For all the above reasons, Jordan attempted to enter bilateral negotiations with Israel despite refusing to sign any agreement with Israel without coordinating with Syria and Lebanon. As a result, on 26 October 1994, a peace agreement between Jordan and Israel was concluded. It was the second peace agreement that Israel had signed with an Arab country since the Camp David Treaty in 1979.

The signing took place before tangible results were reached on the Syrian–Israeli and Lebanese–Israeli tracks and before negotiations were entered for a permanent settlement of the Palestine question. The agreement defined some of the Jordanian and Israeli demands; it stipulated restoring an area of around 380 square kilometres that Israel had occupied in 1967 in Wadi 'Araba and the highlands on the Jordanian side of 'Araba Valley in addition to a small area of land of five square kilometres that Israel had occupied in 1948 in north Jordan. Meanwhile, Israel began to wangle its way out of withdrawing from an area of 117 square kilometres in two areas: the first located in the Aqaba/Eilat triangle, which overlooks the Red Sea, and the second located south of the Dead Sea. Israel proposed exchanging the two areas for an equivalent area of Israeli land.[49] The articles of the agreement covered borders, security, diplomatic ties and bilateral relations, water, economic issues, refugees and displaced people, as well as issues related to places of historical and religious significance, civil aviation, the post, communications, tourism, health and agriculture. The treaty allocated a specific article for each topic, showing how interaction would take place between Jordan and Israel and the way they would be pursued.

It would be fair to say that Jordan succeeded in neutralizing its powerful and dangerous Israeli neighbour and managed to obtain an insurance policy from Israel that no more Palestinians would be deported to Jordan. As for Israel, it was successful in reducing the serious threats against it from the east that were always considered highly dangerous. Furthermore, Israel had managed to cut the ties between the inside circle of confrontational countries, and the outside circle, namely Iraq and Iran, which were the most dangerous. The long-run objective was to strengthen ties to reach successful strategic partnership.[50] The reactions, from both inside and outside of Jordan varied; there were those who supported it and those who opposed it and those who declined to express their views.

The Israeli–Syrian Negotiations

Since the negotiations started there has been no real progress because both parties have demands that are yet to be achieved. Developments on the Syrian–Israeli track would eventually lead to a new regional balance of power. There would be no real problem in signing a comprehensive deal that links complete Israeli withdrawal – as requested by Syria – with providing security and the normalization of ties demanded by Israel. However, the problem with this deal centres on the fact that Israel has not yet determined the scope and price it had to pay to achieve a settlement. The Israeli decision of complete withdrawal from the Golan Heights in that case would be a necessary step as a starting point for resolving the land for peace equation, which brings together the Syrian demand and Israeli goals. The point of contention lies in defining the aims and mechanisms of peace. For Syria, peace is based on the formula of land–peace–security whereas the Israeli view is based on peace–security–land. Israel looks at peace from a wider angle, beyond normalization of ties with Syria or even providing suitable security arrangements in the Golan Heights; the comprehensive deal for Israel includes all fronts and the shape of the region in the future.

Consequently, Israeli–Syrian negotiations entered a vicious circle because of partial solutions that Israel presents as a dire price for peace with Syria; whereas Syria focuses on complete withdrawal from the Golan Heights. Israeli proposals were rejected by Syria. They were intended for local consumption only, in an attempt to win over public opinion regionally and internationally to appear more flexible and improve its image. The difficulties that these negotiations face can be summarized in the following:

1. The lack of trust between the two sides. Whilst Israel questioned Syria's sincerity in normalizing ties, Syria was not convinced of Israel's genuineness about completely withdrawing from the Golan Heights.
2. Israel's belief that Syria is the most difficult partner in the negotiating peace process due to the latter's strategy based on rejecting any solutions that do not ensure complete withdrawal. Accordingly, the Israeli believe that the required price for achieving peace with Syria remains higher than what has been incurred on the Palestinian and Jordanian tracks. The Syrians offered less than others, causing Israel to refuse to give the Syrian track any relative advantage.

On the Israeli–Syrian negotiations track, Bashar Assad, the Syrian President, in an interview with a Japanese newspaper, expressed Syrian readiness to engage in direct negotiations with the American mediators. He said: 'we need the US to play a mediatory role when we move from the indirect talk to direct talk with Israel.'[51] Syria denied that a Syrian diplomat met privately with a high ranking Likud Party representative in Washington in February 2009. The Golan Heights, occupied since 1967, is pivotal to the settlement of the Syrian–Israeli conflict. For Israel the Golan is synonymous with national security, whereas for Damascus, the restoration of Syrian sovereignty is the single most critical act that would remove the stigma of the 1967 war and restore Syria's national pride.[52] It is of exceptional geostrategic value because it offers a commanding position overlooking southern Lebanon, the Golan Plateau, much of southern Syria and north Israel. The Golan is also important for its regional water source.[53] The Golan Heights, today, host more than 10,000 Arabs living in five villages and Jewish settlers are estimated at 15,000, living in more than thirty-five settlements. Syria cannot settle for anything less than a complete Israeli withdrawal to the pre-1967 border, transferring total sovereignty over the Golan to Syria.

Turkey opted to use its good offices and act as a facilitator by hosting indirect talks between the two parties. Hillary Clinton reaffirmed the importance of this track and added that Turkey has played a very important role.[54] Assad pointed out that the indirect negotiations sponsored by Turkey were intended to test the seriousness of the Israeli side. He added: 'we agreed to send our representative to Turkey to facilitate Turkey's role as a mediator.' It is argued that both sides have reached a breakthrough in the indirect negotiations and Ehud Olmert's visit to Ankara, a week before the Israeli invasion of

Gaza in December 2008, was intended to iron out the remaining differences. He promised to discuss the outcome with his government and come back with Knesset approval to move to the second stage, namely direct talks with Syria. However, instead of fulfilling his promises, Olmert chose to invade the Gaza Strip. The Turkish government felt that it had been betrayed by the Israeli Prime Minister Ehud Olmert. Consequently, Turkey strongly opposed the Israeli invasion of the Gaza Strip and Erdogan withdrew from the Dofus conference, on 29 January 2009, in protest against the speech by Shimon Peres and the coordinator's refusal to allow Erdogan enough time to give his comments. Syria, on the other hand, suspended the Turkish-mediated talks in protest against the Israeli invasion of the Gaza Strip, but Syrian officials have not ruled out their resumption, even with the right-wing government. Assad said: 'We will negotiate with any Israeli party in power whether left or right willing to adhere to the peace principles and conditions, namely the return of all the occupied land on the basis of Madrid conference land for peace and the UN Resolutions 242 and 338.'[55]

It is clear that Syria sought to negotiate by playing the zero-sum game. Syria considers time to be the most important factor in exerting pressure in the negotiation process. It is keen on reaching joint Arab security arrangements and ensuring a regional role for Syria as principles that cannot be compromised. As a result, the focus shifted to a security settlement within the framework of peace based on the equation of land for peace.[56] The negotiations would continue without a deadline, as both parties want to achieve specific goals. The continuation of negotiations with the Syrians is considered an achievement in itself. On the one hand, Syria won the respect of others without giving up anything to Israel. On 27 October 2009 Bashar Assad called for the resumption of the indirect negotiations between Syria and Israel.[57] On the other hand, the Syrian government hopes that endless negotiations will inevitably lead to differences of opinion between the US and Israel. For Israel, however, the continuation of negotiations is considered an expression of goodwill and is reflective of its desire to win support both internally and externally. Simultaneously, the process of ongoing negotiations neutralizes the military option between the two sides in the short term. It could be argued that a prolonged negotiation process does not imply in itself a negative effect upon Israel. To the contrary, some Israelis believe that Israel's procrastination will cause Syria to lose international support and will force it to make concessions in the interest of Israel.

5. Effects of the Peace Process

The emergence of the new Middle East structure was not the only outcome of changing world order and regional fluidity. The peace process has inspired other outcomes on the regional level such as:

1. Economic consequences can be seen in the rise in unemployment levels amongst Palestinians internally. It will lead to an increase in emigration from Palestine because of caps that have been placed on the Palestinian labour force and the imposing of a tax on their entry to ensure that no more Palestinian workers can enter Israel, paving the way for a bigger number of Jewish migrants to Palestine. Moreover, the Palestinian–Israeli agreement requires opening the Palestinian markets to Israeli products and guaranteeing the freedom of movement for commodities and free commercial trade between Israel and Jordan and the Palestinian autonomous territories. This would ultimately lead to primary Arab products competing with Israeli advanced products and inspire recession in the Palestinian market. Israel also insist on increasing and merging with the Jordanian market at a later stage. It is worth mentioning here that Israel has earned approximately $1 billion from the Gaza Strip and the West Bank markets.[58] In addition, the importance of the economic market of these three neighbouring and merging entities in what was known as the trilateral economic group, similar to the Benelux union,[59] will make the Palestinian and Jordanian markets subordinate to Israel, because Arab products are less competitive, Arab capital is weak and the Israeli market is limited. Meanwhile, Israeli products would enter the Arab markets disguised as Palestinian products since Israeli products will enter the Palestinian and Jordanian markets freely. It is worth mentioning here the different levels of industrial contribution to the GDP in Israel, Jordan and the West Bank and the Gaza Strip, which are 22, 13 and 7 per cent respectively. The agreement with the Arab states, Jordan and the Palestinian territories would promote the Israeli penetration of the Arab countries through joint projects on roads, power and economic cooperation.
2. Imposing the same price for water in the three countries without recognizing the current dangerous deficit in the process of water distribution (see Chapter 7).

3. Implementing Ben Gurion's strategy of non-Arab countries constricting the Arabs,[60] as the Greater Middle East is designed to do.[61] It is aimed at consolidating leadership of non-Arab countries, Turkey, Iran and Israel, of the new regional order. Israel domination of the new structure will be a fait accompli due to its military and technical superiority.

4. Substituting the Arab regional order with a larger regional system such as the Greater Middle East, the Mediterranean Basin and the Horn of Africa, all of which will be dominated by non-Arab countries. The permanent inter-Arab disputes are considered the main reason for the crisis of the regional Arab order which is attributed to the close political systems, absence of leadership, competition, jealousy and distrust among Arab regimes and the tribal heritage. Others suggest that all these are only symptoms and the real problem lies in the lack of real commitment to joint Arab cooperation.[62] Martin Indyk believes that the US must encourage restructuring the current system in the Middle East by transforming it from a system of balance of power between Israel and the Arabs to a system based to a large extent on the concepts of collective security.[63]

5. Consolidating locality as an antithesis to the prevailing current situation through the so-called state interests at the expense of pan-Arab regional interests. The Arab regional system is defined as a distinguished interactive framework between the Arab countries. This system is distinguished 'as a region with a high density of interaction, which makes a change in any part of it have an effect on the rest of it. This leads, perhaps implicitly, to the recognition of this system on the local, regional and international levels as a distinguished system.'[64]

6. Wealthy Arab countries will be obliged to provide financial support to the Palestinians and compensate Israel[65] because the implementation of the peace accords requires unlimited financial support. The West will expect Saudi Arabia and the oil-rich Arab states to provide the necessary funding at a time when these countries are suffering the most due to the global economic crisis and have no budgets or financial resources to do so. In the end, however, Arab states are obliged to pay the price for any Palestinian–Israeli peace agreement because they are aware of how important achieving peace is for regional political and economic prosperity.[66] On the other hand, they understand the importance of the link between Middle East peace and their regimes' security.

7. Strengthening the relationship between Israel and Arab countries in security fields and the exchanging of intelligence data.
8. Normalizing relations with Israel that would lead its embassies in Arab countries to become headquarters for the Israeli intelligence machine. It is argued that past experience reveals that Israel did not hesitate to spy on the US, its strategic ally, and on that basis Israel could easily do the same with the Arab countries, particularly since the Zionist movement realizes that a permanent peace would be almost impossible.
9. Dependence of Arab countries on the US will increase especially in the areas of security, defence and economic assistance, as illustrated in the concluding of several cooperation agreements in these fields.

On the other hand, peace agreements between Israel and the Arab countries do not necessarily mean that a shift away from the culture of conflict towards a culture of peace is taking place. The ideological, cultural and religious differences between the two parties threaten regional security and stability. The two ideologies are intrinsically against each other and the relations that exist between them represent a zero-sum game. They do not believe in coexistence between Israel as a state and the Arabs. According to the Islamic faith Jews have the right to live in Arab territories and to enjoy all the rights as Arab citizens, but not as a self-proclaimed state on Arab occupied land. This explains the principle behind the refusal of Israel and Hamas to talk to each other. Therefore, normalization of relations between the two foes is considered very difficult if not impossible. The experience between Egypt and Israel is reflective of this because, even though thirty years have passed since the signing of the Camp David Accords, the two parties are yet to achieve permanent peace. Reports from Jordan and Palestine indicate that parties opposing peace, especially Islamists, are working towards thwarting peace efforts between their countries and Israel and they reject any normalization of relations. It is worth mentioning here that Hamas attacks on Israeli targets never ceased since the signing of the Declaration of Principles, in an attempt to abort the peace agreements.[67] On 19 August 1995, a number of religious figures, scholars, jurists and professors of Islamic Shari'ah (law) in Jordan issued religious edicts prohibiting the selling of any land or property owned by Muslims and Arabs in the Greater Syria region to the Jews according to the Shari'ah.[68] Therefore, it is expected that the parties opposing peace will become larger and stronger, through an alliance between Islamists and the residual pan-Arab nationalists. This would strengthen the fundamentalist current and encourage

Arab countries to give secret financial support to the rejectionist groups to buy their security. In turn, this would increase the possibility of distancing the US from its Arab allies in the medium term and cause political change in some Arab regimes. Other scenarios might include the crystallization of strong Palestinian political powers opposing the peace agreements or the way that agreements would be implemented. Islamic reassertion or resurgence might cause instability in Palestine. This is clearly manifested today in the political rivalry and drift between the Palestinian Authority and the resistant groups. It is worth mentioning here that Israeli has orthodox movements, including Agudat Israel, unified in opposing peace agreements with the Palestinians. They have played an important role in Israeli internal politics, as manifested in their decisive vote against the Israeli–Palestinian peace accord. A number of Shas movement members in the Knesset refused to support the agreement.[69] An agreement in the Knesset was reached on 6 October 1995 to expand autonomy for the Palestinians in the West Bank with 61 for and 59 against, following a stormy debate that lasted fifteen hours, in which some of the members of the Labour Party opposed the agreement.[70] The assassination of former Israeli Prime Minister Yitzhak Rabin on 4 November 1995, at the hands of a Jewish extremist, was enough to demonstrate the internal divisions regarding the peace process in the Middle East. Another indication of Israeli militancy against the peace process was the success of the right-wing conservative parties in the February 2009 election.

6. Contentious Issues

The outcome of the peace agreements between Israel and Arab parties is a fragile peace that is liable to collapse at any time. The truce and the limited agreements are merely part of a clash of civilizations. The Arab–Israeli conflict 'will always continue'[71] because there are still a number of issues that have not been resolved. These issues include disarmament, water, the refugees and the settlements.

Disarmament

From the beginning, the Arab–Israeli conflict witnessed a number of arrangements for arms limitation, such as the ceasefire agreements in 1948 and 1949 between Israel on the one hand and Egypt, Syria, Jordan and Lebanon on the other. In 1950, the United States, Britain and France announced that they intended to stop arm deals to the Middle East. These measures were taken to reduce armed conflicts. After the October war in 1973, the issue of limiting armaments entered a new phase as it came to occupy an important part on the agenda of peace negotiations. The most ambitious arrangements came in the Egyptian–Israeli peace agreement in 1979. The agreement achieved a number of important goals including:

1. Reducing the possibility of surprise attacks from Egypt or Israel towards each other.
2. Creating a militarily unbalanced situation in the armed forces for both sides as a way to give Israel security in return for giving up land.
3. Creating a mechanism for military cooperation to oversee the application of agreements with goodwill. On the other hand, the issue of Israeli nuclear armaments was omitted from any arrangement, ensuring Israeli superiority and at the same time presenting an obstacle to permanent peace in the region. Israeli's possession of such strategic non-conventional weapons while the Arabs are denied access to any kind of weapon of mass destruction does not only give Israel the upper hand in the region, but also creates a state of fear within the Arabs and enhances mistrust in the credibility of the peace agreements.

The Refugees

The issue of the refugees is one of the most important elements of the Arab–Israeli conflict. It emerged straight after the 1948 war when large numbers of Palestinians fled their homes to other countries. The number of refugees increased with every war that erupted between Israel and the Arabs or due to the outrageous Israeli ethnic cleansing policy. There was a new wave of Palestinian emigrants during the Israeli invasion of Lebanon. Consequently, groups of varying sizes migrated to other Arab and non-Arab countries, depending on the international political conditions. Today, these immigrants account for more than five million people, mostly living outside of Palestine, 45 per cent of whom are living in inhumane conditions and considered to be refugees supervised by the UNRWA.

The Palestinian refugees issue invokes a number of sensitive and complicated issues in Arab–Israeli peace talks. The Arabs believe that the right of refugees to return to their homes and properties is one that cannot be compromised. They believe that if Israel grants Jews from all over the world the right to return to Palestine, which Israel claims they left thousand of years ago, it should be an

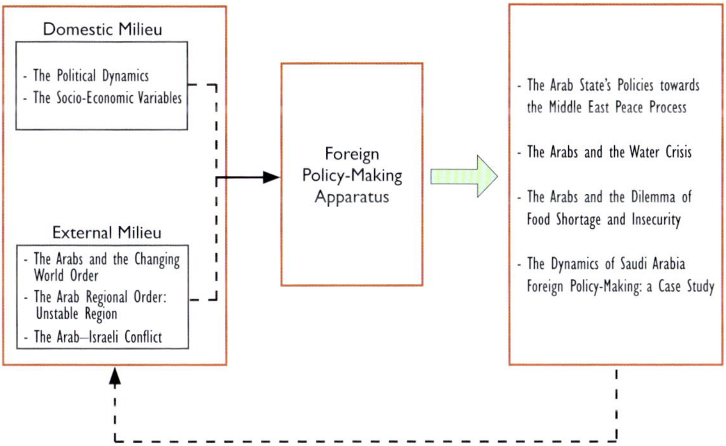

Figure 1: Foreign Policy-Making Process

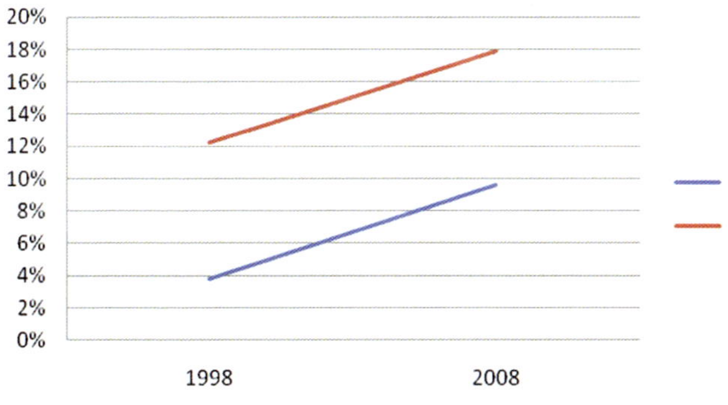

Figure 2: Women Empowerment

Women in Arab Parliaments: Progress, Stagnation or regression, Seminar by the UNDP, Beirut, 9-10/7/2008. http://www.arabparliaments.org/publications/legislature/2008/winp/conceptnote-e.pdf

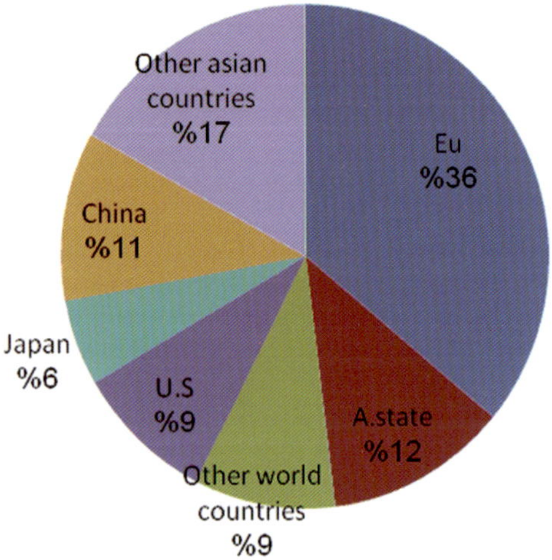

Figure 3: Arab Countries Main Trade Partners (Imports 2007)
Source: *Al-Taqrir al-Iqtissadi al-Arabi 2008*, p. 144

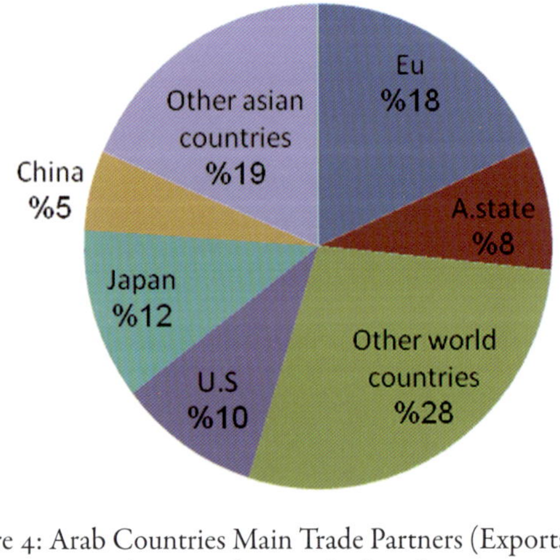

Figure 4: Arab Countries Main Trade Partners (Exports 2007)
Source: *Al-Taqrir al-Iqtissadi al-Arabi 2008*, p.144

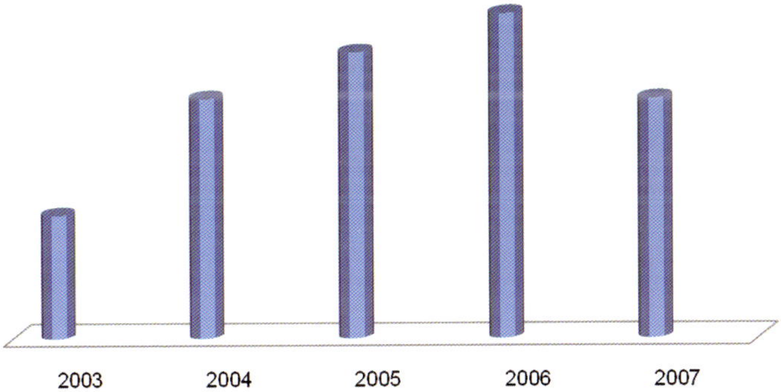

Figure 5: Development of Arab Crude Oil Production (2003–2007)
Source: *Al-Taqrir al-Iqtissadi al-Arabi 2008*, p. 91

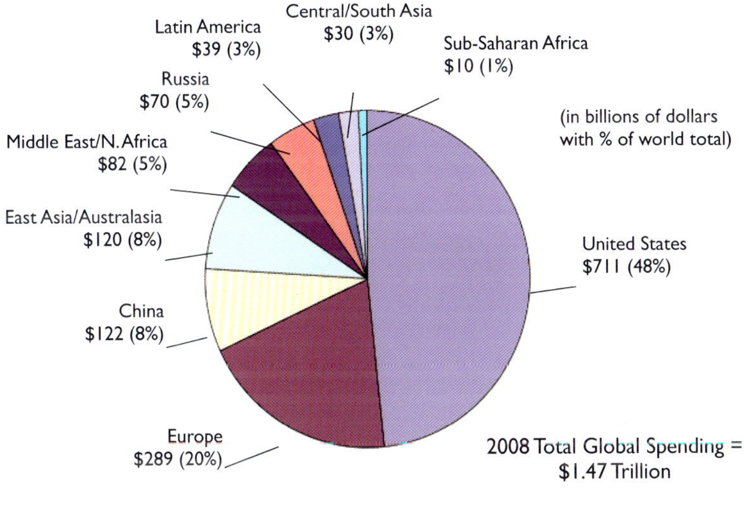

Figure 6: U.S. Military Spending versus the World in 2008

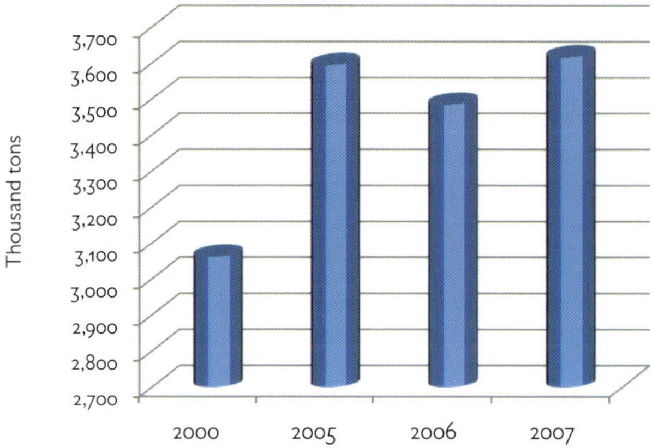

Figure 7: Fish Production in the Arab World (2000–2007)
Source: *Al-Taqrir al-Iqtisadi al-Arabi al-Muwahad 2008*, p.58.

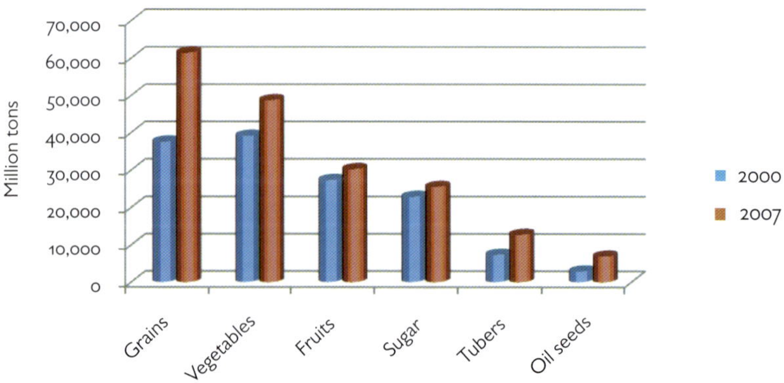

Figure 8: Arab Food Production (2000–2007) (Million Tons)
Source: *Al-Taqrir al-Iqtisadi al-Arabi al-Muwahad 2008*, p. 55

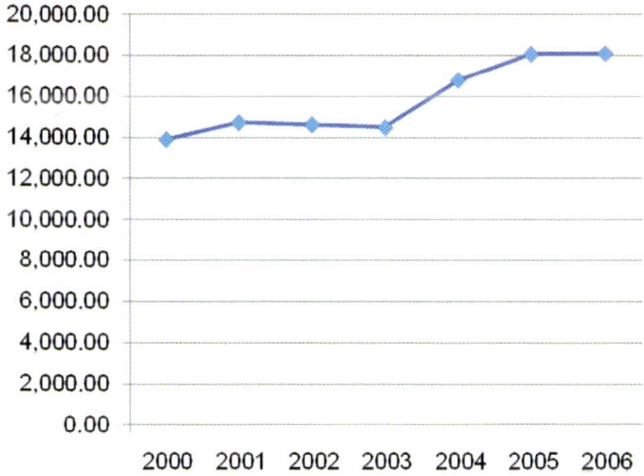

Figure 9: Arab Food Gap Cost (2000–2006) (Billion US$)
Source: *Al-Taqrir al-Iqtisadi al-Arabi al-Muwahad 2008*, p. 63.

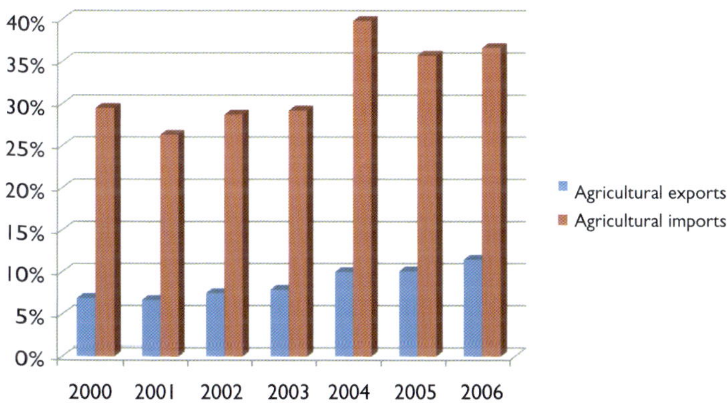

Figure 10: Arab Agricultural Imports and Exports (2000–2006) (Billion US$)
Source: *Al-Taqrir al-Iqtisadi al-Arabi al-Muwahad 2008*, p. 59

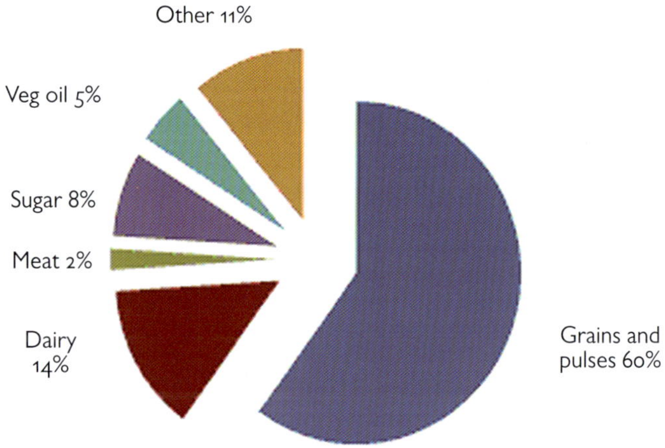

Figure 11: The Structure of the Arab Imports of the Main Food Commodities in 2006
Source: *Al-Taqrir al-Iqtisadi al-Arabi al-Muwahad 2008*, p. 61

Map 1: Saudi-Yemeni Border Agreement

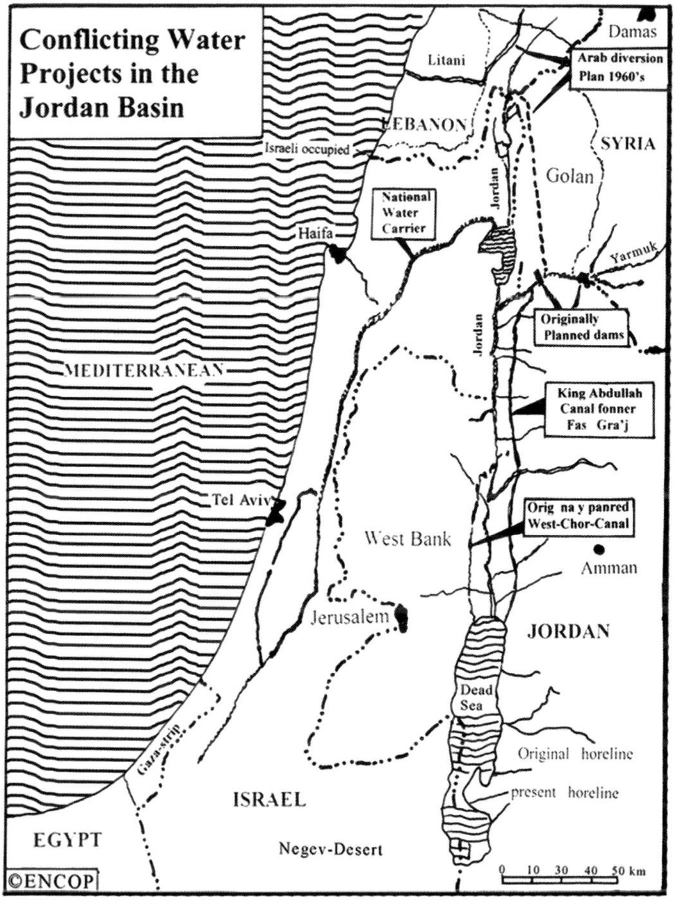

Map 2: Conflicting Water Projects in the Jordan Basin

Map 3: Sources of Euphrates and Tigris Rivers

unalienable right for the Palestinians to return to their home towns that they left six decades ago, or even only few years back. At the same time, Israel believes that the departure of refugees from Palestine was the result of military conflict with Arabs. This led to exchanges in the population as hundreds of thousands of Jews moved from Arab countries to Israel on the one hand and Palestinian Arabs moved to the Arab countries on the other hand. The return of those refugees would change the composition of the Jewish nature of Israel, which was the basis of its founding. Moreover, the return of those Palestinians to the West Bank and Gaza would mean the continuation of unrest and terrorism. The ideal solution to their problem, Israel argues, would be to accommodate them in the countries that they are in and to give them the rights of citizenship, as is the situation in Israel.

As a result of these conflicting points of view, most observers agree that the refugees issue is the most complicated issue for the negotiations, whether bilateral or multilateral. Despite several proposals to solve this problem, there are still projects that no Arab leader could accept, out of fear of creating a social imbalance in their demographic structure, as a result of accommodating Palestinians as citizens in their countries. In addition, no one including the PLO can revoke the rights of the Palestinian refugees to return to their homeland. Such a decision would cause the PLO to lose its legitimacy and strengthen the opposition, especially the Islamist groups who oppose the peace process, particularly Hamas. Finally a failure to attend to the refugees' ambitions would ultimately bring the whole peace process to a dramatic end.

The Settlements

The continuing construction of settlements presents another challenge to the Arab–Israeli peace process. Israel's policy is aimed at demonstrating the importance of Jewish settlements to counterbalance the Palestinian problem and to introduce new ideas and beliefs intended to bully and manipulate international public opinion and to demonstrate the difficulty of abandoning those settlements. Moreover, Israel holds the view that those settlements could act as a bridge for normalization of relations between the Arabs and Israel in any future political settlement.[72] Two hundred thousand settlers in the West Bank constitute a serious problem for any peace agreement because the Israeli government cannot afford to force them out nor can the Palestinians accept to accommodate them.[73] The West Bank has witnessed protests led by Zionist settlers against the Labour government policy on expanding self-government for the Palestinians. On 7 August 1995, Ariel Sharon, a member of the Israeli Knesset from the Likud Party, said that these settlements represented the security of Israel. One settler claimed that the West Bank territories were Zionist territories that were inhabited by their ancestors in the past who did not settle in the coastal towns and that the policies of Rabin's government would lead to the disappearance of Israel. David Ben Gurion said, 'The extremists in Israel who hope to take over Arab territories will strip Israel of its message. If they succeed Israel will not be a Jewish or a democratic state. The Arab population will become the majority and we must take oppressive measures to keep them under our control.'[74] The issue of settlements continues, today, to be the main obstacle confronting any attempt for peace. Analysts believe that they complicate the Israeli negotiations with the Arab parties, the PLO, Jordan and Syria, and that they will continue to block any real and lasting peace between the two sides.

Water

Water has come to represent a major obstacle to maintaining regional peace and stability. The Zionist interest in this issue is due to the climatic and topographical conditions of Palestine, which can take in 15 million people providing the necessary water is available.[75] The importance of water is increasing in the peace negotiations because the two parties expect to suffer from water shortages. Water shortage in Israel is estimated at 800 million cubic metres whereas the water shortage for the Arabs is estimated at 30 billion cubic metres (see Chapter 7). Israel is clinging to the West Bank as it contains a water reservoir that covers 40 per cent of Israeli water consumption at the present time. In July 1995, the Israeli government said that it would withdraw from the West Bank and its subterranean waters but demanded that the water be shared between the two sides.[76] The possibility of water shortages between the Arabs and Israel increases the likelihood of the conflict continuing between the two sides. A few proposals have been put forward to put an end to this problem[77] including the following (see Table 7.3):

1. The Cotton Plan, which aimed at transporting 125 million cubic metres from the Jordan River Basin and 400 million cubic metres from the Litani River to Israel;
2. Transporting between regional countries;
3. The Johnston Plan in 1956, which aimed to divert Jordan River water;

4. Building a canal between the Mediterranean and the Dead Sea;
5. The peace pipeline plan from Turkey;
6. Building huge stations for desalination;
7. Extending the Nile to Israel, the Gaza Strip, the West Bank and Jordan.

None of these has been adopted because of the complexity and sensitivity of the issue. This suggests that, due to water scarcity, the tension between regional states will continue (see Chapter 7).

7. Conclusion

Peaceful settlement does not mean the achievement of a real peace in the region, but is a significant step on the road to peace in the conflict that has been going for around a century. The idea that the current peace process will bring an end to all elements of conflict is completely wrong. It is expected, on the one hand, to take different political and ideological forms in the future and, on the other hand, it is merely a slip-up on behalf of/a manifestation or illustration of the American pragmatic approach.[78] Samuel Toledano, the former deputy security chief of Israel, said that he does not 'see any possibility for peace'.[79] The negotiating teams, whether Arabs or Israelis, realize the seriousness of the issues concerned and cannot ignore them. It shows in the delay in implementing the Declaration of Principles.

The occupied territories represent another obstacle; the land will remain a source of conflict between the Arabs and Jews even if the Jews decide to give up the territories that they occupied in 1967. The issue of the territories occupied in 1948 and the future of its people both inside and outside of these areas will remain. Therefore, land will remain a source of contention causing permanent regional instability. In addition, Israel's adherence to its theory regarding Israeli security dilemmas determines that it has the right to defend the state by launching the first strike against any potential threat, even outside of the Israeli borders. This explains Israel's attack, in 1982, against Iraqi nuclear installations, its attack on a convoy in Sudan, in January 2009, suspected of carrying Iranian weapons to Hamas, and its continuing threat to launch a unilateral attack against Iranian suspected nuclear installations. Therefore, the threat to neighbouring Arab countries from Israel remains a permanent one.

The status of Jerusalem represents another obstacle to the peace process between the Arabs and Israel. The importance of Jerusalem, due to its religious significance for both parties, lies in its 'value' rather than its 'benefit'. The inability of either side to surrender or negotiate the future of Jerusalem is another obstacle to the shift from the culture of conflict to the culture of peace. The current conflict is an eternal conflict. This confirms what is said in the Qur'an: 'And the Jews will not be pleased with you, nor the Christians until you follow their creed.' Also, some Israeli leaders believe that it is impossible to achieve peace even if both sides signed peace agreements. In his book, *The Revolt: Story of the Irgun*, Begin says, 'There will never be peace for the Israeli nation, and not on Israeli territories, and there will never be peace for the Arabs nor in the Arab territories. We will continue liberating our country and all its land from the oppression of Arabs and the war will continue between us even if Arabs signed a peace treaty with us.'

Water scarcity represents an important variable influencing foreign policy-making processes. Water is the only resource countries are inevitably willing to fight for. Both Arab states and Israel will experience water shortage which is likely to obstruct the peace process. Regional countries like Turkey and Iran, having an abundance of water, could become water suppliers or they could use water as a political weapon to bully Arab countries, especially those dependent on water supply from Turkey. Thus, water scarcity is investigated as part of the Arab countries' foreign policy undertakings in the next chapter.

The changes in the Arab world since the beginning of 2011 would inevitably have an impact on the Middle East peace process. The emergence of democratic states in Egypt, Tunisia, Libya and Yemen would invigorate changes in other Arab countries on both levels, domestic and with respect to their foreign policies. A democratic Egypt is expected to push for a sustainable peace in the Middle East based on land for peace formula as has been outlined by the Arab peace initiative. The Arab order would be reengineered to correct the existing imbalanced situation, leading to a more independent course of foreign policy with the Palestinian issue acquiring its position at the centre of Arab politics. Consequently, the challenge for Israel would be to choose between accepting the Palestinian right for self determinations, the two-states solution, or to continue to live in a state of insecurity isolated within its regional context.

Chapter 7

Desertification and Water Crisis in the Arab World

1. Introduction

Water is a source of life in a predominantly desert region. It plays and will continue to play an increasing political, strategic and economical role over the next few decades in the world in general and in the Arab world in particular. It is perhaps the only resource over which any country facing severe shortage will fight, leading some analysts to argue that water war is imminent in the Middle East. The situation is further exacerbated by the global warming. Climate change is posing new challenges for managing water and is altering the assumptions many countries have had for centuries. This chapter considers the position that water is an effective weapon in the hands of Israel during times of war as well as peace. The following questions can be raised. What is the prospect of peace in the region according to the Zionist strategic vision regarding water? What role will water play in the peace process? To what extent will Israel exert pressure on Arabs in the peace process by signalling to utilize this weapon? What kind of position will the water issue occupy in the multilateral negotiations regarding the peace process? And finally, what grave consequences will Israeli water projects have on the development and economic independence of the Arab countries?

In this chapter, I have used the analytical method to uncover the essence of the phenomenon and to determine the relationship between its various components and within the general framework and to uncover the numerous stages that the phenomenon passes through in its development.[1] In addition, I have used the inductive method, which follows an experimental approach to studying the phenomena, which allows us to move from individual facts to general hypotheses.[2] The aim is to understand the future interactions between the Arabs and Israel in consideration of incomplete peace, on the one hand, and their relations with neighbouring countries on the other hand in view of the dialectical nature between water scarcity and the increasing demand for it. Previous studies on the issue warned of the dangerous situation, with the most recent work being *Water in the Arab World: Management Perspectives and Innovations*, edited by Ahmed Shawky Abdel Ghany and N. Vijay Jagannathan, published jointly by the World Bank and the Dutch government.

This chapter seeks to understand the danger that Arab countries are facing as a result of Israel's usurping of water and the policies Israel has adopted to take control of Arab water resources, by highlighting the needs of the concerned Arab countries (the Palestinian Occupied Territories, Jordan, Lebanon, Syria, Egypt and Iraq) in the conflict with Israel for water. The water variable presents an internal constraint as well as an external pressure on Arab states' foreign policy-making apparatus. Here I use reports and statistics about the current situation in order to look to the future. I focus on Israel's water cooperation with regional countries Turkey and Ethiopia and its dangerous implications for the Arab states. It is worth mentioning, however, the difficulties encountered the author due to the absence of official reports and updated statistics and information on the issue. This might be due to the sensitivity of the topic and the secrecy surrounding such figures and statistics. Moreover, research interest on water issues is relatively new to regional studies.

2. Arab Water Scarcity

Reports indicate that total available water in the Arab world is estimated at 300 billion cubic metres per annum. Total available surface and subterranean water resources in the Arab countries are estimated at 277 billion cubic metres per year. The amount that is utilized stands at 180 billion cubic metres, 10 billion cubic metres of which is desalinated and processed. External surface water resources shared with neighbouring countries outside the region account approximately to 57 per cent of the total surface water in the region.[3] On the other hand, the level of self-sufficiency in food reaches 50 per cent of the total need,[4] which is why the Arab world is considered to be suffering from food shortages (see Chapter 8). As we know that the 2 per cent increase in productivity is met by a 3 per cent increase in population and 5 per cent increase in the rate of consumption, this means that there is a 50 per cent food shortage, which will force the Arab countries to import between 40 to 60 per cent of its food needs, equivalent to US$120–200 billion, and over 90 million people of the Arab population will suffer from malnutrition.[5] The situation is further exacerbated by global warming. The 'Intergovernmental Panel on Climate Change (IPCC) model predicts that temperature and water variability will increase in several countries in the region and that water precipitation will also drop by up to 30 per cent by 2050.[6]

Ensuring the continuing flow of water is one of the fundamental national objectives of any nation. In the last few years, the security of water has occupied a top priority and discussing this issue has become equivalent to security. Water resources in the Middle East are scarce by nature, and most of them are trans-boundary. It has become more complicated for the Middle East, especially for Arab areas where the desert occupies 43 per cent of its land and arable land represents 9.4 per cent. A UN Environment Programme study estimates that desert has swallowed up more than two-thirds or 68.4 per cent of total land area of the region.[7] Causes for desertification are the demographic explosion (see Table 7.1), changing social values and norms, and changing the mode of agricultural production.[8] For this reason, analysts such as Hamdi al-Tahir, Nabil Samma'an, Postel, Starr and Allan believe that the shortage of water in the region could lead to an increase in tensions and the outbreak of future wars in the region. Libiszewski believes that such a statement is exaggerated and misleading, as conflicts are still determined by deep political differences. Hydrological matters undeniably represent an additional dimension to the Arab–Israeli conflict, a dimension whose relative importance has been growing over recent years.[9]

Water has long been a scarce resource in the Middle East but the problem has become more acute. Scant rainfall has further strained supplies already restricted by Israel, which largely controls the West Bank's three main aquifers. The dream of establishing Greater Israel from the Euphrates to the Nile is evidence of Israel's vision of the strategic importance of this vital weapon in its confrontation with the Arabs both at present and in the future. The potential of war in the coming decades between Arabs and Israel over water resources is strong, as the two sides will try to secure the success of development projects and to provide food security that relies mainly on water. As early as the 1980s, intelligence experts with the US government identified areas in the world where conflict might broke out over the issue of water. Most of these were in the Middle East. 'The conjuncture of the Middle East population growth and its largely desert climate suggests a very turbulent future.'[10] Regional countries, if they want to avoid war, 'need to work together despite their differences to conserve or find out ways to get water or they will ultimately face a serious problem. Either the water is going to run out, or a war will be fought over the existing water.'[11] There is a dialectical relationship between limited water resources and the increasing need for water due to the rise in population and its multiple uses in various regional states. It has culminated in improper means of consumption and the absence of strategic planning. Whilst the rate of demographic growth has reached 3 per cent, one of the highest rates in the world, the level of water shortage has doubled. The population in the Arab world has increased from 180 to 317 million, representing 5 per cent of the world's population. It is expected to increase from 317 to 743 million between 2007 and 2030 (see Table 7.1); the water shortage will increase in the same period from 30 billion cubic metres to 260 billion cubic metres (see Table 7.2). Statistics show that the Arab countries consumed 71 per cent of their available water between 1996 and 2006, compared to a global rate of 6.3 per cent. More than two-thirds of this amount is used for agricultural irrigation.[12]

Table 7.1. Arab Population Census (1980–2030) (million)

1980	2000	2004	2007	2015	2030
150	300	231.8	317	395	743

Sources: Compiled figures from the joint *Arab Economic Report,* 2008, and *Arab Human Development Report,* 2009.

The Arab countries represent 9 per cent of the world's entire dry land with a rapidly increasing population, whereas its water resources do not exceed more than 0.74 per cent of the entire world's water resources. Sixty-five rivers cross the Arab lands, the biggest of which is the River Nile with an average discharge or outflow of 85 billion cubic metres and the smallest of which is the Miliane River in Tunisia with an average discharge or outflow of 50 million cubic metres, but this network of rivers only partially covers the Arab world's need for water. The figures show that this need will double by the early twenty-first century as the requirement for water in the North African Arab countries stands at approximately 11.4 billion cubic metres; in Egypt and Syria it is 11.1 billion cubic metres; and in the Arabian Peninsula and the Gulf states it is 5.4 billion cubic metres. UAE ground water supply, for example, has fallen by 18 per cent since 2003. Arab countries are in either the arid or hyper arid zone, depending on seasonal rainfall, have very few rivers and often rely on fragile aquifers. 'Consequently, their economies are much more sensitive to the way that water is extracted, conveyed, and consumed than are the economies of other regions.'[13] According to Kilot, territory classified as arid covers 80 to 85 per cent of Jordan, 50 to 65 per cent of Syria and 60 per cent of Israel.[14] 'Over exploitation of subterranean water resources led to numerous problems in the Gulf countries and the Occupied Palestinian Territories (OPT), and elsewhere as a consequent higher salinity level in aquifers.' Water fears caused[15] Saudi Arabia to end grain output. Saudi Arabia plans to halt wheat production by 2016 because of concern about the desert kingdom's scarce water resources. It will begin reducing production annually by 12.5 per cent starting from 2009.[16] The Saudi move represents a significant shift in policy since 1970s to become self-sufficient.

Table 7.2. Fresh Water Availability in Selected Arab Countries (1990)

Country	Yearly Per Capita (in Cubic Metre)	Yearly Population growth & expected pop. Doubling (at current rates)
Palestine (W. Bank & Gaza Strip)	100	3.2% (22 yrs.)
Jordan	220	3.4% (19 yrs.)
Israel	370	2.6% (27 yrs.)
Lebanon	1780	1.9% (34 yrs.)
Syria	2830	3.5% (18 yrs.)
Iraq	5282	3.1% (21 yrs.)
Egypt	1100	2.1% (31 yrs.)
Saudi Arabia	160	3.3% (20 yrs.)
Qatar	55	2.3% (24 yrs.)

Figures on water availability consider only natural renewable resources. Note that the national account includes water amounts which are used or claimed by downstream riparian countries.

Sources: World Resources Institute, *World Resources 1992–93*, New York and Oxford, 1992. Population projections according to UNDP, *Human Development Report 1994*. New York and Oxford, 1994.

Source: S. Libiszewski, *Water Disputes in the Jordan Basin Region and their Role in the Resolution of the Arab–Israeli Conflict*, Centre for Security Policy and Conflict Analysis, Swiss Peace Foundation, 1995, p. 31. www.mideastweb.org/mew_water95.pdf._

Moreover, the average annual rate of water consumption per person does not exceed 1,744 cubic metres whereas the average rate worldwide stands at 12,900 cubic metres. In fact, in some Arab countries the average rate per capita is no more than 1,000 cubic metres per annum, seven times less than worldwide average per capita, which represents 13 per cent of the general average. The percentage of those living on less than 1,000 cubic metres of water per annum represents 53 per cent of the total population of the Arab world, which is considered the highest percentage in the world.[17] According to some reports, population demand for water in 2030 will reach 710 billion cubic metres.[18] It would ultimately reduce per capita share to 460 cubic metres by 2025. The global *Human Development Report* of 2006 confirms that per capita share would be 500 cubic metres.[19] The Arab countries, according to the joint *Arab Economic Report* of 2001, have actually entered a water poverty stage whereby 90 per cent of the Arab population will be living in countries suffering from water shortage.[20] They are heading towards a problematic situation in securing new sources of water to face the increasing demand for water for irrigation, drinking and industry.

Analysts believe that the coming few decades will be marked by water conflicts between the Arabs and Israel, and between the Arabs and neighbouring countries such as Turkey and Ethiopia.[21] Cooperation on water usage and management is heavily affected by prevailing political tensions and ongoing conflicts. Tensions have emerged on sharing resources as the needs of the riparian countries increase.[22] The existence of decisive pan-Arab national security today is strongly linked to the security of water; Israel has been trying to expand and control water security to reinforce the idea that national security is based on water security. The importance of the idea that Israel played a significant role in creating the water crisis in the Arab region is that this region had not faced any such crisis before the establishment of Israel, but did after it began to control Arab territories to expand settlements to accommodate Jewish immigrants. The Israeli policy has been to secure full control over its water needs on one hand and to destabilize the security of Arab water flow by subjecting it to the control of foreign powers on the other hand. It is worth mentioning that 57 per cent of water resources that flow on Arab land spring from outside its borders. Therefore, water security will be a priority for pan-Arab security in the coming years and the water problem will continue to be an obstacle to a comprehensive peace deal in the Middle East. It is argued that 'water will be a key issue in the Arab–Israel peace process'.[23] In US-sponsored peace talks over Palestinian statehood, disputes over water may be overshadowed by more sensitive issues like the future of Jerusalem and refugees. But Palestinian negotiator Saeb Erekat said an accord would be 'unthinkable' without agreement on dividing up the region's water resources. According to Palestinian Water Authority chief Shaddad Attili: 'If you want to have a state, you must have water.'[24] Arab governments have exerted great efforts to secure water for economic uses for their people.

As a result, 'coverage of water needs of the Arab people increased from 83 per cent in 1990 to 85 per cent in 2004'.[25]

Factors causing water to become a source of contention in the Arab–Israeli conflict can be summarized in the following points:[26]

1. The desert climate, which dominates the region, covers an estimated area of 14 million square kilometres and the proportion is used for agriculture makes up approximately 3.8 million square kilometres. This represents 40.2 per cent of land suitable for agriculture.[27] Moreover, 80 per cent of these lands are dependent on the seasonal rains.
2. There has been a steady increase in population, as the population of the Arab world reached approximately 330 million in 2008, and is expected to reach 743 million in 2030, whereas the population of Israel reached 7.2 million in 2008, and despite the rise in immigration to Palestine, will not exceed 12 million by 2030.
3. There has been an increase in the standard of living and in the average consumption of water per person. In the Arab world, the average rate of consumption per person is 100–250 litres per day whereas the average rate of consumption per person in Israel has reached 500 litres per day.
4. Development in the economic and agricultural sectors is relevant, as there is a significant increase in water consumption with the development of the industrial sector, especially industries that rely on water such as copper production. To produce one tonne of copper requires 50 cubic metres of water, one tonne of nickel requires 800 cubic metres of water, and one tonne of paper requires 1,000 cubic metres of water. The agricultural sector consumes more than 80 per cent of the water resources and the industrial sector consumes around 11.5 per cent whereas the level of human consumption stands at approximately 5.5 per cent of all water resources.[28]
5. Security is a very sensitive issue, as national security is a major concern for the Arab states and Israel. Both sides will suffer from water shortage in the foreseeable future, with the annual water shortage for Israel having reached 800 million cubic metres per annum by 2000,[29] and that of the Arab countries having reached 30 billion cubic metres.[30] Therefore, because 'water is scarce and has competing uses, the region needs a management strategy that goes beyond engineering solutions to include revisiting the water rights regime, regulatory framework and public–private partnerships'.[31]

3. Israeli Water Scarcity

The Israeli demand for water is continuously increasing, as Israel, the population of which was no more than 860,000 just before its establishment on 14 May 1948, with a gross consumption of no more than 230 million cubic metres,[32] doubled its level of water consumption because the population increased two-fold. In 1993, the gross consumption of water was approximately 1,754 million cubic metres (see Table 7.3).

Table 7.3. Water Consumption by Sector

<table>
<tr><th></th><th>Population (in million)</th><th>Total Water Consumption (mcm)</th><th>Agric. (in %)</th><th>Industrial (in %)</th><th>Domestic (in %)</th></tr>
<tr><td>Jordan 92</td><td>4.3</td><td>875</td><td>74</td><td>5</td><td>21</td></tr>
<tr><td>Palestine W. Bank & Gaza 90. est.</td><td>1.8</td><td>210</td><td>62</td><td colspan="2">38</td></tr>
<tr><td>Lebanon 90 est.</td><td>3.3</td><td>1060</td><td>74</td><td></td><td></td></tr>
<tr><td>Syria 90 est.</td><td>12.5</td><td>9500</td><td>79</td><td>5</td><td>16</td></tr>
<tr><td>Israel 93</td><td>5.1</td><td>1754</td><td>63</td><td>6</td><td>31</td></tr>
</table>

In the figures for the West Bank and the Gaza Strip domestic and industrial consumption is accounted together. Note that Palestinian water resources, especially in the Gaza Strip, are highly over-used.

Sources: Statistical Abstract of Israel 1994; E. Salameh and H. Bannayan, *Water Resources of Jordan: Present Status and Future Potentials*, Amman, 1993.

Israel, to compensate for its water shortage, seized 2.3 billion cubic metres of water resources from the Arab world. In 2000 Israel water shortage was estimated at approximately 30 per cent. If Israel withdraws from the West Bank, the Gaza Strip, the Golan Heights and southern Lebanon its water shortage will reach 52 per cent.[33] If we take into account the increasing need for water in all countries worldwide due to the increase in population and in the number of economic projects that depend on water, it is expected that the rising need for water in Israel will reach 4 billion cubic metres due to the influx of Jewish migrants from the former Soviet Union and Eastern Europe.[34] In 1991 the cumulative deficit of the entire coastal aquifer was estimated by Israel's state controller at 1.1 billion cubic metres, that is to say, four times the annual replenishment.[35]

Therefore, the water shortage in Israel will reach 2,500 million cubic metres in 2030 instead of 800 million cubic metres in 2000.

Aware of the topographic nature of Palestine, the early Zionist movement realized the necessity of ensuring water availability for the Jewish immigrants. It sent a commission to study the land and water resources of Palestine in 1873. The conclusion of that study, which was published in 1875, was that the land could accommodate a population of 15 million people, provided that suitable water supplies were available for this population.[36] Establishing a national state on partially desert land in Palestine was thought to be too difficult to achieve without securing water resources. Therefore the Zionist movement started working on guaranteeing the required amount of water for establishing the state. The slogan 'From the Nile to the Euphrates, your land, O Israel' reflects the great importance of water for Israel. The creation of Israel is based on borders defined by water; the anticipated borders of this state on Arab land stretch between the Nile and Euphrates, as the two blue lines in the Israel flag represent. Israeli ambitions regarding Arab water resources are old and have not come about as a result of peace negotiations. These ambitions existed even before Israel's formation in 1948, and these ambitions for water would be its jugular vein when it would eventually establish its state on the land of Palestine.[37] Numerous plans for water allocation of Jordan River Basin waters have been suggested over the past nine decades. One of the first proposals was introduced in 1913. Following the League of Nations' grant of a mandate over Palestine to Britain, in 1922, the latter realized that water management and allocation were critical for the region.[38]

The Zionist movement explored various options towards achieving this goal. It made the most of the opportunity of the International Peace Conference after the First World War to promote the water issue. It drew the borders of its future state based on guarantees of water resources.[39] The borders included water resources from the Jordan, Litani and Yarmuk rivers. Furthermore, Zionists also worked towards negotiating with Britain during the time of the British Mandate on Palestine and during British rule of Egypt in 1903, to divert water from the Nile to the Sinai desert.[40] During the era of the British Mandate on Palestine, especially between 1922 and 1948, the Zionist movement managed to obtain licences to carry out water projects as it obtained the right to utilize the Jordan and Yarmuk rivers in 1926. It also gained the right to drain the Sea of Galilee in 1934, which had previously been entrusted to Lebanese individuals. Therefore, the period of the British Mandate on Palestine was a good opportunity for private projects with the help of experts in the water field. Once the establishment of Israel was announced, these projects became a reality on the ground.[41] The main component of the Israeli plan to secure water resources crystallized around the diversion of the upper Jordan waters from Lake Tiberias into a central conduit, completed in 1964, leading through the coastal area up to the north Negev.[42] According to Nurit Kliot, in his book *Water Resources and Conflict in the Middle East* (1994), water conveyance by the conduit gradually increased from 195 mcm in 1965 to an average of 350 mcm per year in the 1970s. In the 1980s the carrier was conveying 420–450 mcm.[43]

The concern for the security of water was one of the implicit factors of Israel's foreign policy towards the Arab and neighbouring countries. The goal of achieving this kind of security is apparent in all the wars Israel launched against Arab countries. One of the aims of the 1956 war was to connect the Suez Canal and the Red Sea. The 1967 war was of great significance to Israel, as it helped Israel take full control of the water resources after it managed to occupy the West Bank, which today provides 40 per cent of Israel's total water consumption, and the Golan Heights, which provides 30 per cent of Israel's needs for water. In the 1967 war, Israel managed to take control of the water resources of the Jordan River, 250 mcm of which are diverted annually to the desert of Negev[44] and to the Suez Canal. In order to accomplish its goal of water security, the Israeli air force launched an attack in 1969 on the buildings of the first stage of a Lebanese project on the Litani River. Moreover, Israel prevented farmers in the south Lebanon from drilling new wells, just as it did to farmers in the West Bank and the Gaza Strip. In 1982, Israel launched a war against Lebanon aiming to control the Litani River and it tried to divert its water towards the Sea of Galilee by using huge pipes buried under the soil. This would provide Israel with an extra 250 mcm of water per annum.[45] The second Israeli policy to ensure water security was to control the mountain aquifer. The aforementioned rivers and lakes are the most visible water resources of the region, but they do not cover the bulk of the water demand in Israel, Jordan and the Occupied Palestinian Territories. In all of these three areas more than 50 per cent of the available renewable water supply is provided by groundwater. In the case of the Palestinians this source makes up nearly the totality of present consumption. The main groundwater basin of the region and also the most critical politically is the aquifer originating on the West Bank. Figures on the potential of the aquifer vary from 600 mcm per year to as much as 900 mcm.[46]

4. Israel's Projects to Usurp Arab Water

Since Israel was established in 1948, successive governments have made every effort in search of water to secure its future needs: from preparing studies and adopting plans to occupying water reservoirs in the Arab territories and usurping and storing water in areas that were under its control. Table 7.4 shows the plans proposed to divide the water between Israel and the Arab countries. Amnesty International accused Israel on 28 October 2009 of taking 80 per cent of the Palestinian water.[47]

Table 7.4. Water Distributions

Plans	The Arab Plan		The Johnston Plan		The Cotton Plan	
State	Water/ Million Cubic Metre	%	Water/ Million Cubic Metre	%	Water/ Million Cubic Metre	%
Syria	132	9.5	45	3.7	30	1.3
Lebanon	35	2.5	-	-	450	19.2
Jordan	1076	76	774	63.8	57	24.5
Arab States	1214	87	819	67.5	1055	45
Israel	182	13	394	32.5	1290	55

Sources: Dakroub Abdelamir, 'Mustaqbal Asiraa Hawla al Miyah fi Asharq Al Awsat', *Al Fikr al Arabi*, vol. 76, Spring 1994, p. 224.

1. The Cotton Plan in 1954 was named after the American expert John Cotton. Its aim was to enable Israel to obtain 125 mcm of the Jordan River water and 400 mcm of the Litani River water. The plan was rejected due to the lack of international supervision.
2. The regional transporting project was achieved in three stages: Stage One in 1951–3 had the aim of draining Al-Hawla lake and deepening the Jordan River; in Stage Two in 1953–5 several canals were dug to control the water of the Jordan River; and in Stage Three in 1955–7, the basaltic layer of the Sea of Galilee was removed to facilitate transporting 12 mcm of Jordan River water resources.[48]
3. The Johnston Plan in 1956 aimed to divert Jordan River water. The Arabs rejected this plan.
4. The two seas canal plan aimed at connecting the Mediterranean Sea and the Dead Sea to generate power by making the most of the difference in sea

> levels. The plan was put on hold by Shimon Peres's government due to the lack of economic benefit.[49] It was one of the projects agreed upon by Israel and Jordan after the countries signed the bilateral peace agreement.

It is evident from Table 7.3 that the agriculture sector represents the greater share of water consumption in general. It is also apparent that water consumption in agriculture can be compared to household consumption as a result of Jewish immigration that took place between 1985 and 1995. Arab water consumption in the Palestinian occupied territories reached approximately 210 mcm in the same period. Israel in its attempts to secure water resources pursued a policy of usurping Arab water on all fronts.

West Bank Water

The importance of the West Bank for Israel lies in its subterranean water reservoir that can hold 200 mcm of water, which is annually renewed by rainwater. This is in complete contrast to the Gaza Strip, and this explains why Israel decided to give up the Gaza Strip but refused categorically to completely withdraw from the West Bank. In the 1967 war, Israel sought to expand its borders and annex the West Bank.[50] The Palestinians control about 200 shallow wells in the West Bank, many of them drilled before the 1967 six-day war in which Israel captured the territory. Those wells produce about 105 million cubic metres per year, but they are meant to supply water to 2.5 million Palestinians. The Israeli authorities, since its annexation of 1967 Arab lands, pursued new water policies to consolidate its control and to import water from the West Bank. They decided that the Arabs could consume 120 mcm of water whilst in reality the Arabs required 400 mcm. The Arabs were prohibited from digging wells deeper than 140 metres whereas Israelis were permitted to dig wells up to 800 metres deep. On the other hand, reports showed that the Israeli settlements in the occupied West Bank were consuming 17 mcm of water, and on an annual basis Israel takes approximately 20 mcm of subterranean water from the West Bank to pump it to other wells that were dug within the Israeli borders of 1948.[51] According to a study published by the Arab League, Israel has usurped 80 per cent of the West Bank water. As a consequence of its control of the West Bank, Israel managed to increase its share of water. In addition, Israel continued to work on merging the water system of the West Bank with the Israeli system out of fear that it would lose this water as part of a peace settlement.[52] The situation is even worse in the Occupied Palestinian Territories where mechanisms of control and monitoring are all but non-existent and knowledge about proper use of chemicals among farmers is insufficient.[53]

The Palestinian Arabs have suffered from discrimination in their basic right to obtain water. Whilst the Zionist settlements and the Israeli military barracks receive water by pipes, the Arab areas receive it by containers under the control of the Jews who draw water from the West Bank villages and resell it to Arab inhabitants. Israel pursued a dual water policy in the occupied Arab lands. Whilst a Jew would get one cubic metre for US$1.5, an Arab would pay US$3.5.[54] Many West Bankers spend between 3 to 5 per cent of their monthly income on water because the tanks are filled up by water tanker services that cost 30 to 40 per cent more than the municipal service. Water Authority chief Attili estimated Palestinian farmers in West Bank and Gaza need 250 mcm of water per year for irrigation, but they get only about 20 per cent of that, or about 50 mcm a year. West Bank Palestinians get 205 mcm annually from their own resources and from Israel. Palestinian officials say Israel controls some fifty West Bank wells with a total capacity of 50 mcm per year.

Around 10 per cent of West Bank communities are surviving on less than ten litres of water per person per day. This figure is well below the World Health Organization (WHO) estimate of average water usage, which is 50 to 100 litres per person per day. West Bank Palestinians supplement their own well supplies by buying up to 45 mcm of water from Israel. Another 5 mcm bought from Israel go to the Gaza Strip, supplementing 50 million from an aquifer. A big part of the problem for Palestinians, officials and rights groups say, is that the amount of water supplied by Israel, set by quotas in interim peace agreements in the 1990s, has not increased in line with Palestinian population growth.[55] As a result, Israeli measures have led to economic damage for the Palestinians, the worst of which has been the rise in unemployment levels and the increase of migration away from the West Bank.[56]

Gaza Strip Water

The situation in Gaza is no better than that in the West Bank. The limitation of water resources in Gaza has become more intense on a daily basis. The Gaza Strip is only 365 square kilometres with a population estimated, in 2008, at 1.5 million, the most overpopulated city in the world, with almost total dependence on rainfall, that occurs in the winter months with an average of between about 400 mm/year in the north and 200 mm/year in the south. According to data released by official Israeli sources in 1992, the natural inflow into Gaza aquifer consists of 47 mcm of rainfall infiltration and about 20 mcm of eastern groundwater.[57] In the course of the years an enormous deficit has accumulated, resulting in a continuous drop in the groundwater level throughout the Strip at an average of 15–20 cm per year. It is estimated that the subterranean water that Israel has taken from the Gaza Strip, during its control of the Strip, on an annual basis reached 200 mcm.[58] The methods that have been used by the Israeli authorities to extract the subterranean water led to the increase of salinity in the water. The salinity of Gaza's groundwater typically increases at average rates of some 10–15 ppm chlorine annually.[59] Today, this level has reached 600 mg per litre, whereas in fact there should be no more than 250 mg per litre. The effect on the inhabitants of Gaza is severe since it is part of the Israeli policy aimed at suppressing Arab inhabitants politically[60] through economic hardship, especially by controlling water resources.[61] The inhabitants of the Gaza Strip, today, are facing real difficulties as a result of water resources being mixed with seawater as well as sewage and the lack of efficient control mechanisms.

The Jordan River

The Jordan River Valley extends from the Golan Heights and Mount Hermon in the north to the Dead Sea in the south and includes Israel, Jordan, Lebanon, Syria and the West Bank. The conflict over the Jordan River's water supplies is a very important part of the Arab–Israeli conflict. This conflict emerged with Israel's plans to take water from the Jordan River for use in real estate works in the Negev desert to accommodate more Jewish immigrants. To achieve this target, the first seven-year plan (1953–60) was enacted intended to increase Israeli water supplies from 810 mcm to 1,730 mcm by the end of 1960. When the Arabs rejected the project, US President Dwight Eisenhower, in 1953, dispatched special envoy Ambassador Eric Johnston to set up a plan to divide the water of the Jordan River. According to the plan, Jordan would get 52 per cent of the Jordan River's water resources, Israel would take 36 per cent, Syria would take 9 per cent and Lebanon would take 3 per cent. The Israelis and the Arabs rejected the proposal, as the Arabs did not want to recognize Israel, and this would have happened if they accepted the quota allocation. On the other hand Israel did not want to restrict itself to a specific quota of the Jordan River.[62] In the mid-1980s, Israel pumped 100 mcm from the Yarmuk River.[63] As a result, Jordan was able to tap no more than 120–30 mcm of water on average from the Yarmuk.[64] It actually contributes 400–500 mcm of water to the basin. Consequently, Jordan relied on its groundwater to make up for the water shortage. Groundwater resources are of particular importance for the country as 90 per cent of municipal supplies are covered by them.[65] In this context, Israel is trying to build a 114-kilometre canal that connects the Mediterranean to the Dead Sea. The project aims to generate electric power, obtain sufficient water for cooling the nuclear power plants in the desert of Negev, set up a station to desalinate seawater in order to irrigate northern Negev, and construct new settlements along the canal to accommodate the new waves of Jewish settlers.[66] In pursuance of its objectives, Israel started limited military manœuvres and skirmishes, especially after the Arab Conference in Cairo in 1964 that rejected diverting the Jordan River. The Israeli launched low-scale border skirmishes that were a prelude to the six-day war of 1967 in which Israel seized the Jordan River and used its water supplies to the utmost, transporting 660 mcm of water per annum to the Negev desert. Israel did not hesitate in 1982 to admit that it had taken up to 600 mcm more than what the Johnston draft agreement has assigned for Israel. Accordingly, Israel has been exploiting more than 50 per cent of the Jordan River's water supplies. Israel drew water from the Jordan River daily even when this process caused water pollution in the southern end of the river. Moreover, Israel has been taking 230 million cubic metres of the Al-Auja River, also known as the Yarkon River. There are indications that if Israel were obliged to give up this quantity of water by replacing it with the desalinated seawater, it would cost it at least US$5 billion per annum. Israel's overexploitation of the Jordan River decreased Jordan's share to 49 per cent. Moreover, on average Jordan groundwater accumulated an annual deficit of about 75–100 mcm, which has been compensated for only in part by heavy rainfalls in recent winters.[67] The impacts of the Jordan water crisis as a result of the overuse of available resources are devastating, including air, water and marine pollution, soil degradation, drying out the Dead Sea and littering the landscape.[68] The deterioration of the Jordanian situation was made evident in the following:[69]

1. Israel nearly completed control of the Jordan River and diverted a large amount of its water to the Negev desert.
2. Jordan's need for water in 2000 reached 1,100 mcm with 25 per cent shortage.
3. The importance of Jordan's water increases with the expected population census rise to 6.2 million by 2010 in addition to 10 per cent of the Jordanians and Palestinians returning to Jordan during the first Gulf war.

4. The dry climate is important, as the desert forms 80 per cent of Jordan topography, as well as the increase in the salinity of the Jordan River due to Israel's overexploitation.
5. Persistent differences between Jordan and Syria led to the failure to build the Unity Dam on the Yarmuk River. According to the proposed project, Syria would receive 75 per cent of electrical power whilst Jordan would receive 10 mcm of water. The World Bank refused to finance the project partly due to the opposition of Israel, which believed that it would be deprived of 15 per cent of the Jordan River's water.

Before signing the bilateral peace agreement with Israel, Jordanian policy was based on awaiting Israeli goodwill around dividing the water resources of the Jordan River.[70] It is worth mentioning here that Israel proposed a number of projects several times to cover Jordan's needs for water.

1. Transporting water from Egypt and Lebanon to Jordan through Israel.
2. Building joint projects such as joint cooperation in Israeli water technology.
3. Cooperation in managing the subterranean water reservoirs.
4. Referring back to the Johnston Plan so Israel would obtain 40 per cent of the Jordan River water, Jordan would receive 45 per cent, and Syria and Lebanon would take 15 per cent, especially as it would cost much less for Jordan to cooperate with Israel than with Syria or Iraq. To transport one cubic metre of water from Iraq to Jordan would cost 50 cents, whilst cooperating with Israel would cost ten times less. It is worth mentioning here that the Jordanian delegation at the fifth round of the multilateral committee on water walked out of the meeting in protest against the ongoing Western blockade that was imposed on the Aqaba peninsula. They had reservations about the proposals made in the conference and its results. Nevertheless, this did not affect the peace talks between Jordan and Israel at a later stage.

As the two countries signed a peace agreement the water issue occupies a priority on the agenda of normalization. They signed a special agreement on constructing a canal linking the Red Sea with the Dead Sea. In the current Israeli–Jordanian peace negotiations, an amount of 70 mcm was assumed to have been the long-term average Israeli diversion quota over the recent decades.

This implies that what Israel had failed to achieve in its war with Jordan became achievable with peace (see Chapter 6).

The Litani River

Historically, the Litani was the basis for territorial demands on the part of the World Zionist Organization and later an object of interest to Israeli governments. Water was at the top of the Zionist movement's interests in Lebanon, especially after the French Mandate of Lebanon began. The French were pressured by the Zionist movement to set the Litani as the Lebanese borders. It is the second largest river of the region. The estimated annual discharge of the Litani averages 700 mcm. The Zionist plan included exploiting the river's water resources in order to develop the Negev desert but this demand was rejected by Lebanon and France.[71] In 1963, the Israeli air force attacked the installations of the first phase of a Lebanese project on the Litani River. One of the main targets of the Israeli invasion of Lebanon in 1978 was to control the Litani River, under the pretext that its water was being wasted in the sea. In fact, the Israeli occupation of southern Lebanon enabled Israel to pump 500 mcm of water from Lebanon on an annual basis. Israel set up projects to transfer water from the Litani River via large underground pipes. These pipes are 27 kilometres long so that they can reach the Sea of Galilee. This way, Israel gains 250 mcm from Lebanon annually.[72] In addition, Israel has linked a water network covering twelve Lebanese villages with its own projects to control the water and charged Lebanese residents of these villages for water. The charge is estimated at 500 Lebanese pounds per cubic metre. Furthermore, it exploited 92 per cent of the Al-Wazzani and Al-Hasbani rivers by linking pipes to the Sea of Galilee. Meanwhile, Israel has prevented farmers in south Lebanon from digging new wells.

With the 1982 invasion of Lebanon, Israel completed its process of usurping the water resources around it, the Al-Wazzani and Al-Hasbani rivers in particular, and was moving towards gaining complete control of the Litani River. Part of the water extracted is presently used for irrigation purposes along the course. Another substantial part of the water is diverted to the Awali River through the Markaba Tunnel for hydroelectric power production. In sum, only 125 mcm of water are left in the lower course of the river, which crosses the Israeli-occupied 'Security Zone'. The Lebanese government sent a memorandum to the United Nations that included all the information on Israel's usurpation of the Litani water and the installations that were erected on Al-Khardali Bridge to draw large amounts of water from the Litani River and store these amounts of water in huge containers in the Israeli settlements that were built in the northern areas of occupied Palestine for this purpose.[73] Despite the Security Council Resolution 425 that called for Israeli withdrawal from south Lebanon, Israel refused to leave the area until it was finally driven out by the Lebanese resistance group. This was not only due to Israel's need for the Litani water resources but also because of the close proximity of the water to the borders, its abundance and its purity.[74] Israeli proposals to cooperate with Lebanon to transport water to Israel and to set up various projects to exploit the water resources and to produce power were rejected by Lebanon. Lebanon decided not to attend the negotiation sessions held by the special committee on water, which was assigned by the peace conference. For example, Lebanon did not attend the fifth session that was held in Amman.[75] The terms of Israeli withdrawal from this area represent the main bone of contention between Israel and Lebanon in the ongoing peace negotiations. This has fed the fears of Lebanese representatives that Israel would use its physical presence in southern Lebanon to divert the river.[76] Israel's unilateral withdrawal from southern Lebanon, however, left the water issue between Israel and Lebanon unsettled.

5. Peace Talks and the Water Issue

Palestinian Authority control of the Gaza Strip and West Bank did not improve the situation. Israel managed successfully to control 95 per cent of the water in the West Bank and the Gaza Strip on an annual basis. It is estimated that these areas contain 930 mcm of water.[77] Israel expressed its interest in Arab waters during the peace conference on the Middle East especially within the framework of multilateral negotiations. The negotiating positions of Arab countries and Israel were far too opposed for there to be any reconciliation. In the Muscat conference for instance, which Syria and Lebanon refused to attend, the Palestinian delegation reinforced its demand to have complete control over Palestinian water. The Palestinian position aimed at redistributing the water resources and to stop Israel usurping Palestinian water, whereas the Israeli position sought to benefit from the technological advances that Israel had achieved in the water domain. The Israeli proposals were based on two principles:[78]

1. Israel deals with its occupation of the Arab territories as an admissible issue. This gives Israel the right to use the water in the Arab occupied territories as it likes.
2. Israel should be the centre of inter-regional water transfer project.

The failure of the first four rounds of talks held by the water committee was due to Israel's insistence on continued occupation of the territories that contain large water reservoirs and diverting these waters by force to the surface waterway resources and draining Arab water by using modern technology that the neighbouring Arab countries have not acquired.[79] It is worth mentioning that Israel obtains 22 per cent of its water from the Golan Heights and 10 per cent from southern Lebanon to help cover its annual consumption of water.[80] The fifth round of talks, which was held in Muscat, was considered the most successful despite the absence of Syria and Lebanon in protest against Israel's positions in previous rounds of negotiation. The most important outcome of the fifth round was that Israel agreed to a Palestinian water authority being formed. Analysts attribute the change in the Israeli position to American pressure.[81] The Oslo II Israeli-Palestinian Water Agreement forms the basis for a future plan under the doctrine of equitable utilization.[82] The signing of the Declaration of Principles between Israel and the PLO in September 1993, following the Gaza–Jericho Agreement, and the Israeli–Jordanian Peace Treaty of October 1994 triggered a dynamic change which makes an about-turn unlikely.[83]

The next conflict in the region will be over water, not oil, and any inaccurate information about the water resources in the current circumstances in which the multilateral peace negotiations are being held might have a negative effect on the Arab negotiators. Israel's current strategic objective is to share the water with the Syrians and Lebanese through official agreements after it managed to share water resources with Jordan. It is the Middle East that is particularly worrisome. Meir Ben Meir, Israel's Water Commissioner, paints a gloomy picture of possible conflict over water between Israel, the Palestinians, Jordan and Syria. In a recent interview with the BBC, Ben Meir said that if there were not sufficient water in the Jordan Valley, 'then we shall doubtless face war'. There is a real likelihood that the water issue could hold up the Middle East peace talks. Palestinian leaders believe that to ensure sustainable peace Israel must release land and water and change the way it uses water supplies. The Jordan Valley is not unique. In other ancient water systems like the Tigris and Euphrates, there is also a danger of conflict over water. Turkey's Grand Anatolia Project, or GAP, is steadily reducing the flow of the Euphrates into Syria and Iraq, heightening political tensions.[84] The recent rapprochement in Turkey's relations with the Arab world could mark the beginning of a new era in the two parties' relations that would ultimately have a positive impact on the issue of water between the two sides.

6. Turkey and the Water Alternative

In the Middle East, a region marked by hostility between nations, obtaining adequate water supplies is a high political priority. Water has been a contentious issue in recent negotiations between Israel and Arab countries. In recent years, Iraq, Syria and Turkey have exchanged verbal threats over their use of shared rivers. 'It should come as no surprise to learn that the words "river" and "rival" share the same Latin root; a rival is someone who shares the same stream.'[85]

Israeli–Turkish cooperation aims at exhausting Arab water resources and controlling them to create a real water crisis in the eastern region of the Arab world. This has been realized so far in the Turkish initiative to build dams along the Euphrates watercourse and on the tributaries of Tigris River, and in its control of the amounts of water flow in these two rivers at the cost of Syria and Iraq. The Tigris and Euphrates rivers have their sources in Turkey, with the latter also flowing through Syria before reaching Iraq. The Grand Anatolia Project, which was inaugurated in 2001, is evidence of this policy. It is a multi-purpose project comprised of thirteen main projects for irrigation and power generation through the building of twenty-one dams, including seventeen on the Euphrates, four on the Tigris, and building seventeen power plants on the two rivers and the tributaries. The total cost of the project is estimated at US$20 billion. The construction of the GAP project achieves many benefits for Turkey's national economy and strengthens its regional role, but reduces the flow of water to Syria and Iraq, impacting particularly on irrigation and power projects in both countries. The problem of water shortage in the Euphrates comes in the absence of an international agreement on water-sharing between the three countries. Negotiations on water distribution started in 1962, but later on were frozen. On numerous occasions, former Turkish President, Suleiman Demirel, announced that the water source is based in Turkey and those who were using these resources could not tell Turkey how to use its own resources (see Map 2). There are oil fields based in many Arab countries and Turkey has no say on their use.

The Turkish government in the late 1980s attempted to open a new chapter in its relations with the Arab states. The then Turkish President Turgut Ozal made an official visit to Syria in July 1987 and Iraq in April 1988. The Turkish approach towards the exploitation of the Euphrates and the Tigris was disappointing for both countries, Syria and Iraq. They believe that the flow of 500 cubic metres of water per second is too low and they have demanded an appropriate share of water, asking for 700 cubic metres per second. Turkey continually refused these demands, arguing that the consumption level per person in Syria and Iraq is much higher in comparison to Turkey. On 23 January 1990, Turkey lowered the flow rate of the Euphrates from 500 cubic metres per second to 120 cubic metres per second. The Turkish projects caused huge losses to Syria and Iraq. Syria lost 40 per cent of the quantity of water that it used to obtain from the Euphrates. This reached 15.7 mcm per annum.[86]

The losses included stopping the operation of seven out of eight turbines at the power station on the Euphrates dam, which provided Syria with 70 per cent of its electricity. This also happened to the Qadissiyah power station in Iraq, which stopped functioning completely in 1991.[87] The losses of Iraq's harvests were estimated at 15 per cent.[88] The accession to power first by the Refah party led by Najmel Din Erbakan, and currently the Justice and Development party AKP led by Erdogan, both with Islamist tendencies, maintained ties with Israel, but helped to ease the tension with the Arab world, particularly Syria and Iraq and Hamas in the Gaza Strip. Erdogan's visit succeeded in improving relations with Syria, with an exchange of visits by dignitaries, including the state visit paid to Turkey by the Syrian President Bashar Assad. Abdullah Gul, the Turkish President, paid his first state visit to Iraq, the first in thirty-three years, and promised to double the amount of water allocated for Iraq from the Tigris and Euphrates river.[89] He also paid, in May 2009, an official visit to Damascus. President Bashar Assad paid another state visit to Turkey on 16 September 2009 where he signed a strategic cooperation agreement with Ankara.[90] Moreover, the Turkish president paid an official visit to Jordan and attended the conclusion of an agreement on 3 December between a Turkish company and the Jordanian government for the construction of a water development plant that will provide Jordan with one million cubic metres of water annually. The two countries also concluded a free trade agreement.[91]

Joint Israeli–Turkish cooperation in the water domain manifested itself in the proposal of a number of joint projects. Among these was a plan to transport water from Turkey to Israel on ships twice a month by Israeli companies. This might develop into extending a sea pipeline between the two countries.[92] The two parties also put forward a project to build Turkish Peace Pipes. This position was reflected in the Peace Pipeline Project that aims to provide Israel, a number of Middle Eastern Arab countries and the Gulf States with water (see

Table 7.5). The project will cost around US$20 billion and it will be financed by the Arab parties. This project aims at handing national security and Arab food security to Turkey through Israel, which would be the greater beneficiary, especially as Turkey wants to bargain water in return for Arab oil. Some observers suggest that, instead of causing future wars, resource shortages will actually encourage a growing trade in water between regional states. They say that an economic interdependence based on water will help avoid conflict. Turkey is one country which apparently supports this view, believing that it can supply fresh water from its southern coast to the Middle East and Mediterranean regions. The Manavgat River flows down towards the Mediterranean, wasting billions of gallons of water every year which Turkey now wants to sell.[93] It would pump water from the Seyhan and Ceyan rivers and transport it to the Arab countries.

Table 7.5. Peace Pipes Distribution

The first line: Transportation of 3.65 million cubic metres	Quotas per Country
Turkey	300,000 cubic metres
Syria	Aleppo 300,000 cubic metres Homs 100,000 cubic metres Damascus 650,000 cubic metres
Jordan	Amman 600,000 cubic metres
Saudi Arabia	Tabuk 100,000 cubic metres Medina 300,000 cubic metres Dammam 200,000 cubic metres Yanbu 100, 000 cubic metres Mecca 500,000 cubic metres Jeddah 500, 000 cubic metres
The second line: transportation of 2.5 million cubic metres	
Kuwait	600,000 cubic metres
Saudi Arabia	Jubayl 200,000 cubic metres Dammam 200,000 cubic metres Khubar 200,000 cubic metres Al Hufuf 200,000 cubic metres
Bahrain	Manama 200,000 cubic metres
Qatar	Doha 100,000 cubic metres

Emirates	Abu Dhabi 280,000 cubic metres Dubai 160,000 cubic metres Sharjah 120,000 cubic metres Ras al Khaymah, Ajman, Al Fujairah and Umm al Quwain 40,000 cubic metres
Oman	Muscat 200,000 cubic metres

Source: Hamdi Al Taher, *Mustaqbal Al Miyah Fil Alam Al Arabi*, 1991, p. 290.

The project, however, was rejected by the Arabs despite Turkey's efforts to persuade them, especially with the low cost incurred. It is worth mentioning that the cost of producing one cubic metre of desalinated water in the Gulf States is US$5. The reasons for the Arab rejection of the Turkish–Israeli plan could be summarized in the following:

1. There is Arab suspicion and distrust of Turkish domination of Arab states by using the weapon of water to pressure them.
2. Israel is the greatest beneficiary whilst usurping Arab water.
3. Syria and Iraq share water resources from the Euphrates and Tigris with Turkey and there is no need to purchase water when they have the natural right to obtain water free of charge. It is worth mentioning that Turkey will gain revenues of US$2 billion annually for selling water.

Israeli–Turkish cooperation came about in conformity with the regional role. Turkey aspires to have an active role in the new Middle Eastern order, with water being a strategic tool to pressure the Arab states for more concessions. Israel hopes to use its relations with Turkey to influence the outcome of the peace process and to pressure Syria for more concessions.

7. Water and the Israeli Policy towards Ethiopia

Ethiopia occupies a high priority in Israel contemporary strategy towards the Arab world because it is one of the main water resources for both Sudan and Egypt as it controls 85 per cent of the River Nile that passes through Sudan and Egypt.[94] Israel is working on encouraging Ethiopia to build a dam along the watercourse of the Blue Nile, which makes up to 80 per cent of Nile water, and to set up other irrigation projects on the Nile, thereby affecting the water level of the Nile in Sudan and Egypt. The proposal includes thirty-three dams, most of which would be situated on the Blue Nile. It would enable Ethiopia to obtain 7 billion cubic metres of water more, in other words, 20 per cent of Egypt and Sudan's shares (see Table 7.6). By cooperating with Ethiopia and Eritrea, Israel seeks to prevent the building of an Arab lake on the Red Sea and to minimize the role of water being used as a weapon against it. The disagreement arising on the allocation of the Nile water stipulated a soft reaction from Egypt. The new government in Egypt called for a dialogue among the Nile states to address any grievances.

Table 7.6. The Egyptian and Sudanese Damage as a Result of Israeli–Ethiopian Cooperation

State	1990	2000	Deficiency
Egypt	55.5 billion cubic metres	70 billion cubic metres	14 billion cubic metres
Sudan	18.5 billion cubic metres	24 billion cubic metres	6 billion cubic metres

Israel was trying to exploit the deteriorating economic and technological situations of the African countries and worked on filling this void. It profited from American plans that aimed at strengthening vital American interests in the region. Israel did not neglect the countries where the River Nile passes: Tanzania, Burundi, Rwanda, Zaire, Kenya and Uganda (see Map 3). Israel cooperated with each of them in the water domain in order to influence the Arab countries.[95]

Israel adopted policies towards Africa intended to impose a blockade on the Arab countries. The Israeli policies include the control of the flow of water from the River Nile, facilitating the immigration of the Jewish Falasha from Ethiopia and controlling small Arab islands in the Red Sea to use them as military bases. The presence of the Jewish Falasha in Ethiopia and Israel's desire to transfer them to Palestine in order to consolidate Israel's demographical weight to balance the considerable increase of the Arab population is another determining factor in pursuance of its foreign policy towards Ethiopia. Israel sent experts to conduct research in Uganda and worked on strengthening its relations with the late separatist leader John Garang in the south of Sudan, supporting his petition for independence. The policy was intended to weaken Sudan and put pressure on Egypt. The construction of the proposed water dams would ultimately affect Somalia as well since the construction of such projects in the Ogaden province would obstruct the water flow to Somalia.

8. Conclusion

The study reflects the reality of the water situation in all Arab countries except Egypt, which has subterranean water estimated at 400 square kilometres in addition to 130 square kilometres of water resources from the Aswan dam. It demonstrates the difficult situation that the Arab world is currently experiencing. Israel controls more than 2.3 billion cubic metres of the Arab water resources. The crisis is worsening and the potential for the outbreak of another regional conflict over water between the Arabs and Israel is strengthened due to the population increase on both sides and the continuing decline in the water reservoirs. The study shows how Israel moved from being in a state of Arab blockade to imposing a blockade on the Arab world through its cooperative relations with neighbouring countries in order to achieve its goals. Israel also succeeded in bridging its relations with Turkey through the marketing of a new Middle East order and the Turkish use of water as a strategic weapon in times of peace and war. Israeli cooperation with African countries through which the River Nile passes shares similar goals. This does not undermine, however, other objectives of the Israeli foreign policy, such as confronting Islamic fundamentalism through its cooperation with Turkey and transferring the Jewish Falasha from Ethiopia.

Israel considers Arab–Israeli cooperation to have great importance because it would contribute enormously to normalization between the two parties and the failure to do so would increase the level of enmity and aversion between the two sides. Water scarcity would exacerbate the situation, trouble the region and threaten the peace process. The effect of the regional water shortage in the region can be summarized in the following points.

1. Israel interest in water did not come about as a result of the peace negotiations; it began with the Zionist movement, which called for a Jewish state extending from the Euphrates to the Nile.
2. Israeli control of the water in the Levant region, and the success of Israel in cooperating with the neighbouring countries, have weakened the Arabs' negotiating position.
3. Israel is the focus of all proposed water distribution plans aimed at establishing a water system, such as the Peace Pipes Project.
4. The increasing need for water in the occupied Arab territories was mainly due to the increase in Jewish migration to Palestine, and the natural

increase of the Arab population in Palestine. If real peace is reached, which would lead to the return of some Arab refugees to Palestine, the need for water will double.

5. The temptations of Israeli technology gained a positive response from the Arab states, especially after the fifth round of the conference on water in Muscat.
6. The damage caused by Israeli cooperation with the countries where the rivers originate for some Arab countries should be one of the main principles in outlining the relations that should be established between the Arabs and the neighbouring countries.
7. Israel exploited the poverty and economic needs of African countries, by sponsoring water projects, to inflict greater damage on the Arab water resources.

Taking into account the zero-sum game whereby any gain for Israel is a loss for the Arabs and vice versa, and with the current imbalance between the two parties, the analysis reveals that any peace that can be reached in the region would be in favour of Israel. In economic terms the crisis is mainly a problem of demand, and in its spatial dimension, a regional challenge.[96] Therefore the peace agreements between Israel and the Arab countries will be nothing more than bilateral settlements; they will not achieve normalization or reach what is known as cultural peace. In the meantime, the continuation of tension over water could lead to the outbreak of economic, political and strategic conflicts between the two parties, which could lead to a war. On the other hand, the chapter emphasizes the necessity to set up an Arab plan on local and pan-Arab levels with steps to focus on determining the priorities in distributing the water resources, rationing consumption, determining the degree of self-sufficiency, exploring new water resources, developing the available resources and using modern technology in desalination. It is necessary to take into account the integration between the surface and subterranean resources and use them in the most efficient way. This requires:

1. Solving the inter-Arab conflicts and water disputes and separating them from any political differences among Arab governments.
2. Forming a water strategy, starting with a precise study on the situation

of the Arab water with all its economic, political and judicial aspects at present and in the future.

3. Completing, updating and coordinating statistics concerning these resources, creating programmes and water surveillance networks and exchanging existing information on coordinated principles.
4. Consolidating water cooperation in building joint dams and canals to achieve the maximum water benefit.
5. Processing the joint subterranean and surface water through building joint reservoirs and setting up integral management of these reservoirs.
6. Using unconventional water resources through desalinating water and processing sewage water for irrigation.
7. Setting up a study centre for Arab water as a subsidiary of the Arab League to observe, adopt and implement Arab and foreign projects related to Arab water resources. It would encourage research and guarantee a cheaper cost for water desalination, including the use of solar energy.
8. Preserving the strategic balance with the neighbouring countries to deter any violation of Arab water rights.

The *Arab Human Development Reports* listed other recommendations[97] to be taken to overcome the critical situation encountered by the Arab countries:

1. Optimization of water allocation.
2. Implementation of an optimal water productivity strategy.
3. Holistic and integrated approaches to water resources, supply and demand planning and management.
4. Capacity building and technical upgrading of all stakeholders.
5. Awareness-raising at all levels, from end users to decision-makers.
6. Issuing and implementing sustainable water policies
7. Development of water resources management models that can stimulate different solution scenarios to select the optimal approach.

Water scarcity has a direct effect on Arab states' ability to secure food sufficiency for domestic consumption. Consequently, food shortage and insecurity are discussed in this book as the third macro-level case study intended to investigate and analyse the different variables involved in shaping Arab states' foreign policy undertakings, being part of the output process and simultaneously part of the input process.

Chapter 8

Food Insecurity in the Arab World

1. Introduction

Food crisis is another dilemma for the Arab countries, playing a detrimental role in shaping their foreign policy-making. It has played a significant role throughout history, shaping the development of civilizations. Securing food has become one of the most serious challenges for humanity since 1974, the year of the global food crisis, which led countries to view it as a component of national security. The UN on the day of eliminating hunger on 16 October 2009 announced that the number of hungry people in the world has reached 1 billion, with an increase of 100 million people due to the global economic crisis and increased food prices[1] and 2.5 billion people suffer from malnutrition. Data also reveal that more than 5 million children die annually because of malnutrition, especially in rural areas where more than 70 per cent of the world's population lives. The UN Secretary-General and the Food and Agricultural Organization (FAO) General Secretary announced on 15 November 2009 that they would go on hunger strike for one day in their attempt to draw world attention to the famine problem.[2] The number of hungry people in the Near East and North Africa was estimated at 42 million.[3] Arab countries are being severely hit by the current global food crisis because they are large net food importers and have to rely on imports to meet almost 50 per cent of their food demands. Food shortage is not only a challenge to the economic system but to the social, political and security variables that form the domestic context of any decision-making apparatus. It is argued that there can be no stability in a world threatened by famine or diseases caused by malnutrition. The dilemma of the food crisis in the Arab world has taken different forms over the last few years. It includes the insufficiency of domestic food production, the decline in the food self-sufficiency rate, the increase in the demand due to relatively high population growth rate and the widening of the food gap.

This chapter argues that the Arab world today is facing a food security dilemma due to the imbalance between demand and supply of locally produced food commodities. The increase in the Arab population to reach 331 million in 2007 combined with a sharp decline in the production of strategic domestic food commodities, and ultimately led the Arab countries to become increasingly dependent on food exporting countries. The crisis transformed the problem into an ongoing political issue because imports of strategic commodities like grain, the most important foodstuff consumed by the Arab people, increased the Arab states' dependency on the outside world, adding further limitations to foreign policy-making.

Here I discuss the potential dilemma of the food shortage in the Arab world and its impacts on the Arab states' foreign policy-makings. It covers the volume of the food gap, highlights the rates of production and compares them with the rates of consumption. It also aims at understanding the causes of this food gap, the required strategy to realize food security and the importance of joint Arab action to achieve Arab targets in this respect. The chapter employs the analytical[4] and inductive approaches[5] in order to investigate the dilemmas of food security in the Arab world. The quantitative approach is also used, with graphs and tables to support the analysis and the results.

There is dialectic between the increase in population levels and the decrease in food production growth. The crisis is no longer merely an economic problem; it has acquired political and security significance. The demographic challenge coupled with the climate changes has led the Arab countries to depend on the United States, Canada and Australia to cover 50 per cent of the food consumption. This is where the danger lies, especially once food has become a strategic weapon in the hands of producing and exporting countries. Thus finding a strategy to achieve food security becomes very important: joint Arab action towards food development is an urgent strategic target that needs to be realized. So what is the required strategy? What is the essence of Arab efforts today to achieve Arab food security?

2. Features of the Arab Food Status[6]

Understanding the main features of the Arab food situation requires looking at some of the main features of Arab food economies and some of the main factors that determine the trajectory of food production. The concept of food security evolved to rest upon four pillars: food availability, food stability, food accessibility and food safety.[7] Previous specialized studies have highlighted the following important facts.

First, Arab states have been facing volatile food conditions as a result of a lack of resources, such as water, desertification, insufficiency of skilled manpower, the decline in per capita income in this sector and the effect of natural disasters such as floods, which cause damage to vast areas of grains and vegetables in countries like Sudan, Egypt, Syria, Lebanon and Arab north Africa.[8] The situation becomes more complex due to the fact that, whilst the majority of the Arab countries are encountering unprecedented population increase, their food production is on the decline. In the 1970s, the growth of agricultural production did not exceed 1.8 per cent whilst the annual demand for food commodities was 4.6 per cent. The period 1975–84 witnessed a rise in the growth of agricultural output to reach 2.5 per cent, but was short of meeting the demands indicator of 6 per cent per annum, causing the Arab self-sufficiency level to drop by 60 per cent and further increasing Arab dependency on the outside market to meet domestic demands for food products.[9] The population has been increasing at a rate of 3 per cent (the population of the Arab world between 1980 and 2007 increased from 150 to 317 million and will reach 743 million in 2030), whereas the growth rate in agriculture will not exceed 2 per cent.[10] The problem is epitomized in the dichotomy between the national ability to produce food and the populations' need for food. This problem develops according to the rates of food consumption and production throughout the years. Since current production does not fulfil consumption needs, reliance on food imports becomes the only viable option. The average rate of consumption development is over double the rate of food production (about 3 per cent); food imports have increased to close the widening gap between food production and consumption and to contain the increasing low level of self-sufficiency with regards to the main food commodities. Therefore, the Arab countries will remain subjected to the pressures of the food exporting countries, especially if these countries insist on having full control of their resources.

Second, the vital domain of agriculture has been limited. Whilst the arable lands in the Arab countries amount to approximately 50 million hectares,[11] only 3.5 per cent of this land is cultivated. In 2007, the Arab population reached 317 million whilst productivity in agriculture has declined and the gap within and between agriculture and other sectors of the economy has widened. Farmers' needs should be attended to and they must receive sufficient incentives to expand production.[12] This requires increasing the amount of land that is cultivated, intensifying production and improving the quality of harvests. It is worth mentioning here that this will be difficult to achieve because the Arab countries have not made the most of the cultivated areas that already exist, let alone of other arable lands.

Third, the scarcity of water is another obstacle to the development of agriculture, as the water resources of the Arab world do not exceed 0.74 per cent of the world's entire water resources and 67 per cent of these resources spring outside of Arab territories. Accordingly, the average annual quota of the Arab citizen does not exceed 1,744 cubic metres.[13] The situation is more complicated with regards to agriculture. It is argued that the Arab countries used 71 per cent of their available water and more than two-thirds of this amount was used for agriculture.[14] Arab cultivated lands relying mostly on rainfall occupy nearly 80 per cent of the total cultivated land (see Table 8.1). It is worth mentioning that the quality and quantity of planted products that depend on rainfall always vary. This is due to the irregularity of the amount of rainfall and its seasons. Therefore the level of pluvial harvests is low compared with those harvests that rely on irrigation. However, the increasing demands for wheat and oat led these products to be planted in lands with insufficient water rather than being left in grazing lands. In addition, the planting of these products has been extended to irrigated lands that do not have sufficient irrigation water. This has a negative effect on the fertility of the land and the level of crops.

Fourth, the rural population in 2006 was 129.2 million, representing 41.9 per cent of the total population, whereas the number of farmers was 87.7 million (see Table 8.1) and the number of those engaged directly in the agriculture sector not more than 32.5 million, making 37.1 per cent of the total farming population. They account for half the labour force in Djibouti and Sudan and 44 per cent in Mauritania and Yemen, between 35.7 and 18.5 per cent in Morocco, Egypt, Oman Syria, Algeria and Tunisia and less than 8.5 per cent in the other Arab countries.[15] Despite the fact that the majority of the workforce depends on agriculture, which is estimated to represent 63 per cent of the population, the real number of those who actually work in this domain does not exceed 28 per cent. Farmers' annual growth is 0.91 per cent whereas the population growth rate is about 2.3 per cent. Food insecurity in the Arab countries has 'partly resulted from the declining per capita productivity in agriculture'.[16] Figures illustrate the low productivity of the Arab farmer and the hidden unemployment in the countryside.[17]

Table 8.1. Agricultural Sector Economic Indicators

	2000	2005	2006	2007
Agricultural Production*	56315	69301	80222	89786
Per Capita	210	230	260	284
% of Agricultural contribution to GDP	8.3	6.4	6.2	6.1
Total Cultivated Land**	65429	71412	71310	n. a.

Rural Population	125956000	130132000	129185000	n. a.
Agriculture Population	86773000	87555000	87741000	n. a.
% of Labour force in Agriculture	31.3	28.1	27.7	n. a.
Per Capita of the Value Added in Agriculture	1855	2156	2466	n. a.
Economic Agricultural Efficiency	0.27	0.23	0.22	n. a.

*Million of tons
**Thousand hectares
Source: *Al-Taqrir al-Iqtisady al-Arabi al-Muahad*, 2008, pp. 295–300.

Fifth, the individual's average share of cultivated land is small in comparison with international averages. This is currently estimated to be about 3.3 duwnam.[18] It was expected to decrease to less than 2,500 square metres by the end of the twentieth century. This means that the individual's share in agricultural production will continue to decrease in comparison to the international average.[19] The small size of property ownership, the multiplicity of ownership systems of arable lands and the lack of stability in Arab countries, along with the absence of coordination, all have a negative effect on the productivity level of the Arab farmer even if he has the means to increase production. This is illustrated by the fact that the productivity of the Arab farmer is not enough to feed three people whereas the productivity of farmers in some developed countries can feed up to 150 people. This is not just about inefficiency: the fertility and the size of the land together with the lack of modern technology play an important role in increasing this failure to achieve self-sufficiency.

Sixth, the small area of cultivated land that is regularly used in the Arab world covers around 435 million hectares, which is equivalent to 4.3 per cent of the world's cultivated areas. It represents 8.2 per cent of all arable lands in the Arab world, which means that only 0.32 per cent of the total Arab area is regularly cultivated.[20] The dominant system that is used in the Arab world of allowing the cultivated land to lie fallow for a year or more[21] reduces the amount of the productive capability. The situation is made worse by the governments' attempts to diversify the economy. New trends include reclaiming agricultural lands for real estate developments and expanding construction works. There are a number of urban development projects being carried out by countries that are in dire need of this kind of land, due to its close proximity to areas of human settlement, in spite of the fact that there are many wastelands unsuitable for agriculture upon which such projects could be built, with no need for the systematic and exhausting processes of desertification that have been occurring due to human and non-human factors, including the demographic explosion, the changing of social values and the changing mode of agricultural production.[22] If the pretext for this is transport and the difficulties in dealing with the desert then the solution lies in setting up an infrastructure that will allow those areas to be moved elsewhere rather than taking agriculture land.

Seventh, small and light farmwork dominates most of the cultivated lands, where production depends often on the available and practical potential. The most important of these types of farmwork are primitive manual work, animal husbandry, seed farming and organic fertilization. This shows that the Arab farmer still does not have the means to buy modern machinery, or the know-how necessary to use sophisticated techniques to achieve more efficiently or increase the productivity level of the cultivated land or to include areas that have not already been cultivated.

Eighth, despite the marginal improvements in food production in 2007 which could be related to the introduction of technology in some Arab countries, it remains lower than the other underdeveloped and developed countries, especially in grains, wheat and barley, with surplus in sugar cane for export (see Table 8.2). The rate of increase in food production varied from 0.3 per cent for wheat, 2.9 for corn, 3 for vegetables and 6.3 per cent for barley.[23] The low productivity rate in grain, wheat and barley, in comparison with the rest of the world, could be attributed[24] to the underdevelopment of the productive agricultural base and primitive means of production, as well as illiteracy and lack of agricultural awareness on the part of the farmers, which demonstrates the deteriorated condition of the cultivated lands, the shortage in irrigated water and the insufficiency of the necessary investment in agricultural development.[25]

Table 8.2. Comparison of Crop Production

	Arab Countries		Developed Countries		Under developed Countries		World	
	2000	2007	2000	2007	2000	2007	2000	2007
Grains	1.4	1.8	3.2	3.6	2.5	2.8	3.0	3.0
Wheat	1.6	2.5	2.5	2.6	2.7	2.8	2.5	2.6
Barley	0.4	1.1	2.7	2.7	1.6	1.7	2.4	2.5
Vegetable	18.2	20.4	20.0	20.0	15.5	16.0	16.0	16.0

Fruits	10.8	7.4	9.5	9.5	9.0	9.0	9.1	9.2
Sugar Cane	100.4	111.8	75.0	75.0	65.0	65.0	66.0	66.0

Source: *Al-Taqrir al-Iqtisadi al-Arabi al-Muwahad,* 2008, p. 56.

For instance, grains are considered the most important Arab crops as they occupy 64 per cent of the cultivated lands. Nevertheless, the average Arab production of grains does not exceed 1.1 tons per hectare, whereas international production reaches 1.9 tons per hectare – a difference of 42 per cent. The average production level of wheat, which is considered the most important Arab harvest, is approximately one ton per hectare whilst in other developing countries it is higher by 20 per cent and internationally by 65 per cent. Meanwhile, the production levels of slender corn and tobacco are both 25 per cent less than the average production level worldwide whereas the production of oats is below the international production level by 50 per cent.[26] Consequently, levels of per capita food availability vary considerably between three groups of Arab countries. The overall quantities range from 2,200 grams per day in Lebanon, where hunger is prevalent for 3 per cent of the population; to 1,500 grams per day in Saudi Arabia, where 4 per cent of the population suffers nutrient deprivation.[27]

Studies have indicated that harvests will continue at this level in the short term and that grains will continue to be the main consumed crops.[28] The cultivation of grains occupies 72 per cent of all cultivated land in the Arab world; estimates indicate a decrease of about 13.8 per cent in the production of all grains due to a decrease in cultivated areas by 4.2 per cent and a decrease in harvest by 5.7 per cent.[29] Therefore the lack of self-sufficiency in grain production along with the high percentage of land that grains occupy will have negative effects on low Arab agricultural productivity in general. Food accessibility is strongly influenced by government economic policies and openness to the world market. The accelerated 200 per cent rise in grain prices since 2001 has made it more difficult to obtain bread in most Arab countries, including the oil-rich states, Saudi Arabia and the UAE. Since October 2007, Egypt, Morocco and Mauritania have witnessed public protests over flattening bread supply and surging prices. Syria, Lebanon and Yemen, too, have found it extremely difficult to obtain bread. In Yemen, prices for wheat and wheat products doubled in one year and this might have already increased national poverty by 6 per cent.[30] Egypt, in early 2008, saw brawls in the bread queues in front of bakeries which caused a number of deaths and wounded.[31] The need for grains in Arab countries, which still import half of the grains they consume, makes the shift towards cultivating other crops a very important, viable and logical alternative. The first step could be in educating the consumers about alternative food products in order to minimize the total Arab consumption of grains. The next step would be to call for the local planting of various agricultural crops to lessen the burden on the state budget as a result of policies of subsidies and imports – reducing its subordination to the exporting countries and avoiding the exhaustion of the land. Increasing food insecurity in the region requires higher Arab investment in agriculture. Strategic stores should also be created to achieve food security and stability for society in the face of changes in climate conditions.

Ninth, livestock production in the Arab countries suffers in the same way as crop production. This is reflected in the low level of unit productivity as well as of general production growth. Arab countries have some 373 million heads of livestock, mostly in Sudan. However, the average size of livestock is estimated at 135 kilograms, in comparison with 182 kilograms in some European countries, America, New Zealand and Australia. The average rate of slaughtered livestock reaches 13.2 per cent, whereas on an international level it reaches 18.3 per cent. Moreover, the average weight of a slaughtered unit in the Arab world is approximately 120–130 kilograms whereas the world average is roughly 179 kilograms. In addition, the growth in the number of livestock is low as the average is no more than 2.3 per cent annually.[32] The importance of livestock production lies in the fact that it cannot be excluded from the food security issue. Furthermore, the emphasis in the field of livestock production in the Arab countries is on assessing marketable livestock production. The livestock growing in several Arab countries is based on the personal or tribal initiative for mainly tribal or social reasons rather than economic incentive, such as export for instance, or even for self-consumption. Animals are used for economic purposes: they carry or pull loads and tools; they are also used for ploughing and softening land. The absence of an active policy on livestock production led to a drop in the growth of meat production in the Arab countries, due to the shortage in concentrated forage, the lack of pasture, the spread of diseases and the low productivity of genetic composition. As a result of these factors, the Arab economy has a heavy burden to cover the deficit in the balance of trade to secure the requirements for livestock products. Fish, however, could present an alternative to make up for the red meat shortage (see Figure 7). The region has 22.2 thousand kilometres of coastline and 16.6 thousand kilometres of rivers. It produces 3.8 million tons of fish annually, mostly in Morocco, Mauritania, Egypt, Yemen and Oman.[33]

Dairy production is stagnant. At the beginning of the 1970s, dairy production reached a level of 7.2 million tons but a few years later the production growth stopped. Reports revealed that only 40 per cent of production capacity in Arab factories is actually being used.[34] This is due to the lack of growth in numbers of milking cattle that stand at around 6.6 million and to the decrease in the annual level of production per head. Whilst the international level of production per head reaches 1,910 kilograms per annum, the production in Egypt, Sudan and Mauritania, for instance, reaches half, one-third and one-sixth respectively of that figure. [35]

Table 8.3. Arab Food Gap for Main Crops (2000–2006) (%)

Group/Year	2000	2001	2002	2003	2004	2005	2006
All Grains	46.4	49. 7	48.2	57.3	55.2	49.7	56.3
Wheat	46.0	48.2	46.4	58.3	53.73	49.93	57.99
Barley	21.2	44.9	39.0	56.1	51.6	32.4	41.6
Rice	67.8	66.2	74.8	74.4	73.18	70.62	74.61
Corn	38.5	39.5	36.4	40.5	44.3	36.2	38.2
Potato	98.3	98.4	97.8	99.1	100.6	100.6	101.2
Sugar	37.8	33.9	32.6	33.8	34.8	38.5	33.5
Pulses	57.6	61.1	61.5	64.4	62.12	56.2	59.82
Oils & Fats	45.6	39.3	39.6	35.1	31.1	28.1	27.8
Vegetables	99.2	99	99.7	99.4	100.1	100	99.7
Fruits	97.3	95.5	96.2	96.5	96	95.9	96.8
All Meats	85.9	85.7	85.4	82.7	83	80.9	81.3
Dairy Products	71.5	68.9	68.4	69.9	71	71.4	71
Eggs	96.8	97.4	98.1	98.7	96.3	95.9	96.4
Fish	108.3	102.7	107.4	102.9	101.6	103	103.8

Source: *Al-Taqrir al-Iqtisadi al-Arabi al-Muwahad,* 2008, p. 310.

Statistics show a fall in the averages of food self-sufficiency since 1970 with few exceptions. Table 8.3 illustrates the percentage of food self-sufficiency amongst the most important food groups in the Arab world between 2000 and 2006. The table shows a clear food gap in all food crops, which inevitably presents a dilemma for decision-makers and further challenges the quest for food self-sufficiency. The table also reveals the efforts made by some Arab countries in the agricultural sector where improvement in some food crops production was clear, especially in fish, potato, vegetables and eggs where production represented 96 per cent and above whilst a gap continued to exist in some other food products like oils and fat, sugar, corn and legumes at less than 50 per cent. Date was another crop with significant increase. Tunisia's date production was expected to increase by 11 per cent in 2009 to 155,000 tons. It occupies the first list of date-producer countries where 80 to 85 per cent of the total production is exported.[36]

3. Development of the Food Gap in the Arab World

The food gap is defined as the size of the gap between local production and net imports of all food commodities. The gap increases as a result of growing demand rates surpassing the rates of production growth. The shortage in production in comparison to increased levels of consumption in the food domain in the Arab world led to a huge deficit in the trade balance of all main food commodities (as demonstrated in Table 8.3). Arab food imports in 2006 amounted to $27 billion, with an increase of 1.6 per cent in terms of price.[37] The dangers of overdependence on international markets to secure food needs came home sharply in the spring of 2008 when global food prices skyrocketed. In most Arab countries 'the price increases impose a heavy fiscal burden on governments, apart from creating social and political unrest'.[38] By mid-2008, food prices were 40 per cent higher in comparison with the same period the year before. The impact was felt in virtually all Arab countries, including the oil-rich countries. Prices of wheat increased by 200 per cent, driving up the prices of food commodities in general by 75 per cent since the beginning of the twenty-first century.[39] 'Food price increases are likely to increase poverty in the short run. The poor in urban areas, the rural landless and small and marginal farmers stand to lose.'[40]

The food gap in most Arab countries puts them in a vicious circle: dependency on foreign markets for food commodities cause budget deficits in the less fortunate Arab countries that have to be closed again through borrowing from the foreign markets, increasing their debts and weakening their purchasing power while at the same time promoting their dependency on the outside world. Their cash flow was used in securing food necessities instead of being reinvested in developing the agricultural sector. The increasing demand for food products and the inability of the Arab countries to meet the demands locally leave them vulnerable to outside pressures and threaten their security and stability. All food-importing Arab countries with the necessary resource capabilities adopted self-sufficiency policies in grain and particularly in wheat. One of the countries reported to have met its goal is Syria.[41] Another is Saudi Arabia, which not only achieved self-sufficiency but also realized a surplus over market demands at the expense of its scarce subterranean water resources.[42] Only three Arab countries achieved surplus in their food trade balance in 2006 – Syria, Tunis and Mauritania – whilst Saudi Arabia, Kuwait, Jordan, Somalia, Bahrain, Egypt and Iraq had largest trade deficits, with Saudi Arabia being the most affected. The UAE, Algeria, OPT, Lebanon, Djibouti and Sudan had recorded a small increase of 3.4 per cent in their food imports in the same year.[43] The prevalent situation hinders development, as a constant food shortage means these countries are exposed to fluctuations in the world markets and at the mercy of international monopolies. In contrast to the food production growth rates of 1.5–2 per cent per annum, the rate of food consumption increased by 5 per cent per annum. The consumption rate being twice as much as the production rate contributed to the widening of the food gap and the decrease in self-sufficiency rates and to a greater dependency on foreign entities to meet food demands.[44]

There is an interchangeable movement between deficit and surplus in most world regions, but the Arab world suffers from a continuous trade balance deficit. The reason for this is its failure to grow strategic commodities especially grains, the level of consumption of which surpasses that of any other region with a similar population census. Grain and wheat represented 36.2 per cent of total Arab food imports in 2006, down 4 per cent in terms of prices and 7.5 per cent in terms of quantity. Wheat is the main commodity in the grain group in terms of importance, accounting for 43 per cent of the total grain price in 2006[45] since it remains the foremost ingredient in the Arab meal.[46] Factors contributing to the heavy dependence of the Arab states on food imports are water scarcity, scarce arable land and desertification, the high rate of population increase, fluctuations in world markets and local and regional conflicts. A brief review of the situation in some Arab countries like Yemen, Jordan, Saudi Arabia and Syria substantiates the argument. Yemen, a low-income state, with low agricultural productivity estimated at 15 per cent of the GDP and employing 50 per cent of the labour force, cannot keep pace with the country's rapid population growth. Jordan has an agricultural output of only 2 per cent of the GDP and employs only 10 per cent of the labour force, making food imports essential to meet local demand; however, it is heavily influenced by external factors such as oil prices and regional conflicts. In Saudi Arabia, with a high GDP, agriculture currently accounts for 5 per cent of the GDP and employs 7 per cent of the labour force, and it is becoming entirely dependent on food imports. Syria, a middle-income country, where agriculture occupies a third of the country's land area, contributes 50 per cent to the GDP and engages 33 per cent of the active population, is the only Arab country to achieve self-sufficiency in the most important foodstuffs and also to improve the performance of its export trade in fruits, vegetable, pulses, grain and olive oil.[47]

This situation represents a permanent burden on the states' balance of payments sheets. In Saudi Arabia, if the current condition persists without any increases in production, the food gap will widen and the deficit will continue to rise[48] because, after the government decision to reverse its policy to achieve self-sufficiency in wheat due to water scarcity (see Chapter 7), its wheat imports will reach 3.4 million tons by 2016, which could place the kingdom in the top fifteen largest importers of cereals. Currently Saudi Arabia imports a negligible amount of wheat, while producing 2.5 million tons annually. Egypt is the world's second largest importer of wheat.[49] On the other hand, exports of strategic food commodities from the Arab world are limited and its exports represent a very slight surplus of secondary commodities such as fruits that can be easily spared by the importing countries easily and do not serve as a balanced score card regarding the international supply of the commodities and food products necessary to people's lives (see Figure 8).

The Arab countries earmark a lot of their resources for food commodities. The payments are increasing every year. The demand for food commodities is continuously on the rise. This is reflected in the increasing cost of imports, as the food gap widened between 1971, 2000 and 2006 from $2.2, $31.5[50] to $36.6 billion.[51] Consequently, the Arab region spent around $375 billion throughout the twentieth century to meet local demand for food (estimated according to 1985 prices). This amount is astronomical, especially if compared with what has been invested in agricultural development in the Arab countries.

4. Dimensions of the Food Gap

The shortage in the main food commodities started to be noticed clearly at the beginning of the 1960s when the net of wheat imports were estimated at 2.4 million tons. But the deficiency increased enormously, reaching 8.8 million tons in 1975, which meant the annual level of deficiency stood at 10 per cent during that period. Sugar imports also increased during the same period from 1.3 million tons to 2.2 tons, an annual deficiency of 4 per cent. The gap for meat increased from 62,000 tons to 330,000 tons also during the same period. This meant an annual increase of 12.7 per cent. With regards to value, the total value of the food gap for all food commodities increased from $1.11 billion in the middle of 1971–3 to $4.7 billion in 1975. This means an average annual development of 48 per cent. The rate of the Arab food gap jumped between 1974 and 1977 in comparison with previous periods. It reached 13.7 per cent for wheat, 15 per cent for sugar, 34.6 per cent for meat and 35 per cent for dairy products.

The improvement in the standard of living in some Arab countries coupled with high birth rates, in addition to the changes in diet and attitudes towards food consumption, caused the food gap to record a sudden jump in the demand for meat and dairy products at the beginning of the 1970s compared with wheat and sugar. As a result the gap in dairy products was estimated, in the period between 1974 and 1977, at 13.7 per cent per annum. The situation further deteriorated in the 1980s with regards to most agricultural products. During the period between 1985 and 1992, the gap varied in correlation with average production and the average demand for food products. Whilst during the 1980s the average rate of food production improved to reach $12.7 billion annually, with an average growth rate of 3.5 per cent, the value of the food gap in all Arab countries in 1991 reached about $10.3 billion, to record for the first time a decrease of 21.6 per cent in comparison with 1990. This was due to a number of factors including the fall in prices of some food commodities, such as grains, sugar and oil. The statistics in the Arab world for the period 2000–6 reveal that the region suffers from shortages in most important food commodities, including grains and wheat (see Table 8.5).

Analysing the agricultural development plans, and reading production growth vis-à-vis population increase and the GNP vis-à-vis the food commodities trade balance, reveal the intensity of the deficiency in the main food commodities such as grains, oil, meat and dairy products, which show that there would be a far greater deficiency by 2016. The deficiency in grains has increased from 11.2 million tons in 1975 to 26.1 million tons in 2000 and it constituted 36.2 per cent of the total strategic food commodities' imports in 2006.[52] Wheat deficiency also increased from 8.8 million tons in 1975 to approximately 19.2 million tons in 2000. As for sugar, the gap increased from 2.2 tons to 3.5 million tons in the same period. Similarly, the deficiency in meat reached one million tons by 2000. Deficiency in the trade balance of expensive food commodities, such as animal products and oils, will also increase due to production inadequacy and the increasing demand for such products. Table 8.3 shows that there was an improvement in the production of some food crops such as potatoes, fruits and vegetables, whilst the deficiency increased in some strategic food commodities such as grains and sugar in the Arab countries, despite the decrease in the total value of grain imports. The change was from 46 to 58 per cent between 2000 and 2006, as shown by Table 8.3, clearly revealing that the Arab world dependency on the food exporting countries will further increase.

Table 8.4. The Food Gap (1975–2000)

Commodity	Deficiency before 1975	Deficiency after 1975	Deficiency in 2000
Wheat	2.4 million tons	8.8 million tons	19.2 million tons
Sugar	1.3 million tons	2.2 million tons	3.5 million tons
Meat	62 thousand tons	330 thousand tons	1 million tons
Dairy Products	-	1.6 million	5.5 million tons

Source: Adnan Hiza' al-Bayyati, 'Attassahur wa Azmat al Ghida fil Watan al Arabi' (Desertification and Food Crisis in the Arab Homeland), *Shu'un Arabiya*, vol. 74, 1993, p. 191.

As for value, the food gap increased from $14.133 billion in 1980 to $16.641 billion in 1989. The deficiency in food commodities accounted for $14.3 billion in 2000 (according to 1975 prices), hence the Arab countries paid around $200 billion by the end of the twentieth century (based on the 1975 prices) to cover the costs of the food gap.[53] The accumulative value of food imports in the 1980s reached around $190 billion, which further exacerbated and complicated the situation.[54]

The value of the food gap in the Arab countries was US$10.3 billion in 1991, less by $2.1 billion than 1990. This was due to the fall in prices of some food commodities such as grains, sugar and oil, whereas the average value of the food gap in the 1980s was around $12.7 billion per annum. In other words, there was an annual average growth rate of 3.5 per cent. Table 8.4 shows an increasing trend in the development of the food gap in Arab countries in 1975 and 2000. The food gap since the beginning of the twenty-first century again witnessed steady increase. Statistics released by the Arab Monetary Fund reveal an increase from $13.9 to $18 billion between 2000 and 2006 as shown in Table 8.5. The level of shortage in grains went down in 2006 to 53.7 per cent; in wheat to 43 per cent; in dairy products to 20 per cent; in oil to 13 per cent; in meat to 12 per cent; in sugar to 11 per cent. The accumulative value of the food gap in the 1980 to 1992 accounted for $42 billion made up of grains ($15 billion), dairy products ($13 billion), meat ($9 billion), vegetable oils and sugar ($9 billion).[55] In contrast, there was a surplus in fruits and vegetables, whereas sugar recorded an increase in the rate of self-sufficiency for sugar (reaching 5 per cent) and meat (10 per cent). The main agricultural commodities witnessed an average annual growth of approximately 2.7 per cent against an increase in demand for those commodities that reached an average annual rate of 1 per cent. In 1991 there was an improvement in the levels of self-sufficiency as there was an increase in most of the produced food commodities, most prominently grains that increased from 52 to 57 per cent and meat from 84 to 88 per cent. In 1992 Arab agricultural production witnessed a fall of about 2 per cent due to the shrinking of the crops area by a rate of 2.4 per cent because of bad weather conditions and less rainfall.[56] The food gap, between 1992[57] and 2007, increased from about $9.8 to $18.1 billion and is expected to reach $32 billion dollars by the year 2012.[58]

Table 8.5. The Arab Food Gap for Major Food Commodities (2000–2006) (millions US$)

	2000	2001	2002	2003	2004	2005	2006	% CHANGE
Grains	6378	7554	7412	6997	8506	9661	9042	4.5
Wheat	2752	3856	3796	2936	4453	4497	4220	7.4
Barley	956	772	867	857	868	1400	1372	6.2
Rice	1120	1102	859	1048	1245	1470	1331	2.9
Corn	1323	1350	1520	1423	1555	2098	1893	6.2
Potatoes	92	96	148	140	98	104	54	-8.5
Sugar	1163	1390	1377	1270	1209	1359	2035	9.8
Pulses	414	352	378	341	381	414	391	-1.0
Oil & Fat	1101	1158	1326	1569	2473	1960	2113	11.5
Vegetables	265	244	195	117	6	-66	-70	—
Fruits	285	591	401	300	310	448	423	6.8
All Meat	1439	1498	1583	1845	1990	2610	2422	9.1
Dairy	1914	2105	2135	2211	2633	2859	3014	7.9
Eggs	64	43	36	14	42	57	60	-1.1
Fish	-252	-305	-362	-314	-858	-1343	-1437	33.7
Total	19014	21806	21671	144586	20210	24426	26933	4.5

Source: *Al-Taqrir al-Iqtisadi al-Arabi al-Muwahad*, 2008, p. 310.

Figure 9 shows that the cumulative value of the food gap in 2006 reached US$18.1 billion, showing a slight increase of 0.2 per cent because of stability in the prices of some commodities like oil and sugar. The annual average value during the period 2000 to 2006 was $15.8 billion. This was also due to the development of local production which reduced the volume of imports of some commodities; grain by 6.4 per cent due to the increase in production especially in Syria and

Morocco, all meats by 7.2 per cent, pulses by 5.7 per cent, potatoes by 47.9 per cent and fruits by 5.5 per cent. At the same time, the food gap increased by 49.8 per cent for sugar, oils by 7.8 per cent, dairy by 5.5 per cent and eggs by 4.7 per cent. On the other hand, the Arab countries recorded a surplus in other food commodities like fish and vegetable by 7 and 5.5 per cent respectively.[59] However, Table 8.6 shows that the Arab world is still short of securing self-sufficiency in the main food commodities, especially grains.

Table 8.6. The Percentage of Change in the Food Gap Cost (2000–2006)

Commodity	2000-2006	2005-2006	Commodity	2000-2006	2005-2006
Grain	6.0	-6.4	Oils & Fat	11.5	7.8
Wheat	7.4	-6.2	Vegetable	—	5.5
Potatoes	-8.5	-47.9	Fruits	6.8	-5.5
Sugar	9.8	49.8	Meats	9.1	-7.2
Pulses	-1.0	-5.7	Milk Dairy	7.9	5.5

Source: *Al-Taqrir al-Iqtisadi al-Arabi al-Muwahad,* 2008, p. 63.

5. Arab Food Imports and Exports

The exports and imports of food commodities parameter shows the disparity between the amount of consumed imported and exported foods. Consequently it explains better the extent of the lack of food in some areas. The imported food commodities in 1991 went down by 15.1 per cent in value and by 2 per cent in quantity due to market forces. Food imports constituted about 72 per cent of total agricultural imports. The Arab states differ in the level of dependency on the outside world in securing their food needs. The level of imported food commodities in the Arab world oscillated between 1980 and 2006, reaching its highest point in 2006 to make $36.6 billion and to its lowest level in 1991 to $13.96 billion.[60] Estimates indicate that the value of the Arab agricultural imports witnessed a slight increase in 1992 of about 4 per cent in comparison with 1991, but was only 2.5 per cent in 2006, due to the increase in local demand for food commodities, whilst the cost of food imports increased from 14.7 to $36.6 billion in the period 1992–2006, with an alarming annual growth rate of 3.5 per cent. Table 8.7 shows the size of imports and exports of some food commodities between 2000 and 2006. There are some positive signs, such as the 9 per cent increase in annual growth of agricultural exports, whereas there was a decline in the rate of increase of Arab imports to an average of 3.7 per cent over the same period, showing a deficit of 1.7 per cent. However, the structure of the imports differs significantly from that of the exports in importance because they import strategic commodities like grains, wheat, sugar, meat and dairy, whilst exporting the surplus of the less strategic ones for the majority of inhabitants of the Arab world, like fish, vegetables and fruits.[61]

Table 8.7. Arab Agricultural Exports and Imports (2000–2006) (billions US$)

	2000	2001	2002	2003	2004	2005	2006	% Annual Growth	
								00-06	05-06
Exports	6.9	6.7	7.5	7.9	10.0	10.1	11.5	9.0	14.3
Imports	29.5	26.3	28.7	29.2	39.8	35.7	36.6	3.7	2.5
Trade Deficit	22.6	19.5	21.2	21.4	22.8	25.6	25.0	1.7	2.1-
% of Exports to Imports	23.3	25.7	26.1	26.9	30.5	28.3	31.6		

Source: *Al-Taqrir al-Iqtisadi al-Arabi al-Muwahad,* 2008, p. 59.

The other interesting phenomenon centres on the fact that, firstly, despite the Arab heavy agricultural investment in the field of grains producing 29.9 million tons, the largest part of their imports is made up of grains, as they imported 11.2 million tons, costing about $1900 million, in the early 1990s. The situation in 2006 became worse, with the import of grain making 36.2 per cent of the total value of Arab imports of the main food commodities estimated at $27 billion. The total value indicates a 1.6 per cent increase as a result of the soaring prices in the world market, despite the fact that there was a decrease in quantity level by 2.2 per cent.[62] Secondly, Table 8.5 shows that the Arab world's production of fruits and vegetables is less than the production of grains, whilst the size of the Arab countries' exports of fruits and vegetables exports exceeds that of grain exports. Fruit and vegetables are the only commodity to exceed one million US dollars in exports. As for the value of food exports and imports in the twenty-first century we find that this varies from one commodity to another (see Figure 10).

Trends in the foreign trade of food commodities in the Arab countries will now be summarized.

Food Imports

Arab countries encountering food shortages are forced to become increasingly dependent on the foreign markets to reduce the food gap, exposing their vulnerability to external pressures. The Arab world's 'net food imports account for 5–10 per cent of total imports in most Arab countries with wheat being the most popular foodstuff'.[63] Table 8.8 shows, first, that the Arab countries paid between $22.6 and $25 billion for food commodities alone. Second, the per capita figure for net imports differs on the basis of the country's income and its population size and it had declined between 2000 and 2006 with the exception of the GCC states. A review of the trends in the Arab countries' food imports since 1980s, and despite the improvement in the agricultural production, shows a steady increase in the Arab countries' payments for imported food, which more than doubled from $17 billion to $36.6 billion in 2006. The increased demand for food commodities due to the high rate of population, the instability in market prices, desertification due to water depletion and salinity, and the changes in the dietary habits explain the antithesis of the steady increase in the total cost of food imports, despite the success achieved by some Arab countries like Syria in attaining self-sufficiency in food production and an increase in food exports. Figure 11 clearly illustrates the food imports tendency in the Arab world since the beginning of the twenty-first century.

Table 8.8. Net Arab Agricultural Imports (2000–2006)

	Net Imports (Million US$)		Per Capita of Net Imports (US$)	
	2000	2006	2000	2006
Arab States with Agricultural Resources*	9735	8474	48	37
GCC Countries**	9663	13132	330	374
Other Arab States***	3206	3207	70	65
Total	22604	25033	81	79

*Algeria, Egypt, Iraq, Morocco, Sudan, Syria & Tunisia.
**Bahrain, Kuwait, Qatar, Oman, Saudi Arabia & UAE.
*** Djibouti, Jordan, Lebanon, Libya, Mauritania, Palestine & Somalia.
Source: *Al-Taqrir al-Iqtisadi al-Arabi al-Muwahad,* 2008, p. 60.

To understand the heavy burden of the payments devoted only to food imports the Arab countries can be divided into three categories:

1. The first group consists of the Arab countries with agricultural resources showing a decline in the accumulative value of their food imports from $9.7 to $8.4 billion between 2000 and 2006, estimated at around 75 per cent.
2. The second group includes only the GCC countries: Bahrain, Kuwait, Qatar, Oman, Saudi Arabia and the UAE. They represent a large part of the total value of the Arab food imports, with an increase from $9.6 to $13.1 billion in the same period. The increase is significant: going from being almost equal to the first group in 2000 to more than 60 per cent of the total Arab food imports, despite the fact that their population, at only 38.3 million, does not exceed 13 per cent of the total Arab population of 317 million. The GCC countries are importing 100 per cent of their staple foods, but have the cushion of oil revenue.[64] The only explanation for this is the high standard of living which has led to changes in food habits in the oil-rich societies of the Gulf. Demand will also have increased as a result of the high proportion of migrant workers, from all corners of the world, causing not only an unbalanced social structure, but also an unbalanced economic life. Finally, water scarcity and desertification have also contributed to the increase in food imports.
3. The third group consists of Djibouti, Jordan, Lebanon, Libya, Mauritania, Palestine and Somalia. This group includes countries which are either impoverished or politically instable or suffer from water scarcity and desertification. There is a constant trend in the value of their imports between 2000 and 2006, amounting to $3.2 billion.

Food Exports

The contribution of food exports to GNP was minimal throughout the 1970s, estimated at $4–$5 billion per annum. The volume and value of food exports began to pick up by the end of the twentieth century, with a positive contribution from surpluses in some agricultural commodities, especially fish, vegetables, dates and fruits. The data in Table 8.9 show a steady increase in the volume of exports for some agricultural commodities. Arab food exports in 2006 saw a growth rate of 10.4 per cent in terms of quantity and 7 per cent in value. Fish shows an increase of 6.7 per cent in quantity and 4.7 per cent in terms of value, followed by fruit at 1.6 per cent in quantity and 1.3 per cent in value. The contribution of the other Arab food commodities was less significant. Arab countries are divided into three groups according to the relative importance of their food exports:

1. The first group consists of Sudan, Morocco, Egypt, Tunisia, Syria, Mauritania and Lebanon. They make almost 70 per cent of the total Arab food and agricultural exports.
2. The second group consists of Saudi Arabia, the UAE, Oman, Yemen, Jordan, Iraq and Algeria. They account for 30 per cent of the total Arab food and agricultural export.
3. The third group consists of Libya, Qatar, Kuwait, Bahrain, Djibouti and Somalia. This group, for different reasons, was not among the food exporting Arab states.

It is apparent from the above that countries with agricultural resources like Syria, Morocco and Egypt occupy the list of the Arab exporting countries. However, Syria is the only Arab country to have succeeded in achieving self-sufficiency, whilst Egypt and Morocco are still major importers of food and agricultural commodities. Other Arab countries like Sudan, known in the Arab literature as the bread basket of the Arab world, Tunisia, Iraq, Algeria, Yemen and Lebanon have great potential to contribute significantly and to meet the increasing Arab demand for food. Unfortunately, however, five out of the six are torn by internal conflicts, civil wars, political chaos and foreign occupation. Sudan is home to the largest hungry population, followed by Yemen.[65] They are the most severely affected by undernourishment and hunger.[66] No positive contribution from them is expected until political stability is achieved.

The above analysis of trends in Arab exports and imports of food commodities highlights the extent to which Arab food security is vulnerable, and raises serious questions about the obstacles that the agricultural sector faces and its future prospects. The size of the food gap in the Arab countries is growing wider and shows the extent to which the Arab world is vulnerable to becoming the first region in the world that is incapable of meeting its food needs, being dependent on imports and foreign aid.[67] It is also one of two world regions in which the number of undernourished has risen since the beginning of 1990s – from 19.8 million in 1992 to 25.5 million in 2004, representing 10 per cent of its total population.[68] Even in wealthy countries like Saudi Arabia, Kuwait and the UAE segments of the population do not obtain sufficient nourishment. It could be argued, however, that this is possibly related to the changing food diet and the increasing dependence on fast food or 'junk food' more than to actual deprivation of healthy food.

Table 8.9. Arab Agricultural Exports and Imports (millions US$)

	Agricultural Exports			Growth %	Agricultural Imports			Growth %
	2000	2004	2006	00-06	2000	2004	2006	00-06
Arabs	29482	32836	36578	3.7	6878	10016	11545	9
Jordan	907	1611	1660	10.6	313	932	965	20.7
UAE	3129	2902	3103	0.1-	1178	788	920	4.0-
Bahrain	449	466	564	3.9	107	118	181	9.1
Tunisia	1083	1453	1344	3.7	841	1589	1803	13.6
Algeria	2782	4773	4677	9.1	111	154	165	6.8
Djibouti	119	117	126	1.0	19	17	20	1.2
Saudi Arabia	5402	6716	9620	10.1	475	1060	1314	18.5
Sudan	1213	602	1217	0.1	202	567	488	15.9
Syria	791	1142	1055	4.9	571	816	1528	17.9
Somalia	46	55	40	2.3-	5	12	15	20.1
Iraq	1720	1650	1510	2.2-	7	7	10	6.1
Oman	1097	1519	730	6.6-	399	950	381	0.8-
Palestine	600	—	260	13.0-	86	—	39	12.5-
Qatar	672	243	410	7.9-	125	7	10	35.0-
Kuwait	1276	1355	1637	4.2	78	110	128	8.6
Lebanon	1223	1460	1520	3.7	135	309	320	15.5
Libya	559	799	807	6.3	299	5	7	46.4-
Egypt	3659	2874	3420	1.1-	579	1242	1036	10.2
Morocco	1904	1979	1870	0.3-	1106	960	1590	6.2
Mauritania	72	8	7	32.2	156	172	360	15.0
Yemen	779	1132	1000	4.3	86	200	266	20.7

Source: *Al-Taqrir al-Iqtisadi al-Arabi al-Muwahad*, 2008, p. 304.

Food and agricultural issues are not confined to a number of Arab countries; it is a crisis for the entire Arab world. Since the Arab countries are reliant on foreign countries for food, food security has become a major concern and requires more joint and urgent efforts from Arab countries. Dependency on foreign supply of food threatens state sovereignty, exposing it to fluctuations in food markets, conflict of interests, regional and international conflicts and human abuses or natural disasters inflicting political, economic and social consequences. To what extent are the current institutions in Arab countries capable of finding effective solutions to this crisis in the short and longer terms? What is the nature of the political obstacles that stand in the way of any joint Arab strategy to confront the crisis? What are the political and strategic implications?

6. The Capability of Arab Institutions

The Arab world has witnessed many bilateral, trilateral and multilateral initiatives concerning agricultural cooperation and project coordination. In the domain of freeing agricultural commodities from national restrictions and facilitating their exchange, the Arab countries concluded an agreement in 1953. It confirmed facilitating commercial exchange, organizing transit trade and excluding customs duties on a wide range of agricultural and livestock commodities, which was considered an important precedent. A pan-Arab institution called the Arab Organization for Agricultural Development was founded, as well as the Arab Center for the Studies of Arid Zones and Dry Lands, along with the foundation of unions concerned with the food crisis, most prominently the Arab Agricultural Engineers Union. In the meantime, several Arab companies were founded for joint investment, such as the Arab Company for Livestock Production, the Arab Fisheries Group, the Arab Authority for Agricultural Investment and Development and many other bilateral companies whose activities include agricultural development. These companies were founded as joint ventures between oil-producing countries that have the funds and other Arab countries that have the agricultural resources and the potential for agricultural and industrial investment. Perhaps the most important Arab legislation in this field is the Unified Agreement for the Investment of Arab Capital in the Arab States that was ratified at the Amman Summit in 1980, 'providing a suitable environment for investment in order to activate Arab economic resources in the field of joint Arab investment which requires setting up legal investment regulations in a clear and stable juristic framework that works to facilitate the movement of Arab capital and invest them in the Arab states in a way that will serve the development, liberation and growth, and raise the standard of living of their citizens'.[69]

To consolidate Arab food security some programmes for developing the production of main food commodities were created, in addition to the National Strategic Consolidation Programmes for Grains. The commodity development programmes, however, were based on the availability of water and land resources between the Arab countries, on removing the obstacles facing production and restricting its capacities and development, and finally acting on a macro level rather than the micro, which requires settling not only intra-Arab, but also inter-Arab contentious issues. These programmes should be founded on the expansion of cultivated land and increased production, to be sustained by research and agricultural projects, countryside development projects, as well as infrastructure consolidation projects. The commodity development programmes were intended to focus on strategic commodities, including the programmes for growing grains, oil harvests, growing sugar, livestock and domestic animal production and fish production. According to official study by the Arab Organization for Agricultural Development the programme was intended to stimulate production increases that would meet domestic consumption needs in the Arab countries with agricultural resources like Iraq, Sudan, Syria, Yemen, Somalia, Tunisia, Morocco and Mauritania. Food surpluses would be exported to Arab countries suffering food shortages. This would help to alleviate the burdens incurred, reduce external dependency and would inevitably reduce Arab foreign payments. Consequently, the expected cumulative value in production would increase from $13 to $16 billion between 1985 and 2000 and the food gap would be lowered by nearly half in 2000 from $14.268 to $7.366 billion as a result of implementing these programmes.[70] However, macro efforts have not yet been successful. Saudi Arabia, a high-income country, fares no better than Syria, a middle-income country, in terms of prevalence of hunger – at 4 per cent in each country according to World Bank data in 2008.[71]

Private Arab investment in the agricultural sector is still very limited in scope for several reasons, the most important of which is the decline in capital owners making such agricultural investments. Other reasons include the scarcity of scientific expertise and skilled labour in agricultural development, the absence of suitable advanced technology in the Arab cultural environment and, last but not least, the national regulatory laws and measures for private investment in the agricultural domain.[72] Arab efforts in this domain, despite their importance and increase, still fell short of achieving food security.

It is apparent that, despite joint Arab efforts, the reality of food production in the Arab countries reflects the variation of the food situation from one Arab country to another. The Iraq–Iran war had an effect on the food situation in Iraq, as the average consumption per person in 2005 went down to 2300 calories per day.[73] The international embargo due to the 1990 Kuwaiti predicament, followed by the American occupation of Iraq since 2003, have worsened the situation, driving the Iraqi people into chaos and causing poverty, hunger and malnutrition. The average intake per person of national food produce in Iraq went down by 32 per cent. National food production did not cover more than 20 per cent of the required levels in 1990s. Consequently it became necessary to import 5 million tons of food to fill the gap.[74] At the same time the average daily consumption per person exceeded 3,000 calories in the United Arab Emirates, Syria, Kuwait, Lebanon, Libya and Egypt.[75] It is worth mentioning that these figures and data do not reflect the real tragic situation that the Arab people are encountering in other parts of the Arab world – such as Somalia, wracked by a civil war, or Sudan, still suffering from the problem of the south, or the Occupied Palestinian Territories or Iraq since 2003. In 1988 the average consumption per person in Somalia did not exceed 1,736 calories per day. The situation further deteriorated with the outbreak of the civil war, causing the death of more than a quarter of children under the age of 5 because they did not have access to food.[76] Statistics indicate that, in the period 1980 and 1991, the individual rate of consumption of national food products went down by 20 per cent. In the meantime the civil war in Somalia or Sudan or Lebanon, or any country plagued with regional or domestic conflict, led to the destruction of the agricultural base, as mines were planted in the agricultural lands. Warring parties have always used food as a strategic weapon, stopping aid supplies reaching the end users who were in critical need of them. Food deprivation was responsible for a death rate of over 250 people per 1,000 in some regions of Sudan. The Arab food condition is critical and alarming. People will become prey to hunger and malnutrition. Arab regimes will suffer too because of their total foreign dependence for food commodities, infringing their state sovereignty. The above analyses clearly reveal that Arab efforts in achieving self-sufficiency in food commodities are still in their infancy. In the fight against hunger, not much success has been achieved towards goal one of the Millennium Development Goals (MDGs) to halve, between 1990 and 2015, the proportion of people who suffer from hunger. Djibouti, Kuwait and Mauritania have made the greatest progress towards lowering the prevalence of undernourishment. Sudan has also made progress, but still experiences serious hunger prevalence. Egypt, Jordan, Lebanon, Morocco, Saudi Arabia and Yemen, on the other hand, recorded increases in both the absolute numbers and prevalence of undernourishment, while Syria and Algeria achieved very small reductions in the prevalence of undernourishment, but no reduction in the numbers of undernourished.[77] So what are the obstacles to the Arab food strategy?

7. Constraints on the Arab Food Strategy

The Arab world occupies vast areas of land, estimated at around 14 million square kilometres. Total arable land made up 36.2 per cent of the total agricultural land in 2006. However, the actually cultivated areas cover only 47.3 million hectares or about 3.5 per cent of the total Arab land. This represents 3.2 per cent of the cultivated lands worldwide. Pastures and meadows cover about 256 million hectares, or 19 per cent of the total area of the Arab world, whereas forests cover 127 million hectares or 10 per cent of the Arab areas. The area covered by desert is estimated at 43 per cent. It is worth mentioning that the shortage of cultivated lands in the Arab world can be attributed to a combination of natural, human and political factors.

Natural Factors

Natural factors include several aspects such as climate change and prevailing weather conditions, soil fertility and water resources.

(a) *The climate*

The agricultural industry in the Arab countries is characterized by being unstable due to the climate change. Climate plays an important role in agriculture. It constitutes one of the main pillars of support for – or obstacles to – agricultural production. The weather of most Arab countries varies between a Mediterranean and a dry-hot climate, where the high temperatures cause soil to lose stored humidity as a result of evaporation. Humid weather encourages the rapid growth of insects and parasites which feed on and destroy plant leaves. Arab countries are also constrained by the short of rainfall. Rain is the most important factor for agriculture as it still determines the modes of production and the amount of productivity. The low production of Moroccan wheat in 1992 shows the effect of changes in weather on Arab agriculture as wheat reached 66.5 per cent and oats reached 67 per cent of their normal levels.[78] The rates of rainfall in the entire Arab world are low as a result of the prevailing desert weather, as the desert stretches in a belt from the in the Atlantic west to the Gulf in the east. The amount of rain per annum in most Arab countries does not exceed 250 millimetres and there are areas that receive less than their share, especially areas within the desert. In 2007, Moroccan agricultural output declined by 2.5 per cent because of the reduced rainfall. Simultaneously, the growth of agricultural outputs in other Arab countries in the same year was related to the increase in rainfall.[79] Saudi

Arabia decided to amend its agricultural policy and stop growing wheat starting from 2009 due to water scarcity, and decided to invest in external markets with agricultural resources to secure its domestic needs for food commodities. It is putting $800 million into a public company that will invest in overseas agricultural projects. The move signals a large change in Riyadh's efforts to outsource supply for the kingdom's increasing food needs.[80]

(b) *Rainfall*

The abundance of rain is confined to the highlands and to the northern and southern edges of the Arab world. The amount of rain on the mountains that border the Arab nation from the north is 750–1000 millimetres per annum. But in the other areas it is considerably less: average rainfall does not exceed 400–500 millimetres and often it drops to 200–50 millimetres only. There is a strong link between the amount of rainfall and agricultural production in the Arab world. The more rain that falls, and spread over a longer period in the year, the greater the harvest and vice versa. But despite the scarcity of rain in some Arab countries, the Arab people have not made the most of the rain that they get. Most of the rain that falls lands in ravines that the thirsty soil absorbs, or evaporates due to high temperatures, or gathers in larger ravines, forming rivulets and rivers that empty into the sea, and so it is lost. It is apparent that rainfall is not sufficient for agriculture in the Arab countries and that irrigation should use different sources of water. Availability of water is absolutely indispensable for growing plants. The inadequacy of water supplies represents a major obstacle to any agricultural expansion in the Arab world.[81]

(c) *Soil*

Most Arab soils are short of nitrogen and many organic materials, except alluvium that exists in the sedimentary regions, especially in the Nile Valley and Delta, and in the lands adjacent to the Tigris and Euphrates. As for the physical characteristics of the Arab soil, it has both good and bad qualities, since it does not have high levels of clay which makes manual farming work or work that depends on animals quite difficult because the soil becomes sticky as soon as it is exposed to water and once it dries out it forms deep cracks. Most of the Arab world's soil is soft, such as in the land situated between Iraq and Syria, as the thickness of the soil does not exceed 90 centimetres and most of it is less than 50 centimetres thick. It is well known that soil that does not exceed 90 centimetres in depth is very shallow and it cannot preserve sufficient humidity from one seasonal harvest to another in the dry agriculture system.

Human Factors[82]

Arab countries undertook from the mid-1970s a unilateral policy for agricultural development on the micro level whereby each Arab state sought to secure food self-sufficiency regardless of its agricultural resources. Each Arab state relied on its own natural, financial and human resources in setting up and implementing an economic plan for development. This policy was irrational and doomed to fail because agricultural resources are distributed unevenly across the region. The unintegrated approach to agricultural development did not achieve high return rates and had come about as an inevitable outcome of the ununified state of the Arab world. It is a representation of the distrust and competitive nature of inter-Arab relations. Human constraints can be summarized as follows.

(a) *Lack of agricultural funding*
Unilateral agricultural development delayed the priority of agricultural funding by the Arab funds, and caused a huge financial gap. It has affected the rates of investment and production growth in those Arab countries which have agricultural resources but no financial resources.

(b) *Delay in prioritizing the agricultural sector*
Despite the low level of agricultural production development, as a result of unilateral national development and lack of funding, national development plans have not devoted enough shares of investment to the agricultural sector out of the total resources for national development. This demonstrates the failure of Arab governments to prioritize agricultural development.

(c) *Marginal contribution made by the private sector*
The contribution made by the private sector in agricultural investment is very low, and even some of these investments were taken from agricultural banks that are subsidiaries to the public sector. Public funding has mostly been geared towards financing big projects such as irrigation, land reclamation and drainage projects, whilst there are some other important, economically sound, projects that could be realized within agriculture.

In addition to these human factors, there are other difficulties such as the lack of use of advanced technology in Arab agricultural development, the lack of skilled manpower, ownership of limited agricultural lands that are not enough for the familial needs of the farmer, the shortcomings of the infrastructure (for example, roads, power, etc.) and the legal and political barriers in the interregional food commodities trade, which all present obstacles to making the most of the available resources.[83]

Political Factors[84]

Food security can be achieved when all people at all times can obtain basic foodstuffs, materially and economically. Therefore the main political foundations are an important part of realizing food security. Despite the clear overlapping of human factors and political factors, it is possible to divide the political factors into:

1. Absence of political stability in several Arab agricultural countries.
2. State control of most economic activities.
3. The lack of a protection policy or stimulus package for national products.
4. Corruption, particularly manifested in compelling foreign investors to share projects with local investors.
5. Restrictions imposed on the movement of capital in a number of agricultural Arab countries.
6. Unstable economic conditions.
7. Inability to gain a strong level of control on the project.
8. Lack of transparency in tax relief policies and data release.
9. Inability to achieve high returns on agricultural investments.
10. Unavailability of production elements like seeds, fertilizers and modern technology.
11. The lack of availability of hard currency.
12. The instability of the world food commodities market.
13. Fluctuation of local currency value or purchasing power.
14. Underdeveloped infrastructure.
15. Lack of promoting investment agencies.
16. Lack of studies on investment opportunities and small research funding. (Studies indicate that the size of Arab expenditure on scientific research in the agriculture domain has not exceeded 0.3 per cent whereas it reaches about 8.3 per cent in the developed world.[85] Arab expenditure on agricultural

scientific research was estimated at 0.2 per cent of GDP in 2005, compared with 2.8 per cent in the developed world.[86])

17. The increase in defence expenditure at the expense of other development projects.[87]

These are some of the factors with negative influences on Arab agricultural investment. The availability of some production components in one Arab country is often countered by factors impeding production in the same country. Political instability deters investors. Political and economic instability, along with the freedom of investment, the high return and the commitment of states and governments to binding laws and bylaws setting out the rules of the game, are the most prominent factors that will attract or put off investment.[88] The ease of obtaining licences, carrying out investment and dealing with the officials concerned, is considered one of the most important factors behind investors' decisions.

8. Arab Food Strategy

The importance of joint Arab action regarding agricultural development is based on the following:

1. Achieving food security for the Arab region as a whole. It consists of countries with agricultural potential but without the necessary financial surplus, except Iraq and Algeria, to achieve fast development in food production, whereas most of the Arab countries that enjoy financial surplus do not have agricultural resources to meet their food needs.
2. The need to invest the Arab financial surplus within Arab countries has become more urgent since 1975 with the global food crisis.
3. The social and political aspects of agricultural development and food security are in need of joint Arab action. Arab farmers have an income that is much less than their counterparts in the urban areas. Therefore, joint Arab action in this domain would improve the social and economic level of these farmers[89] and help improve the political stability of Arab countries.
4. The work towards eliminating the Arab food gap, especially with regards to strategic crops such as grains and meat, requires regional cooperation and coordination of policies.

5. Achieving fair distribution of food. This can be achieved through exchanging utilities, services and resources in a way that Arab resources will serve Arab development.

6. Strengthening and developing the infrastructure, as joint Arab action will be aiming to establish institutions that work to serve and develop Arab societies and to achieve balanced and integrated development.

7. Achieving flexibility and dynamism, as Arab agriculture should reach the stage of flexibility and dynamism so that it will be able to interact and adjust to deal with international changes, whether within the Arab regional order or the international order.[90]

8. Through Arab cooperation, Arab farmers will be able to obtain their agricultural requirements at reduced prices and in large quantities. For instance, there is a low level of agricultural production in the Arab lands due to the lack of technology, modern machines and fertilizers, at a time when the Arab world has a surplus of nitrogen, phosphate and potassium fertilizers. If the fertilizer-producing countries cooperated with farmers in have-not countries to supply them with fertilizers, the Arab farmer would be able to obtain what he needs in large quantities and at cheaper prices than he would pay if the fertilizer came from the outside world.[91]

All these targets underline the necessity of joint Arab action to achieve food security, especially as there are positive conditions that would bring benefit to the Arabs from such action:

1. The vastness of arable land resources in the whole Arab world means that the agricultural area has the potential to be expanded by nearly 15 million hectares.

2. Great efficiency could increase water resources by nearly 82 billion cubic metres, which would double the irrigated lands.

3. The Arab countries encompass different environmental areas that would help to produce different crops and increase the opportunities for integration, reducing their dependency on the outside world.

4. There are huge capabilities of intensifying agricultural production through the introduction of modern use of fertilizers, machines and improved technology, and prohibiting cultivated land from lying fallow.

5. Available manpower reaches 27.7 million workers who could take in modern production devices through training and guidance.
6. Technical staff are available in a number of Arab countries and with more training and incentives it should be possible to raise the technological level of production and carry out advanced scientific and agricultural research.
7. Employing the large money surpluses of oil-rich Arab countries in agriculture investment in Arab states with agriculture resources would consolidate food development and close the existing food gap. Contemporary joint Arab actions to achieve food security are not bad, but have been inadequate.

9. Conclusion

A few questions come to mind about the future of food security in the Arab world. If the Arab countries cannot close the food gap at a time when their revenues are high, will they be able to close it when their financial resources start to decline as a result of the fluctuation in oil prices and the purchasing power of their local currencies? If they managed to do so would they succeed in breaking through the international monopoly markets and competing with other buyers? Moreover, the Arab world is not a priority in the field of marketing, which will have a negative effect and will further consolidate its subordination to the exporting countries. The Arab countries might be obliged to buy the scraps from the international markets, especially if the existing political situation in the Arab world is taken into consideration and the fact that the latter does not own the strategic commodities, apart from oil, that would enable it to negotiate.[92]

We can summarize the most important political and strategic consequences of the food crisis in the following points:

1. The subordination of Arab countries to food exporting countries, especially if we take into account the current international variables, the limitations of the main producing countries of food harvests where grains top the list, the nature of the dominant political and economic systems and their abilities in political manœuvring, and the control of multinational companies in trade and production of food worldwide. If Arab countries continue being dependent on importing food from abroad this will increase their subordination to the exporting countries regardless of their other potential.[93] As for the oil states, and despite their ability

to buy food, they would be subjected to certain international pressure from the exporting countries. During the October 1973 war, the US threatened the Arab oil-producing states, especially the Gulf States, with banning food products being exported to them, after these countries used oil as a strategic weapon to benefit Arab causes. Dependency on foreign markets for food will drain national budgets and cause liquidity shortages as well.

2. The backwardness of the food industry sector would weaken the interaction between the fields of agriculture and industry, and these two sectors and the public sector.
3. The deterioration of farmers' incomes and purchasing power. This widens the class disparity and deepens the incompatibility between the countryside and urban Arab society.[94] Table 8.8 shows the increasing ratio of the dependency of most Arab countries on the outside world, where the GCC countries' imports represent more than 50 per cent of the total Arab agricultural imports and the food gap in 2007 stood at US$18.1 billion.

Escaping this dark tunnel requires effective joint Arab efforts that could be expensive in the short term. Arab countries should act collectively in pursuance of the following policies:[95]

1. Secure an updated and efficient infrastructure of roads, storage facilities, modern technology, water, power, fuel and healthcare.
2. Adopt local pricing policies in accordance with the goals of increasing production as well as the farmer's income.
3. Secure the necessary seasonal and mid- and long-term funding to enable the Arab farmer to achieve his tasks.
4. Intensify agricultural advice and offer services that help farmers understand the nature of soil and the best fertilizers and plants for it.
5. Educate farmers on the importance of convergence or linkage between personal interest and the national interest.
6. Democratize the decision-making process in the agricultural sector.
7. Support scientific research, publish findings and make them accessible to all.

8. Set up management information systems to allow information transparency, providing weather updates, information on plant diseases, advice and crop rotation instructions to farmers throughout the year.
9. Carry out research on the soil, how to improve it and how to deal with salinity and desertification.
10. Prepare farming administration cadres.
11. Coordinate plans with agricultural strategies.
12. Carry out efficient marketing for local agriculture products.
13. Carry out joint irrigation and land reclamation projects.
14. Carry out joint projects related to fertilizers and pesticides.
15. Improve mobilization of wealth and manpower for agricultural investment.
16. Fund agricultural development projects in the Arab countries with agricultural resources and potential.

The implementation of these policies would eventually help the Arab countries secure self-sufficiency in food commodities, removing domestic constraints due to the dilemma between population increase and decline in local agricultural outputs. Achieving food security locally will reduce the vulnerability of the Arab world to external pressures and free their decision-making processes, allowing them to play a more independent role in global politics.

Chapter 9

Determinants of Saudi Arabia's Foreign Policy-Making

1. Introduction

Foreign policy, as I discussed in Chapter 1, is defined as the outcome of interaction that take place between variables in the domestic milieu and the external milieu. The two contexts have human and non-human constituents. In the domestic milieu these are located outside of the framework of the political regime and within the social periphery, whereas the external milieu is defined as the human and non-human elements that reside outside the social periphery. It is viewed as a process of selecting policies, all of which at times are desirable but are contradictory or unwanted as a whole and it is necessary to choose one of them. Therefore, foreign policy is a process of finding the balance between the foreign commitments of a given state and its domestic determinants or constraints to fulfil such commitments.

This chapter considers Saudi foreign policy as the outcome of interaction between domestic constraints and external pressure. It aims to identify the various internal and external dimensions that determine the Saudi foreign policy decision-making process, as Saudi Arabia has gained great importance in shaping Arab foreign policy since 1967 and regional and international changes influence the future of this role. This chapter does not include the outputs or the 'dependent stage', as James Rosenau called it, except in relations whereby these outputs become part of the inputs or part of the independent variables. It covers the domestic milieu, comprising geographical, historical, ideological, political, demographic, social, economic and military factors. Regarding the external milieu, the following contexts will be discussed: the regional, the international and that of the international organizations. In the final section I analyse the different apparatuses that are involved in shaping and implementing Saudi foreign policy. This study is based on different primary and secondary resources.

It is worth mentioning that a large number of books have been written about Saudi Arabia, and it could be argued that the most distinguished among them are *Saudi Foreign Policy since 1945*, by Ghassan Salamah; *The History of Saudi Arabia*, by Alexei Vassiliev; *Saudi Arabia: The Ceaseless Quest for Security*, by Nadav Safran; *State, Society and Economy in Saudi Arabia*, by Tim Niblock; *Saudi Arabia in the Oil Era: Regime and Elites: Conflict and Collaboration*, by Mordechai Abir and *The Kingdom*, by Robert Lacey.

The study in this chapter is intended to be a case study for the analyses of the foreign policies of Arab states on the micro level. Saudi Arabia was chosen because (1) it is the oldest regime in the Arab world, (2) it has a prolonged history of relative stability, (3) it enjoys a geopolitical importance on the regional and international levels for many reasons and (4) other Arab regional powers have retreated from playing a major role in the affairs of the region.

2. The Domestic Milieu

The domestic milieu includes all the human and non-human variables existing within the national frontiers of a state.

The Geographical Variable

Geography is important in directing the foreign policy of any state since it determines the priorities of the state's foreign relations. If a country is in a region that is characterized by political instability and security tensions this inevitably has an effect on the foreign policies of that country and its regional and international alliances. Saudi Arabia is close to numerous Arab and non-Arab countries, such as Iran, Iraq, Egypt, Yemen and Ethiopia. This places particular serious responsibilities on Saudi Arabia, and grants it a strategic advantage.[1] The effect of the geographical factor on foreign policymaking is distinguished by the position and by the area. Saudi Arabia is the largest Arab country covering an area of 2,240,000 square kilometres. It is larger than any of the other regional countries; Iraq covers an area of 434,924 square kilometres and Iran covers 1,247,000 square kilometres. Saudi Arabia has to make the most of this area in order to diversify its sources of revenue. With the desert forming the largest part of the land surface, Saudi Arabia has had to depend on other countries in securing its food requirements and this has restricted its relations with the exporting countries. On the other hand, the Saudi territories are home to the largest oil reservoir in the world. This has strengthened the influence of the

Saudi kingdom on the courses of regional and international political events in accordance with its national interests. The large area of Saudi Arabia and its position in a region dominated by rivalry between the main regional powers has strengthened the sense of insecurity amongst the decision-makers in the kingdom. This has led to an increase in military spending, on the one hand, and searching for allies regionally and internationally, on the other hand. This has consolidated Saudi Arabia's dependency on the wider world.

The readiness shown by the US to defend Saudi Arabia reflects the geopolitical importance of the kingdom. It is located on two waterways that are vital to American interests – the Arab Gulf and the Red Sea – and consequently has control of two strategic water exits: the Straits of Hormuz and the Suez Canal. Saudi Arabia has the largest world oil reserves and hence controlling the kingdom means controlling the destiny of the entire whole world, at least for the foreseeable future, making the kingdom a priority for American regional strategy. The closeness of Saudi Arabia to the former Soviet Union strengthened its status in US strategy, especially during the cold war.

The Historical Variable

Understanding the making of foreign policy in any country often requires awareness of the historical dimension. Although I have reservations about using the historical method to study international relations,[2] I believe it is necessary to understand the foreign policy of any given state. The Saudi state that I discuss in this chapter is the third Saudi state, declared after the unification of the Najd and Hejaz regions as one independent and sovereign state known as the Kingdom of Saudi Arabia. Although some historians state that this took place in January 1902 when Abdalaziz Ibn Abdul Rahman Ibn Saud managed to regain Riyadh, his sovereignty was incomplete, as in May 1914 he accepted Ottoman sovereignty and in return the Ottomans recognized him as the governor of Najd with the title of Pasha, ensuring that his sons and grandsons would succeed him to the throne, which is still the main rule that has been used for the succession of power in the kingdom. Paragraph B of Article 5 of the Basic System of Governance that was announced in 1 March 1992 says: 'The dynasty right shall be confined to the sons of the founder, King Abdalaziz Ibn Abdul Rahman Al Saud (Ibn Saud), and his offspring. The most eligible among them shall be invited, through the process of "Baya'a" [pledging allegiance] to rule in accordance with the Book of God (Qur'an) and the Sunnah of the Prophet.'[3]

With the outbreak of the First World War, Ibn Saud's ties with Britain entered a new phase. He exploited the dispute between Britain and the Ottoman Empire effectively to consolidate his ambitions and to gain British recognition of his independence in Najd and Al-Ihsa' and to obtain money and weapons,[4] which were used to impose his control of Hail and the Mountain of the Shummar. Ibn Saud did not officially abandon his subjection to the Ottoman Empire until he had managed to guarantee the security and independence of his kingdom. After twelve months of negotiations, Ibn Saud signed his first agreements with Britain on 26 December 1915, in which Britain recognized Ibn Saud as an independent ruler in Najd and Al-Ihsa' and the surrounding areas and pledged to help him if there were any cases of external aggression against his territories. In return, Ibn Saud pledged not to contact any foreign power or to relinquish any part of his land to any foreign country, to respect the political status quo of the British protectorates in the Gulf and to protect the routes of pilgrimage.[5] It was the first regional role to be given to the kingdom. In 1927 another agreement was signed between the two parties in which Britain recognized Ibn Saud as the king of Najd and Hejaz and the two parties adhered to the principles of the agreement of 1915.[6]

Britain wanted to see stability in the Arab Peninsula. To achieve this it had to put all its political weight behind Ibn Saud. After 1929 it abandoned its 'divide and rule' policy and adopted a supportive policy for Ibn Saud's efforts to unite the Arab Peninsula by providing him with weapons through the British government in India.[7] In January 1930 Britain became the first country to provide Ibn Saud with airplanes along with their British crews for civilian and military use, to help him connect the provinces of his vast kingdom.[8] Britain took on the responsibility of providing Ibn Saud with financial aid during the first four years of the Second World War. This aid was estimated at a total of £3 million, in the form of commodities or silver money.[9] Britain also helped Ibn Saud to eliminate the Ikhwan Movement that threatened his rule.[10] Despite the surrender of Sultan Ibn Byjad, the leader of the Ikhwan Movement, and the termination of its direct influence, Faisal al-Dwaish and Dhidhan Ibn Hithlain continued to oppose Ibn Saud until Britain refused Faisal al-Dwaish's request (when he contacted Captain Dixon in Kuwait at the end of October 1929) to protect the women, children and old men of his tribe and its possessions in the north of Najd, and to let him settle in Kuwait.[11] This refusal led to Dwaish's surrender to the Kuwaiti authorities on 10 January 1930, marking the end of the Ikhwan Movement's opposition to Ibn Saud.

This shows how Britain supported Ibn Saud politically, materially and morally and contributed actively to establishing the modern Saudi state. The development of relations between Saudi Arabia and the West during the rule of Abdalaziz Ibn Saud was attributed to his conviction that he was indebted to the West for founding his kingdom and ties with the West were at the centre of Saudi foreign policy. Nevertheless, the era of cooperation did not prevent the emergence of some disputes between the two countries, which dated back to the first discoveries of oil in the Arabian Peninsula in 1933. These disputes came about as a result of Britain's commitment to its agreements with Oman and the Emirates of the Omani Coast, as well as Britain's desire to monopolize the processes of searching for oil in the region, especially when Ibn Sauds decided to hand over this privilege to an American company[12] for better royalties.

Despite the continuation of disputes[13] between the two parties, Britain became more willing to reach a peaceful settlement with Ibn Saud on the border disputes between Saudi Arabia and the sheikhdoms, even if this came at the expense of the latter.[14] Britain had realized that its influence in the Middle East was declining. It saw the possibility that the power of Abdalaziz Ibn Saud would become the dominant one in the region and possibly become a candidate to protect Western interests after its withdrawal. The regional events that the Arabian Peninsula had experienced – the Yemeni revolution in 1962 and the intervention of Gamal Abdel Nasser in supporting the revolutionaries against the Imam who was supported by Saudi Arabia, as well as the enmity of the Saudi royal family to the popular freedom movements in the Gulf and the Peninsula region – played an important element in shaping the Saudi royal family decision to freeze its demand of annexing Al Buraymi Oasis and resuming its diplomatic relations with Britain in January 1962. These relations had been severed since 1956. Consequently, the emergence of pan-Arabism and liberation movements in the Arab Peninsula and the Gulf region prompted the Saudi government to freeze its regional ambitions with the aim of ending the gains that those movements had achieved. The Saudi government began to view the sheikhdoms as the bulwark of its own security. This would explain the Saudi view today of the security link between the kingdom and the Gulf Cooperation Council member states. In brief, the desire of Britain and Saudi Arabia to preserve the political status quo in the Gulf and the Arabian Peninsula, along with the fear of the pan-Arabism and left-wing movements, helped to make Saudi Arabia the 'legitimate successor' of Britain. This change, coupled with the US–Saudi rapprochement from the 1930s, connected the region to the Western camp. Consequently, the conservative Saudi and pro-Western trends are among the main factors that determine contemporary Saudi foreign policy.

The Ideological Variable

Ideology has been one of the most effective factors in determining the foreign policy of any given country. It is argued that 'the ideological conservatism of the Saudi family precluded it from establishing permanent ties with the country that was first to recognise the new Kingdom (in 1926) and to offer economic assistance."[15] The significance of the ideology to Saudi foreign policy lies in the fact that the Saudi regime takes its legitimacy from three overlapping basic elements: tribalism, religion and the Wahabi movement,[16] due to its connection to the religious and social ideology of the Wahabi movement.[17] The existence of the two holy cities – Makkah and Medina – strengthened the use of Islam as an effective ideology in forming Saudi foreign policy, for example in Saudi–Iranian relations in 1987. The importance of ideology increases as it is dominant in social customs and traditions and it controls the positions of public opinion, and especially the Islamic elite, as was the case in the first Gulf crisis. It leads to specific policies being followed that are justified by the system of values on which the legitimacy of the political system is based,[18] such as adopting the decision to take part in the oil embargo in 1973 despite King Faisal's belief that oil should not be used as a strategic weapon in the war against Israel.[19] Similarly, Saudi Arabia opposed the Camp David agreements and committed itself to the Baghdad Summit resolutions, despite Saudi having been one of the Arab countries that hoped that President Anwar Sadat's peace initiative would achieve positive results.[20]

Moreover, the Saudi regime uses Islam as a means to mobilize public support to give legitimacy to its foreign policy undertakings. The Saudi leaders used Islam to justify their positions towards Gamal Abdel Nasser in the 1960s[21] and to confront the pan-Arab wave[22] by calling for an Islamic bloc, which was embodied at a later stage in the founding of the Organization of the Islamic Conference based in Jeddah. It also used Islam to justify its positions against Colonel Muammar Gaddafi's government in Libya in the 1980s. Saudi Arabia has sought to direct its foreign aid to Islamic countries in order to export its conservative ideology and this is what crystallized into its support to Pakistan.[23] It is worth mentioning that 96 per cent of Saudi foreign aid[24] goes to the Islamic countries, with approximately 70 per cent going mainly to Arab countries. The conservative Saudi ideology strove to prevent the establishing of permanent relationships with the Soviet Union and it adopted anti-Marxist and anti-Soviet Union policies.[25]

The effect of ideology differs according to the personality that leads the political hierarchy. For instance, in accordance with his conservative conviction and political views, Abdalaziz Ibn Saud opposed the reform movement in Kuwait and Bahrain in 1938. He believed that the masses should not be encouraged to share power and that power should remain in the hands of those who rule. These events were not harmonious with his perception of constitutional measures in an Arab and Muslim state.[26] Contemporary Saudi-held perceptions of the democratic measures in Kuwait and Bahrain are similar to the position of the founder of the third Saudi state.

Faisal Ibn Abdul Aziz's fear of the pan-Arab movement was behind the call for Britain to delay its decision to withdraw from the east of Suez. During his visit to Britain on 19 May 1967, King Faisal demanded that Britain should commit itself to defend the area against any aggression from the United Arab Republic or by the pan-Arab movements.[27] He expressed his country's willingness to help in fininancing the continuity of the British presence in the region.[28] King Faisal, stemming from his religious beliefs, looked at Zionism and Communism as two sides of the same coin, representing 'the axis of evil'.[29] On the other hand, the keenness of the political elite in Saudi Arabia to display the Islamic characteristics of Saudi foreign policy did not necessarily mean a pure Islamic policy or that it only served Islamic goals, since the relations of the kingdom are determined by political, economic and strategic considerations.[30] Therefore Islam is not the main motivator of Saudi foreign policy but its conservative philosophy. This is clearly manifested in the following:[31]

1. Saudi Arabia's support of the conservative tribal systems in the small Gulf States, which appears in its military and security alliance. It offered financial and military aid to Sultan Qaboos's government against the Dhofar revolution despite its political and sectarian differences with the Omani government. This culminated in founding the Gulf Cooperation Council.
2. Saudi Arabia's implicit support of the role that Iran under the Shah used to play as the policeman of the Gulf, and playing a similar role on the Arab side of the Gulf. It also supported Iran–Iraq rapprochement in 1975.
3. The close cooperation with the United States and its acceptance of an increasing US role in the region. This appears in its implicit approval of a US presence in Juffair, Bahrain, and of American aid given to Sultan Qaboos in return for granting the American forces facilities in Mua'sirah Island and in the Musandam Peninsula,[32] in addition to the facilities granted to the American forces in the Saudi territories of Dhahran, Dammam,[33] Khams Mishit, al-Jubail, Yanbu and Hafar al Batin and the invitation to American

forces on 7 August 1990 to use Saudi territory against Iraq, despite the outcry of some of the religious leadership and their disapproval.

The Political Variable

What concerns us in this section is getting to know the nature and dynamics of the political system, the degree of political participation and the degree of its stability. The Saudi political system is known as a closed hereditary monarchy. Before his death, Abdalaziz Ibn Saud demanded that his thirty-six sons promise him that they would work together after his death and, if they disagreed, to seek to reconcile their differences within the family domain. Nevertheless, this did not prevent the emergence of some disputes amongst royal family members, especially when Prince Talal Ibn Abdalaziz criticized the political system in his country and called for the establishment of a democratic constitutional monarchy.[34] Prince Talal had his passport confiscated in Beirut. The other dispute occurred between King Saud and Prince Faisal, which eventually led to the dethroning of King Saud and his exile in Egypt at the order of the royal family council. Faisal was made king of the country and Saud attempted to retake the throne by force.[35] In addition there were several ongoing disputes between the late King Fahd and Crown Prince Abdullah on key issues concerning ties with the US and relations with Arab countries. The lack of trust between the two parties was reflected in Prince Abdullah's refusal to relinquish the position of commander-in-chief of the National Guard, which he considered a safety valve in order to preserve the political balance with the king, his brothers, the Sedaris group, and sons who have been given a number of important ministerial posts such as the (ministers of) Crown Prince, first and second Deputy Prime Ministers (PM), Defence, Interior, and Governor of Riyadh, etc.

There are numerous reasons for these disputes, the most important of which is personal ambition. Abdalaziz Ibn Saud married into prominent families such as al-Thinyan, Al Al-Shaykh, al-Sedaris and al-Jalwi, as an important way to unite the Ibn kingdom and to ally with the tribes. As he married fourteen women his sons were not full brothers but half-brothers and so rivalry for power is inevitable. For example, Saud belongs to Ar'ar tribe who are part of Banu Khalid, whereas Faisal belongs to Al Al-Shaykh, and Fahd and his brothers – Turki, Sultan, Nayef, Abdul Rahman, Selman and Ahmad – belong to the al-Sedaris family, whereas Abdullah belongs to the Shummar tribe. As for Talal, Nawaf, Mansur, Mutayib, Misha'al and Majid, their mother was Armenian, whereas Mamduh and Masha'ur were born to a Syrian mother.[36] If the members of the royal family have so far managed to overcome their differences in accordance with the will of their father, what will happen in the next few coming decades when all of Abdalaziz's sons have died; who will take over and how? This question casts a shadow over the future of the monarchy in Saudi Arabia. It is argued that aging brothers and changing society assume a leadership crisis[37] as, even with the Basic System of Governance, which was issued by King Fahd Ibn Abdalaziz on 1 March 1992, choosing a king will become more complicated. King Abdullah, then aged 84, formed, in 2006, a family council consisting of thirty-five family members assigned the power to choose the Crown Prince once Prince Sultan, the incumbent crown prince, is sworn in to the throne. He, however, was the first to go back on this when he decided to elevate 74-year-old Prince Nayef, the Interior Minister, to third place in line for the throne as the second deputy premier due to Prince Sultan's ailing health. The move raised speculation that Prince Nayef will succeed his brother Sultan if the later passes away before King Abdullah. A dissenting voice came from within the al-Saud royal family. Prince Talal urged the king not to bypass the allegiance council.[38] Prince Nayef is known for being a tough, uncompromising conservative who does not support the political reforms initiated by his brother King Abdullah. King Abdullah has continued the cautious reform programme begun when he was crown prince. To promote increased political participation, the government held elections nationwide from February to April 2005 for half the members of 179 municipal councils. (However, the Saudi government decided in May 2009 to put the short-lived experiment on hold for two years.[39]) In December 2005, King Abdullah completed the process by appointing the remaining members of the advisory municipal councils. The king instituted an Inter-Faith Dialogue initiative in 2008 to encourage religious tolerance on a global level; in February 2009, he reshuffled the cabinet, which led to more moderates holding ministerial and judicial positions, and appointed the first female to the cabinet.[40]Reforms undertaken in Saudi Arabia remain short of people's aspirations and demands. It was argued the 'the patriarchal Saudi state must embrace progressive liberalisation and popular participation in the decision- making process.'[41]

The Saudi political system has not been stable since it was founded. In addition to political disagreements and the power struggle within the royal family, there were several attempts to overthrow the regime, from the mutiny of the Ikhwan Muslimeen (brothers) to the numerous coups d'état and plots in 1966, 1967, 1969,[42] 1977[43] and 2008. The year 1979 also witnessed the takeover of the Grand Mosque, led by Juhayman al-Utaibi who accused the regime of corruption and violation of Shari'ah (Islamic law). This incident represented the first Islamist challenge to the Saudi regime, which kept using Islam to justify its internal and foreign policies and to legitimize the regime. The years of 1980 and 1981 witnessed political disturbances in Sharqiya (Eastern Province) led by Shi'ite groups that believed that they were being subjected to persecution.[44] Some Islamic scholars[45] also opposed the mobilization of American and Western forces in the Arab peninsula against Iraq. Several prominent Islamist figures were arrested due to their opposition to the kingdom's participation in the Moscow Conference, in January 1992, to discuss the regional issues of the Middle East with the participation of the Arabs and Israel. The turning point in Saudi political life was a 2003 petition called 'A vision for the present and the future of the homeland', signed by Islamist reformers and liberals. The document is founded on the principles of confessional and political diversity in the kingdom. They broke the taboo of speaking about Wahabism. The Islamists called for free elections, freedom of expression and association, an independent judiciary and fairer distribution of wealth – in short a constitutional democracy.[46] Ten Saudis involved in petitioning the king were arrested in February 2007, and at the time of writing eight of these remain in custody, but have not been charged.[47] Saudi Arabia in the late 1990s and early twenty-first century witnessed a series of deadly attacks against Saudi and American installations and bases. In a further development revealing the inter-family power feud, Saudi sources confirmed reports which revealed that in late 2008 Russia unveiled to the Saudi government an attempted coup d'état engineered by Prince Bandar bin Sultan bin Abdalaziz, former long-time Saudi ambassador to Washington, with the help of former associates and of military commanders at Riyadh Aviation Base, and with the blessings of senior American officials in George W. Bush's administration. Sources also confirm that Prince Bandar is under house arrest and that many military officers have been arrested; however, their names and numbers have not been revealed and remain unconfirmed.[48]

The Saudi political regime obtains its legitimacy from several factors. The most important of them are the following:

1. Tribalism; the Saudi regime is based on a tribal alliance established through affinity or distributing wealth to the tribal chiefs in order to gain their loyalty or by attracting certain tribal figures to work as part of the National Guards and the Armed Forces.

2. The Wahabi movement, which is based on the blind obedience to the Imamate[49] represented by the Saudi government.

3. Islam, as the Saudi government attempts to exploit the religious factor in order to grant its existence political legitimacy. This can be seen in the absence of a written constitution until the Basic System of Governance was issued on 1 March 1992, on the grounds that the constitution is the Qur'an. The royal family was persistent in consulting Islamic scholars on a regular basis, as King Abdalaziz was committed to meet them every day after Maghreb (sunset) prayer, whereas King Faisal used to meet them on a weekly basis and King Khalid devoted every Monday to meeting the scholars, as did King Fahd and King Abdullah. The scholars participated in drawing up social policies, enacting laws and interpreting outcomes. They dominate some ministries and institutions and the headquarters of policy-making in education, judiciary, pilgrimage affairs, religious endowments, Da'awa (preaching) activities and religious research, and in the promotion of virtue and prevention of vice.

4. The wealthy elite community on which the government relied to finance the governmental treasury between 1926 and 1932. This financial support became secondary after 1947. Although the role of this group of people has changed since the discovery of oil, they are still essential to the monarchy in preserving the present state. The role of this group can be summed up in the process of Saudi foreign policy-making, its support to the capitalist economy system, and the rapprochement with the West and enmity towards communism.

The main features of the Saudi regime can be summed up as follows:

1. Individuality – the process of decision-making is in the hands of the king in his capacity as head of both the executive and legislative authorities and he can also exercise the juristic authority at times.[50] Politically analysing the Basic System of Governance in Saudi Arabia shows that this law has granted the king the constitutional legitimacy to lead both the executive and legislative authorities.

2. A closed political system – as it is a hereditary system and the critical decisions are taken by the most influential members of the royal family council.[51] The Saudi regime is characterized by the absence of parties and trade unions.

3. The absence of any active political participation. Although personal decisions can be influenced through personal discussions that take place in the king's public assemblies, allowing citizens to enter the daily assembly does not legitimize the view that the Majlis system is a form of democratic representation, due to the fact that the ability to express an opinion to the decision-maker is not equal to possessing the right to determine the substance of the decisions taken by the king. Therefore, these kinds of meetings, albeit important, do not represent a constitutional channel with a real effect on state policies.[52]

In compliance with the demands of the intellectual elite put to the king after the end of the first Gulf crisis in July 1991, which led to constitutional reforms embodied in the forming of a representative council and the adoption of the principle of competence and fighting corruption, King Fahd announced on 1 March 1992 a package of political reforms, including the formation of a sixty-member consultative council – the Shura Council. Without belittling these reforms, especially if they are followed by more important and effective steps, these are nothing more than formalities and are merely cosmetic. This is because:

1. Its role is merely consultative.
2. Its members are appointed by the king, so they are accountable to the king not the people.
3. Its number is not proportionate to the kingdom's population.
4. The powers of the council to question the ministers are conditioned by the king's approval. The king too is the arbitrator between the council and the government.

The role of technocrats in the decision-making process is limited despite their increasing numbers in the government throughout the previous period because al-Saud dominate the country in nearly all spheres. They represented six out of fourteen ministers in the first government under King Faisal in 1965, then sixteen out of twenty-seven ministers in the government that was formed under King Fahd, and significant numbers of them were appointed to the Shura Council. The intellectuals play an indirect role in the process of foreign policy-making in Saudi Arabia through their participation in the governmental bureaucracy as ministry deputies, ambassadors, diplomats, administrative directors, civil servants, etc. in addition to the political weight that they gain through their various posts and their effective presence as one of the main groups of society, and the regime cannot ignore their ambitions. Therefore, the most effective social groups in decision-making in the kingdom are the scholars, the tribal chiefs, the merchants and the intellectuals. However, although the kingdom has built a modern government and bureaucracy, members of the royal family hold the most senior posts: the King, Crown Prince, Prime Minister and his Deputy, and the ministers of Defence and Aviation, Interior and Security, Foreign Affairs and the National Guard in addition to less significant ministerial posts like Public Work and Housing.[53]

The conservative nature of the political system is reflected in the Saudi foreign orientations that are based on three main points:

1. Animosity to Communism. This was demonstrated through its rejection of establishing diplomatic relations with the former socialist bloc until the early 1990s and in its alliance with the West and mainly with the United States, and in its support to anti-communist regimes, for example, its financial aid to the Contras in Nicaragua.
2. Fighting against the democratic attempts in neighbouring countries or in the states affiliated to its regional system, whether these countries are Gulf, Arab or Islamic states; for example, its position towards the democratic attempts in Bahrain and Kuwait.[54]
3. Animosity to any Islamic revolution as this would affect the legitimacy of the Saudi regime. Therefore the Saudi government will adopt a negative position towards Islamic revolution, as was the case regarding the Iranian revolution and the Sudan's Revolutionary Command Council for National Salvation government due to its connections to the National Islamic Front, and its position on the political developments witnessed by Algeria where the Islamic Salvation Front won the election and achieved a landslide victory in 1992. The Saudi position was manifested in the visits that L'Akhdar el-Ibarhimi made to Saudi Arabia and the statements he issued.[55] Alternatively, Saudi Arabia attempts to gain allies among the revolutionary groups to prevent the hardliners from taking power and to gain influence regarding the political changes. An example of this was Afghanistan. The Saudi position towards the political changes taking place in Afghanistan was demonstrated by supporting the coalition government that comprised all groups, including the secularists, instead of letting the Islamic 'fundamentalists' take over power.

The Demographic Variable

The demographic factor plays an important role in determining how far any state can influence the policies of other countries in a way that would meet its foreign aims. Population and diversity might be the most important elements as the population and the degree of cohesion of any society form the basis upon which the foreign policy of any country can be built. This section will focus on the size of the population of the kingdom, the ratio of nationals to non-nationals and the main communities and minorities in Saudi society.

It is worth mentioning first that, with the absence of the official local statistics, it is difficult to determine the real numbers of the Saudi population, therefore I rely on the estimates given by concerned special international organizations. The estimates indicate that the kingdom's population level has quadrupled in the last five decades – with annual growth rate at 4 to 2.44 per cent and improved average life expectancy age to 72 years – from 6 million in 1965[56] to 13.8 million in 1988,[57] 24 million in 2007[58] (see Table 9.1), 28.6 million, including 5.6 million non-nationals, in 2009, and with an expected decline in the annual population growth rate to 1.8 per cent,[59] it will come to 33.7 million in 2015. Sources in 2001 estimated nationals to account for 73 per cent of which Bedouin make up to 10 per cent and Shi'ites 6 per cent, with expatriates at 27 per cent of which Asians make 20 per cent, Arabs 6 per cent and others at 1 per cent.[60]

Table 9.1. Saudi Arabia Population (1965–2009) (million)

1965	1980	1988	1995	2007	2009
6	9	13.8	16	24	28.6

Oil played an enormous role in changing the social life in the kingdom. There has been an increase in internal migration levels, with people leaving the countryside for the cities: the population in the cities increased from 65 per cent of the total Saudi population in 1980 to 74 per cent in 1987,[61] whereas the countryside population decreased from 35 per cent to 27 per cent in the same period, and declined to 18.2 per cent by 2000.[62] The ratio of rural (nomads) to urban population went down from 50 per cent of the population in the 1970s to approximately 34 per cent in the 1980s to 12 per cent in 2006.[63]

Furthermore, like other Gulf societies, despite a significant percentage of government spending being allocated for education, Saudi society suffers from the shortage of a skilled labour force. The Saudi expenditure on education in the period 1995 to 2005 was estimated at 27.6 per cent of total government expenditure,[64] leading to a sharp decline in the illiteracy rate to 19.6 per cent in 2005.[65] The local workforce (15–65 years old) reached only 37 per cent in 2006 with annual growth at 3.1 per cent.[66] Despite all the economic progress that Saudi Arabia has witnessed, several failing aspects have hindered the process of development. The most urgent problem lies in the lack of a trained workforce to carry out planned works for the development process.[67] It is reflected in the fact that 85.2 per cent of the Saudi workforce is in the service sector, with only 7.8 per cent in the industrial sector and 7 per cent in the agricultural sector.[68]

Saudi Arabia relies on a foreign workforce to carry out development projects in the country. Despite discrepancies in estimates of the size of the foreign workforce, it is no less than 50 per cent of the total population. The estimates indicate that, until the first Gulf crisis, the Yemeni community formed a large proportion, estimated at 2–3 million before around two-thirds of them were deported. The Egyptian and Jordanian communities represent the second and third largest Arab communities that form the Saudi workforce. The non-Arab foreign workforce is represented by Indians, Pakistanis, Bengalis, Koreans and other Asians. There is a large proportion of Americans and Europeans also, especially in the military and technical fields.[69] Therefore the kingdom lacks the skilled labour to shoulder the burden of development, which has forced the state to rely on an immigrant workforce. This has had a serious effect on Saudi foreign policy towards the countries of origin of the foreign workforce and has had economic, social and cultural effects on Saudi society.

Sectarianism is also a destabilizing factor in Saudi society, as there is a Shi'ite minority that numbers approximately 1.5 to 2 million people. Although it does not exceed 8 per cent of the total population, its importance lies in the success of the Iranian revolution and their geographic proximity to Iran, and the possibility of sabotage through the infiltration of Iranian aid, in addition to political and psychological support – as illustrated in the frequent calls by some Iranian clergy to export the revolution to the Arab Gulf States or to express claims to Bahrain, which makes them a source of continuous anxiety to the Saudi government.[70] Their location has increased their importance because they reside in the areas of the Saudi oil reservoirs. Sources have indicated that they have begun to make their voices heard since the success of the Iranian revolution. In 1979 they disputed the laws that forbid observing the Ashura ceremony marking the martyrdom of Imam Hussain. They organized a festival in February 1980 to commemorate the first anniversary of Khomeini's return to Iran. This led to clashes with the security forces in Al Qattif, where four demonstrators were killed.[71] Saudi Shi'ite clergy have repeatedly voiced their discontent, criticized the government policies of 'oppression' against the Shi'ite community and called for autonomous rule or session from the kingdom. Therefore this minority plays an important role in directing kingdom's policy towards Iran and internally.

The Social Variable

Looking at the role played by the social variable on Saudi foreign policy-making requires the study of the social structure of Saudi society, the social strata, communities and social groupings, and prominent families. However, it is important to note that Gulf societies are relatively young and have not yet formed a class structure, given the flexibility of social mobility. Hence, the investigation of the social role would not use a 'class' to describe the social divisions in Saudi society. Like other societies, Saudi society takes on a pyramid shape where the upper social stratum comprises the royal family, the 'Ulama (religious scholars), tribal leaders, landowners and the prominent families such as al-Sedaris, al-Thinyan, al-Ashaykh and al-Jalwi. This group has ruled the country since the formation of the third Saudi state. It has benefited from the regime economically and politically and it has interests in the current political situation. However, the status and influence of the 'Ulama and prominent families have diminished 'mostly because of growing social complexity and their reduction to salaried government servants.'[72] On the other hand, the traditional middle stratum is very small. It consists of a modest number of shop owners, the lower ranked civil servants, professionals and manual craftsmen. This class has not enjoyed any power or influence and it has not carried out any activity that links it to the influential class.

As a result of the discovery of oil and the spread of education, a new middle stratum has appeared. It is made up of a mixture of those who are employed mainly by the state, such as civil servants, scientists, university lecturers, medics, teachers, engineers, lawyers and judges. This stratum also includes merchants, landowners and other similar groups. Members of this stratum originate from the traditional middle stratum. The importance of this stratum lies in the continuous need for all kinds of services that it offers and the increase in demand for them. But despite the continuous expansion of this stratum and the legitimacy of its political aspirations in playing a political role, the lack of active political institutes and suitable constitutional channels has excluded this stratum from the decision-making process and helped maintain the royal family's monopoly of power internally and externally.[73] As a result, the political system came to give the monopoly of power by the royal family constitutional legitimacy. The new middle stratum has exerted its influence through the leading posts that some of its members occupy. Since the decision-making process is still in the hands of the royal family through the king and royal family council, the 'the middle social strata exerts its influence in shaping economic policy more than it does politically'.[74] Meanwhile, the role of this stratum in politics is represented by princes who studied abroad and were influenced by Western governing values and by their peers who belong to this stratum. As for the lower social stratum, it is large, weak, poor and ineffective. It is comprised mainly of unsettled nomads and unskilled workers and the land leaseholders in the countryside. This stratum does not have any political role and has not carried out any activity to change the social structure of Saudi society. Nevertheless, it is difficult to say that this poor class has no influence, as the political system cannot ignore its aspirations regardless of how weak it may be. Therefore, one could say that the higher a social stratum moves up the hierarchy echelon, the more it will influence the decision-making process.

The Economic Variable

Saudi Arabia has an oil-based economy with strong government controls over major economic activities. The Saudi economy depends mainly on oil (see Chapter 2). The oil sector accounts for roughly 80 per cent of budget revenues, 45 per cent of GDP, and 90 per cent of export earnings.[75] According to the Geneva Agreement signed on 15 January 1992 the Saudi quota reached 7.887 million barrels a day, increased in 2007 to 8.754 million barrels a day (mbd) and returns of $179 billion. Saudi Arabia increased its oil production capacity to a record 12.5 mbd keeping almost one-third of its capacity shut down.[76] The estimates indicate that the Saudi reserve of oil reached in 2007 the level of 266.8 billion barrels, making the kingdom home to the largest oil reserve, with 20 per cent of the world reserve. The kingdom possesses a large natural gas reserve, which in 2007 was estimated to be 7.2 trillion cubic metres. Meanwhile, its annual production reached 88,209 million cubic metres.[77] Consequently, the 'kingdom not only influences the fate of the world's oil consumers; it holds power over the world's other oil producers.'[78]

The economic indicators demonstrate the extent to which the Saudi economy has suffered as a result of its dependence on oil. Its GDP was US$582.8 billion in 2008 due to a sharp increase in oil revenues before the beginning of the global economic crisis. Oil contribution to the GDP in 2006 was $178.4 billion. Its economic exposure can also be seen in the extent of its vulnerability to oil market fluctuations and the instability of the dollar. This was clearly reflected in the drop of Saudi GDP from $131.3 billion in 1981 to $100.5 billion in 1985[79] due to the decline of oil revenue between 1981 and 1988, from $119 billion to $16.6 million,[80] as a result of the drop in the oil prices that led to budget deficit increase from $12.8 billion in 1984[81] to $17.6 billion in 1985.[82] As a result of the decline of oil prices compared with the prices of the early 1980s and the first Gulf crisis, the kingdom became an indebted state. Its external debts were estimated in 1990 to be approximately $22.2 billion.[83] The improvement in the international oil prices in 1987 led to a relative revival in the Saudi economy. The linkage between oil prices and economic growth is clear in the fluctuation of growth percentage over the period 1984–2008. It went down from 9 per cent in 1984 to 8.7 per cent in 1986, to 2.4 per cent in 1987, back to 7.2 per cent in 1990 and to 4.2 per cent 2008. In the meantime the rate of inflation was up from 2 per cent in 1990 to 10.3 per cent in 2008 and the unemployment rate was estimated at 8.8 per cent in 2008[84] while it remained dependent on foreign workers for menial occupations. The Saudi budget, due to the sharp increase in the oil prices until mid-2008, showed a huge improvement, whereby the budget witnessed a jump from a deficit of $5.5 billion in 2002 to a surplus of $46.1 billion in 2007.[85] High oil prices through mid-2008 have boosted growth, government revenue, and Saudi ownership of foreign assets, while enabling Riyadh to pay down domestic debt. Consequently, the annual average per capita is constantly affected by the fluctuation of the GDP as illustrated by the increase from 8,850 dollars in 1985[86] to 20,700 dollars in 2008.[87] Moreover, the instability in oil prices affected cash flow as it went down from $145 billion in 1981 to $85 billion in 1986.[88] However, the increase in the oil prices in early twenty-first century helped Saudi Arabia to pay off its debts and to accumulate foreign reserves of $33.5 billion in 2007.[89]

The Saudi government, from the beginning of the 1970s, has showed increasing interest in diversifying sources of revenue. It embarked on the first five-year plan for the period 1970–5, in the sectors of agriculture, industrial development and communications. This can be seen in the participation of other sectors in the gross domestic product.[90] As part of the first five-year plan, two dams were built in Wadi Jizan and Abha, and agricultural lands were reclaimed. At the same time, several oil refineries were built in Riyadh and Jeddah. The second five-year plan included the construction of an 800-mile pipeline to transport oil from the eastern region to Yanbu. Another oil refinery was built in Yanbu with a capacity of 500,000 barrels a day. Consequently, Saudi Arabia became the leading Arab country in refining crude oil locally as its productivity rose from 750,000 barrels a day in 1975 to 1.4 million barrels in 1985[91], to 2 million barrels in 2007.[92] In the agricultural domain, Saudi Arabia's attempt to produce wheat was successful in terms of quantity, with an increase in the level of production from 150,000 tons per annum to two million tons in the last two decades. The kingdom is the third largest Arab country in wheat production. Its whole agricultural production increased in 1979–81 by 240 per cent.[93] Saudi Arabia produces dates, wheat, barley, tomatoes, melons, citrus, mutton, chicken, eggs and dairy.

Despite the Saudi limited success in the agricultural sector, which was demonstrated by the decrease in the gross Saudi imports of foodstuffs in 1984–5 by $400 million,[94] Saudi Arabia is still suffering from a lack of self-sufficiency as its agricultural imports in 2006 were estimated at $9.6 billion, with an annual increase of 10 per cent.[95] This shows that, although a great deal of effort was exerted in the agricultural domain and there was improvement in its productivity, the kingdom is still dependent on foreign countries to secure its food requirements. For instance, in 1980, the kingdom imported one billion dollars worth of foodstuffs from the United States.[96] This was due to a number of factors but mainly the kingdom's environmental conditions and topographical factors, as although it covers a vast area, the areas suitable for cultivation do not exceed 4,500 hectares, of which 1,135 hectares were already cultivated. This represents about 25 per cent of the total cultivable land in Saudi Arabia. The shortage in national manpower represents one of the main impediments that the development plans face as the number of farm workers is no more than 4,672.[97] Recent data shows that no more than 7 per cent of the workforce was engaged in the agricultural sector in 2006.[98] Since the beginning of the twenty-first century, the agricultural sector contribution to the GDP has been declining from 4.9 in 2000 to 2.8 per cent in 2007.[99] The inability to achieve food self-sufficiency represents a further domestic constraint and increases the kingdom's vulnerability to external pressures, shaping its foreign policy towards the exporting countries. As part of its effort to attract foreign investment and diversify the economy, Saudi Arabia acceded to the World Trade Oraganization (WTO) in December 2005 after many years of negotiations. The government has announced plans to establish six 'economic cities' in different regions of the country to promote development and diversification.[100]

The kingdom, thanks to its oil wealth, has managed efficiently to use its foreign aid to influence the foreign policy undertakings of recipient countries. For this purpose, in 1987, Saudi Arabia designated about 3.32 per cent of its GNP to foreign aid.[101] Between 1973 and 1987, Saudi Arabia was one of the top five donor countries in the world.[102] Due to its religious standing,[103] it was able to influence the policies of developing countries, Islamic countries in particular. In this way it managed to influence the course of regional and international events to a large degree.[104] In the Gulf region, the kingdom acted to disturb political reform in the Gulf States. In 1975, it offered Bahrain $350 million to dissolve parliament. It invested its financial power in weakening the popular movements to liberate Oman and the Gulf, as it gave the Omani government, between 1975 and 1979, approximately $3 million to invest in the development field and to prevent another revolution. It also offered North Yemen the same amount of money to persuade that country to force out a number of Russian experts and to reduce its dependency on the former Soviet Union, whilst it gave the government of South Yemen around $125 million in return for stopping its support of liberation movements in the region.[105] On the regional level, with regards to the countries of the Gulf, Saudi participated actively during the Iraq–Iran war by supporting the Iraqi military endeavour. King Fahd announced in 1991 that Saudi Arabia gave Iraq around $25 billion during the war with Iran.[106] On the other hand, Saudi Arabia paid the biggest share in financing the Allied forces against Iraq during the Kuwait crisis. On the Arab level, Saudi Arabia gave Egypt approximately $2.6 billion between 1967 and 1975 in return for Egypt pledging not to interfere in the internal affairs of the states of the Arabian peninsula. Meanwhile, the risk of freezing the $600 million of aid to Syria was the reason why Syria sent its military forces into Lebanon in 1976. In 1989, Saudi Arabia gave Jordan financial aid estimated at $200 million[107] to consolidate the Jordanian monarchy and to weaken the Arab Economic Council.

The Military Variable

The military variable represents one of the main factors determining the extent to which the state can achieve its foreign policy objectives in such a troubled world. The gauge with which the force of the state is measured depends on two main points: the number of active personnel and the weapons. To measure each of them requires looking jointly at both quantity and quality, and despite all the efforts the Saudi government has made to consolidate and strengthen its military capacity, allocating 10 per cent of its GDP in 2005 to military expenditure,[108] its capability is still lagging behind, as was clearly evident in the first Gulf crisis. The Saudi forces were estimated in 2004 at 124,500 soldiers at best, plus 75,000 active National Guard.[109] Accordingly the kingdom is ranked seventh among the Middle East states, whilst non-Saudis represent 50 per cent of the army (see Chapter 4).

The Saudi military strategy is based on having a force that enables it to deter any external threat until the arrival of military support from allied states, especially the United States, as was the case in the first Gulf crisis. Military expenditure has increased 400 times from 1962 to 2007. In 2007, the kingdom was ninth in world rank after the United States, China, Russia, United Kingdom, France, Japan, Germany and Italy (see Chapter 3). Saudi military expenditure between 1987 and 1990 has almost doubled from $16,235 million (representing 35.8 per cent of total governmental expenditure)[110] to $31.86 billion, which included the Saudi share in financing the American–British campaign against Iraq. However, the actual defence budget was $13.86 billion.[111] Saudi military expenditure reached $29.5 billion in 2007 (see Table 4.2).

The kingdom depends on the West to provide its military needs. Between 1973 and 1977, Saudi Arabia bought weapons from Britain, France and the United States. That included 735 medium-sized tanks, 250 light tanks, 700 armoured vehicles, troop carriers, F5 fighter jets, three Mirage planes, a helicopter, transport planes, Hawk missiles air-air, field guns, anti-aircraft guns and military boats.[112] In addition, in 1981, the United States sold to Saudi Arabia five AWACS E-3A planes for a total of $5.8 billion. The kingdom owns around 700 medium-sized tanks, 240 light tanks, 1,700 field guns, eight frigates, twelve warships, four minesweepers, twenty armed helicopters, twenty-four unarmed helicopters, 253 fighters, including sixty F-15c as well as twelve training planes, fifty-three Tornado planes and fifty-two F-5E planes.[113] Saudi defence equipment in 2004 included 315 M-1A2 Abram, 290 AMX-30, 450 M60A3, RECC 300 AML-60/-90, AIFV 570+ AMX-10P, 400 M-2 Bradley, APC 3000 M-113A1/A2/A3, twelve attack helicopters AH-64 TPTHEL, SAM Crotale, 500 Stinger, 500 Redeye, 291 combatants aircraft, ASM Maverick and AAM Sidewinder Missiles, eight principal surface combatants, twenty-six patrol and coastal combatants, seven mine warfare, seven support and miscellaneous, and twenty-one armed helicopters.[114]

Saudi military demands often were faced with reluctance either from the US administration or from Congress. On 22 October 1980, President Jimmy Carter refused to sell the kingdom F-15 fighter jets and Congress refused to sell to Saudi Arabia forty fighter jets in 1985 and Stinger missiles in 1986. On 11 June 1987, the Senate also refused to sell to the Saudis 1,600 air-air Maverick missiles in fear that they would one day be used against Israel.[115] Due to these recurring US positions, the kingdom sought to diversify its weapon imports, seeking alternative sources. Consequently it signed two contracts in 1986 with the UK. The first was known as the Yamama 2. It contained a pledge of the second party to provide the first with 132 war planes including 72 Tornados, and other devices and services related to these planes. Then, in 1988, another contract called Yamama 3 was signed. It was worth $20 billion. It included purchasing war planes, Tornados and Hawks, in addition to six minesweepers of the Sandown Class for $540 million. In addition Saudi Arabia signed a series of military contracts with France. In 1988, the two parties signed a contract to strengthen the Saudi defence system for $546 million and another contract in the same year for $517 million. Saudi Arabia tried to obtain missile systems, Automat, to protect its coasts, in addition to two sea surveillance planes.[116] In June 1989, the two parties concluded two further military contracts for $2.7 billion; they included 3,000 Mistral surface-air missiles similar to the American Stinger and helicopter carriers.[117] Another contract was concluded in 2009 whereby the British government would supply Saudi Arabia with seventy-two Euro fighters (Typhoon) for $39.9 billion as part of the al-Salam deal. However, the deal is awaiting US approval due to the fact that it includes the transfer of US technology.[118] The Saudis also bought an unknown number of Chinese Silkworm missiles. They are surface-surface missiles with a range of 2,700 kilometres, meaning that they can reach Iran, Israel, the Islamic republics in the southern part of the former Soviet Union and India.[119] The Saudi–Chinese deal caused political differences between Saudi Arabia and its strategic ally the United States, leading the Saudis to declare that the US ambassador to the kingdom was persona non grata. Meanwhile, Israel threatened to carry out a pre-emptive strike against Saudi's new missiles. As a result of the Saudi move, the US Senate approved new regulations on arms deals that Saudi Arabia requested:

1. The US administration pledged to Congress that the Saudis would not obtain nuclear heads or chemical weapons that could be installed on the missiles that were purchased from China.
2. The size of the Saudi air fleet would be limited to sixty F-15 fighters.
3. The updating and replacement of the existing Saudi planes should be within this limit.[120]

The continuing presence of foreign troops on Saudi soil after the liberation of Kuwait became a source of tension between the royal family and the public until all operational US troops left the country in 2003.[121] From the above, we can conclude that the military factor plays a major role in steering Saudi foreign policy, especially with regards to its relations with the main neighbouring states and the weapons-exporting countries, especially the United States, that reflects the importance of the domestic constraints imposed on Saudi foreign policy-making.

3. The External Environment

The Regional Order

Given the inherited weakness of the power components, foreign policy-makers in Saudi Arabia opted to adopt foreign policies based on the principle of containment and alliance, on one hand, and the exploitation of the self-interest of the main powers in order to achieve its own national interests, on the other hand. In the subsidiary Gulf regional order, the kingdom occupies the lowest position in comparison to the main regional actors in all power components.[122] Therefore it has tried to ignore its differences with the smaller Gulf States to focus instead on cooperation and coordination between them as part of its regional coordinator role to meet the looming challenge of Gulf security. This culminated in the establishment of the Gulf Cooperation Council playing the linchpin of the organization and until 1990 adopting a policy of manœuvre and bullying among the major regional countries – Iraq and Iran. This approach was demonstrated through its alliance with Iran to contain Iraq on one occasion and its alliance with Iraq on another. The kingdom also pursued a policy of co-opting the Arab consensus in dealing with regional issues to contain any threat that could come from any state in the subsidiary regional order or from any of the radical Arab countries, or that could emerge as a result of not settling the Arab–Israeli conflict. Saudi Arabia also worked on avoiding the conflict between the superpowers by adopting the non-alliance policy, but its fear of the former Soviet Union or any 'radical' government in the region made the kingdom more lenient towards the West, particularly the United States.

Saudi's belief that it was surrounded by hostile countries was a source of anxiety and a continuous feeling of insecurity.[123] This played a paramount role in shaping the kingdom's policies towards those powers and towards the members of the GCC. Before 1979, Saudi Arabia cooperated with Iran to contain the threat of the Ba'ath government in Iraq. It sought to exploit Iraq–Iran rapprochement in 1975 by using Iraq to foil the Shah's plans to control the Gulf through the conclusion of a joint defence agreement between the regional Gulf States. It also exploited Iran's self-interest to halt the Iraqi ambition to lead the Arab states in the Gulf.[124]

After the fall of the Shah's regime in Iran and the establishment of a revolutionary Islamic government in accordance with the Shi'ite doctrine, the regional threat shifted from Iraq to Iran. That led to a change from the regional alliance represented by the Saudi Arabia–Iran axis to the Saudi Arabia–Iraq alliance, which was manifest in the kingdom's support of Iraq during the Iraq–Iran war. But Iraq's attempt to annex Kuwait in 1990 led the Saudis to work towards re-establishing their alliance with Iran. The new Saudi position towards Iran was demonstrated in the endorsement of the GCC member states, during the Doha Summit in December 1990, of a role for Iran in any regional security arrangements in the future. This new policy was also manifest in the exchange of visits carried out by senior officials of the two countries, including the visit of the Saudi Foreign Minister Saud Al Faisal to Tehran in May 1991 and the announcement of an upcoming visit that the Saudi King would undertake to Iran. The policy was seen in the development of relations with these two states and in Saudi's positions towards the political developments in the Gulf region.

(a) *Iran*

Saudi–Iran ties are determined by a number of variables, the most important of which is the geographical location. As the Gulf is the most important passageway for Iran to the outside world, this is the main reason behind Iran's desire to dominate it. Saudi–Iranian relations underwent two stages – one during the era of the Shah and the second that began with the rule of the revolutionary Islamic government. During the first stage, Saudi–Iranian relations were categorized by cooperation as the two states ended their borders disputes during the Shah's visit to the kingdom in 1968, and his acceptance of the rights of Bahrainis for self-determination led to his relinquishing the demand to annex Bahrain, in accordance with Saudi's request. Iran, with the support of the United States, assumed a self-appointed role as the 'Policeman of the Gulf'. The Shah's government sought to coordinate its policies with the Saudi government in order to contain 'Marxist' or 'pan-Arab' threats and this was illustrated, in 1975, in Iran's role in putting down the Omani revolution. The two countries eventually became part of the 'Twin Pillar' policy of the Nixon Doctrine for Gulf security. Saudi Arabia was the second pillar in that American strategy for Gulf security. But that does not suggest that Saudi Arabia was not dismayed by the Shah's expansionist ambitions in the region.[125]

Since 1979, the success of the Iranian revolution has represented a different kind of threat to the Saudis:

1. Iran was transformed from a strategic shield to a potential threat.
2. Saudi Arabia was stuck between two similar regimes as far as hostility was concerned.
3. Iran became a threat to the freedom of navigation in the Gulf.[126]

Iran also challenged the Islamic legitimacy of Saudi Arabia's regime. It did not hesitate to engineer riots and demonstration organized by Iranian pilgrimages during the 1987 and 1989 haj seasons[127]. Fear of the new Iranian government was a factor in adjusting Saudi foreign policy regionally and internationally. On the regional level, it led to an increase in cooperation and coordination with Iraq on one hand, and working towards getting Egypt back to the Arab fold on the other hand. As for the international level, Saudi Arabia began to distance itself from US policy in the region and began cautious cooperation with the socialist camp. This was demonstrated by the visits of some Saudi officials to Moscow as part of Arab or international delegations and in purchasing Silkworm missiles from China.

Saudi Arabia faced a regional security dilemma concerning developments in neighbouring Iran. On the one hand, it remains very concerned with the extreme nature of President Ahmedinejad's government, Iran's military build-up and the dubious Iranian nuclear programme. One option was to join the anti-Iranian coalition consisting of pro-Western countries including Israel. Prince Bandar bin Sultan, Saudi Advisor of National Security, met with an Israeli Minister, Avi Dichter, in Amman on 6 September 2006[128] to foster a coalition that would include Israel but this option seems to have been ruled out since the alleged coup led by Bandar. A second option centres on accommodation or engagement of Iran whereby Iran must change its course and reach a modus vivendi with its neighbours and the world. In a third option, the kingdom sought to improve 'relations with Tehran because they see realistic possibilities for removing Iranian antipathy.'[129] This is illustrated in the Saudi decision in the autumn of 2006 to set up a high-level contact with Iran whereby meetings took place in various Arab capitals including Beirut, Baghdad and Riyadh. The Saudi engagement policy towards Tehran culminated in the exchange of senior dignitaries' visits by Iranian officials including Akbar Hashemi Rafsanani in 1998, President Mohammed Khatami in 1999 and President Ahmadinejad in Makka in March 2007. Interestingly enough, the two sides embarked on discussing security arrangements culminated in the signing of a security pact in 2001 during Prince Nayif bin Abdulaziz's visit to Tehran.[130] Saudi Arabia also refrained from criticizing the Iranian nuclear programme openly. Riyadh's objectives centre on securing Iran's commitment not to retaliate against Saudi Arabia or any of the GCC countries in retaliation to American or Israeli attack on Iran and to limit Iranian influence in various parts of the Arab world. The Saudi regional policy towards Iran provoked Martin Indyk to write, 'We seem to have backed the wrong Saudi.'[131]

(b) *Iraq*

Iraq represents the second main power in the Gulf subregional order, which has an ambition not only to consolidate its Gulf status but also to become the centre of Arab policy. The geographic position of Iraq, and its pan-Arab commitment since 1958, formed a barrier to developing strong relations with conservative Arab Gulf States. For a long time, the struggle to dominate the Arab side was one of the characteristics that distinguished the interaction between Saudi Arabia and Iraq. This was demonstrated by the Saudi support enjoyed by Kuwait in confronting the Iraqi threat in the early 1960s,[132] whereby the Saudis sent their troops to help the Kuwaiti forces to resist Iraqi forces.[133]

Despite the fact that the Kuwaiti issue was resolved through the Arab League, the Saudis continued to perceive Iraq's secularist pan-Arab ideology as a potential threat that would threaten their security and their stability. This was due to Iraq's attempts to weaken if not eliminate conservative and pro-Western regimes in the region. Iraq hosted Saudi Ba'athists and other opposition groups and allowed them to use Baghdad radio to broadcast their political messages to the people of the Arabian Peninsula and to issue a magazine called *The Vanguard Voice*.[134]

In their attempts to ensure their security and stability the Saudis have worked towards finding allies on the regional and international levels as a precautionary measure against any Iraqi ventures. This was demonstrated by the emergence of the Saudi Arabia–Iran axis and the alliance with the United States. In the meantime they tried to improve their relations with Iraq, especially after the Algiers Agreement as Iraq, up until 1981, became a member of all the integrative projects of the Arab Gulf states: the Gulf News Agency, the Gulf University, the Centre of Studies and Documentation Centre, the Gulf Folklore Centre of the Gulf Arab States, the Gulf Organization for Industrial Consulting, etc., and the Gulf Soccer Tournament.

The Iraq–Iran war gave the kingdom an important opportunity to contain the Iranian threat and to exclude Iraq from any future Gulf security arrangement that concerned Arab Gulf States. The Saudis succeeded in setting up an exclusive club through the founding of the GCC on 25 May 1981. In the meantime, Saudi Arabia supported the Iraqi war endeavour morally, materially and politically. It dedicated all its media outlets to supporting the Iraqi position in the war. The kingdom gave Iraq over $25 billion in financial aid and, along with Kuwait, it designated the revenues of 300,000 barrels of oil of its production to compensate Iraq for the fall of its oil production due to the war. Saudi Arabia allowed Iraq to build a pipeline to transport 1.5 million barrels a day of its oil to the Red Sea to avoid the Iranian blockade in the Gulf.[135]

Despite the improvement in the relations between the two countries, distrust and animosity continued to be dominant in the policies of both parties towards each other, especially after the radical changes that Iran had witnessed. The Saudis considered the National Charter that Saddam Hussein promulgated on 8 February 1980 as an indirect challenge to its influence in the Gulf. The kingdom expressed its disapproval of the new Iraqi initiative and believed it to be condemning it for its ties with the United States.[136] Due to its mistrust of Iraq, Saudi Arabia resumed building a military city near the Iraqi borders at a cost of $8 billion, known as the Military City of King Khalid, intended to accommodate more than 70,000 people by the beginning of 1990s, where three frigates would be based.[137]

Since the end of the Iraq–Iran war, relations have fluctuated; they have moved from cautious cooperation to the highest level of conflict. In the first stage, relations between the two countries witnessed a noticeable development, represented by the exchange of dignitaries' visits between the two sides at the highest levels. The most important of these was possibly King Fahd's visit to Baghdad, 23–26 March 1989 that was considered the first of its kind since the success of the 14 July Revolution that toppled the monarchy there. During that visit the two parties signed an agreement to delineate the borders between the two countries. Some sources believed[138] that the visit made by the Saudi king and the signing of the border agreements and agreements for non-interference in the internal affairs of the other side reflected a sense of mistrust among the Saudis, especially after the emergence of the Arab Cooperation Council that the kingdom saw as an Iraqi attempt to dominate the region, whereas these agreements can be seen as Iraqi recognition of the central role of Saudi Arabia in the Gulf Cooperation Council, and Iraq's aim was to reassure the other Arab Gulf states that Iraq did not pose a potential threat to their security.[139] Nevertheless, those agreements were revoked by Iraq during the first Gulf crisis.

The first Gulf crisis that started on 2 August 1990 terminated the cautious Saudi–Iraqi rapprochement. Despite Saudi's public warning to Kuwait that the kingdom would not be able to protect it against Iraq's anger,[140] the Iraqi invasion of Kuwait gave the Saudi governing elite the impression that the next step would be the toppling of the royal family and regime change in Saudi Arabia, as had happened in Kuwait.[141] Therefore Saudi Arabia became determined to prevent Saddam Hussein from dictating peace or war in the future.[142] King Fahd was solid in his stance and rejected any indication of reaching a peaceful settlement of the crisis.[143] The Saudis were prepared to support any military campaign against Iraq to destroy Iraq's chemical weapons and its nuclear programme. This was demonstrated in King Fahd's immediate calling on the aid of US forces. George Bush sr did not hesitate to answer the Saudi call and gave his immediate orders on 7 August 1990 to deploy US forces on Saudi territories. However, Saudi Arabia viewed post-Saddam Hussein Shi'ite-dominated governments with suspicion.[144] Despite the kingdom's supportive role in the changing of regimes in Iraq by the American forces, relations with Shi'ite-dominated Iraqi governments have never been warm. Officials in both countries have exchanged public criticisms. The sending of a Saudi ambassador to Baghdad, due to the American pressure, failed to alleviate the differences. On the one hand, the Saudis 'objected to the idea that Iraq would be ruled by Shi'ites and did not trust the Shi'ite-led government of Nuri al-Maliki'[145] and expressed concerns over its 'dubious' ties with Iran. On the other hand, the al-Maliki government accused Saudi Arabia of backing Sunni insurgents.

Iraqi annexation of Kuwait on 2 August 1990 drew Saudi Arabia closer to the US.[146] As a result of the first Gulf crisis, the kingdom became a public supporter of the US presence in the region[147] as the backbone of any regional security forces. Some analysts stated that it would be hard to believe that the Saudis would take any harmful action against the United States.[148] Meanwhile, the oil historian Daniel Yaring described the new chapter in the Saudi–American relations as special, and that they 'became more special'.[149] The special relation was demonstrated in the emergence of the US as the main commercial beneficiary in the region. In 1991, American exports increased in the Middle East by 60.8 per cent to reach $10 billion. The share of the kingdom was three-quarters of the total exports of the United States to seventeen countries in the Middle East. This was an increase of 63 per cent compared to previous years.[150]

(c) *The Arab–Israeli Conflict*

Saudi Arabia has been subject to criticism from both Arab radicals and some Western conservatives for distancing itself and being actively involved in the conflict. Each party has its own interpretation, though conflicting, for the potential Saudi role in the conflict. Arab radicals criticize passivity and alliance with the US, the strategic ally of Israel. Western conservatives, on the other hand, view Saudi Arabia as a potential threat, particularly because of its ties to the US, to Israel security[151] that should be denied American support and military aid until it recognizes Israel and softens its trade and commercial policies. King Faisal complained strongly to the American ambassador to Saudi Arabia, saying that they (the Americans) did not make the task of their friends easy for them: 'You ignore their interests and weaken their influence in the region.'[152] Despite the two countries, Saudi

Arabia and Israel, being on America's side, Israel includes the kingdom in the second out of three circles that it should extend its influence to.[153] Israel during the 1956 Trilateral aggression on Egypt and the six- days war of June 1967 occupied several Saudi islands in the Gulf of Aqaba, 'returning them to Egyption control in connexion with its withdrawal from Sinai in 1982."[154] The build-up of Saudi military force invoked Israeli fears of the possibility that these weapons could fall into hostile hands. This led the Israeli air force to penetrate the Saudi airspace by flying over Tabuk in 1977 and 1978, and throwing empty barrels on runways as a way of demonstrating their capabilities.[155] Israel is actually one of the states that threaten Saudi security; Saudi capability cannot engage with Israeli forces or deter Israeli attack because it lacks the advanced technologies such as the modern air-air missiles, air control, the early warning capability, the maintenance, the military bases and the military leadership structure to avoid heavy casualties.[156] Strategic analysts believe that AWACS planes have no effect on offensive operations because they were not provided with smart sign detectors that Israeli planes have. They are known as 'EC2/Hawk'. It is worth mentioning that the Saudi AWACS lack the necessary advanced sonic and tactile information joints to prevent the Israelis from using anti-electronic measures. Besides, the radars on the Saudi AWACS cannot survey military land movements.[157] The F-15 Saudi jets lack the offensive capabilities that the similar Israeli planes have, including the capability to undertake air strikes, the long-range radars or even the defensive air, sea and land missiles. It is argued that 'whilst the normal "ferry range" of an F-15 is 2800, those supplied to al-Riyadh could fly only about one thousand miles' and of the sixty F-15s only forty-five are actually combat planes, the rest being trainers.[158] Consequently, the Israeli threat in March 1988 to carry out a pre-emptive strike against Silkworm missiles that Saudi Arabia had bought from China[159] made King Fahd announce on 8 April that these missiles do not carry nuclear warheads and they would not be used against Israel (see Chapter 5).[160]

The Israeli–Ethiopian association at the time of Mengistu Haile Miriam is another issue concerning Israel and the kingdom because closing Bab al-Mandab at the entrance to Red Sea meant that Saudi Arabia would ultimately be deprived of the necessary commodities for development. It would also disturb Saudi oil exportation through the Suez Canal.[161]

The Saudi position towards the Camp David agreement was somewhat ambiguous. The Saudis wanted to gain the potential benefits for their long-term interests provided by the initiative. At the same time, they wanted to avoid paying the price for supporting the initiative, in fear of the reactions of the Arab opponents to the peace agreement between Egypt and Israel.[162] During the visit of American State Secretary Cyrus Vance, between 22 and 24 September 1978 to win over Saudi support for the initiative, the Saudis described the initiative as an important primary step towards peace. During the Arab Summit in Baghdad in November, they also tried to mobilize support against imposing sanctions on Egypt.[163]

However, because of fear of Arab criticism of the Saudi–American alliance, in addition to the divisions among the Saudi royal family on this issue, the Saudi government felt, during the Arab Summit in Tunis in 1979, that it was obliged to take an opposing position to the Egyptian–Israeli peace accord sponsored by the United States.[164]Yet the Saudi Arabia 'sought to play a moderating role in Arab politics, to promote the prospects of peace, and to persuade its Arab allies to keep open channels for negotiation'.[165] The kingdom, through the King Fahd peace initiative that became later King Fahd's initiative and then the GCC initiative, and the King Abdullah peace initiatives, offered Israel more than the Camp David agreement had. At the Fes Summit on 6 September 1982, it granted Arab recognition to Israel and the right to exist, whereas the Camp David agreement was limited to only Egypt's recognition. Analysts attributed this initiative to King Fahd's attempt to prove Saudi Arabia's goodwill towards Israel to obtain American acceptance for the arms deal that Saudi Arabia requested, which included AWACS planes and spare parts for F-15 jets.[166] Although the Saudi initiative did not provide any positive results in achieving peace between the Arabs and Israel due to Israeli rejection, Saudi Arabia accepted George Bush's initiative, which emerged after the first Gulf crisis, even though that initiative did not achieve the minimum of Fahd's initiative. Saudi Arabia participated in the Madrid Conference in October 1991, represented by its ambassador to the United States Prince Bandar Ibn Sultan. It also participated through its Foreign Minister Prince Saud al Faisal in the regional conference that was held in Moscow on 31 January 1992. This did not reflect an essential change in the Saudi strategy towards the Arab–Israeli conflict as was the case with Camp David agreement. It reflected more a change in dealing with this issue. It is worth mentioning that the Saudi stance towards the PLO changed after the latter allied itself with Iraq during the first Gulf crisis. The Arab Peace Initiative, a comprehensive peace initiative, was first proposed by Crown Prince Abdullah to be endorsed on 13 February 2002 at the Beirut Summit of the Arab League, and was reconfirmed at the Riyadh Summit in March 2007. The initiative is based on the principle of land for peace, calls for a two-states solution and reaffirms the right of the Palestinian refugees to return in accordance with the international resolutions.

The International Order

The struggle between great powers in the Gulf and Arabian peninsula region shaped the modern history of the region. The end of the Second World War brought with it the waning of the traditional powers and created new superpowers represented by the United States and the Soviet Union. Until the beginning of the 1990s, the international bipolar system affected the development of the region's relations with the wider world. According to this system the two states had interests and goals in the region. Since the end of the Second World War, the American strategy has been based[167] on preventing any other hostile power from gaining control in the Gulf and ensuring the free flow of oil to it and to its allies. Meanwhile, the Soviet strategy was based on driving the US out of the region and gaining access to the region's oil.[168] The discovery of oil increased the importance of Saudi Arabia in the realm of international politics, making the kingdom a focal point, and intensified the international polarization and rivalry to win the region over. The development of the US–Soviet relationship had a tremendous effect on the development on US–Saudi relations and of Soviet–Saudi relations.

(a) *The United States*

US policy towards the Gulf region is part of the overall US strategy towards the Middle East. It centres around three main principles: securing oil supplies to industrial countries, ensuring Israeli security and preventing any hostile power from controlling the region, whether local or international. 'The US has been the main defender of Saudi Arabia in terms of offsetting military threats, as well as being the Kingdom's main supplier of weapons.'[169] The US has made Saudi security a red line that Washington could not tolerate its infringement. Roosevelt was the first US president to declare that 'the defence of Saudi Arabia was a US national interest.'[170] The kingdom, on the other hand, has served as an important regional ally and partner of the US.[171] Saudi Arabia's importance to the United States lies in its capacity as a trade partner and in the presence of 400 American oil companies in the kingdom since 1974.[172] Some analysts believe that the monopoly of the Saudi oil by American oil companies forms one of the main factors determining US policy-making towards the Gulf.[173] US imports of Saudi oil increased from 486 barrels to 1,337 barrels per day between 1973 and 1990.[174] Since 1974 the kingdom has blocked the attempts of some OPEC members to try and increase oil prices, especially during the Iraq–Iran[175] war and the second and third Gulf crises.

Saudi Arabia invested around 80 per cent of its oil revenues in the United States.[176] The external trade patterns in the period 1972 and 2007 show that Saudi Arabia was gradually absorbed into the Western economy, especially the US economy, at the expense of Saudi Arabia's trade with other countries in the world.[177] Yet Saudi Arabia has also opened up to China, Russia and other Asian countries. In 1975, the cultural bonds between the two countries were consolidated officially with the formation of the American Joint Committee on Economic Cooperation, which was implicitly concerned with Saudi education.[178] The United States is the biggest exporter of arms to Saudi Arabia. If we take into account the conditions that the United States imposes on arms-importing countries, the kingdom has been restricted by its relations with the United States and in its capability to use these weapons. Saudi Arabia unofficially accepted the American condition of not placing F-15 fighter jets in the two military bases that are close to Israel, Tabuk and Hafar Albatin. If the kingdom wanted to risk severing military and technical support then it would require at least a month to transport the ammunition to Tabuk. This would not be possible without risking a pre-emptive Israeli strike.[179] The restrictions imposed on Saudi Arabia include the manner in which it could use combatant aircraft, the Saudi need for assistance from the US in using these jet fighters until 1993,[180] the cap on numbers and the monopoly of the United States of the spare parts, training and the like.

Saudi Arabia's keenness to preserve its ties with the United States can be seen in its attempt to calm America's concern when King Fahd confirmed in a letter to the former American President Ronald Reagan in April 1988 that Silkworm missiles bought from China did not carry nuclear warheads, that they were for defensive purposes and would never be used against Israel.[181] The Saudis informed the Israelis through Washington that they were committed to the principle of not being the first to use missiles against Israel.[182] After twenty years of abstaining from signing the agreement, upon the suggestion by US Defense Secretary Frank Carlucci to reassure the Israelis, the Saudi Foreign Minister Saud Al Faisal on 26 April 1988 announced that the Saudi cabinet approved adhering to the Non-Proliferation Treaty. The Saudi decision reflects the degree of the external milieu influence on Saudi foreign policy-making. After the Kuwaiti predicament, Saudi Arabia concluded a bilateral defence agreement with the United States. From 1999 to 2006, Saudi Arabia received $6.5 billion under arms transfer agreements with the United States, an annual average of $815 million in inflation-adjusted fiscal year 2006 dollars; and in July

2007 Washington announced the sale of $20 billion in advanced weaponry to Saudi Arabia and its neighbours in the Gulf Cooperation Council.[183]

The American influence on Saudi Arabia's foreign policy-making is illustrated not only in issues of global concern but in regional issues of great importance to regional security and stability as well as in the Arab national cause. In 2003 during the Anglo-American invasion of Iraq, although the Saudis voiced their concern about Iranian regional ambitions and decided not to join the American–British coalition, at the start they refrained from criticizing the American occupation of Iraq but later on and in a significant move King Abdulla, in March 2007, described it as illegal . In a further development that possibly caused a rift in the Arab consensus, the Saudis did not hesitate to blame Hezbollah for the 2006 Israeli war on Lebanon and have been supportive of the American interventionist policy in Lebanon trying to influence the outcome of Rafiq al-Hariri affairs. Saudi Arabia pursued a policy closer to the American perspectives towards the intra-Palestinian power struggle between the 'revisionist group' led by Mahmoud Abbas and the 'resistance group' led by Hamas. Although Saudi Arabia worked out a short-lived deal between the two groups known as the 'Makkah Accord', it has been an active supporter of the pro-West Mahmoud Abbas government in the Palestinian Authority. They did not hesitate to blame Hamas for the twenty-two days of Israeli aggression against the Gaza Strip in December 2008–January 2009. Saudi Arabia also has been an active supporter of the US policy towards Iran and Afghanistan. The US push for Middle East peace is coming under increasing strain on all sides. Saudi antipathy to concessions put a strain on President Obama's diplomacy and called on the US to withhold Israel aid.[184] Saud al Faisal, Saudi Foreign Minister, rebuffed Washington's central idea of Arab 'confidence-building' measures for Israel's freeze on settlements.[185] Saudi Arabia, because of its fear of any Iranian retaliation, opted for detaching itself from the US policy towards Iran, refusing to be a member of an anti-Iranian coalition. The Saudi government is compelled to somehow come to terms with the sharpening tension between its dependence on the US for its security and popular discontent with American policies towards the Arab world.[186]

(b) *Russia*

The Soviet strategy towards the Gulf used to be based on two main principles: geopolitical location and oil. The importance of the geographical position lies in the close proximity of the Gulf to the southern national Soviet borders and its position in the warm waters. The importance of Gulf oil in Soviet strategy lay in two main factors: the dependency of the West and Japan for the foreseeable future and the potential of the Soviet Union becoming an oil-importing country. The importance of Saudi Arabia in Soviet strategy was not external to this general framework of the importance of the Gulf region. Despite this importance, interaction between the two parties in all fields was weak, although the Soviet Union was one of the first countries to recognize Ibn Saud's kingdom, giving him moral and economic support, and diplomatic ties were frozen. On the eve of the Second World War the Soviet Union unilaterally took the decision to end its diplomatic mission in Riyadh after it realized that its relations with the kingdom were not achieving its objectives.[187] Saudi Arabia took up hostile positions against Soviet interests in the region and against its policies towards the Third World, especially the Arab world, and justified its positions in all these cases with ideological pretexts.

Soviet influence on Saudi foreign policy was indirect as the Soviet Union strengthened its relations with the kingdom's neighbouring countries. Saudi Arabia worked to break the Soviet siege (Rim Land) against it. Saudi decision-makers found that their country was located within a Soviet triangle made up of Afghanistan, Ethiopia and South Yemen, in addition to the Soviet Union's ties with some neighbouring Arab countries like Iraq, Syria, Egypt and North Yemen. 'Saudi Arabia sought to prevent a situation that would allow the Soviet Union to come to the aid of radical Arab states.'[188] This explains why Saudi Arabia supported some of the Afghan Mujahedeen groups and provided financial support to Somalia and the Eritreans' revolution against Ethiopia. It also helped South Yemen financially. Saudi Arabia influenced the changing foreign policy orientation of several Arab countries, especially Egypt, Somalia and North Yemen.[189] Riyadh, in 1974, offered financial aid to Somalia on condition that they expelled the Soviet military personnel.[190] The kingdom played an important role in Egypt's acceptance of the Rogers' Initiative and the change of Egypt's course under Anwar Sadat from the Soviet Union's orbit to that of the United States. It gave Somalia financial aid estimated at $400 million in 1978 in return for expelling the Soviet military experts and $200 million for its military endeavour against Ethiopia.[191] 'The Saudi leaders' anti Soviet attitude was reawakened after the Soviet invasion of Afghanistan in December 1978.'[192] With the efforts by the Soviet Union to improve its relations with the Gulf Cooperation Council, and mainly Saudi Arabia, and the 'New Thinking' policy that the Soviet leader Mikhail Gorbachev had adopted, which started with the withdrawal of Soviet troops from Afghanistan, condemned the Israeli threat of carrying out a pre-emptive strike against the Saudi Silkworm missiles,[193] and rejected Iraqi claims to Kuwait, the Soviet threat was removed from the Saudi security agenda. Regional and international developments inspired a new era in relations between the two countries. The two sides decided on 17 December 1990 to exchange diplomatic relations. In the meantime, a Saudi Kazakhstan oil company was formed to encourage Saudi investment in the Soviet Union. It was also announced that the kingdom would join the United Arab Emirates and Kuwait in lending the Soviet Union $4 billion as a token of appreciation for its position during the first Gulf crisis.[194]

Relations with Russia have improved significantly, as illustrated in the exchange of visits by dignitaries, including King Abdullah's visit, as Crown Prince, the most senior Saudi official since 1932, to Moscow in September 2003, followed by President Vladimir Putin's visit, the Russian first head of state, to the kingdom in February 2007 and the Saudi Crown Prince Sultan's visit to Moscow in November 2007. Prior to the 1990s, trade between Russia and the kingdom was virtually non-existent. It was only from the mid-1990s onwards that significant trade between the two countries took hold. Russia's exports to Saudi Arabia in 1997 were valued at $112 million, which made it the 34th largest exporter to the kingdom. By 2006, Russia was ranked 24th, with total exports amounting to $693 million, an increase of 533 per cent. Within that growth, the years 2005 and 2006 were the best yet in the history of Saudi–Russian trade relations. Russian exports for 2004 had reached $237 million, but jumped by 51 per cent in 2005 to $400 million and by a further 77 per cent in 2006. In 2007, Saudi imports from Russia were expected to achieve a record $826 million.[195]

The developments in the Russian–Saudi relationship reflect Moscow's more muscular foreign policy as well as wariness among Gulf States over US foreign policy in the region.[196] Saudi Arabia and Russia have established a truce, but many issues threaten their fragile rapprochement. 'An agreement about military-technical collaboration between Russia and Saudi Arabia was signed on 14 July 2008, in the presence of Prime Minister Vladimir Putin, by Federal agency on VTS head Mikhail Dmitriev and National Security Council of Saudi Arabia Secretary General Prince Bandar bin Sultan bin Abdalaziz.'[197] According to Mark N. Katz, 'Saudi–Russian relations have been negatively affected by differences over several issues in recent years. These include oil pricing policy, investment and trade, Russian allegations about Saudi policy towards Chechnya and other Muslims in the former USSR, and Saudi security concerns about Russian arms transfers as well as the growing Russian–Israeli relationship.'[198] Today, Saudi Arabia and Russia are the largest oil producers in the world, with Russia exceeding the Saudis by 2 mbd because the latter decided to cut its oil production capacity by one-third.[199] It was reported that despite King Abdullah's decision to call off a deal with Russia for the purchase of combat helicopters, a deal concluded by Prince Bandar in July 2008,[200] the Russians discovered the abortive coup engineered by Prince Bandar in late 2008 and informed the Saudi government.[201] Russia, as result, came to occupy an important position in the Saudi monarch's perception of world politics.

Since the collapse of the Soviet Union, Saudi Arabia has attempted to gain influence in the new independent Muslim republics of the former Soviet Union. Since 1990, the Saudi government sought to welcome the pilgrims of Central Asian republics at its own cost. It also sent them many copies of the Qur'an and granted scholarships for students from these republics to study in Saudi universities. Meanwhile, many high-ranking Saudi officials visited these countries, most importantly Saud Al Faisal, the Saudi Foreign Minister, who visited Tajikistan, Azerbaijan, Turkmenistan and Uzbekistan in February 1992. Straight after that visit, the exchange of diplomatic missions was announced. The Saudi ambassador to Moscow, Dr Abdalaziz Khoja, denied that his country wanted to compete with Turkey and Iran to gain influence in these republics. Al Khoja said that his country 'approves of the legitimate interests of each country in establishing relations with other countries. Moreover, we welcome and encourage all Muslim countries to consolidate relations with the new Central Asian countries.'[202]

(c) *International Organizations*

The network of the international organizations plays a significant role in shaping the foreign policy undertakings of member states. However, the degree of influence depends on many factors related to the member's capability and role in the organization and differs from one organization to another according to its importance to the state. Saudi Arabia is a member of several international and regional organizations as it is a member of the Gulf Cooperation Council, the Arab League, Organization of the Islamic Conference (whose headquarters are in Jeddah), the Non-Aligned Movement and the United Nations. It is also a member of a number of specialized government organizations, the most important of which are OPEC and OAPEC. Those interested in understanding Saudi's ties to these organizations will see that Saudi Arabia had an effect on the regional and international organizations and vice versa and that the degree of influence of the regional organizations was until the beginning of the 1990s bigger than international organizations. This was evident on many occasions. For instance, Saudi Arabia adhered to the resolutions of the Arab Summit that was held in Tunis in 1979 with respect to Egypt's signing of the Camp David agreement – as an example of the way Saudi Arabia was influenced by its membership of the Arab League – whereas the Arab leaders accepted King Fahd's initiative at the Fes Summit in September 1982 after they have rejected it earlier in November 1981. It shows the degree of Saudi influence on the Arab League's resolutions in a way that would serve its national interests on the one hand and illustrates the Saudi desire to purse a 'regional coordinator' policy[203] on the other. On 13 February 2002 Saudi Arabia won the Arab states' endorsement for the new Saudi peace initiative during the Arab League Summit in Beirut later and was reconfirmed during the Riyadh Arab Summit in 2007. Saudi Arabia's acceptance to join the oil embargo against the United States and the Netherlands during the October war in 1973 and being forced to join the anti-Egyptian block putting them in conflict with the US[204] show the effect of the kingdom's membership of the Arab of regional organization. The founding of the Organization of Islamic Conference by the kingdom reflects its desire to reduce the pressure exerted upon it by the Arab League and contains pan-Arab influence on Arab states' politics. The utilization of the Gulf Cooperation Council and the Arab League by the Saudis during the first Gulf crisis to legitimize inviting foreign forces to counter Iraq demonstrates the importance of these organizations in Saudi foreign policy-making, and also the degree of the kingdom's influence on these organizations. Saudi commitment to the resolutions of the Non-Aligned Movement towards South Africa, its support of the liberation, non-Communist movements of the Third World and the provision of foreign aid to poor countries are examples of indirect influence of the movement on Saudi foreign policy-making. However, anybody who follows Saudi foreign policy will note how the kingdom, since the mid-1970s, stopped giving importance to the Non-Aligned Movement – seen through the irregularity of the Saudi king's attendance at its summit meetings. As for the United Nations, its influence on the Saudi foreign policy-making was weak until the end of the 1980s. This is shown by its refusal to sign UN agreements and its rejection of becoming a member of the Non-Proliferation Treaty of Nuclear Weapons until 1988. The effect of the United Nations on Saudi foreign policy-making in the early twenty-first century will depend on the role the United States chooses to play through the United Nations in the unstable international order.

4. The Decision-Making Apparatus

The decision-making apparatus of any state is a transitional stage between the independent variables that include the input process and the dependent variables making the output or implementation of these policies. Although it transforms the inputs into outputs, it does not do that automatically; rather, the formation of decisions takes place within a framework of ideology, the cultural and social background of the decision-makers themselves, since some policies are the product of their cultural and historical background.[205] Despite the king being the main person making decisions regarding foreign affairs, some other parties participate in the decision-making process: the royal family council, the cabinet and the foreign ministry.

The King

The king in the Saudi political system is considered the most senior executive, diplomatic and legislative power. At times he practises judicial authority.[206] He is both the chief of state and head of government. The importance of the role of the king in foreign policy-making lies not in the executive power, over which he presides, but in being the highest diplomatic authority in the state too. The Saudi ambassadors to other countries are called the Ambassadors of the Servant of the Two Holy Cities, not the Ambassadors of Saudi Arabia, because the whole state is represented by the king himself. However, although the king plays the main role in the Saudi foreign decision-making, he is not the only person who takes important decisions, as a group of the royal family – called the Allegiance Council or the Supreme Committee – shoulders part of the responsibility.

The Allegiance Council

The Allegiance Council is next to the king in the political hierarchy. Although this council used to specialize in the internal affairs in the era of King Faisal, foreign policy has become one of its concerns since the era of King Khalid.[207] The council holds regular meetings to study state affairs. However, its role in influencing the process of Saudi policy-making depends on the personality of the king and the nature of the relationship between the king and his crown prince. The role of the council in the kingdom's political affairs increases if the king is less charismatic, unpragmatic, or weak, becoming less influential in politics, especially in dealing with issues related to power, as was the case during the reign of King Saud when the Allegiance Council decided to entrust power to Crown

Prince Faisal. Its role also increases if the head of power (i.e. the king) is weak and the crown prince wants to monopolize or manipulate power to influence the Allegiance Council to have an impact on a specific policy. Its role during the eras of King Saud and King Khalid was stronger than that under King Faisal, King Fahd and King Abdullah. During the period of King Khalid, Prince Fahd, then crown prince, relied heavily on the support of his full brothers, the al-Sedaris, to promote his power. King Abdullah, in 2006, empowered the council with the responsibility to choose the crown prince when the post becomes vacant. This body often works on settling foreign issues if they are related to regional positions and policies.

The Cabinet

The cabinet occupies the third place in importance after the king and the Allegiance Council. It is appointed by the monarch every four years and includes many royal family members. The Saudi cabinet's importance lies in its combining executive and legislative powers and its being presided over by the king personally. The cabinet is considered the king's right arm. It carries out the tasks of legislation and implementation of the kingdom's internal and external policies. As for the external domain, and in the case of what are known as Programme Decisions, the cabinet takes suitable decisions according to the advice of the Foreign Ministry regarding regional and international affairs. It also adopts the nominations of the diplomatic corps.

Foreign Ministry

The Saudi Foreign Ministry undertakes the task of gathering and analysing information obtained through diplomatic channels. It also chooses and prepares the national cadre politically and diplomatically through its Diplomatic Institute. In addition, future diplomats take part in intensive external courses abroad. All this training enables them to carry out administrative responsibilities and the kingdom's foreign policy tasks efficiently. The importance of the Foreign Ministry is heightened due to the fact that its minister is a member of the royal family and he enjoys membership of both the cabinet and the Family Council. The Saudi Foreign Minister also occupies the post of the king's political adviser. He is a member of what is known as the Inner Circle, which is responsible for Saudi foreign decision-making and consists of the foreign, defence and oil ministers, and the intelligence director and other selected members of the royal family.

Majlis Ashura

Majlis al-Shura is a unicameral consultative body with the powers to discuss local issues and recommend policies. King Fahd fortified the foundations of counselling (or Shura) in the kingdom by issuing the new Majlis Ash-Shura Law on 24 November 2000. He launched the first term of the council with a speaker and sixty members. In the second term, the council consisted of a speaker and ninety members. In the third term, the council included a speaker and 120 members. Since the fourth term, the council consisted of a speaker and 150 members, six of them women, and a chairman appointed by the monarch for four-year terms. The Saudi monarch deliberately targets the intelligentsia for its composition as a means to avert criticism for the lack of political participation. The Majlis's role in foreign policy is minimal, despite having a foreign affairs committee among its twelve committees, giving support to government foreign policy undertakings. The Saudi government introduced election for half of the local and provincial councils but the Shura council is still made up of appointed members. However, the Council of Ministers announced in October 2003 its intent to introduce elections for a third of the members of the National Consultative Council or Majlis al-Shura incrementally over a period of four to five years, although to date no such elections have been held or announced. Prince Nayef, the second Deputy Premier and Interior Minister, rebuffed the idea of electing the members of Ash-Shura saying 'there is no need for that'.[208] Moreover, the first Saudi experiment of electing members of the local and provisional councils came to a standstill with the royal decision in 2009 to freeze it.

5. Conclusion

The proceeding analyses of the dynamics of Saudi Arabia foreign policy-making reveal the following:

1. Saudi foreign policy-making is similar to that of other states: a by-product of interaction between internal and external variables.
2. The effect of the internal milieu on Saudi policy-making is two-fold. It has increased its dependency on external factors but it has consolidated its ability to have an influence on international politics due to the natural and strategic resources that it owns. On the other hand, it was argued that 'economic and social changes have engendered pressure for political change.'[209]

3. Since the 1990s, the external milieu came to play an increasingly significant role in Saudi foreign policy-making.

4. Despite the role that effective social groups play in the process of foreign decision-making in Saudi Arabia, the process of taking a decision is characterized by a unilateral approach and is almost exclusively the king's prerogative.

5. All the different variables discussed do not enjoy the same political weight or priority in all policies. Whilst geography, history, ideology, the political system, the military system, the economic system, and regional and international rivalry are the most effective factors in determining the course of Saudi foreign policy regionally, ideology and economy are the factors that steer Saudi foreign policy towards the Third World. Saudi foreign policy-making is constrained by its relatively small population and a proportionately small and weak military establishment. Simultaneously, geography, ideology, economy, the military factor and international rivalry are the most important variables in determining the course of Saudi foreign policy internationally.

6. Saudi Arabia, unhappy with the changes that took place in Tunisia and Egypt and the likely outcome of democratization in other Arab countries – Yemen, Libya, Jordan and Syria – currently at the time of writing this book and witnessing social and political uprisings, has no alternative but to interact with the new democratic governments in these countries. It is likely that the Saudis will have to join the new camp on issues of foreign policy, especially with respect to Palestine and the peace process.

Epilogue

Political reforms adopted by Arab governments do not meet the aspirations of the masses for a share of power. People are not optimistic about a gradual and peaceful transition to a power-sharing form of government. Existing regimes 'think only of how to maintain power'. Western support for tyranny, autocracy and indulgence of corruption in the Arab world, far from securing regional stability, breeds extremism and failed states. Western support for oppressive Arab regimes has thwarted democratic attempts. The absence of a peaceful transfer of power has left the Arab people with no peaceful mechanism to change governments, inspiring instead a different form of mass uprising, as exemplified by the Tunisian, Egyptian, Yemeni, Libyan, Jordanian, Algerian, Syrian and Bahraini experiences. The fact that the Arab political systems are faced with lost political legitimacy and being undemocratic enhances the argument that, on the one hand, inter-Arab relations are unstable and would continue to fluctuate between cold war and détente and, on the other hand, the absence of accountability and checks and balances inevitably causes domestic and regional instability.

Despite the fact that the Arab world has the potential for development – huge oil and gas reserves, a large skilled and unskilled labour force, vast area and abundant natural resources – the performance of the Arab countries in the field of socio-economic development is unsatisfactory. Arab states continue to rely on the outside world to secure their domestic needs and are, despite their oil and gas reserves, economically vulnerable. Policies adopted by the contemporary Arab governments have widened the gap between the governing and the governed, consolidated the patriarchal culture, enhanced social, religious, ethnic and sectarian cleavages and class division, increased the gap between the haves and have-nots in Arab societies creating social imbalance, inspired corruption, intensified inter-Arab competition, emphasized the disintegrative factors in Arab politics, promoted the dependency theory on the cultural and economic levels and alienated the intelligentsia.

The Arab world since the Second World War came to acquire a significant importance in the foreign policy agenda of the main international actors. The international variable weight in the foreign policy-making of the less developed countries exceeds by far their inputs into world developments. The Arab countries as part of the international community are by no mean immune from being affected by international changes. However, although the Arabs played a significant role in bringing about changes in the world order, their impacts on the Arab world were minimal. Arab states were fearful of domestic and regional threats and needed a supplementary power to compensate for their inherent weakness, prompting closer cooperation between the moderate Arab countries and the US and thus depriving them of an independent foreign policy. The Arabs, despite their geostrategic location and the fact that they possess nearly half of the world oil reserves, chose to ally with the US, Israel's strategic ally.

Arab countries' foreign policy-making is constrained by the fact that they exist in an unstable region. Developments following the second Gulf crisis in August 1990 promoted significant changes in the international world order and have played a major role in shaping Arab countries' foreign policy undertakings. Interregional relations have not been stable and the Arab world has been divided into two camps: the 'moderate' and the reluctant. The Arab regional order has been weakened by multiple factors including the distrust and mismanagement of inter-Arab differences, the Israeli threat, the Iranian challenge, Turkey's regional ambition and the dependence on the US for security.

The Arab–Israeli conflict continues to be a further destabilizing factor. The cold war between the former USSR and the US led to greater polarization of the conflict, with each power taking sides. The second Gulf crisis, followed by the collapse of the Soviet Union, inspired tremendous change in the contemporary world order. These changes deprived Arab countries of their ability to play one superpower against the other to achieve their national interests and prompted the contemporary world powers to show greater interest in the settlement of the conflict through the peace process. The Arab–Israeli conflict is mainly an ideological conflict because, in essence, it is a conflict between civilizations: the Islamic civilization on one hand and the Western, Jewish-Christian, civilization on the other. Western support given to the Zionist movement, later Israel, caused a prolonged regional conflict between the two sides, not only threatening Arab security, but also posing a serious threat to world peace and security. The international factor has been significant in the development of the Arab–Israeli conflict and dictates times of peace or war in the region. It is likely that the changes in Egypt will bring Egypt back to leading the Arab order hence profoundly affecting the Arab–Israeli conflict.

Regional and international developments since summer 1990 marked the beginning of a transformation in the Arab countries' foreign policy towards the conflict, from a military doctrine to peace as an Arab strategic option. The shifting balance of power in favour of Israel brought with it fragile peace agreements. The issues encountering the peace process that have been discussed will impede the achievement of a real peace. Jerusalem, refugees, settlements, water and land will remain contentious issues hindering any possible peace agreements. The limitations of the land will remain a source of conflict between the Arabs and Jews, even if the latter decided to give up the territories that it occupied in 1967. The issue of the territory occupied in 1948 and the future of its people both inside and outside of those areas will remain. The nature and status of Jerusalem represent another obstacle to the peace process between the Arabs and Israel. The importance of Jerusalem, due to its religious significance for both parties, lies in its 'value' rather than its 'benefit'. The inability of either side to surrender or negotiate the future of Jerusalem is a main obstacle to the shift from a culture of conflict to a culture of peace.

The analysis of the water condition in the Arab world demonstrates the complex situation that the Arab countries are currently experiencing. Israel controls more than 2.3 billion cubic metres of the Arab water resources. This indicates that the crisis is worsening and the potential outbreak of another regional conflict over water between the Arabs and Israel remains stronger due to the population increase on both sides and the continuing decline in water reservoirs. The continuation of tension over water could lead to the outbreak of economic, political and strategic conflicts between the two parties that would inevitably lead to a war in the future. On the other hand, the study emphasizes the necessity to set up an Arab plan on the local and pan-Arab levels to address the issue of water scarcity, with steps to focus on determining the priorities in distributing the water resources, rationing consumption, determining the degree of self-sufficiency, exploring new water resources, developing the available resources and using modern technology in desalination. Water scarcity would ultimately have a direct effect on Arab states' ability to secure food sufficiency for domestic consumption.

Food shortage and the increasing numbers suffering hunger and malnutrition is another dilemma for the Arab countries, playing a detrimental role in shaping their foreign policy undertakings. The demographic challenge coupled with climate change and global warming has led the Arab countries to depend on the United States, Canada and Australia to supply 50 per cent of the food consumed. This is where the danger lies, if food becomes a strategic weapon in the hands of producing and exporting countries. The situation is getting more and more complicated in light of food monopoly policies in the international markets. It will further consolidate Arab states' subordination to the exporting countries. They might be obliged to buy the scraps of the international markets.

The preceding analysis of the Arab foreign policy-making in the twenty-first century, confirms a number of points:

1. The world has witnessed fundamental changes but, although the Arabs helped bring them about, directly and indirectly, they have had no part in their consequences.

2. The Arabs have not reaped any benefits from the winds of change sweeping the world since the early 1990s, because the costs of change have been too great for their governments. On the contrary, these changes have tightened the regimes' iron grip even further, increased Arab dependence on the United States, upset the balance of power in the region, escalated internal Arab divisions and weakened the Arab regional order. It has dragged the region once again into an era of direct colonialism, as evidenced by the American occupation of Iraq and the role the US is playing in the Middle East peace process.

3. The prevailing condition of the Arab countries is the main obstacle facing reformers and advocates of change, since it is a natural consequence of the Arab regimes' underdevelopment, evidenced by their underdeveloped institutions, political behaviour, constitutions and legal frameworks, not to mention the absence of mechanisms to gauge efficiency and transparency. The Arab world has been led by its own leaders into a dark tunnel, from which there is no escape except through a fundamental change in the very character and nature of the regimes themselves.

4. The Arabs today are grappling with a civilizational challenge. In the age of globalization, Arab countries suffer from an identity crisis and cultural alienation that has rendered them incapable of dealing with the fast-moving developments around them, let alone actively contributing to forging the future.

5. Readings and analyses of internationally accepted development indicators and yardsticks confirm that the Arab states are still underdeveloped. We can therefore say that, for the past few decades, these states have been generally impoverished, since they have been largely characterized by weak economies and social, intellectual and political underdevelopment, and have failed to find the right equilibrium between security and development.

6. On the basis of the present study's findings, the outlook for the Arab world is for more fragmentation, more division, dependence on the outside world, more ominous economic and social developments, and the loss of Arab rights in Palestine, Iraq and Sudan. Rights might be also lost in regions that currently appear secure, especially where citizens live

as minorities in their own countries. The division of Arab countries into small entities and political cantons is but another scenario within the framework of America's globalization policy, a scenario that will continue to haunt advocates of Arab and Islamic nationalism alike. Shifting towards a more optimistic scenario requires a qualitative transformation in the nature of the regimes themselves towards democracy. Their power, which they should owe to the people, should rest on efficacy, transparency and the rule of law. If this comes about, a new reading of the situation will emerge, based on entirely different indicators from those we have today. Until this happens, the Arab individual will continue to suffer from a crisis of personality and intellect because he is, after all, a mere product of the crisis conditions under which he lives.

Notes

Prelude

1. For more details see Hassan H. al-Alkim, *The GCC States in an Unstable World*, Saqi Books, 1994, pp. 17–31.
2. Charles Maynes, 'The Middle East in the Twenty-First Century', *Middle East Journal*, vol. 52, no. 1, Winter 1998, p. 9.

Introduction

1. Samuel Huntington, *The Clash of Civilizations*, Free Press, 2002, p. 130.
2. Ibid, pp. 116–17.
3. *Sharjah TV*, 8 Oct. 2009.
4. Huntington, *Clash of Civilizations*, p. 83.
5. *Towards a Contemporary Islamic View,* 1992, pp. 13–15.
6. UNDP (United Nations Development Fund) *Human Development Report,* 2005, p. 254.
7. Hassan al-Alkim, 'Al-Arab, Amrika, wa al-Nidham al-Dawli al-Jadid' (The Arabs, America, and the New World Order), *Arab Journal of International Studies*, Summer/Fall 1993.
8. Huntington, *Clash of Civilizations*, p. 29.
9. For more details, see Shimon Peres, *Ma'rakat Al-ssalam: Yuwmiyat* (The Battle for Peace: Diary), trans. Ammar Fadhil wa Malik Fadhil, Amman: Al-Ahliya lil Nashr wa al-Tuwzi, 1995.
10. Comprises the entire Middle East and Muslim world; it stretches from the Muslim world's frontiers with China, to Morocco and Mauritania, and it includes, according to foreign policy studies, the Arab world, Israel, Central Asia and the Caucasus.
11. A. Ghafli, *Gulf Strategic Report*, pp. 194–5.
12. A. Abdallah, *Al-Waqt*, 23 Oct. 2007.
13. A. Gafli, *Khaleej*, 20 Oct. 2009.
14. A. Ghafli, *Gulf Strategic Report*, p. 74.
15. David Easton, *A Framework of Political Analysis*, Prentice-Hall, 1965.
16. Roy Macridis (ed.), *Foreign Policy in World Politics*, Prentice-Hall, 1962, pp. 5–6.
17. Richard C. Snyder, H. W. Bruck and Burton Spain, *Decision-Making as an Approach to the Study of International Politics*, Free Press, 1962. Also George Modelski, *A Theory of Foreign Policy*, Pall Mall, 1962.
18. James Rosenau, *The Scientific Study of Foreign Policy*, Nichols, 1980.
19. W. D. Coplan and Charles W. Kegley (eds), *A Multi-Method Introduction to International Relations*, Markham, 1971, p. 155.

Chapter One

1. See Abdal Muna'im al-Mashat, *Al-Tanmiah al-syassiah fi 'alam al Thalyth* (Political Development in the Third World), Al-Ayn: Al-Ayn li-al-Nashr wa-al-Tawza', 1988, ch. 2.
2. Samuel Huntington, *The Clash of Civilizations*, Free Press, 2002, p. 113.
3. Mashat, *Al-Tanmiah*, p. 79
4. Huntington, *Clash of Civilizations*, p. 114.
5. *Arab Human Development Report,* 2009, p. 54.
6. C. Gary and D. Kaufmann, 'Corruption and Economic Development', *Finance and Development* (March 1998), pp. 7–8, cited in Yousef Khalifah al-Yousef, 'Dirasat Halat Al-Imarat al-Arabia al-Mutahidah (Corruption: The Case of the UAE), in *Al-Fasad wa al-Hukum al-Salh fi al-Dawal al-Arabiah* (Corruption and Good Governance in Arab Countries), Beirut: Centre for Arab Unity Studies and the Swedish Institute in Alexandria, 2004, pp. 577–8.
7. Yousef Khalifah al-Yousef, 'When Rulership Becomes Privileged Booty (ghanimah): The Condition of the Gulf Cooperation Council', *Contemporary Arab Affairs*, vol. 1, no. 4, Oct. 2008, p. 633.
8. J. E. Peterson, Saudi Arabia and the Illusion of Security, Adelphi Paper 348, London: the International Institute for Strategic Studies, 2002, p. 56.
9. Ghassan Salama, 'Al-Ta'adadiah wa al-Tahyyid al-Mutabadil: Al-Illaqat al-Arabia- al-Arabiah fi al-Rahyn wa al-Muhtamal' (Pluralism and the Interdependent Neutralism: Contemporary Inter-Arab Relations and the Potential), *Al-Mustaqbal al-Arabi*, vol. 115, Sept. 1988, pp. 102–3.
10. Abdullah al-Naqrash, 'Al Andhimah al Siassia al- Arabia wa al- Nidham al-Arabi' (Arab Political Regimes & The Arab Regional System) *Arab Journal of Political Science*, vols. 3 and 4, Sept. 1989, p. 83.
11. Bernard Lewis, 'The West and the Middle East', *Foreign Affairs*, vol. 76, no. 1, Jan./Feb. 1997, p. 119.
12. *Arab Human Development Report,* 2009, pp. 72–3.
13. Bernard Lewis, 'The West and the Middle East', p. 638.
14. Kemal Dervis and Nemat Shafik, 'The Middle East and North Africa: A Tale of Two Futures', *Middle East Journal*, vol. 52, no. 4, Autumn 1998, p. 512.
15. *Arab Human Development Report,* 2009, p. 69.
16. http://www.anhri.net/reports/libya.
17. Dervis and Shafik, 'Middle East and North Africa', p. 511.
18. Charles Maynes, 'The Middle East in the Twenty-First Century', *Middle East Journal*, vol. 52, no. 1, Winter 1998, p. 12.
19. Mahmoud Abulfadil, 'Al-Tashkilat al-Ijima'iah wa al-Takuyn al-Tabaqi fi al-Watan al-Arabi' (Social Formation and the Class Emergence in the Arab Homeland), *Al-Mustaqbal al-Arabi*, vol. 115, Sept. 1998, p. 85.
20. *Arab Human Development Report,* 2009, p. 54.
21. Ibid.
22. *Financial Times*, 17 Aug. 2008.
23. There are many such examples, among which we might mention the arrest by the Egyptian, Moroccan and Tunisian authorities of dozens of Islamists, and the arrest in Syria and Bahrain of a number of reformists. *Jazeera TV* (Arabic), 25 Dec. 2007.
24. A number of dismissed UAE teachers staged a demonstration in front of the Ministry of Education headquarters in Dubai. *Gulf News,* 20 Nov. 2007.
25. *Khaleej*, 13 Nov. 2007.

26. *Arab Human Development Report,* 2006, p. 36
27. Huntington, *Clash of Civilizations*, p. 114.
28. John E. Peterson, *Saudi Arabia and the Illusion of Security*, Adelphi Paper 348, London: the International Institute for Strategic Studies (IISS), 2002, p. 54.
29. *Financial Times*, 17 Aug. 2009.
30. *Financial Times*, 6 Sept. 2009.
31. http://www.hrw.org/middle-eastn-africa/saudi-arabia, 10 Aug. 2009.
32. *Financial Times*, 17 Aug. 2009.
33. A. Abdullah, 'Al-Imarat wa Taqarir Haquq Al- Insan' (UAE & Human Rights Report) Al-Waqt, 16 Feb. 2010.
34. *Financial Times*, 22 July 2009, and http://www.telegraph.co.uk/news/worldnews/middleeast/saudiarabia/5882406/Amnesty-criticises-Saudi-Arabias-shocking-human-rights-violations.html, 22 July 2009.
35. http://en.wikipedia.org/wiki/Social_Contract_(Rousseau).
36. Yousef Khalifah al-Yousef, *Al-Fasad wa al-Hukum*, 2004, p. 580.
37. J. E. Peterson, Saudi Arabia and the Illusion of Security, op. cit., p. 53.
38. Sadah Habashinah, 'Al-Siassa al-Urbiah Tijah al-Arab Munthu Harib 1973 Hta Mutamar Barcelona al-Thani 2005' (The European Policy towards the Arabs from the 1973 War to the Barcelona 2nd Conference 2005), *Mu'atah*, vol. 22, no. 5, 2007, pp. 204–5.
39. Salama, 'Al-Ta'adadiah wa al-Tahyyid al-Mutabadil', p. 123.
40. *Arab Human Development Report,* 2009, p. 54.
41. Sa'd El-Din Ibrahim, 'Sinariuhat al-Mustagbal al-Arabi' (Scenarios of Arab Future), a paper presented to the Egyptian Committee on the Afro-Asian People Solidarity, pp. 3–5. Cited in Ahmed Yusif, *al-Mustaqbal al- Arabi*, vol. 115, Sept. 1988, p. 85.
42. Strobe Talbott, 'Democracy and the National Interest', *Foreign Affairs*, vol. 75, no. 6, Nov./Dec. 1996, p. 62.
43. James A. Bill and Carl Leiden, *Politics in the Middle East,* 2nd edn, Little, Brown & Co., 1979, p. 27.
44. Mohammed Abid al-Jabri, 'Al-Waqa' al-Siassy al-Arabi' (The Contemporary Arab Status Quo), a paper presented to a conference in Amman, Dec. 2001, pp. 8–9.
45. *Arab Human Development Report,* 2009, p. 73.
46. Ibid., pp. 30–1.
47. John E. Peterson, *Dwal al-Khalij al-Arabia: Khatawat Nhwa Almusharaka al Siassiah* (*The Arab Gulf States: Steps toward Political Participation*), trans. Dham Musa al-Atawnah, D. A. Publication, 1989, p. 138.
48. Rosemarie Zahlan, 'King Abdul Aziz's Changing Relationship with the Gulf States during the 1930's', in Tim Niblock (ed.), *State, Society and Economy in Saudi Arabia,* Croom Helm, 1982, p. 65.
49. Robert Lacey, *The Kingdom,* Fontana Paperbacks, 1982, p. 341.
50. *Financial Times*, 29 April 2009.
51. Riad El-Rayyes, *Al-Khalij al-Arabi wa Ryah al-Taqyr* (*The Arab Gulf and the Wind of Change*), Riad El-Rayyes Books, 1987, p. 49.
52. Ali al-Kuwarri, *Oil Revenues in the Gulf Emirates,* Bowker, 1978, p. 20.
53. Tim Niblock, 'Social Structure and the Development of the Saudi Arabian Political System', in Niblock (ed.), *State, Society and Economy in Saudi Arabia,* Croom Helm, 1982, p. 95.
54. *Khaleej*, 31 Dec. 1982.
55. Majid al-Majid, *Majlis al-Ta'awun* (*The Cooperation Council*), Ta Ha Publishing, 1986, p. 12.

56. Adeed Dawisha, 'The Middle East', in Christopher Clapham (ed.), *Foreign Policy Making in Developing States*, Saxon House, 1977, p. 20.
57. Adeed Dawisha, 'Saudi Arabia's Search for Security', *Strategic Studies,* 1979, p. 20.
58. *Los Angeles Times*, 14 April 1991.
59. Nasir al 'Abaidly, 'Al-Dimucratia al-Kuwaitia Latazal Masdr Qalaq Li al-Andhima Khaleejiah' (Kuwaiti Democratization: A Source of Anxiety for the Gulf Regimes), *Al-Quds Al-Arabi*, 24 Nov. 2009.
60. J. E. Peterson, *Dwal al-Khalij al-Arabia: Khatawat Nhwa Almusharaka al Siassiah*, op. cit., p. 50.
61. Tim Niblock (ed.), *State, Society and Economy in Saudi Arabia*, Croom Helm, 1982, p. 89.
62. *Khaleej*, 9 July 1991.
63. *Al-Wafd*, 10 July 1991.
64. *Los Angeles Times*, 14 April 1991.
65. *Al-Rai al-'am*, 8 Jan. 1992; and *Khaleej*, 1 March 1992.
66. *Khaleej*, 31 July 1991 and 2 Aug. 1991.
67. *New York Times*, 5 June 1991.
68. Mary Ann Tetreault, 'Civil Society in Kuwait: Protected Space and Women's Rights', unpublished, p. 277.
69. *Los Angeles Times*, 5 June 1991.
70. *Khaleej*, 13 Jan. 1992.
71. *Arab Human Development Report,* 2009, p. 69.
72. *Khaleej*, 1 Aug. 1991 and 28 March 1992.
73. *Al-Islah*, vol. 175, 20 Feb. 1992, pp. 9–10; *Al Khalij*, 16 April 1992; *Khaleej*, 3 Sept. 2009.
74. *Al-Wattan*, 14 Feb. 1992; *Khaleej*, 9 April 1991.
75. *Al-Sha'ab*, 1 May 1991.
76. *Al-Sha'ab*, 21 May 1991.
77. Abdulatif al-Mahmuwd, 'Dawr al-Musharakah al-Sha'abiah fi Sun'a al-Qarar al-Siassy wa Mustaqbal al-Dimuqratiah fi al-Mantaqah' (The Role of Political Participation in Decision-making and the Future of Democracy in the Area), a paper presented to a conference in Kuwait, 7–9 Dec. 1991, unpublished, pp. 13–14.
78. *Al-Nahar*, 11 Dec. 1991.
79. *Al-Safir*, 19 Dec. 1991.
80. Daniel Pipes and Patrick Clawson, 'Ambitious Iran: Troubled Neighbors', *Foreign Affairs*, vol. 72. no. 1, 1993, p. 133.
81. Eric Hooglund, 'The Sultanate of Oman: Oman Charts its Next 25 Years', *Middle East Insight*, vol. 12, no. 1, Nov.—Dec. 1995, p. 57.
82. *Al-Ittihad*, 5 Jan. 1992.
83. For more information see Hoogland, 'Sultanate of Oman', p. 57.
84. *Al-Ittihad*, 5 Jan. 1992.
85. *Al-Madinah*, 4 June 1992.
86. *Financial Times*, 3 Sept. 2009.
87. J. E. Peterson, Saudi Arabia and the Illusion of Security, op. cit., p. 51.
88. On 25 June 1996, an attack was carried out on a military compound in Khobar in the Eastern Province, blowing up a building, killing 23 Americans, and wounding about 300 soldiers.
89. *Middle East Monitor,* Dec. 1992, p. 28.
90. A council member who prefers to be anonymous.
91. *Al-Hayat*, 24 June 1996; and *Al-Sharq al-Awsat*, 6 May 1996.

92. *Al-Hayat*, 8 May 1996.
93. *Al-Ittihad*, 27 Jan. 1996; and *Al-Hayat*, 24 Feb. 1996.
94. *Al-Ittihad*, 11 June 1996.
95. *Al-Siassa*, 6 June 1996.
96. *Al-Hayat*, 11 June 1996.
97. *Arab Human Development Report, 2009, p. 69.*
98. *Jazeera TV* (Arabic), 21 Aug. 2009.
99. *Jazeera TV* (English), 22 Feb. 2010.
100. http://www.anhri.net/reports/libya.
101. https://www.cia.gov/library/publications/the-world-factbook/geos/sa.html.
102. http://groups.google.com/group/akhbar_alkhaleej?hl=en; http://www.frontlinedefenders.org/ar/node/1752.
103. Yousef Khalifah al-Yousef, *Al-Fasad wa al-Hukum*, 2004, pp. 583–8.
104. *Sharjah TV*, 13 Oct. 2009.
105. *Financial Times*, 20 April 2009.
106. http:/www.rsf.org/article.php3?id_article=29889uae05.01.09.
107. Yousef Khalifah al-Yousef, *Arab Contemporary Affairs,* vol. 1, no. 4, Oct. 2008, p. 634.
108. *Financial Times*, 7 April 2009.
109. *Al-Shuruq*, 23–29 April 1992, p. 6.
110. For more details, see Tetreault, 'Civil Society in Kuwait', p. 289. According to a confidential source, some nominees paid about 4,000 Kuwaiti dinars (about $12,000) for every vote.
111. *Financial Times*, 10 April 2009.
112. 126 http://www.telegraph.co.uk/news/worldnews/middleeast/saudiarabia/5882406/Amnesty-criticises-Saudi-Arabias-shocking-human-rights-violations.html, 22 July 2009.
113. *Financial Times*, 10 April 2009.
114. Madeline Albright, 'The Testing of American Foreign Policy', *Foreign Affairs*, vol. 77, no. 6, Nov./Dec. 1998, pp. 63. *Al Arab*, 10 Dec. 1992.
115. A. Abdullah, *Al-Nidham al-Iqlimy al Khalijy* (*The Gulf Regional System*), al-mu'sasah al Jama'iah Lidrasat wa al Nashr, 1998, p. 29.
116. *Financial Times,* 3 Sept. 2009.
117. *Financial Times*, 10 April 2009.
118. For more details on the Omani experience see Abdullah Juma Al-Haj, 'The Polities of Participation in the Gulf Cooperation Council States: The Omani Consultative Council', *Middle East Journal*, vol. 53, no. 4, Autumn 1996, pp. 560–71.
119. http://www.telegraph.co.uk/news/worldnews/middleeast/saudiarabia/5882406/Amnesty-criticises-Saudi-Arabias-shocking-human-rights-violations.html, 22 July 2009.
120. *Khaleej*, 9 March 2009.
121. Talbott, 'Democracy and the National Interest', p. 56.
122. *Arab Human Development Report,* 2009, p.70.
123. For more details see Hassan Hamdan al-Alkim, 'The Prospect of Democracy in the GCC States', *Critique,* Fall 1996.
124. *Financial Times*, 6 Sept. 2009.
125. Talbott, 'Democracy and the National Interest', p. 57.
126. Maynes, 'Middle East in the Twenty-First Century', p. 11.
127. Lewis, 'The West and the Middle East', p. 123.
128. Emile A. Nakhleh, 'Political Participation and the Constitutional Experiments in the

Arab Gulf: Bahrain and Qatar', in Tim Niblock (ed.), *Social and Economic Development in the Arab Gulf*, Croon Helm, 1980, p. 175.
129. Mohammed Abid al-Jabri, 'Al-Waqa' al-Siassy al-Arabi', 2001, p. 10.
130. Cited in Talbott, 'Democracy and the National Interest', p. 61.
131. Abdullah al-Naqrash, op. cit., pp. 96–97.
132. Abdullahh al-Shaji, 'Fragmented and Teetering Arab Order', *Gulf News*, 5 Jan. 2009.
133. Reuters, 29 March 2009.
134. *Jazeera TV* (Arabic), 5 Jan. 2009.
135. *Sharjah TV*, 16 Oct. 2009.
136. http://jta.org/news/article/2009/10/12/1008440/abbas-defends-goldstone-vote-deferment-decision?gclid=CITR35OQxJoCFQMupAod4grDtA.
137. Mark N. Katz, 'Yemen Unity and Saudi Security', *Middle East Policy*, vol. 1, no. 1, 1992, p. 120.
138. Mordechai Abir, *Saudi Arabia: Government, Society and the Gulf Crisis*, Routledge, 1993, pp. 162–8.
139. *The Estimate*, 30 June 2000.
140. *Yemen Post*, 9 Feb. 2007.
141. Katz, 'Yemen Unity and Saudi Security', p. 129.
142. Pipes and Clawson, 'Ambitious Iran', p. 133.
143. Ibid., pp. 130–1.
144. Nadav Safran, *Saudi Arabia: The Ceaseless Quest for Security*, Belknap Press of Harvard University Press, 1985, p. 265.
145. Tim Niblock, 'Iraq's Policies towards the Arab States of the Gulf', in Niblock, *Iraq: The Contemporary State*, Croon Helm, 1982, p. 156.
146. Herman Elliots, 'Ma'tiyat al Aman fi Khalij al Farsi', UAE Foreign Ministry Archive, 1981, pp. 18–19, unpublished.
147. Ibid., p. 26.
148. Sophia Beernaerts, 'Economic, Political and Legal Aspects of Co-operation between the European Economic Community and the Countries Parties of the Charter of Co-operation Council in the Arab States of the Gulf', (dissertation presented to the Institute of European Studies, Université Libre de Bruxelles, 1989), p. 18 (English version, UAE Foreign Ministry Archive).
149. *Al-Ittihad*, 17 Jan. 1991.
150. Hassan H. al-Alkim, 'Al-'Alaqat al-Arabiah al-Khalijiah ma' Iran: R'wiah Mustaqbaliah', (The Arabian Gulf Relations with Iran: A Future Perspective), *Arab Journal for International Studies*, Winter 1990, p. 24.
151. Beernaerts, 'Economic, Political and Legal Aspects', p. 18.
152. See document no. S/16574.
153. See document no. S/RES/552 (1984).
154. Abdul Ridha Assiri, *Kuwait's Foreign Policy: City State in World Politics*, Westview Press, 1990, p. 102.
155. *Middle East Economic Digest (MEED)*, 29 Nov. 1986, pp. 4–5.
156. *The Soviet Union and the Middle East*, vol. 6, no. 12, 1990, p. 25.
157. *Washington Post*, 15 Jan. 1991.
158. Hassan H. al-Alkim, 'Al-'Alaqat al-Arabiah al-Khalijiah ma' Iran', p. 6.
159. Cited in Beernaerts, 'Economic, Political and Legal Aspects', p. 20.
160. *The Soviet Union and the Middle East*, vol. 6, no. 12, 1990, p. 25.
161. *Al-Taqrir al Iqtisadi al Arabi al Muahd 1992*, The Arab Monetary Fund, 1993.
162. Pipes and Clawson, 'Ambitious Iran', pp. 131–2.

163. Bernard Lewis, 'Rethinking the Middle East', *Foreign Affairs*, Autumn 1992, vol. 74, no. 4, p. 101.
164. Before the Iraqi invasion of Kuwait, Saudi Arabia was producing a quarter of OPEC's oil.
165. *New York Times*, 18 June 1992.
166. Salama, 'Al-Ta'adadiah wa al-Tahyyid al-Mutabadil, p. 104.
167. David Long, 'Saudi Arabia and its Neighbors: Preoccupied Paternalism', in Richard Singelar and J. E. Peterson (eds), *Crosscurrents in Gulf*, Routledge, 1988, p. 190.
168. Lewis, 'The West and the Middle East', p. 125.
169. Magda Abu Fadil, 'Bitter Words between Neighbours', *The Middle East,* 1 May 1993.
170. http://correlator.sandbox.yahoo.net/index.php/people/Qaruh+Island.
171. For more details see Hassan H. al-Alkim, *The Foreign Policy of the United Arab Emirates*, Saqi Books, 1989.
172. KUNA (Kuwait News Agency), 30 June 2005.
173. KUNA, 1 July 2005.
174. *Khaleej Times*, 1 July 2005.
175. http://groups.google.com/group/akhbar_alkhaleej?hl=en.
176. A. Abdullah, 'Al-Imarat wa al-Qarar al-Saudi' (UAE and the Saudi Decision), *Khaleej*, 26 Aug. 2009.
177. *Khaleej*, 27 Aug. 2009.
178. *Khaleej*, 29 Aug. 2009.
179. Salama, 'Al-Ta'adadiah wa al-Tahyyid al-Mutabadil', p. 123.
180. Interview with Bashar al-Assad, *Khaleej*, 9 March 2009.
181. Ahmed Yousef, 'Mustaqbal al-Sira'at al-Arabiah- al-Arabiah' (The Prospect of Inter-Arab Struggles), *Al-Mustaqbal al-Arabi*, vol. 115, Sept. 1989, p. 83.
182. Reuters, 29 March 2009.
183. Abdullahh al-Shaji, op.cit., *Gulf News*, 5 Jan. 2009.
184. Anwar Gargash, 'Iran, the GCC States, and the UAE: Prospects and Challenges in the Coming Decade', in Jamal S. Al Suwaidi, Iran and The Gulf: A Search for Stability, London: I. B. Tauris, 2002, p. 136.
185. Reuters, 30 March 2009.
186. Ibid.
187. *Arab Strategic Report 2007–8*, Centre for Political and Strategic Studies, 2009, p. 204.
188. Ibid., pp. 202–3.
189. Reuters, 29 March 2009.
190. *Arab Strategic Report 2007–2008*, p. 205.
191. *Financial Times*, 14 Jan. 2009.
192. SANA (Syrian News Agency), 19 Aug. 2009.
193. *Khaleej*, 29 Aug. 2009.
194. *Khaleej*, 31 Aug. 2009.
195. *Khaleej*, 1 Sept. 2009.
196. *Khaleej*, 6 Sept. 2009.
197. *Khaleej*, 9 Sept. 2009.
198. *Jazeera TV* (Arabic), 9 Oct. 2009.
199. *Khaleej*, 10 Sept. 2009.
200. Reuters, 29 March 2009.
201. *Arab Strategic Report 2007–8*, pp. 205–6.
202. *Khaleej*, 5 March 2009.

203. *Khaleej*, 12 March 2009.
204. *Khaleej*, 8 Oct. 2009.
205. *Khaleej*, 9 March 2009.
206. *Arab Strategic Report 2007–8*, pp. 206–7.
207. Reuters, 30 March 2009.
208. *Los Angeles Times*, 14 April 1991.
209. *Financial Times*, 10 April 2009.

Chapter 2

1. Basil al-Bustani, *Al-Tanimiah al-Bashriah al-Mustadamah* (A Sustained Human Development), Centre for Arab Unity Studies, 2009, p. 44.
2. Samuel Huntington, *The Clash of Civilizations*, Free Press, 2002, p. 130.
3. Ibid., pp. 116–17.
4. *Arab Knowledge Report*, 2009, p. 17.
5. For more details, see Ali al- Hut, Al- Iqtrab al- Thaqafi. Cultural alienation, Majallat al-Wihda, no. 39, December 1987, 137–147. And Jalal Amın, *Al-Mahriq al-Arabi wa al-Maghrib* (The Arab Mashreq and Maghreb), Beirut: Centre for Arab Unity Studies.1981.
6. John E. Peterson, *Saudi Arabia and the Illusion of Security*, op.cit. p. 56.
7. Ahmed al-Barsan, "Masadr al-Quwah al-Arabiah wa al-Siassa al-Kharijiah al-Amrikyah"(Sources of Arab Power & the American Foreign Policy), *Arab Journal of Political Science*, No. 13, Winter 2007, p. 12 .
8. Abdulilah Balaqziz, 'Muqadimat litahlil al-Khitab al-Siassi al-Arabi (Introduction to the Analysis of Arab Political Speech), *Al-Mustaqbal al-Arabi*, vol. 123, May 1989, p. 10.
9. Cited in Ahmed Salim al-Bursan, 'Massadr al-Quwah al-Arabia wa al-Siassa al-Kharjiah al-Amerikia' (Sources of Arab Power and American Foreign Policy), *Arab Journal of Political Science*, Winter 2007, pp. 11–12.
10. Albert Hourani, *Arabic Thought in the Liberal Age*, Oxford University Press, 1962, p. 49.
11. Cited in Muhammad al-Rwmayhi, *Khaleej laysa Nafta* (*The Gulf is Not Oil*), Dar Kathima, 1983, p. 253
12. Taha Hussein, *Mustaqbal al-Thaqafah* (*Future of Culture*), Dar al-Kitab al-Libnani, n.d., p. 47.
13. Ikram Diyn al-Umari, *Al-Turath wa al-Hadatha* (*Heritage and Modernity*), UAE National Student Union, 1986, p. 15.
14. A. Abdallah, 'Al-Islah al-Jam'ayi fi al-amarat' (University Reforms in the UAE), *Al-Waqt* (Bahrain), 23 Oct. 2007.
15. For details, see Ismail Kilani, *Fasl Adiyn 'an al- Dawlah* (Separation of State and Religion), Islamic Bureau, 1980.
16. Huntington, *Clash of Civilizations*, p. 129.
17. Ibid., p. 125.
18. For more details, see Ziauddin Sardar and Devies Merry Wyn, *Why Do People Hate America*, trans. Ma'ain al-Imam, Obeikhan Publishers, 2005.
19. Said Hareb, 'Language and Identity', *Al-Arab* (Qatar), 23 Feb. 2009.
20. Huntington, *Clash of Civilizations*, p.106.
21. It is worth mentioning that the ministerial meeting of the Organization of Islamic

Conference, held in Jakarta in Dec. 1996, had called on all non-Arab Muslim countries to use Arab script.

22. *Towards a Contemporary Islamic View,* 1992, working paper, p. 30.
23. Huntington, *Clash of Civilizations*, p. 126.
24. Abdul Rahman al-'Uways, *Khaleej*, 27 Dec. 2007.
25. Hareb, 'Language and Identity'.
26. *Arab Knowledge Report,* 2009, p. 46.
27. *Towards a Contemporary Islamic View, Conference Proceedings,* 1992, pp. 13–15.
28. Hisham Sharabi, *Nationalism and Revolution in the Arab World*, Van Nostrand, 1966, p. 19.
29. Ahmed Sidqi al-Dajani, 'Al-Fikr al-Qarbi wa al-Taqiyir fi al-Mujtama'a al-Arabi' (Western Thought and Change in the Arab Society), in *Al-Turath waal-Tahdiat al 'Asr fi al-'Alam al-'Arabi* (*Heritage and Challenges of the Age in the Arab World*), Centre for Arab Unity Study, 1985, pp. 318–19.
30. *Arab Knowledge Report,* 2009, p. 46.
31. Ali al-Ghafli, al- Taqrir al- Istratijy al-Khalijy (*Gulf Strategic Report),* 2006, p. 70.
32. Mohammed Abid al- Jabiri, Ishkaliat al-Assalah wa al-Hadathah fi al-Fikr al- Arabi al-Mua'sir: Sira' Tabaqi awu Mushkilat Thaqafah (The originality vs. modernity dilemma in contemporary Arab thought: a class struggle or cultural problem? In: *Al-Turath wa Tahadiat al-A'sr fi al-A'alam al-Arabi* (*Heritage and challenges of the age in the Arab world*). Beirut: Centre for Arab Unity Studies, 1985, pp. 29–33.
33. Huntington, *Clash of Civilizations*, p. 109.
34. http://www.topuniversities.com/university-rankings/world-university-rankings/2009/results.
35. *Arab Knowledge Report,* 2009, p. 22.
36. W. Nathmi, *Qadhaia al Tanmiah wa al Takhaluf* (*Issues of Development and Underdevelopment*), Arab Institute for Studies and Publication 1985, p. 26
37. George Masri, 'Mushkilat al-Bahth al-Ilmi fi al-'Alam al-'Arabi: Halat al Jama'at' (Scientific Research Problem in the Arab World: The Case of Universities), *Mustaqbal al-'Alam al-Islami,* vol. 12/13, Fall 1994, p. 119.
38. *al-Wai al-Islami* 2007.
39. *Al- Hayat* 2005.
40. Abd al-Latif Zarnaji, *Majallat al-Muhandis al-Arabi*, no. 123, 1996.
41. *Arab Parliament* 2001.
42. Ibid.
43. *Ilaf* 2006.
44. Ibid.
45. *Majallat al-Muhandis al-Arabi*, vol. 123, 1996.
46. *Al-Kifah al-Arabi* 2005.
47. Arab Parliament 2001.
48. Cited in W. Nathmi, *Qadhaia al Tanmiah*, p. 190.
49. Ibid., pp. 64–70.
50. Al-Wai al-Islami 2006.
51. *Arab Knowledge Report,* 2009, p. 23.
52. *Arab Human Development Report,* 2009, p. 157.
53. Mohammed Naqbi, *Gulf Strategic Report 2004–2005*, 2006, p. 176.
54. *Al-Mawqif al-Arabi*, vol. 274, 10 March 2007.
55. *Jazeera TV* (Arabic), 1 Oct. 2007.
56. *Arab Knowledge Report*, 2009, pp. 10–11.
57. *Arab Human Development Report,* 2009, pp. 132–3.

58. Nathmi, *Qadhaia al Tanmiah*, p. 59.
59. *Human Development Report*, 2005, p. 250.
60. Ibid., p. 21.
61. Zaghlul Raghib al-Najjar says that the Arabs spend 20 cents per capita on training and education programmes, whereas Japan spends $51 (Nathmi, *Qadhaia al Tanmiah*, pp. 50–1). These figures seem rather exaggerated and need further scrutiny (ibid.).
62. *Human Development Report*, 2005, p. 254.
63. *Taqrir al-Iqtissadi al-Arabi al-Muahad*, 1994, p. 25. (*Arab Economic Report*)
64. *Arab Knowledge Report*, 2009, p. 20.
65. *Arab Human Development Report,* 2009, p. 239.
66. *Arab Human Development Report*, 2006, p. 78.
67. Nathmi, *Qadhaia al Tanmiah*.
68. *Arab Human Development Report*, 2006, pp. 20–1.
69. The Kuwaiti high court recently ruled that women can travel without seeking written approval from their guardian. *Jazeera TV*, 26 Oct. 2009.
70. Amani Kamal, 'Tathir 'Asr al Naft fi wadh'a al Nisaa al Arab' (Impact of the Oil Era on the Status of Arab Women). *Social Affairs*, vol. 19, Fall 1988, pp. 213–18.
71. *Human Development Report*, 2005, p. 311.
72. Ibid., p. 316.
73. Muza Ubayd Ghabbash, 'Tathir al-Qayam ala 'Amal al-Mar'at fi Mujtama'a al Imarat' (The Impact of Values on Working Women in UAE Society), *Social Affairs*, vol. 18, Summer 1988, pp. 133–55.
74. 'Women and Empowerment in the Arab World', *Arab Studies Quarterly*, 22 Sept. 2003, http://www.thefreelibrary.com/Women+and+empowerment+in+the+Arab+world-a0117186910.
75. Women in Arab Parliaments: Progress, Stagnation or Regression, Seminar by the UNDP, Beirut, 9–10 July 2008. http://www.arabparliaments.org/publications/legislature/2008/winp/conceptnote-e.pdf.
76. http://www.arabparliaments.org/publications/legislature/2008/winp/conceptnote-e.pdf.
77. Nathmi, *Qadhaia al Tanmiah*, p. 59.
78. The ratio of male to female students at the UAE University is 3:1.
79. Basil al-Bustani, *Al-Tanmiah al-Bashariah al-Mustadamah* (*Sustainable Human Development*), Centre for Arab Unity Studies, 2009, p. 44.
80. *Human Development Report*, 2005, p. 254.
81. For more details see Abdal Muna'im Al-Mashat, *Al-Tanmiah al-syassiah fi 'alam al Thalyth* (*Political Development in the Third World*), Al-Ayn: Al-Ayn li-al-Nashr wa-al-Tawza, 1988.
82. *Arab Knowledge Report*, 2009, p. 12.
83. *Jazeera TV* (Arabic), 15 Nov. 2009.
84. https://www.cia.gov/library/publications/the-world-factbook/geos/it.html.
85. *Taqrir al-Iqtissadi al-Arabi al Muahad,* 2008.
86. For more information, see Hassan Hamdan al-Alkim, 'Azmat al-Ghytha fi al-Watan al-Arabi' (The Food Crisis in the Arab World), *Asiassa al-Dawlya,* vol. 123, Jan. 1996.
87. *Taqrir al-Iqtissadi al-Arabi al-Muahad,* 2006.
88. Ibid.
89. Majallat al-Muhandis al-Arabi, vol. 123, 1996.
90. E. Sahliyeh, 'The Limit of State Power in the Middle East', *Arab Studies Quarterly*, Fall 2000.
91. *Khaleej*, 13 Nov. 2007.

92. *Arab Human Development Report*, 2009, pp. 132–3.
93. *Taqrir al-Iqtissadi al-Arabi al-Muahad* 2008, p. 147.
94. *Arab Knowledge Report*, 2009, p. 12.
95. Ibid., p. 19.
96. *Taqrir al-Iqtissadi al-Arabi al-Muahad* 2008, p. 145.
97. Ibid., pp. 145–6.
98. Ibid., p. 90.
99. http://en.wikipedia.org/wiki/OPEC.
100. http://english.sina.com/technology/1/2005/1011/48989.html.
101. *Taqrir al-Iqtissadi al-Arabi al-Muahad* 2008, p. 92.
102. *CIA World Fact* book, as of 1 Jan. 2009.
103. *Arab Human Development*, 2009, p. 79.
104. Women in Arab Parliaments, seminar 2008. http://www.arabparliaments.org/publications/legislature/2008/winp/conceptnote-e.pdf

Chapter 3

1. Hassan al-Alkim, 'Al-Arab, Amrika, wa al-Nidham al-Dawli al-Jadid' (The Arabs, America, and the New World Order), *Arab Journal of International Studies*, Summer/Fall 1993.
2. For more details, see Shimon Peres, *Ma'rakat Al-ssalam: Yuwmiyat* (*The Battle for Peace: Diary*), trans. Ammar Fadhil wa Malik Fadhil, Amman: Al- Ahliya lil Nashr wa al-Tuwzi, 1995.
3. Comprising the entire Middle East and Muslim world, it stretches from the Muslim world's frontiers with China, to Morocco and Mauritania, and it includes, according to foreign policy studies, the Arab world, Israel, Central Asia and the Caucasus.
4. *Jazeera TV* (Arabic), 25 Dec. 2007.

4a. According to Shimon Peres, the Arabs had no source of weapons and less political support: The old antagonistic Soviet Union that once supported the Arabs against Israel is now gone, replaced by a democratic Russia that supports the peace process.

5. A. Ghafli, *Gulf Strategic Report*, p. 73.
6. Munir Shafiq on *al-Hiwar TV*, 16 June 2007.
7. Jewish settlers living in the occupied territories focused their attack on Rabin's peace moves by pressing political party SHAS to pull out of the coalition, *Independent,* 11 May 1993.
8. It is apparent that there was compulsion in the attempt of the leadership of South Yemen headed by Ali Salim al Baidh to secede and engage in war with the unity government headed by Ali Abdullah Saleh for sixty-six days, which ended in the defeat of the separatists. Yemen was unified. For more details, read Jamal Sanad al Suwaidi (ed.), *Harb Yemen 1994: Al Asbab wa Nata'ij* (*Yemen 1994 War: Causes and Implications*), Saqi Books, 1995.
9. *Investigative Leads,* vol. 9, June 1989, published by the Executive Intelligence Review.
10. *Khaleej*, 11 Nov. 1989.
11. *Investigative Leads*, vol. 9, June 1989.
12. *Institution Analysis*, vol. 39, 1988, published by Heritage.
13. *Los Angeles Times*, 3 June 1991.
14. *New York Times*, 1 June 1991.
15. *Al-Ittihad*, 26 May 1989.

16. F. Sarrah, 'Al-Yahwdiah wa al-Sahiwniah fi al-Ittihad al Suwvity' (Judaism and Zionism in the Soviet Union), *Sh'wun Filistiniah*, Feb. 1990, p. 91.
17. *Al-Ittihad*, 25 Feb. 1990.
18. Shafiq Maghar, *Dhahirat Gorvachev* (*Gorvachev's Phenomenon*), Riyadh al Rays Li al-Kutub wa Al-Nashir, ND., p. 442.
19. Ibid., pp. 113–19.
20. Sarrah, 'Al-Yahwdiah wa al-Sahiwniah', p. 96.
21. Maghar, *Dhahirat Gorvachev*, pp. 138–9.
22. *Al-Khalij*, 12 Sept. 1990.
23. *New York Times*, 4 Jan. 1991.
24. Ibid.
25. Abu Awda, Adnan, 'Al-Amil al-Dimughraphy fi al-Sira' al-Arabi-al-Israili', (The Demographic Factor in the Arab Israeli Conflict), the annual symposium on diplomacy, UAE Foreign Dhabi, on 30 Jan. 1990, pp. 5–21, unpublished.
26. Ibid., p. 13.
27. *Al-Ittihad*, 30 Apr. 1990.
28. *Al-Khalij*, 12 Nov. 1990.
29. M. Jalla Nu'man, 'Al Mutaghirat Al Jadidah fi Al Ittihad Al Suwvity wa Atharaha ala Al Sharq Al Awsat' (The Changes in the Soviet Union and their Impacts on the Middle East), *Al-Arabi*, vol. 12, Sept. 1987, p. 14.
30. Shahi Feldman, 'Missiles and CBW Proliferation: The Middle East', American Association for the Advancement of Science, Proliferation of Ballistic Missiles Policy Options for the Future, proceedings of the annual meeting symposium, New Orleans, LA, 19 Feb. 1990, p. 14.
31. *Al-Ittihad*, 13 Sept. 1990.
32. *Al-Khalij*, 24 Feb. 1990.
33. Abdul Aziz, Al Qazaz, 'Al Masalih al-'ulya li Dwal Aurwba fi al-'Alam al-Arabi' (The European States' Vital Interests in the Arab World), a lecture given at the United Arab Emirates University on 21 May 1990.
34. David Neoman, 'The Jewish Settlements', a lecture given at University of California Los Angeles on 17 April 1991.
35. http://www.undp.ps/en/newsroom/publications/pdf/other/dtpov.pdf.
36. http://www.indexmundi.com/israel/unemployment_rate.html.
37. *Khaleej*, 24 Feb. 1990.
38. Feldman, 'Missiles and CBW Proliferation', p. 14.
39. *Al-Ittihad*, 13 Sept. 1990.
40. *New York Times*, 21 Jan. 1991.
41. Feldman, 'Missiles and CBW Proliferation', p. 14.
42. *Washington Post*, 15 Jan. 1991.
43. *Washington Post*, 15 Nov. 1991.
44. Document on Persian Gulf War: US Costs and Allied Financial Contributions, CRS IB 91019, 21/9/1992.
45. SU and ME, vol. 6, no. 12, 1990, p. 11.
46. *New York Times*, 6 June 1991.
47. *New York Times*, 18 June 1991.
48. Hassan H. al-lAkim, *The Foreign Policy of the United Arab Emirates*, Saqi Books, 1989, pp. 79–81.
49. *Los Angeles Times*, 5 June 1991.
50. A high-ranking UAE military officer has informed the author that US officials have approached the UAE for such an arrangement but the UAE government declined on

the ground that the UAE continues to adhere to its principles of non-alignment and to its Arab obligations. The argument is substantiated by the fact that up till writing of the paper, no such thing has materialized.

51. *Al-Hayat,* 11 May 1991.
52. Document on Arms Sale to Saudi Arabia: Current Status, Congressional Report Services, (CRS) IB91007, 25 Feb. 1993.
53. *Sunday Telegraph,* 27 Sept. 1992.
54. Document on Arms Sale to Saudi Arabia: Current Status, CRS IB 91007, 25 Feb. 1993.
55. Document on Middle East Arms Supply: Recent Control Initiatives, CRS IB 91113, 22 March 1993.
56. *Khaleej*, 21 Aug. 1991.
57. Clyde Prestowitz, *Rogue Nation: American Unilateralism*, trans. Fadhil Jatkar, Al-Hiwar Athaqafi, 2003, p. 47.
58. Associated France Press, 3 April 2009.
59. Ziauddin Sardar and Devies Merry Wyn, *Why Do People Hate America*, trans. Ma'ain al-Imam, Obeikhan Publishers, 2005, p. 11.
60. Ibid. p. 137.
61. Ibid., pp. 80–1.
62. William Blum, *Rogue State*, Monroe, IL: Common Courage Press, 2005, pp. 12–13.
63. Prestowitz, *Rogue Nation: American Unilateralism*, trans. Fadhil Jatkar, Al-Hiwar Athaqafi, 2003, pp. 212–15.
64. Mekhled Mubaideen, 'Al-Muqif al-Amiriki Tijah al-Barnamj al-Nawawi al-Irani' (The American Attitude towards the Iranian Nuclear Programme), *Dirasa* (Jordan), vol. 34, 2007, p. 784.
65. Prestowitz, *Rogue Nation*, pp. 19–20.
66. Reuters, 1 April 2009.
67. Blum, *Rogue State*, pp. 26, and Prestowitz, *Rogue Nation*.
68. Charles Maynes, 'The Middle East in the Twenty-First Century', *Middle East Journal*, vol. 52, no. 1, Winter 1998, p. 11.
69. Kemal Dervis and Nemat Shafik, 'The Middle East and North Africa: A Tale of Two Futures', *Middle East Journal*, vol. 52, no. 4, Autumn 1998.
70. Khalid Tahsin Ali, *Al-Mustaqbal al-Arabi*, vol. 123, May 1989, p. 105.
71. Prestowitz, *Rogue Nation*, p. 20.
72. Ibid., pp. 245–7.
73. Reuters, 7 March 2009.
74. Mubaideen, 'Al-Muqif al-Amiriki Tijah al-Barnamj al-Nawawi al-Irani', p. 782.
75. Shahram Chubin and Jerrold Green, 'Engaging Iran: A US Strategy', *Survival*, vol. 40, no. 3, 1998, p. 153.
76. Mubaideen, 'Al-Muqif al-Amiriki Tijah al-Barnamj al-Nawawi al-Irani', p. 774.
77. Associated France Press, 25 March 2009.
78. www.chinaview.cn, 1 April 2009, 07:55:02.
79. Chubin and Green, 'Engaging Iran', pp. 157–8.
80. http://news.yahoo.com/s/ap/20090420/ap_on_re_eu/un_un_racism_conference.
81. BBC R4, 20 April 2009.
82. Associated France Press, 27 April 2009.
83. Strobe Talbott, 'Democracy and the National Interest', *Foreign Affairs*, vol. 75, no. 6, Nov./Dec. 1996, p. 52.
84. Samuel Huntington, 'The West Unique, Not Universal', *Foreign Affairs*, vol. 75, no. 6, Nov./Dec. 1996, pp. 40–1.

85. Prestowitz, *Rogue Nation*, p. 339.
86. Chubin and Green, 'Engaging Iran', p. 160.
87. For more details see Hassan Al-Alkim, 'Al Suhywniah al Yahwudiah al Amirikyah wa Tathiraha 'Ala Syassat al Wilayat al Mutahidah al Kharijiah Tijah al 'Alim Al Arabi' (The American Jewish Zionism and its Impacts on US Policy towards the Arab World), *Shu'un Arabiah*, vol. 56, Dec. 1988.
88. Sardar and Wyn, *Why Do People Hate America*. p. 103.
89. Blum, *Rogue State*, pp. 244–64.
90. Bulent Aras, 'Post-Cold War Realities: Israel Strategy in Azerbaijan and Central Asia', *Middle East Policy*, vol. 5, no. 4, Jan. 1998, p. 70.
91. Prestowitz, *Rogue Nation*, p. 23.
92. Charles Maynes, 'Middle East in the Twenty-First Century', p. 14.
93. Blum, *Rogue State*, pp. 244–64.
94. Sardar and Wyn, *Why Do People Hate America*, p. 70.
95. Blum, *Rogue State*, p. 245.
96. Ibid., p. 265.
97. Prestowitz, *Rogue Nation*, p. 22.
98. BBC News-Arabic Service, 12 April 2009.
99. http:// www.en.wikipedia.org/wiki/Kyoto_Protocol.
100. BBC News, 12 April 2009.
101. http://unfccc.int/meetings/cop_15/items/5257.php
102. Richard Haass, 'What to Do with American Primacy', *Foreign Affairs*, vol. 78, no.5, Sept./Oct. 1999, p. 39.
103. Samuel Huntington, *The Clash of Civilizations,* Free Press, 2002, p. 35.
104. Huntington, 'The West Unique, Not Universal', p. 29.
105. http://www.time.com, 5/4/2009.
106. Haass , op. cit., p. 37.
107. A. Abdullah, 'Al-Nidham al-Dawli al-Jadid' (The New World Order), a lecture given during a symposium on 'the International Changes and its Impacts' held at the UAE Foreign Ministry, Abu Dhabi, on 20 Feb. 1990.
108. Muhammad Zakaria Ismail, 'Al Nidham Al Dawli Al Jadid: Al Wahm Al Khadia' (The New World Order: Falseness and Deception), *Al-Mustaqbal Al Arabi,* 143, Jan. 1991, p. 7.
109. *Los Angeles Times,* 26 June 1991.
110. M. Gorbachev, *Al Byrystrwika* (*The Perestroika*), trans. Abdul Jawad, 8th edn, Dar al Shurwq, 1989, p. 59.
111. *Jazeera TV* (Arabic) 3 April 2009.
112. World Economic Outlook Update, Global Economic Slump Challenges Policies, January 28, 2009, http://www.imf.org/external/pubs/ft/weo/2009/update/01/
113. *Jazeera TV* (Arabic), 10 April 2009.
114. *Jazeera TV* (Arabic), 15 Nov. 2009.
115. http:// www.cia.gov/library/publications/the-world-factbook/geos/us.html
116. *Arab Strategic Report 2007–2008*, Cairo. 2009, p. 10.
117. Forecast made by the employers' organization the CBI, the Ernst and Young ITM Club and the Centre for Economics Research. *City A.M.*, 20 April 2009.
118. BBC R4, 22 April 2009.
119. *City A.M.*, vol. 874, 20 April 2009.
120. http://www.armscontrolcenter.org/policy/securityspending/articles/fy09_dod_request_global/
121. Reuters, 18 June 2009.

122. Charles Maynes, 'Middle East in the Twenty-First Century', pp. 12–13.
123. Mohammed Selim, *Al-Arabi*, 13 April 2009.
124. *Khaleej*, 21 Aug. 1991.
125. *The Military Balance 2002/2003*, pp. 88–94.
126. http://www.cia.gov/library/publications/the-world-factbook/geos/us.html.
127. Muhammad Z. Ismail, 'Al Nidham Al Dawli Al Jadid ', p. 12.
128. *Daily Telegraph*, 17 May 1993.
129. Associated France Press, 21 March 2009.
130. Mekhled Obaid Mubaidheen, 'Al-Syn al-Sha'biah wa Imkaniat Tahwlah ila Qutb Dawli Fa'il' (China and the Probability of Becoming an Effective International Power), al-Manara, 2004, p. 160.
131. *Jazeera TV* (Arabic), 15 Nov. 2009.
132. *The Military Balance 2002/2003*, pp. 145–8.
133. http://www.cia.gov/library/publications/the-world-factbook/geos/us.html.
134. *The Military Balance 2002/2003*, p. 141.
135. Prestowitz, *Rogue Nation*, p. 330.
136. *New York Times*, 14 March 2009.
137. *Jazeera TV* (Arabic), 5 April 2009.
138. Associated France Press, 7 April 2009.
139. http://news.yahoo.com/s/ap/20090917/ap_on_re_eu/eu_eastern_europe_missile_defense.
140. *Khaleej*, 19 Sept. 2009.
141. http://www.delawareonline.com/article/20090920/NEWS02/909200341/1006/NEWS.
142. George McCovern, 'The Future Role of the United States in the Middle East', *Middle East Policy*, vol. 1, no. 3, 1992, p. 1.
143. CBS TV, 6 April 2009.
144. Associated France Press, 7 April 2009.
145. Reuters, 7 March 2009.
146. *Khaleej*, 9 March 2009.
147. *Khaleej*, 12 March 2009.
148. Chubin and Green, 'Engaging Iran', p. 162.
149. Reuters, 8 March 2009.
150. Chubin and Green, 'Engaging Iran', p. 160.
151. Dubai TV, 20 March 2009, 8:30pm UAE local time.
152. Reuters, 21 March 2009, 6:30pm.
153. Reuters, 23 March 2009.
154. Reuters, 21 March 2009, 8:30 pm.

Chapter 4

1. The GCC is a subregional organization that was set up in Abu Dhabi on 25 May 1981. It consists of six Gulf countries: Bahrain, Kuwait, Oman, Qatar, Saudi Arabia and the United Arab Emirates (UAE). The objectives of the Council are to cooperate in economic matters, security and defence
2. Abdullah al-Naqrash, op.cit., p. 88.
3. Ali Edin Hillal and Jamil Matter, *Al-Nidham al-Iqlimy al-Arabi*, Centre of Arab Unity Studies, 1979, p. 28.

4. 'Asam Nu'aman, 'Nahwa Mashru'a Distur Itihadi 'Arabi' (Towards an Arab Federal Constitutional Project), *Al-Mustaqbal al-Arabi*, vol. 123, May 1989, p. 29.
5. Abdullah al-Naqrash, op.cit., p. 91.
6. Siar al-Jamal, 'Al-Khitab al-Tarikhy al-'Arabi ma bin al-Harbin al-'Udhmiyn' (Historical Arab Speeches between the Two World War), *Al-Mustaqbal al-Arabi*, vol. 123, May 1989, p. 75.
7. Samuel Huntington, 'The West Unique, Not Universal', *Foreign Affairs*, vol. 75, no. 6, 1996, p. 130.
8. *Khaleej*, 3 June 2009.
9. Abdel Mun'am al-Mashat, 'Tadris al Amn al Qawmi al Arabi' (Teaching Arab National Security) *Arab Journal of Political Science* vol. 3 & 4, Sept. 1989, p. 208.
10. Charles Maynes, 'The Middle East in the Twenty First Century', *Middle East Journal*, vol. 52, no. 1, 1998, p. 16.
11. Abdullah al-Naqrash, op. cit., p. 95.
12. Brenda Seaver, 'The Regional Sources of Power-Sharing Failure: The Case of Lebanon', *Political Science Quarterly*, vol. 115, no. 2, Summer 2000, p. 284.
13. Richard Haass, op. cit., p. 44.
14. Kemal Dervis and Nemat Shafik, 'The Middle East and North Africa: A Tale of Two Futures', *Middle East Journal*, vol. 52, no. 4, Autumn 1998, p. 507.
15. Cited in Seaver, 'Regional Sources', p. 251.
16. Ghassan Salama, 'Al-Ta'adadiah wa al-Tahyyid al-Mutabadil: Al-Illaqat al-Arabia al-rabiah fi al-Rahyn wa al-Muhtamal' (Pluralism and the Interdependent Neutralism: Contemporary Inter-Arab Relations and the Potential), *Al-Mustaqbal al-Arabi*, vol. 115, Sept. 1988, p. 120.
17. Richard Haass, op. cit., p. 44.
18. Ahmed Yousef, op. cit., p. 87.
19. Seaver, 'Regional Sources', p. 262.
20. Abdel Mun'am al-Mashat, 'Tadris al Amn al Qawmi al Arabi', op.cit, pp. 207–8.
21. Mauritania decided in early 2009 to sever its diplomatic relations with Israel.
22. *Arab Strategic Report 2007–2008*, pp. 208–12.
23. Ghassan Salama, 'Al-Ta'adadiah wa al-Tahyyid al-Mutabadil', p. 103.
24. Seaver, 'Regional Sources', p. 264.
25. Bulent Aras, 'Post-Cold War Realities: Israel Strategy in Azerbaijan and Central Asia', *Middle East Policy*, vol. 5, no. 4, Jan. 1998.
26. Abdullah al-Naqrash, op.cit., p. 97.
27. Charles Maynes, op, cit., p. 15.
28. Dervis and Shafik, 'The Middle East and North Africa', p. 506.
29. Bulent Aras, 'Post-Cold War Realities'.
30. Salama, 'Al-Ta'adadiah wa al-Tahyyid al-Mutabadil', p. 112.
31. Ahmed Yousef, op.cit., p. 95.
32. Regional organization created in 1991 by the Treaty of Asuncion. It encompasses four Latin American countries: Argentina, Brazil, Paraguay and Uruguay.
33. Mohammed Selim, *Al-Ahram*, 5 Nov. 2008.
34. http://ec.europa.eu/external_relations/mercosur/index_en.htm.
35. Sadah Habashinah, 'Muhadidat al-Siassa al-Kharijiah al-Iraniah Tijah al-Wilaiat al-Mutahidah al-Amrikiah 1979–2007' (The Determinants of Iran's Foreign Policy towards the US 1997–2007), *Mu'atah*, vol. 23, no. 5, 2008, p. 21.
36. http://arabic.arabia.msn.com/news/middleeast/AFP/2009/June/814770.aspx.
37. World Factbook, http://www.cia.gov/library/publications/the-world-factbook/geos/ir.html#Econ.

38. Shahram Chubin and Jerrold Green, 'Engaging Iran: A US Strategy', *Survival*, vol. 40, no. 3, Autumn 1998, p. 154.
39. Ibid.
40. *Arab Strategic Report 2007–2008*, p. 126.
41. http://en.wikipedia.org/wiki/User:Arcayne/busywork_3.
42. *Al-Hayat*, 14 Aug. 2005.
43. *Arab Strategic Report 2007–2008*, p. 129.
44. Tim Niblock, State, Society and Economy in Saudi Arabia, p. 127.
45. Shahram Chubin, 'Iran and Regional Security in the Persian Gulf', *Survival*, vol. 34, no. 3, Autumn 1992, p. 65.
46. Anwar Gargash, 'Iran, the GCC States, and the UAE: Prospects and Challenges in the Coming Decade', p. 138.
47. Chubin, 'Iran and Regional Security', p. 66.
48. Ibid., p. 64.
49. Ibid., p. 68.
50. Ibid., p. 69.
51. Nadav Safran, *Saudi Arabia: The Ceaseless Quest for Security,* Boston, MA: Belknap Press of Harvard University Press, 1985, p. 234.
52. Jamal S. al-Suwaidi, 'Gulf Security and the Iranian Challenge', *Security Dialogue,* vol. 27, no. 3, 1996, p. 277.
53. http://en.wikipedia.org/wiki/User:Arcayne/busywork_3.
54. *Arab Strategic Report 2007–2008*, p. 126.
55. Ibid., p. 135.
56. World Factbook, http://www.cia.gov/library/publications/the-world-factbook/geos/ir.html#Econ.
57. *Khaleej*, 9 March 2009.
58. Chubin and Green, 'Engaging Iran', p. 153.
59. Associated France Press, 27 April 2009.
60. Charles Tripp, 'Iraq and the Gulf States', *Survival*, vol. 34, no. 3, Autumn 1992, p. 52.
61. *Al-Arab*, 10 Dec. 1992.
62. *The Military Balance, 1998/99*, p. 117.
63. Antony Cordesman, 'Al Quadrat al 'Askaria al-Iranyah' (Iran's Military Capabilities), *Dirasat 'Alamiah,* Emirates Centre for Strategic Studies and Research, 1996, p. 18.
64. Habashinah, 'Muhadidat al-Siassa al-Kharijiah al-Iraniah Tijah', p. 22.
65. *The Military Balance 2002/2003*, pp. 103–5.
66. *The Military Balance, 1998/1999*, p. 117.
67. *Sunday Telegraph,* 27 Sept. 1992.
68. Daniel Pipes and Patrick Clawson, 'Ambitious Iran, Troubled Neighbors', *Foreign Affairs*, vol. 72. no. 1, 1993, p. 127.
69. *AlMajalla,* 8 Dec. 1996, p. 17.
70. Total invested $2 billion in the development of the Sirri oil and gas fields after CONOCO was forced to abandon a nearly concluded deal.
71. Simon Serfaty, 'Europe and the United States in the Persian Gulf,' *Middle East Journal,* vol. 52, no. 3, summer 1998, p. 342.
72. John Calabrese, 'China and the Persian Gulf: Energy and Security', *Middle East Journal,* vol. 52, no. 3, summer 1998, p. 354.
73. Chubin, 'Iran and Regional Security', p. 62.
74. *Independent,* 30 Dec. 1992.
75. Sources believe that Iran obtained missiles of different types including: 60–100 SSN-22, 60–100 C-801 and C-802, Hawk, Stinger, WF-6, 250–300 SCUDS-B, 60-70

SCUDS-C, 150–200 CSS-8/25/30, 50–60 Silkworm, SA-5, SA-7, AT-3, AT-4, SA-2, SA-10, SA-12, SA-14, SA-16, CS-802, HN-5, NO-DONG-1. Al-Suwaidi, 'Gulf Security', p. 282; Cordesman, 'Al Quadrat', pp. 70, 88 and 104.

76. Pipes and Clawson, 'Ambitious Iran', p. 127.
77. Al-Suwaidi, 'Gulf Security', p. 283.
78. They were closed in March 2009 by the Nuri al Malki government in Baghdad as a sign of goodwill to Tehran.
79. They are made through members of the religious establishment: www.chinaview.cn, 20 Feb. 2009. http://news.xinhuanet.com/english/2009-02/20/content_10852316.htm.
80. Al-Alkim, *The Foreign Policy of the United Arab Emirates*, Saqi Books, 1989, pp. 140–4.
81. *Al-Quds al-Arabi*, 2 Sept. 1992.
82. *The Times,* 2 Sept. 1992.
83. Charles Tripp, op.cit., pp. 52–3.
84. *Al-Ittihad,* 17 Nov. 1996.
85. Serfaty, op.cit., p. 341.
86. Shamlan al Essa, *Al Khilafat al Hududiah wa al Iqlimiah bin al Arab wa Iran, Al Ilaqat al Arabiah al Iranyah* (Arab–Iranian Border & Regional Differences & Arab- Iranian Relations), Centre for Arab Unity Studies, 1996, p. 444.
87. *Al-Khalij,* 12 Nov. 1996.
88. See *The Military Balance 2008*, IISS, 2008.
89. Ibid.
90. Mekhled Mubaideen, 'Al-Muqif al-Amiriki Tijah al-Barnamj al-Nawawi al-Irani' (The American Attitude towards the Iranian Nuclear Programme), *Dirasat* (Jordon), vol. 34, 2007, p. 773.
91. http://en.wikipedia.org/wiki/Nuclear_program_of_Iran.
92. *Khaleej*, 20 Oct. 2009.
93. *Arab Strategic Report 2007–2008*, p. 131.
94. Shahram and Green, 'Engaging Iran', pp. 159–61.
95. http://www.globalsecurity.org/wmd/world/iran/bushehr.htm.
96. http://www.globalsecurity.org/wmd/world/pakistan/khan.htm.
97. http://www.globalsecurity.org/wmd/world/iran/khan-iran.htm.
98. http://www.globalsecurity.org/wmd/world/iran/bushehr.htm.
99. Arms Control Association, April 2005, http://www.armscontrol.org/act/2005_04/Bushehr.
100. *The Military Balance 1998*, p. 117.
101. *Front Line*, May 2005, http://www.pbs.org/frontlineworld/stories/iran403/background.html
102. Cordesman, 'Al Quadrat', pp. 122–4.
103. *The Military Balance 1998*, p. 20.
104. Mubaideen, 'Al-Muqif al-Amiriki Tijah', p. 776.
105. *Independent,* 30 Dec. 1992.
106. Amir Taheri, 'Iran has Started a Mideast Arms Race', *Wall Street Journal*, 23 March 2009, http://online.wsj.com/article/SB123776572203009141.html.
107. Reuters, 9 April 2009.
108. Reuters, 29 Oct. 2009.
109. Reuters, 7 March 2009.
110. Times online, 29 March 2009: http://www.timesonline.co.uk/tol/news/world/middle_east/article5993094.ece

111. Reuters, 18 April 2009.
112. Reuters, 9 April 2009.
113. *Jazeera TV* (Arabic), 20 Oct. 2009.
114. Reuters, 17 April 2009.
115. *Jazeera TV* (Arabic), 20 Oct. 2009.
116. Reuters, 22 Oct. 2009.
117. *Jazeera TV* (Arabic), 22 Oct. 2009.
118. Reuters, 29 Oct. 2009.
119. *Jazeera TV* (Arabic), 15 Nov. 2009.
120. *Daily Mail*, 30 Nov. 2009.
121. *Al-Arab,* 10 Dec. 1992.
122. *Al-Ittihad,* 17 Nov. 1996.
123. *Arab Strategic Report 2007–2008*, p. 129.
124. For more details see Hassan H. al-Alkim, *The GCC States in an Unstable World: Small States Foreign Policy Dilemmas*, Saqi Books, 1994, pp. 145–8.
125. Malik Mufti, 'Daring and Caution in Turkish Foreign Policy', *Middle East Journal*, vol. 52, no. 1, Winter 1998, pp. 33–4.
126. Bulent Aras, 'Post-Cold War Realities: Israel Strategy in Azerbaijan and Central Asia', *Middle East Policy*, vol. 5, no. 4, Jan. 1998, p. 70.
127. For more details of the treaty see http://wwi.lib.byu.edu/index.php/Treaty_of_Lausanne.
128. http://www.incirlik.af.mil/library/factsheets/factsheet.asp?id=5469.
129. Samuel Huntington, *The Clash of Civilizations*, Free Press, 2002, p. 126.
130. *Arab Strategic Report 2007–2008*, p. 157.
131. Reuters, 7 March 2009.
132. Mufti, 'Daring and Caution', p. 35.
133. *Arab Strategic Report 2007–2008*, p. 159.
134. Mufti, 'Daring and Caution', p. 45.
135. William Hill, 'Siassat Turkia al-Kharjiah fi 'Asr ma Ba'd al-Harb al-Barida wa al-Sharq al-Awsat' (Turkey Foreign Policy in Post Cold War Age and the Middle East), *Arab Researcher*, vol. 48, July–Oct. 1998, p. 11.
136. https://www.cia.gov/library/publications/the-world-factbook/geos/tu.html.
137. *The Military Balance 2004–2005*, pp. 71–2.
138. https://www.cia.gov/library/publications/the-world-factbook/geos/tu.html.
139. Said Hareb, 'Turkia al-Jadida' (New Turkey), http://www.alarab.com.qa/details.php?docId=102965&issueNo=675&secId=15.
140. World Factbook, https://www.cia.gov/library/publications/the-world-factbook/geos/tu.html.
141. It included large parts of the contemporary Arab world; however, over time and with the western colonial powers' incursion since the beginning of the 19th century most parts of the Arab homeland especially north Africa became western colonies. The Ottomans until their final collapse after WW1 maintained weak control of Palestine, Syria, Iraq, part of today's Saudi Arabia and Yemen.
142. Hassan al-Alkim, *Qadhaya Islamiyya Mua'sira* (*Contemporary Islamic Issues*), Centre for Asian Studies, University of Cairo, 1997.
143. http://en.wikipedia.org/wiki/Sykes-Picot_Agreement.
144. Masauwd Dhahir, 'Al-Fadha' al-Arabi wa Ma'zaq al-Ta'wun ma' Duwal al-Juar al-Iqlimi fi Matala' al-qarn al-Wahd wa al-'Ashrin" (Arabs and the Problem of Cooperation with Neighbouring Countries in the 21st Century), a paper presented to the conference on the Arab in the 21st Century, Amman, 7–8 Nov. 2001.

145. Ibid., p. 5.
146. Mufti, 'Daring and Caution', p. 43.
147. Ibid., pp. 44–5.
148. *Jazeera TV* (Arabic), 7 Aug. 2009.
149. *Jazeera TV* (Arabic), 29 Oct. 2009.
150. Mufti, 'Daring and Caution', p. 39.
151. *Arab Strategic Report 2007–2008*, p. 218.
152. Tracking no. 452798, http://www.fas.org/news/iran/1996/960816-452798.htm.
153. *Khaleej*, 27 Dec. 2009.
154. *Arab Strategic Report 2007–2008*, p. 133.
155. *Jazeera TV* (Arabic), 27 Dec. 2009.
156. *Arab Strategic Report 2007–2008*, p. 162.
157. Ibid., pp. 162–3.
158. Ibid., p. 216.
159. Ibid.
160. *Khaleej*, 9 March 2009.
161. Associated France Press, 22 March 2009.
162. *Jazeera TV* (Arabic), 22 Oct. 2009.
163. A report on Turkish–Israeli military cooperation, http://www.arabicnews.com/ansub/Daily/Day/010305/2001030508.html.
164. Bulent Aras, 'Post-Cold War Realities: Israel Strategy in Azerbaijan and Central Asia', *Middle East Policy*, vol. 5, no. 4, Jan. 1998, pp. 70–1.
165. *Al-'Usbu' al Arabi*, 7 Feb. 1994, p. 23.
166. Mufti, 'Daring and Caution', pp. 47–8.
167. Aras, 'Post-Cold War Realities', p. 78.
168. Mufti, 'Daring and Caution', p. 45.
169. Aras, 'Post-Cold War Realities', p. 71.
170. Ibid., pp. 70–1.
171. *Arab Strategic Report 2007/2008*, p. 164.
172. 'Triple Alliance: The US, Turkey, Israel', http://www.military-quotes.com/forum/triple-alliance-us-turkey-israel-t30320.html
173. Hill, 'Siassat Turkia al-Kharjiah', p. 10.
174. 'Triple Alliance: The US, Turkey, Israel'.
175. *Arab Strategic Report 2007/2008*, p. 165.
176. Ibid., p. 163.
177. A report on Turkish–Israeli military cooperation, http://www.arabicnews.com/ansub/Daily/Day/010305/2001030508.html.
178. *Arab Strategic Report 2007/2008*, pp. 164–5.
179. *Jazeera TV* (Arabic), 5 Jan. 2009.
180. Ibid.
181. Ibid.
182. Dervis and Shafik, 'The Middle East and North Africa', p. 515.
183. *Khaleej*, 19 Sept. 2009.
184. Abdulmina'm al-Mashatt, 'Tadris al-Amn al-Qawmi al-Arabi' (Teaching the Arab National Security), *Arab Journal of Political Science*, vols 2/3, p. 193.
185. Al-Alkim, *Foreign Policy of the UAE*, p. 175.
186. Sophia Beernaerts, 'Economic, Political and Legal Aspects of Cooperation between the European Economic Community and the Countries Parties to the Charter of Charter of Cooperation Council for the Arab States of the Gulf', dissertation, 1989, p. 22.

187. William Quandt, *Saudi Arabia in the 1980s: Foreign Policy, Security, and Oil,* Brookings Institution, 1981, p. 61.
188. *Khaleej,* 27 March 1988.
189. *Khaleej,* 9 April 1994.
190. Hassan H. al-Alkim, 'Bi'at Sun'a al-Qarar al-Kharijy al-Sa'udi' (The Environment of the Saudi Foreign Policy), *Arab Journal of Political Science,* vol. 7, Nov. 1992, p. 66.
191. *Washington Post,* 20 April 1993.
192. William Wallace and Jan Zielonka, 'Misunderstanding Europe', *Foreign Affairs*, vol. 77, no. 6, Nov./Dec. 1998, p. 74.
193. Simon Serfaty, op.cit., p. 339.
194. *Khaleej*, 19 Sept. 2009.
195. For more details see Al-Alkim, *GCC States in an Unstable World.*
196. Interview with Dr Adnan abu 'Udah, Jordanian permanent representative to the UN, New York, 29 April 1993, cited ibid.

Chaper 5

1. Yitzhak Shamir, 'Israel's Role in a Changing Middle East', *Foreign Affairs*, Spring 1982, pp. 789–801.
2. A. Ghafli, *Khaleej*, 21 Oct. 2009.
3. We might refer here to the Arab Popular Committee against normalization, which includes a number of well-educated individuals from several Arab countries, and to similar committees in individual Arab countries.
4. *Jazeera TV* (Arabic), 27 Nov. 2007.
5. *New York Times*, 27 Nov. 2007.
6. For more information, see al-Alkim, Al-Salam Bin al-Arab wa Israil: Drasa Istrafiyah (Peace between the Arab & Israel: A Futuristic Study) *Journal of the Social Sciences*, vol. 24, no. 4, winter 1996, p. 97.
7. We might refer here to the political developments in Gaza, in June 2007, including the confrontations between Hamas and Fateh.
8. *Jazeera TV* (Arabic), 27 Nov. 2007.
9. D. Stout, 'Israel's Nuclear Arsenal Vexed Nixon', *New York Times*, 29 Nov. 2007.
10. *Jazeera TV* (Arabic), 27 Nov. 2007.
11. *Jazeera TV* (Arabic), 25 Dec. 2007.
12. *Jazeera TV* (Arabic), 28 Dec. 2007.
13. Conflict can be defined as a clash of wills and powers between two rivals or more. The aim of each party is to destroy the other either completely or partially so one side will dominate the other. That party will then be able to end the conflict in such a way that its goals will be achieved.
14. Mahjub Omar, *Al-Sira' al-Arabi al-Israeli wa Sidam al-Hadharat* (*Arab–Israeli Conflict and the Clash of Civilizations*), Centre for Research and Strategic Studies, 1995, p. 120.
15. Ibid., p. 116.
16. Jalal al-Alim, *Qadat al-Gharb Yaquluwn* (*The Sayings of Western Leaders*), UAEU Student Union, 1979, p. 47.
17. Ziyad Abu Ghanima, *Al Haraka al Islamiyya wa Qadiya Filistin* (*The Islamic Movement and the Palestinian Issue*), Amman: Dar al Farqan for Publication and Distribution, 1985, p. 15.

18. Tawfiq Hasso, *Wa'd Balfur wa al Halaqah al Mafquda* (*Balfour Declaration and the Missing Link*), al-Ain: Dar al Kitab al Jama'I, 1986, p. 85.
19. Hassan al-Alkim et al., *Qadhaya Islamiah Mua'sirah* (*Contemporary Islamic Issues*), Centre for Asian Studies, Cairo University, 1997, pp. 145–7.
20. Jalal Tani, *Al Ikhwa al Za'ifa,* trans. Ahmed al Bazuri, Mu'asasat al-Risala, 1983, p. 18.
21. T. Ismael, *The Middle East in World Politics*, Syracuse University Press, 1974, p. 99.
22. M. I. Goldman, *Soviet Foreign Aid*, Praeger, 1967, p. 74.
23. *Arab Record and Report*, 1971, p. 73.
24. See W. Laqueur, *The Struggle for the Middle East*, Macmillan, 1969.
25. *Arab Record and Report*, 1967, p. 381.
26. *Arab Record and Report*, 1968, p. 175.
27. *Arab Record and Report*, 1970, pp. 5–34 and 36.
28. *International Herald Tribune*, 9 May 1969.
29. *Daily Telegraph*, 30 Sept. 1970.
30. *Al-Siassa al-Dawlya* (Cairo), vol. 9, July 1967, p. 188.
31. *Al-Siassa al-Dawlya* (Cairo), vol. 10, Oct. 1967, pp. 188–9.
32. Mahmoud Riyadh, *Al Bahth 'an Aslaam wa Sira' fi Asharq al Awsat 1948–1978* (*The Search for Peace and the Struggle in the Middle East*), Al-Mu'asasa al-Arabiya lil Dirasat wa Nashr, 1981, pp. 93–151.
33. Ibid., p. 13.
34. Ibid., p. 123.
35. *Arab Record and Report*, 1971, p. 176.
36. Ismael, *The Middle East*, p.112.
37. *Arab Record and Report*, 1972, p. 471.
38. *Middle East Journal*, vol. 27, no.2, Spring 1973, p. 61.
39. *Arab Record and Report*, 1972, p. 270.
40. Ibid., p. 535.
41. Mohammed Numan Jalal, 'Atughayurat al Jadida fil Ittihad Asufiyati wa Athruh ala Sharq al Awsat' (The New Changes in the Soviet Union and its Implication on the Middle East), *Al Bahith al Arabi* (London, The Arab Researcher), vol. 12, June 1987, p. 14.
42. *Khaleej* (Sharja), 3 July 1987.
43. John Ward Anderson, 'Fewer Come to Israel, and Many are Leaving', *Washington Post Foreign Service,* 23 April 2004; p. A17, http://www.boykotisrael.dk/fewer_come_to_israel.htm.
44. http://countrystudies.us/russia/88.htm.
45. Bulent Aras, 'Post-Cold War Realities: Israel Strategy in Azerbaijan and Central Asia', *Middle East Policy*, vol. 5, no. 4, Jan. 1998, p. 72.
46. Mark N. Katz, 'Putin's Foreign Policy toward Syria', *Middle East Review International,* vol 10, no. 1, March 2006, http://meria.idc.ac.il/journal/2006/issue1/jv10no1a4.html.
47. http://www.worldtribune.com/worldtribune/WTARC/2005/eu_russia_01_26.html
48. Katz, 'Putin's Foreign Policy'.
49. http://countrystudies.us/russia/88.htm.
50. http://www.ynetnews.com/articles/0,7340,L-3213707,00.html.
51. http://en.wikipedia.org/wiki/Russia_and_the_Arab%E2%80%93Israeli_conflict#Russia.27s_return_to_the_Middle_East.
52. Katz, 'Putin's Foreign Policy'.
53. http://www.un.org/apps/news/story.asp?NewsID=31245&Cr=gaza&Cr1.
54. http://www.voanews.com/english/archive/2009-06/2009-06-26-voa35.cfm?CFID=

265224999&CFTOKEN=33108596&jsessionid=00304700b0ae081e65593b434b532c232ef2.

55. http://www.palestinefacts.org/pf_1991to_now_israel_us_support.php.
56. Stephen Green, *Al-Inhiyaz: 'Alaqat Amrika al-Sirriya bi Isra'il* (*Taking Sides: America Secret relations with Israel*), Mu'asasa Adirasat Filistiniya, 1985, pp. 9 and 17.
57. Gideon Raphael, *Destination Peace: Three Decades of Israeli Foreign Policy*, Stein & Day, XXXX,ND., p. 7.
58. http://www.palestinefacts.org/pf_1991to_now_israel_us_support.php.
59. Yula al-Batl, *Al Ittifaq al Askari fi Isra'il Khilal 35 'Ama'* (*Military Accord in Israel in Thirty-Five Years*), Mu'asasat Adirasat Filistiniya, 1984, p. 50.
60. John G. Stoessinger, *Crusaders and Pragmatists: Movers of Modern American Foreign Policy*, W. W. Norton Co., 1979, p. 121.
61. Herman Finer, *Dulles over Suez*, Quadrangle, 1964, p. 6.
62. Green, *Al-Inhiyaz*, p. 163.
63. Ibid., p. 153.
64. http://www.palestinefacts.org/pf_1991to_now_israel_us_support.php.
65. Yula al-Batl, *Al Ittifaq al Askari*, p. 12.
66. US House of Congress, Committee on Foreign Affairs, *Sub-Committee on Europe and the Middle East for Assistance Legislation for Fiscal Year 1984/1985*, US Government Printing Office, 1983, p. 22.
67. Stout, 'Israel's Nuclear Arsenal Vexed Nixon', *New York Times*, 29 Nov. 2007.
68. Avner Cohen, *Israel and the Bomb*, New York: Colombia University Press, 1998.
69. Najib Saleh, *Al-'Asr al-Isra'il min Qanat al Swuyis ila Bab al Mandab* (*The Israeli Era from the Suez Canal to Bab al-Mandab*), Dar Aqra, 1983, p. 267.
70. http://www.mfa.gov.il/MFA/Peace+Process/Guide+to+the+Peace+Process/US-Israel+Memorandum+of+Understanding.htm.
71. Yula al-Batl, *Al Ittifaq al Askari*, p. 22.
72. http://www.aipac.org/Publications/AIPACAnalysesIssueBriefs/31-Issue_Brief_Strategic_Coop.pdf.
73. *Isra'il al 'Am 2000* (*Israel in the Year 2000*), Dar al Jil lil Nashr, 1987, p. 39.
74. Stephen D. Isaacs, *Al-Yahud wa Siassa Al Amrikiya* (The Jews and the American Policy), Dar al Ittihad, 1987, p. 227.
75. Yula al-Batl, *Al Ittifaq al Askari*, p. 13.
76. *Khaleej*, 23 Dec. 1987.
77. *Khaleej*, 11 Dec. 1987.
78. Al-Siassa *Al-Dawlya*, vol. 88, April 1987, p. 304.
79. Ibid.
80. http://www.palestinefacts.org/pf_1991to_now_israel_us_support.php.
81. *Al-Ittihad* (Abu Dhabi), 10 Aug. 1979.
82. Munir al-Hur and Tariq al-Mussa, *Mashari' Ataswiyya lil Qadiya Filistiniya 1947–1982* (*Peace Projects for the Palestinian Question*), Dar al Jalil lil Nashr, 1983, p. 75.
83. Aras, 'Post-Cold War Realities', p. 68.
84. http://middleeast.about.com/od/arabisraeliconflict/qt/me081129a.htm.
85. Nadia Mustafa, *Uruba wal Watan al Arabi* (*Europe and Arab Home Land*), Silsilat Athiqafa al Qawmiya, 8, Markaz Dirasat al Wahda al Arabiya, 1987, pp. 79–81.
86. http://www.ena.lu/oil_crisis_netherlands-020703488.html.
87. Mustafa, *Uruba wal Watan al Arabi*, p. 92.
88. Ibid., p. 103.
89. Sadah A. al-Habashinah, 'Al-Siassa al-Urubiah Tijah al-Arab munth Harb 1973 Ila

Mutamar Barshalunah' (The European Policy towards the Arabs between the 1973 war and Barcelona Conference), *Mu'atah*, vol. 22, no. 5, 2007, p. 201.
90. http://www.knesset.gov.il/process/docs/venice_eng.htm.
91. Habashinah, 'Al-Siassa al-Urubiah Tijah', p. 201.
92. Ibid., pp. 197–9.
93. http://www.europa-eu-un.org/articles/en/article_1726_en.htm.
94. http://www.ejpress.org/article/news/eu-israel_affairs/5538.
95. http://www.ejpress.org/article/news/western_europe/6352.
96. http://euobserver.com/9/28260.
97. http://www.haaretz.co.il/hasen/spages/902066.html.
98. http://www.scoop.co.nz/stories/WO0812/S00591.htm.
99. Abdul Fattah al Ahbabi, 'Ifriqia Bayn Ataghalghal al Isra'ili wa al Mawqif al Arabi' (Africa between Israel Inflitration and the Arab Position), *Al-Siassa al-Dawlya*, vol. 78, 1984, p. 153.
100. http://chr.sagepub.com/cgi/pdf_extract/18/5/17.
101. http://209.85.229.132/search?q=cache:jyByz7hU5vIJ:www.ajcarchives.org/AJC_DATA/Files/888.pdf+China+starts+diplomatic+relations+with+Israel&cd=1&hl=en&ct=clnk&gl=uk.
102. Ibid.
103. http://meria.idc.ac.il/journal/2004/issue4/jv8no4a6.html.
104. http://www.haaretz.com/hasen/spages/1042322.html.
105. http://en.wikipedia.org/wiki/India%E2%80%93Israel_relations.
106. Aras, 'Post-Cold War Realities', p. 77.
107. *Al-Kitab Asanawi lil Qadiya al Filistiniya lil 'Am 1968* (*The Year Book for the Palestinian Question 1968*), Mu'asasa al Dirasat al Filistiniya, 1971, p. 954.
108. Halmi Abdul Karim, 'Al Qarah al Ifriqiya wal wliyatuha fi al-Siassa al- Kharijiya al Isra'iliya' (Africa and the Israeli Foreign Policy), *Al Mustaqbal al Arabi* (Beirut), vol. 76, 1985, p. 42.
109. Regina Sharif 1977, http://www.jstor.org/pss/2536530.
110. http://cbs5.com/national/Venezuela.israel.gaza.2.901451.html.
111. http://www.haaretz.com/hasen/spages/1053454.html.
112. Amal al-Shazli, 'Al Atmaa' al Isra'iliya fi al Qurn al Ifriqi' (Israel Ambition in the Horn of Africa), *Al-Siassa al-Dawlya*, vol. 54, 1978, pp. 51–3.
113. Majdi Hammad, *Isra'il wa Afriqiya* (*Israel and Africa*), Dar al Mustaqbal al Arabi, 1985, p. 26.
114. Al-Hur and Al-Mussa, *Mashari' Ataswiyya*, p. 28.
115. Ibid., p. 82.
116. http://daccessdds.un.org/doc/RESOLUTION/GEN/NR0/288/65/IMG/NR028865.pdf?OpenElement.

Chapter 6

1. An 'analytical approach' reveals the essence of the phenomenon, and defines the links between its elements and the way they are formed within its framework, and the revealing of the various stages that the phenomenon passes through in its development. An 'inductive approach' follows the experimental method in studying phenomena in which a researcher moves from individual facts to general hypotheses so that predictions can be made (Mohammed Mahmoud Rabi', *Manahij al Bahath Fi 'alm Asiassa*, Maktaba al Falaah, 1987, pp. 246 and 253).

2. Peace in its linguistic sense is the opposite of conflict. More precisely, it is the stabilization of forces within a legal framework that is dominated by fair treatment and the rule of law. The system would become legal if the rules that shape it are respected by all forces. With relation to the Arab–Israeli conflict, real peace cannot be achieved by settlements that ignore the root causes of the conflict. Any political settlement that is imposed by force without solving the essential problem is merely 'a pause' in the conflict. Nizam Mahmoud Barakat, 'Al Istitan wa Sira' al Arabi al Isra'ili: Al Janib Asiyyasi', *Journal of Social Science* (Kuwait), vol. 23, no. 1, Spring 1995, n. 1, p. 187.
3. Political settlement is conciliation between the aims of all parties involved in the conflict, whether partially or completely, in accordance with the balance of power at the time of conciliation. That means that agreement at that moment expresses the real power of the signatories but it does not express their essential interests and this is what distinguishes it from the peace process.
4. Tawfiq Hasso et al., *Qadhaya Dawliah Mua'sirah* (*Contemporary International Issues*), al-Ain Publishing, 1989, pp. 421–18
5. Reuters, 17 April 2009.
6. *Financial Times*, 17 Jan. 2009.
7. *Jazeera TV* (Arabic), 3 April 2009.
8. Associated France Press, 30 March 2009.
9. http://www.alarab.com.qa/details.php?docId=101011&issueNo=661&secId=15.
10. Associated France Press, 25 March 2009.
11. Ahmed Nofel et al., *Al-Qahyah al-Filistiniah fi Arbaa'un A'ama* (*The Palestinian Question in Forty Years*), Centre for Arab Unity Studies, 1989, pp. 190–2.
12. Hasso et al., *Qadhaya Dawliah Mua'sirah*, p. 211.
13. *Jazeera TV* (Arabic), 16 Dec. 2008.
14. *Jazeera TV* (Arabic), 3 April 2009.
15. Hassan al-Alkim, 'Al Suhywniah al Yahwudiah al Amirikyah wa Tathiraha 'Ala Syassat al Wilayat al Mutahidah al Kharijiah Tijah al 'Alim Al Arabi' (American Jewish Zionism and its Impacts on US Policy Towards the Arab World), *Shu'un Arabiah*, vol. 56, Dec. 1988, pp. 212–26.
16. David Stout, 'Israel Nuclear Arsenal Vexed Nixon', *New York Times*, 29 Nov. 2007.
17. Martin Indyk, *Ma Wra Tawazin al-Qwah: Khyar Amrika fi al-Sharq al-Awsat* (*Beyond the Balance of Power: America's Option in the Middle East*), Centre for Research and Strategic Studies, 1992, p. 9.
18. Richard Nixon, *Ma Wra' al-Salam* (*Beyond Peace*), trans. Malik 'Abbas, Al-Ahlya for Publishing and Distribution, 1995, p. 159.
19. Martin Indyk, 'Siassat Klintun Hial al-Sarq al-Awsat' (Clinton's Policy towards the Middle East), *Drasat Filistiniah*, vol. 15, Summer 1993, pp. 163–52.
20. Associated France Press, 1 April 2009.
21. Bob Woodward, *State of Denial*, Pocket Books, 2007, p. 76.
22. *New York Times*, 22 Nov. 2007.
23. *Jazeera TV* (Arabic), 27 Nov. 2007.
24. Associated France Press, 25 March 2009.
25. Reuters, 7 March 2009.
26. Prestowitz, *Rogue Nation*, p. 358.
27. *Jazeera TV* (Arabic), 3 April 2009.
28. *Investigative Leads*, vol. 9, June 1989.
29. *Los Angeles Times*, 3 June 1991.
30. *New York Times*, 1 June 1991.

31. Munir al Hur and Tariq al Mussa, *Mashari' Ataswiyya lil Qadiya Filistiniya 1947–1982* (*Peace Projects for the Palestinian Question*), Dar al Jalil lil Nashr, 1983, pp. 200–1.
32. Shai Feldman, 'Missiles and CBW Proliferation', Proceedings of the Annual Meeting Symposium, New Orleans, 1990, p. 14.
33. Hassan Al Alkim, 'The Arabs and the Changing World Order', *The Middle East and African Studies*, 1993, p. 343.
34. Shimon Peres, *Ma'rakat Assalam: Yuwmiyat* (*The Battle for Peace: Diary*), trans. Ammar Fadhil wa Malik Fadhil, Al Ahliya for Publication and Distribution, 1995, pp. 379–68.
35. Nixon, *Ma Wra' al-Salam*, p. 158.
36. A. Abdullah Wild Abah, 'Al-Taswyah fi al-Sharq al-Awsat wa Mustaqbal al-Nidham al-Arabi' (Middle East Settlement and the Future of the Arab System), *Al-Mustaqbal al-Arabi*, vol. 192, Feb. 1995, p. 34.
37. *Al Khaleej*, 11 Nov. 1989.
38. Peres, *Ma'rakat Assalam*, p. 370.
39. Ghassan Salama, 'Al Arab wa Isra'il wa Amrika wal Mufawadat' (The Arab and Israeli American Conflict', *Al-Mustaqbal al Arabi*, vol. 172, June 1993, pp. 8–6.
40. *The Economist*, 26 March 2009.
41. Bashir Nafi, 'Ittifaq Ghaza-Ariha: Nuqat al Da'af wal Quwwa' (Gaza–Jericho Agreement), *Shu'un Asharq Al Awsat*, vol. 24, 1993, pp. 20–19.
42. Ibid., p. 20.
43. Peres, *Ma'rakat Assalam*, p. 372.
44. Ibid., p. 381.
45. Ibid., pp. 428–9.
46. See the economic development programme for the region, article B of the fourth supplement specializing in the Arab–Israeli cooperation protocol in development programmes in the region and the Declaration of Principles regarding the arrangements for transitional self-government, Sept. 1993.
47. A. Abdullah Wild Abah, 'Al-Taswyah fi al-Sharq al-Awsat', pp. 37–41.
48. The majority support continuing negotiations with Israel, *Al Watan*, 2 May 1992.
49. Jamal Mazloum, 'On the Thirtieth Anniversary of Arab–Israeli Peace Negotiations', *Al Ittihad*, 26 Oct. 1994.
50. Za'if Shayf, 'Al Maksab al Istratijji li Isra'il wal Urdun', *Dirasat al-Filistiniya*, vol. 20, Autumn 1994, p. 113.
51. *Khaleej*, 12 March 2009.
52. M. Muslih, 'The Golan: Israel and Syria: Strategic Calculation', *Middle East Journal*, vol. 47, no. 4, 1993, p. 625.
53. *Al-Mussawar*, 2 Dec. 1994, p. 25.
54. Reuters, 7 March 2009.
55. *Khaleej*, 9 March 2009.
56. Ayman Abdel Wahhab, Assayed, 'Al Massar al Suri al Isra'ili wa Ma'uqat al Safqa al Kamila', *Al-Siassa al-Dawlya*, vol. 120, April 1995, p. 221.
57. *Jazeera TV* (Arabic), 28 Oct. 2009.
58. Ghassan Salama, 'Afkar Uwliya 'an Asuq Asharq Awsatiya' (Preliminary Thoughts on the Middle Eastern Market), *Al Mustaqbal al Arabi*, vol. 179, Jan. 1994, p. 68.
59. Belgium, Holland and Luxembourg.
60. Salama, 'Afkar Uwliya 'an Asuq Asharq Awsatiya', p. 75.
61. Bernard Lewis, 'Rethinking the Middle East', *Foreign Affairs*, vol. 74, no. 4, Autumn 1992, p. 10.

62. Mohammed Sayyed Said, 'Mustabal Anizam al Iqlimi al Arabi', *'Alam al Ma'rifa*, vol. 158, Feb. 1992, pp. 40–1.
63. Indyk, *Ma Wra Tawazin al-Qwah*, p. 19.
64. Said, 'Mustabal Anizam al Iqlimi al Arabi', p. 16.
65. Hassan al-Alkim, *The GCC States in an Unstable World: Foreign Policy Dilemmas of Small States*, Saqi Books, 1994, p. 121.
66. Riyad Najeeb Arris, *Riyah Asumuh* (*The Western Winds*), Riyad Arris lil Kutub wal Nashr, 1994, pp. 190–1.
67. *International Herald Tribune*, 22 Aug. 1995.
68. *Al Ittihad*, 20 Aug. 1995.
69. Peres, *Ma'rakat Assalam*, pp. 332–3.
70. *Al Khaleej*, 7 Oct. 1995.
71. Mahjub Omar, *Al-Sira' al-Arabi al-Israeli wa Sidam al-Hadharat* (*Arab–Israeli Conflict and the Clash of Civilizations*), Centre for Research and Strategic Studies, 1995.
72. Nizam Mahmoud Barakat, 'Al Istitan wa Sira' al Arabi al Isra'ili' (Settlements and Arab– Israeli Conflict), *Journal of Social Science* (Kuwait), vol. 23, no. 1, Spring 1995, p. 166.
73. Samuel Toledano, *Jazeera TV* (Arabic), 10 April 2009.
74. Nixon, *Ma Wra' al-Salam*, p. 158.
75. Hassan al-Alkim, 'Azmat al-Miyah fil Watan al Arabi' (Water Crisis in the Arab Homeland), *Journal of Social Science* (Kuwait), vol. 23, no. 3, Autumn 1995, p. 12.
76. *Khaleej*, 7 Oct. 1995.
77. Al-Alkim, 'Azmat al-Miyah fil Watan al Arabi', p. 19.
78. Omar, *Al-Sira' al-Arabi al-Israeli*, p. 120.
79. Interview with *Jazeera TV* (Arabic), 10 April 2009.

Chapter 7

1. Mohammed Rabi', *Manahij al Bahath Fi 'alm Asiassa*, Maktaba al Falah, 1987, p. 246.
2. Ibid., p. 253.
3. *Arab Human Development Report,* 2009, p. 37.
4. *Khaleej*, 21 July 1993.
5. *Al-Ittihad*, 11 Dec. 1993.
6. http://go.worldbank.org/JGN8LCSFPO.
7. *Arab Human Development Report*, 2009, p. 3.
8. Ibid., p. 41.
9. Stephan Libiszewski, *Water Disputes in the Jordan Basin Region and their Role in the Resolution of the Arab–Israeli Conflict*, Centre for Security Policy and Conflict Analysis, Swiss Peace Foundation, 13 Aug. 1995, p. 7.
10. Charles Maynes, 'The Middle East in the Twenty-First Century', *Middle East Journal*, vol. 52, no. 1, Winter 1998, p. 15.
11. www. Scribd.com/water in the middle east.
12. *Arab Human Development Report,* 2009, p. 139.
13. http://go.worldbank.org/JGN8LCSFPO.
14. Cited in Libiszewski, *Water Disputes*, p. 12.
15. *Arab Human Development Report,* 2009, p. 139.
16. *Financial Times*, 27 Feb. 2008.
17. *Al Ittihad*, 20 Jan. 1994.

18. *Al-Taqrir al-Iqtisadi al-Arabi al-Muahad* (*Unified Arab Economic Report*), Arab Monetary Fund, 1993, p. 81.
19. *Arab Human Development Report,* 2009, p. 38.
20. Ibid., p. 39.
21. Despite the existence of conflicts over water between some Arab countries and the consequent effects on Arab water security, this study has dealt with the Arabs as one political unit in facing the external dangers that threaten Arab national security.
22. *Arab Human Development Report,* 2009, p. 37.
23. Maynes, 'Middle East in the Twenty-First Century', p. 16.
24. Reuters, 18 March 2008.
25. *Arab Human Development Report,* 2009, p. 39.
26. *Al-Iqtisad al-Islami*, vol. 150, Oct. 1993, pp. 45–61.
27. Mahmoud Ahmed, *Israil wal Miyah al Arabiya* (*Israel and the Arab Water*), Dar al Mustaqbal al Arabi, 1991, p. 208.
28. Abdul Amir Dakroub, 'Mustaqbal Asiraa' Huwla al Miyah fi Asharq Al Awsat' (The future of the Conflict over Middle Eastern Water), *Al Fikr al Arabi,* vol. 76, Spring 1994, p. 210.
29. *Al-Ittihad*, 4 March 1993.
30. *Al-Ittihad*, 31 May 1993.
31. http://go.worldbank.org/JGN8LCSFPO.
32. *Al-Hawadith*, 18 Feb. 1994.
33. Abbas Qassim, 'Al-Amtaa' bil Miyah al Arabiya wa Ab'aduha Ajiyulitikiya', *Al-Mustaqbal al-Arabi*, 174, Aug. 1993, p. 18.
34. *Al-Ittihad*, 25 Oct. 1993.
35. Libiszewski, *Water Disputes*, p. 21.
36. *Al-Ittihad*, 28 Feb.1994
37. Ahmad, *Israil wal Miyah al Arabiya*, p. 208.
38. *Environmental Law Reporter*, vol. 33, no. 10207, 2003.
39. *Al-Hawadith*, 18 Feb. 1994.
40. Nabil Samman, *Israil wa Miyah al Arabiya: Harb al Miyah min al Furat ila Nil* (*Israel and the Arab: Water War from the Nile to Euphrates*), N.P., 1990, p. 87.
41. Dakroub, 'Mustaqbal Asiraa' Huwla al Miyah fi Asharq Al Awsat', p. 222.
42. Libiszewski, *Water Disputes*, p. 13.
43. Cited ibid., p. 13.
44. *Al-Ittihad*, 31 May 1993.
45. *Al-Ittihad*, 25 Oct. 1993.
46. Libiszewski, *Water Disputes*, p. 16.
47. *Jazeera TV* (Arabic), 29 Oct. 2009.
48. *Al-Ittihad*, 3 March 1994.
49. Hassan Bakr, 'Al Mandhour al Maee lil Sira' al Arabi al Israili' (Water Perspective in the Arab–Israeli Conflict), *Al-Siassa al-Dawlya*, April 1991, vol. 104, p. 140.
50. Hamdi al-Tahir, *Mustaqbal al Miyah Fil Alam al Arabi* (*Water Prospects in the Arab World*), 1991, p. 332.
51. *Al-Ittihad*, 25 July 1993.
52. Bakr, 'Al Mandhour al Maee lil Sira' al Arabi al Israili', p. 133.
53. Libiszewski, *Water Disputes*, p. 23.
54. Ibid., p. 141.
55. Reuters, 18 Sept. 2008.
56. *Al-Ittihad*, 31 May 1993.
57. Libiszewski, *Water Disputes*, p. 19.

58. *Al-Ittihad*, 25 Oct. 1993.
59. Libiszewski, *Water Disputes*, p. 20.
60. Samman, *Israil wa Miyah al Arabiya*, 1990, p. 90.
61. *Al-Ittihad*, 25 Oct. 1993.
62. *Al-'Usbu' al Arabi*, 14 March 1994, p. 21.
63. Libiszewski, *Water Disputes*, p. 15.
64. Ibid., p. 13.
65. Ibid., p. 22.
66. *Al-Siassa*, 29 March 1993.
67. Libiszewski, *Water Disputes*, p. 22.
68. Ibid., pp. 23–8.
69. Al-Tahir, *Mustaqbal al Miyah Fil Alam al Arabi*, pp. 346–7.
70. Fathi A. Hussain, "Al-Miyah fi al- Mufawadhat Muta'adidat al-Atraf" (Water in the Multi Parties Negotiations) *Al-Siassa Al- Dawlya*, no. 108, April 1992, p. 346.
71. *Al-Hawadith*, 18 Feb. 1994, p. 17.
72. Al-Tahir, *Mustaqbal al Miyah Fil Alam al Arabi,* 1991, p. 356.
73. *Al-Ittihad*, 25 Oct. 1993.
74. Samman, *Israil wa Miyah al Arabiya*, p. 141.
75. *Al-Wasat*, 24 April 1994, p. 23.
76. Libiszewski, *Water Disputes*, p. 16.
77. *Al-Siassa*, 29 March 1993.
78. Majdi Subhi, "Azmat al- Miyah fi al- Mufawadhat al-Muta'adidah" (Water Crisis in the Muti Parties Negotitations) *Al-Siassa Al-Dawlya*, no. 114, Oct. 1993, p. 129.
79. *Al-Ittihad*, 25 Oct. 1993.
80. *Al-Ittihad*, 4 March 1993.
81. *Al-Wasat*, 24 April 1994, p. 22.
82. *Environmental Law Reporter*, vol. 33, no. 10207, 2003.
83. Libiszewski, *Water Disputes*, p. 7.
84. Peter Allison, 'Water Wars: The Global Viewpoint', *Global Water Intelligence*, www.itt.com/waterbook/worldiasp, 8 April 2009.
85. 'Global Water Shortage Looms in New Century', http:/ag.arizona/AZWATER/awr/dec99/feature2.htm.
86. *Al-Safir*, 11 Oct. 1993.
87. *Al-Ittihad*, 31 May 1993.
88. *Al-Safir*, 11 Oct. 1993.
89. Associated France Press, 25 March 2009.
90. *Khaleej*, 17 Sept. 2009.
91. *Jazeera TV* (Arabic), 3 Dec. 2009.
92. *Al-Bayan*, 3 April 1992.
93. Allison, 'Water Wars'.
94. Abdullah Al Sultan," 'Athyubia: al-Bahr al-Ahmar wa al- Sira'a al-Arabi al-Israili wa al-Tanafis bin al-Astratyjitayin'(Ethiopia: the Red Sea and the Arab- Israeli Conflict and the Competition between the Two Strategies) Beirut, Centre for Arab Unity Studies, 1984, p. 93.
95. Qassim, 'Al-Amtaa' bil Miyah al Arabiya wa Ab'aduha Ajiyulitikiya', p. 37.
96. Libiszewski, *Water Disputes*, p. 28.
97. *Arab Human Development Report,* 2009, p. 39.

Chapter 8

1. *Sharjah TV*, 17 Oct. 2009.
2. *Jazeera TV* (Arabic), 15 Nov. 2009.
3. Said Hareb, 'Thaqafa wa Juw'a' (Culture and Hunger) http://www.awan.com/pages/oped/228887
4. 'Analytical methods' reveal the essence of the phenomenon and define the relationship between its elements and how they are formed within a general framework. They reveal the various stages the phenomenon passes through in its movement and development. Rabi', *Manahij al Bahath Fi Uluwm Assiyasiyya*, p. 246.
5. The 'inductive approach' means following the experimental method in studying phenomena in which a researcher moves from individual facts to general hypotheses so that predictions can be made. Ibid., p. 253.
6. 'The Food Problem in Arab Countries', a study prepared by the Arab Organization for Agricultural Development, presented to the organization's council 11th session (Damascus, Dec. 1980), *Shu'un Arabiya*, vol 11, Jan. 1982. Adnan Hiza' al Biyati, 'Attasahur wa Azmat al Ghida fil Watan al Arabi', *Shu'un al Arabiya*, vol. 74, 1993.
7. *Arab Human Development Report,* 2009, p. 138.
8. *Al Usbu' al Arabi*, 29 Nov. 1993
9. Khalid Tahsin Ali, 'Azmat al-Ghitha wa al-'Amal al-'Arabi al- Mushtarak' (Food Crisis and the Joint Arab Work), *Al-Mustaqbal al-Arabi,* vol. 123, May 1989, pp. 99–100.
10. *Ataqrir al Iqtisadi al Arabi al Muwahhad (Arab Economic Report),* 1993; *Human Development Report*, 1993.
11. One hectare (= 10,000 square metres).
12. *Arab Human Development Report,* 2009, p. 141.
13. Hassan Hamdan al-Alkim, "Azmat al-Miyah fil Watan al-Arabi' wa al-Harb al-muhtamilah (Water Crisis in the Arab Homeland and the Potential of War)', *Journal of Social Science* (Kuwait), vol. 23, no. 3, Autumn 1995.
14. *Arab Human Development Report* 2009, p. 139.
15. *Al-Taqrir al-Iqtisadi al-Arabi Al-Muwahad,* 2008, pp. 49–50.
16. Ibid., p. 141.
17. George Fu'ad, 'Azmat al Aman al Ghida'i al Arabi'(Arab Food Crisis), *Al-Ittihad*, 23 Feb. 1993.
18. One dunum is an agricultural measurement: one is equivalent to 1,000 square metres.
19. Abdatniyan al-Thanyan, *Al Aman al Ghida'i wal 'Amal al 'Arabi al Mushtarik (Food Security & The Arab Joint Efforts)*, Dar al Firk al Mu'asir, 1990, p. 30.
20. George Fu'ad, op.cit..
21. Fallow – whereby the land is left for over a year without seeding.
22. *Arab Human Development Report,* 2009, p. 41.
23. *Al-Taqrir al-Iqtisadi al-Arabi al-Muwahad,* 2008, pp. 54–,5.
24. *Arab Human Development Report,* 2009, p. 140.
25. *Khaleej,* 10 April 1993.
26. Food Problem in Arab Countries, *Shu'un Arabiya*, vol. 11, Jan. 1982. Adnan Hiza' al Biyati, 'Attasahur wa Azmar al Ghida fil Watan al Arabi', *Shu'un al Arabiya*, vol. 74, 1993, p. 97.
27. *Arab Human Development Report.* 2009, p. 128.
28. Al-Thanyan, *Al Aman al Ghida'i,* p. 30.
29. *Taqrir al Iqtisadi al Arabi al Muwahhad*, 1993, pp. 80–2.
30. http://go.worldbank.org/3SRT6N96H0, issued on 2 July 2008.

31. *Arab Human Development Report*. 2009, p. 136.
32. Al-Thanyan, *Al Aman al Ghida'i*, p. 30.
33. *Arab Human Development Report,* 2009, p. 139 .
34. *Khaleej*, 10 March 1993.
35. The Food Problem in Arab Countries, *Shu'un Arabiya*, vol. 11, Jan. 1982. Adnan Hiza' al Biyati, 'Attasahur wa Azmar al Ghida fil Watan al Arabi', *Shu'un al Arabiya*, vol. 74, 1993, pp. 79–80.
36. *Al-Bayan*, 5 Oct. 2009.
37. *Al-Taqrir al-Iqtisadi al-Arabi al-Muwahhad*, 2008, p. 61.
38. http://go.worldbank.org/3SRT6N96H0, issued on 2 July 2008.
39. *Arab Human Development Report,* 2009, p. 135.
40. http://go.worldbank.org/3SRT6N96H0, issued on 2 July 2008.
41. *Jazeera TV* (Arabic), 22 Oct. 2009.
42. *Arab Human Development Report,* 2009, p. 138.
43. *Al-Taqrir al Iqtisadi al Arabi al Muwahhad*, 2008, p. 60.
44. 'The Food Problem in Arab Countries', p. 80.
45. *Al-Taqrir al Iqtisadi al Arabi al Muwahhad*, 2008, p. 61.
46. *Financial Times*, 27 Feb. 2008.
47. *Arab Human Development Report,* 2009, p. 131.
48. Abdullahl-Thanyan, *Al Aman al Ghida'i,* p. 44.
49. *Financial Times*, 27 Feb. 2008.
50. Hassan H. al-Alkim, 'Azmat al-Ghitha fi al- Wattan al-Arabi (Food Crisis in the Arab Homeland), *Al-Siassa al-Dawlya*, vol. 123, Jan. 1996, p. 14.
51. *Al-Taqrir al Iqtisadi al Arabi al Muwahhad,* 2008, p. 59.
52. Ibid., p. 61.
53. 'The Food Problem in Arab Countries', pp. 80–1.
54. Adnan Hiza' al Biyati, 'Attasahur wa Azmar al Ghida fil Watan al Arabi', *Shu'un al Arabiya*, vol. 74, 1993, p. 191.
55. *Al-Taqrir al Iqtisadi al Arabi al Muwahhad (Arab Economic Report),* 1994, p. 42.
56. *Al-Taqrir al Iqtisadi al Arabi al Muwahhad,* 1993, pp. 80–2.
57. *Al-Taqrir al Iqtisadi al Arabi al Muwahhad,* 1994, p. 42.
58. *Khaleej*, 7 Oct. 2009.
59. *Al-Taqrir al Iqtisadi al Arabi al Muwahad* 2008, p. 63.
60. *Al-Taqrir al Iqtisadi al Arabi al Muwahad,* 1993, p. 89.
61. *Al-Taqrir al Iqtisadi al Arabi al Muwahad,* 2008, p. 61.
62. Ibid.
63. http://go.worldbank.org/3SRT6N96H0, issued on 2 July 2008.
64. Ibid.
65. *Arab Human Development Report,* 2009, p. 123.
66. Ibid., p. 126.
67. George Fu'ad, op. cit..
68. *Arab Human Development Report,* 2009, p. 123.
69. Abdullahl-Thanyan, *Al Aman al Ghida'i*, pp. 488–9.
70. 'The Food Problem in Arab Countries', pp. 89–93.
71. *Arab Human Development Report*. 2009, p. 133.
72. Mohammed al Amadi, 'Al Aman al Ghada'i wa Ta'awan al Arabi' (Food Security and the Inter Arab Cooperation), *Shu'un Arabiya*, vol. 23, Feb. 1983, p. 37.
73. World Socialist web site, http://www.wsws.org/articles/2005/may2005/iraq-m18.shtml
74. *Human Development Report,* 1994, pp. 42–3.

75. Adnan Hiza' al Biyati, 'Attasahur wa Azmar al Ghida fil Watan al Arabi', *Shu'un al Arabiya*, vol. 74, 1993, pp. 190–1.
76. George Fu'ad, op. cit..
77. *Arab Human Development Report,* 2009, p. 124.
78. *Al-Taqrir al Iqtisadi al Arabi al Muwahad,* 1993, pp. 80–2.
79. *Al-Taqrir al Iqtisadi al Arabi al Muwahad,* 2009, p. 44.
80. *Financial Times*, 14 April 2009.
81. For further detail please see Hassan al Alkim, 'Azmat al Miyah fil Watan al Arabi.
82. George Fu'ad, op. cit..
83. 'The Food Problem in Arab Countries'.
84. Mohammed al Amadi, 'Al Aman al Ghada'i wa Ta'awan al Arabi', *Shu'un Arabiya*, vol. 23, Feb. 1983, pp. 39–40.
85. Tawfiq Abdul Azim, *Asafeer*, 1 Jan. 1993.
86. *Al-Taqrir al-Iqtisadi al-Arabi al-Muwahad* 2008, p. 53.
87. *Human Development Report,* 1994, pp. 50–1.
88. Please see interview with the UAE businessman in *Shorouk*, vol. 163, 22 May 1995, pp. 30–5.
89. Khaled Tahseen Ali, 'Al Aman al Ghada'I wal Amal Arabi al Mushtarik, Malaf al Aman al Qawmi al Arabi', *Shu'un Arabiya*, vol. 35, Jan. 1984, pp. 125–7.
90. Abdullahl-Thanyan, *Al Aman al Ghada',* 1990, p. 480.
91. Mohammed al Fara, *Nahu Istratijiyya Muwahhada li Muwajiha Mushkilat al Intaj al Arabi min al Ghida* (*Towards a Unified Strategy to Counter The Problem of Grain Production*), p. 70.
92. Bernard Lewis, 'Rethinking the Middle East', *Foreign Affairs*, vol. 75, no. 4, Autumn 1992.
93. Al Fara, *Nahu Istratijiyya Muwahhada,* op.cit., p. 73.
94. Tawfiq Abdul Azim', 'Al Aman al Ghida'i al Arabi', *Asafeer*, 1 Jan. 1993.
95. Mohammed al Amadi, 'Al Aman al Ghada'i wa Ta'awan al Arabi', *Shu'un Arabiya*, vol. 23, Feb. 1983, pp. 39–40.

Chapter 9

1. Hussein Abu Talib, 'Asus Assyassa al Kharijiya Asa'udiya', *Al-siassa al-Dawlya*, vol. 90, Oct. 1987, p. 38.
2. For further details see Ismail Sabri Muqalled, *Al-Illaqat al-Syassya al-Dawlya* (International Political Relations), 5th edn, Thaat al Salasil, 1978, pp. 14–15.
3. *Al-Ittihad*, 2 March 1992.
4. J. B. Kelly, *Arabia, the Gulf and the West*, Weidenfield & Nicolson, 1980, p. 229.
5. Ibid.
6. Ibid., p. 236.
7. Robert Lacey, *The Kingdom*, Fontana Paperbacks, 1982, p. 216.
8. David Holden and Richard Johns, *The House of Saud*, Pan Books, 1983, p. 104.
9. Lacey, *Kingdom*, p. 263.
10. Sluglett and Marion Farouk-Sluglett, 'The Precarious Monarchy: Britain and Abdalaziz Ibn Saud', in Tim Niblock (ed.), *State, Society and Economy in Saudi Arabia*, Croom Helm, 1982, p. 37.
11. Lacey, *Kingdom*, p. 219.

12. Kelly, *Arabia the Gulf and the West*, p. 64.
13. For more information see Hassan H. al-Alkim, *The Foreign Policy of the United Arab Emirates*, Saqi, 1989, pp. 108–36.
14. Rosemary Zahlan, *The Origin of the United Arab Emirates*, Macmillan, 1978, pp. 69–70.
15. Fred Halliday, 'A Curious and Close Liason: Saudi Arabia's Relations with the United States', in Tim Niblock (ed.), *State, Society and Economy in Saudi Arabia, London: Croom Helm, 1982, p. 126.*
16. Amil Nakhla, *Amrika wa Sa'udiya (America & Saudi Arabia)*, Dar al Hikma lil Nashr, 1980, p. 59.
17. James Buchan, "Secular and Religious Opposition in Saudi Arabia', in Tim Niblock, *State, Society and Economy in Saudi Arabia*, p. 107.
18. Adeed Dawisha, 'Saudi Arabia Search for Security', *Strategic Studies*, 1979, p. 9.
19. *Arab Record and Report*, 1973,
20. *The Memoirs of Cyrus Vance*, 2nd edn, Al Markaz al Arabi lil Ma'lumat, 1974, p. 64.
21. Adeed Dawisha, 'The Middle East', in Christopher Clapham (ed.), *Foreign Policy Making in Developing States*, Saxon House, 1977, p. 55.
22. Lacey, *Kingdom*, p. 374
23. William Quant, *Saudi Arabia in the 1980s*, Brookings Institute, 1981, p. 10.
24. Fred Halliday, op. cit., p. 126.
25. Morris Mehrdad Mottale, *The Arms Buildup in the Persian Gulf*, University Press of America, 1986, p. 114.
26. Rosemary Zahlan, 'King Abdul-Aziz's Changing Relationship with the Gulf States during the 1930s', in Tim Niblock (ed.), *State, Society and Economy in Saudi Arabia*, p. 65.
27. Harold Wilson, *The Labour Government 1964–1970: A Personal Record*, Weidenfeld & Nicolson, 1971, p. 396.
28. F. Gregory Gause, 'British and American Policies in the Persian Gulf 1968–1973', *Review of International Studies*, vol. 11, no. 4, Oct. 1985, p. 253.
29. Lacey, *Kingdom*, p. 385.
30. Talib, 'Asus Assyassa al Kharijiya Asa'udiya', p. 48.
31. Nakhla, *Amrika wa Sa'udiya*, pp. 98–9.
32. Dawisha, 'Saudi Arabia's Search for Security', p. 22.
33. For more information see Hussein Musa, *Al Ittifaqiyat al-Ma'quda bayn al-Wilayat al-Mutahida wa Duwul Majlis al-Ta'wan* (*The Concluded Agreements between the US and the GCC States*), Al Haqiqa Press, 1987.
34. Lacey, *Kingdom*, p. 341.
35. Ibid., pp. 376–8.
36. Kelly, *Arabia the Gulf and the West*, p. 239.
37. J. E. Peterson, Saudi Arabia and the Illusion of Security, op. cit., p. 43.
38. *Financial Times*, 30 March 2009.
39. http://arabic.arabia.msn.com/news/middleeast/Reuters/2009/June/829440Update.aspx.
40. https://www.cia.gov/library/publications/the-world-factbook/geos/sa.html.
41. J. E. Peterson, Saudi Arabia and the Illusion of Security, op.cit., p. 57.
42. Lacey, *Kingdom*, pp. 374–82.
43. Dawisha, 'Saudi Arabia's Search for Security', p. 7.
44. For more information, see *Intifada al Mantiqa Asharqiya*, Manzama Athuwra al-Islamiyya fi al-Jazeera al Arabiya, 1981.

45. Please see Safar Abdul Rahman al Hawali, *Kashaf al Ghimma 'an 'Ulama al Umma* (*Unveiling the Hidden for the Muslim Nation Scholars*), Iqra Publication, 1991.
46. *Financial Times*, 10 April 2009.
47. *Financial Times*, 17 Aug. 2009.
48. http://www.dp-news.com/pages/detail.aspx?articleId=16755.
49. Derek Hopwood, 'The Ideological Bases, Ibn Abdul Wahad, Muslim Revival', in Niblock (ed.), *State, Society and Economy in Saudi Arabia*, p. 30.
50. Enver Khoury, *The Saudi Decision-Making Body: The House of Saud*, Institute of Middle Eastern and North African Affairs, 1978, p. 16.
51. Ibid., p. 36.
52. Tim Niblock, 'The Saudi Political System', in Niblock (ed.), *State, Society and Economy in Saudi Arabia*, op. cit., pp. 88–90.
53. J. E. Peterson, Saudi Arabia and the Illusion of Security, op.cit., p.p. 48- 50.
54. Dawisha, 'Saudi Arabia's Search for Security', p. 20.
55. Please see the interview with Lakhdar Brahimi in *Ukkaz*, 20 Nov. 1992.
56. Baghat Korany and Ali H. Dessouki, *The Foreign Policies of Arab States*, Westview Press, 1984, p. 245.
57. *Al-Taqrir Istratiji al Arabi 1988*, Mu'asasa al Ahram, 1989, p. 11.
58. *Al-Taqrir al-Iqtisadi al-Arabi al-Mwahad* 2008, p. 282.
59. https://www.cia.gov/library/publications/the-world-factbook/geos/sa.html.
60. *The Military Balance 2001- 2002, p. 145.*
61. *Al-Taqrir al-Iqtisadi al-Arabi al-Mwahad,* 1988, p. 212.
62. Ibid., p. 317.
63. *Al-Taqrir al-Iqtisadi al-Arabi al-Mwahad*, 2008, p. 283.
64. Ibid., p. 287.
65. *Al-Taqrir al-Iqtisadi al-Arabi al-Mwahad*, 2008, p. 288.
66. Ibid., p. 292.
67. *Al-Taqrir al-Iqtisadi al-Arabi al-Mwahad*, 1985, p. 323.
68. *Al-Taqrir al-Iqtisadi al-Arabi al-Mwahad*, 2008, p. 292.
69. Nakhla, *Amrika wa Sa'udiya*, p. 43.
70. Kelly, *Arabia the Gulf and the West*, p. 251.
71. Talib, 'Asus Assyassa al Kharijiya Asa'udiya', pp. 40–1.
72. J. E. Peterson, op.cit., p. 49.
73. Buchan, 'Secular and Religious Opposition', in Niblock (ed.), *State, Society and Economy in Saudi Arabia*, pp. 117–18.
74. Talib, 'Asus Assyassa al Kharijiya Asa'udiya', p. 47.
75. https://www.cia.gov/library/publications/the-world-factbook/geos/sa.html.
76. *Financial Times*, 6 Sept. 2009.
77. https://www.cia.gov/library/publications/the-world-factbook/geos/sa.html.
78. *Financial Times*, 8 Sept. 2009.
79. *Al-Taqrir al-Iqtisadi al-Arabi al-Mwahad*, 1986, p. 382.
80. *Al Nashara al Iqtisadiya*, (*Water Security for the GCC States*), Riyadh: The GCC Secretariat, 1990, p. 97.
81. *Al-Taqrir al-Iqtisadi al-Arabi al-Mwahad*, 1987, p. 311.
82. *Al-Taqrir 'an Tanmiyya fil 'Alam 1987*, published by the World Bank, June 1987, trans. by al Ahram for translation and publishing, Cairo, p. 221.
83. *The Military Balance 1986–87*, 1976, p. 106.
84. https://www.cia.gov/library/publications/the-world-factbook/geos/sa.html.
85. *Al-Taqrir al-Iqtisadi al-Arabi al-Mwahad*, 2008, p. 346.
86. *South*, Nov. 1987, p. 49.

87. https://www.cia.gov/library/publications/the-world-factbook/geos/sa.html.
88. *Al-Taqrir al-Iqtisadi al-Arabi al-Mwahad*, 1982, p. 333.
89. *Al-Taqrir al-Iqtisadi al-Arabi al-Mwahad*, 2008, p. 372.
90. *Al Nashara al Iqtisadiya*, op.cit., pp. 93–4.
91. *The Military Balance 1991–92*, 1991, p. 117.
92. *Al-Taqrir al-Iqtisadi al-Arabi al-Mwahad*, 2008, p. 318.
93. *The Military Balance 1987–88*, 1986.
94. Khalid Tahsin Ali, 'Azmat al Ghida wa al-'Amal al Iqtisadi al Mushtarak' (Food Crisis and the Shared Economic Hope) *Al-Mustaqbal al-Arabi*, vol. 123, May 1989, p. 103.
95. *Al-Taqrir al-Iqtisadi al-Arabi al-Mwahad,* 2008, p. 304.
96. *Al-Taqrir al-Iqtisadi al-Arabi al-Mwahad,* 1990, p. 267.
97. Mahmoud al Maraghi, *Nufuz min Tiraz Khas: Dirasa Hawl Ahwal al Nafd wa Mutaghayarat al-Thamaniyat* (*Influence of Special Nature*), Dar al Mustaqbal al Arabi, p. 19.
98. *Al-Taqrir al-Iqtisadi al-Arabi al-Mwahad*, 2008, p. 292.
99. Ibid., p. 295.
100. https://www.cia.gov/library/publications/the-world-factbook/geos/sa.html.
101. Ismail Mohammed Da'is, 'Al Musa'dat al Kharijiya al Imrikiyya wal Musa'dat Asa'udiya', *Dirasa Sau'ida*, vol. 5, 1991, p. 100.
102. Ibid., p. 98.
103. *Al-Taqrir al-Iqtisadi al-Arabi al-Mwahad*, 1987, p. 267.
104. Nakhla, *Amrika wa Sa'udiya*, p. 56.
105. Talib, 'Asus Assyassa al Kharijiya Asa'udiya', p. 42.
106. *Al-Ittihad*, 17 Jan. 1991.
107. Dawisha, 'Saudi Arabia's Search for Security', pp. 20–1.
108. https://www.cia.gov/library/publications/the-world-factbook/geos/sa.html#Military.
109. *The Military Balance 2004–2005*, p. 135.
110. *Khaleej,* 16 April 1989.
111. *The Military Balance 1991–1992*, pp. 117–18.
112. Kelly, *Arabia the Gulf and the West*, p. 264.
113. *The Military Balance 1991–1992*, pp. 117–18.
114. *The Military Balance 2004–2005*, pp. 135–6.
115. BBC World Service, Arabic Service, 11 June 1987.
116. *Khaleej*, 16 April 1989.
117. *Al-Ittihad*, 16 June 1989.
118. *Financial Times*, 17 April 2008.
119. *Khaleej*, 18 April 1989.
120. *Al-Ittihad*, 19 May 1988.
121. https://www.cia.gov/library/publications/the-world-factbook/geos/sa.html.
122. *The Military Balance 1991–92*, 1991, pp. 105–18.
123. David Long, 'Saudi Arabia and its Neighbours: Preoccupied Paternalism', in Richard Sindelan and J. E. Peterson (eds), *Cross Current in the Gulf*, Routledge, 1988, p. 190.
124. Nadav Safran, *Saudi Arabia: The Ceaseless Quest for Security*, Belknap Press, 1985, p. 265.
125. Long, 'Saudi Arabia and its Neighbours', p. 192.
126. Safran, *Saudi Arabia*, p. 234.
127. J. E. Peterson, Saudi Arabia and the Illusion of Security, op.cit., p. 15.
128. Joseph Kostiner, 'Saudi Arabia and the Arab-Israeli Peace Process: The Fluctuation

of Regional Coordination', *British Journal of Middle Eastern Studies*, vol. 36, no. 3, December 2009, p. 425.
129. J. E. Peterson, Saudi Arabia and the Illusion of Security, op.cit., p. 16.
130. Ibid., p. 15.
131. Martin Indyk, 'The Honeymoon's Over for Bush and the Saudis', *Washington Post*, 29 April 2007, cited in Joseph Kostiner, op.cit., p. 428.
132. John A. Duke, 'Aspects of Saudi Arabia's Relations with Other Gulf States', in Niblock (ed.), *State, Society and Economy in Saudi Arabia*, p. 160.
133. Tim Niblock, 'Iraqi Policies towards the Arab States of the Gulf', in Niblock (ed.), *Iraq: The Contemporary State*, Croom Helm, 1988, p. 133.
134. M. Abir, *Saudi Arabia in the Oil Era*, Croom Helm, 1988, p. 112.
135. Hassan al-Alkim, 'Al 'Alaqaat Khaleejiya al-Arabiya ma' Iran' (Arab Gulf Relations with Iran), *Arab Journal of International Relations*, Winter 1990, p. 64.
136. Herman Elliots, 'Ma'tiyat al Aman fi Khalij al Farsi', UAE Foreign Ministry Archive, 1981, pp. 18–19, unpublished.
137. Quant, *Saudi Arabia in the 1980s*, p. 52.
138. Sophia Beernaerts, 'Economic, Political and Legal Aspects of Cooperation between the European Economic Community and the Countries Parties Charter of Cooperation Council for the Arab States of the Gulf', dissertation, 1989, p. 21.
139. Al-Alkim, 'Al 'Alaqaat Khaleejiya al-Arabiya ma' Iran', p. 45.
140. M. A. Adelman, Harindar De Silva, and Michael F. Koehn (1991) 'User Cost in Oil Production, *Resources & Energy*, Vo1.13, 1991, p. 6.
141. Abdul Khaliq Abdullahh, *Azmat al Khalij: Khalfiyat al-Azma duwr al-Adrak wa al-Adrak al-Khadi' fi Azmat Khaleej wa Taday'ha 'ala al-Watan al-Arabi* (*Gulf Crisis: Its Background and Implications*), Centre for Arab Unity Studies, 1991, p. 91.
142. Cited in Beernaerts, 'Economic, Political and Legal Aspects', p. 20.
143. *The Soviet Union and the Middle East*, vol. 6, no. 12, 1990, p. 25.
144. J. E. Peterson, Saudi Arabia and the Illusion of Security, op.cit., p. 16.
145. Joseph Kostiner, op.cit., p. 425.
146. J. E. Peterson, Saudi Arabia and the Illusion of Security, op.cit., p. 17.
147. Ibid., p. 11.
148. *New York Times*, 6 June 1991.
149. *New York Times*, 18 June 1991.
150. BBC World Service, Arabic Broadcasting, 14 April 1992.
151. J. E. Peterson, Saudi Arabia and the Illusion of Security, op.cit., p. 23.
152. Elliots, 'Ma'tiyat al Aman fi Khalij al Farsi', p. 19.
153. Beernaerts, 'Economic, Political and Legal Aspects', p. 22.
154. J. E. Peterson, Saudi Arabia and the Illusion of Security, op.cit., p. 23.
155. Quant, *Saudi Arabia in the 1980s*, p. 61.
156. Antony Cordesman, 'Al-Iwaks wa al-Bahth al-Imriki 'an Istiqrar Istratiji fi Asharq al-Adna', (AWACS & the American Search for Strategic Stability in the Near East), Dirasat Istratigiah, No. 46, 1981, p. 66.
157. Ibid., p. 64.
158. Fred Halliday, op.cit, pp. 140-141.
159. *Khaleej*, 27 March 1988.
160. *Khaleej*, 9 April 1988.
161. Quant, *Saudi Arabia in the 1980s*, p. 44.
162. Safran, *Saudi Arabia*, p. 259.
163. Ibid., pp. 262–3.
164. Ibid., p. 238.

165. J. E. Peterson, *Saudi Arabia and the Illusion of Security*, op.cit., p. 8.
166. Ibid., p. 333.
167. *New York Times*, 8 March 1992.
168. Hassan al-Alkim, 'Mas'alat al-Amn fi Khaleej' (The Issue of Gulf Security), *Al-Wahdah*, vol. 53, Feb. 1989, pp. 115–17.
169. Joseph Kostiner, op.cit., p. 424.
170. Fred Halliday, op.cit., p. 125.
171. J. E. Peterson, Saudi Arabia and the Illusion of Security, op.cit., p. 7.
172. Gene Lindsey, *Saudi Arabia*, Hippocrene Books, 1991, p. 325.
173. Mohammed Hijazi, 'Al Tanmiyya al Mabtura wal Hijra al Ajnabbiya al Mutazima', *Majallat al Khalij al Arabi*, vol. 11, no. 6, 1979, p. 661.
174. *New York Times*, 18 June 1991.
175. Quant, *Saudi Arabia in the 1980s*, p. 266.
176. *Dirasat Istratijya*, vol. 39, May 1981, p. 36.
177. Korany and Dessouki, *Foreign Policies*, p. 266.
178. M. Abir, *Saudi Arabia in the Oil Era*, p. 47.
179. Cordesman, 'Al-Iwaks wal Bahth al Imriki', p. 66.
180. *Salsalat Dirasat al Istratijiya*, vol. 10, al 'Alam al Thalath lil Dirasat wa Nashr Centre, 1982, p. 87.
181. UAE Television, Dubai, 8 April 1988.
182. *Washington Post*, 20 Dec. 1988.
183. http://www.jamestown.org/programs/edm/single/?tx_ttnews%5Btt_news%5D=33812&tx_ttnews%5BbackPid%5D=166&no_cache=1.
184. *Financial Times*, 7 June 2009.
185. *Financial Times*, 3 Aug. 2009.
186. J. E. Peterson, Saudi Arabia and the Illusion of Security, op.cit., p. 57.
187. W. Quant, *Saudi Arabia in the 1980s*, pp. 64–5.
188. Joseph Kostiner, op.cit., p. 418
189. *Khaleej*, 26 March 1988.
190. Fred Haliday, op.cit., 1982, p. 134.
191. For more details see Antony H. Cordesman, *The Gulf and the Search for Strategic Stability*, Westview Press, 1984, pp. 34–5.
192. Joseph Kostiner, op.cit., p. 422.
193. *The Soviet Union and the Middle East*, vol. 6, no. 12, 1990, p. 28.
194. Dawisha, 'Saudi Arabia's Search for Security', p 20.
195. http://www.arabnews.com/?page=6&section=0&article=103811&d=21&m=11&y=2007.
196. http://www.saudi-us-relations.org/articles/2007/ioi/071124-sultan-russia.html.
197. *Eurasia Daily Monitor,* vol. 5, no. 137, 18 July 2008.
198. http://www.accessmylibrary.com/coms2/summary_0286-27165870_ITM.
199. *Financial Times*, 6 Sept. 2009.
200. http://www.dp-news.com/pages/detail.aspx?articleId=16755.
201. Ibid.
202. *Majallat al Majalla*, vol. 635, 14–18 April 1996, p. 30.
203. Joseph Kostiner, op.cit., p 429.
204. Ibid, p. 418.
205. Quant, *Saudi Arabia in the 1980s*, p. 38.
206. Khoury, *Saudi Decision-Making Body*, p. 16.
207. Paul Stevens, 'Saudi Arabia's Oil Policy in the 1970s: Its Origins, Implementation and

Implications', in Niblock (ed.), 'State, Society and Economy in Saudi Arabia', op.cit., p. 219.

208. http://arabic.arabia.msn.com/news/middleeast/Reuters/2009/June/829440Update.aspx

209. J. E. Peterson, *Saudi Arabia and the Illusion of Security*, op.cit., p. 9.

Bibliography

Books

Abdul Wahhab, Ayman Assayed, 'Al Massar al Suri al Isra'ili wa Ma'uqat al Safqa al Kamila', *Al-siassa Al- Dawlya*, vol. 120 (April 1995), pp. 223–19.

Abud, Sami, *Jighrafiya al Miyah wa Istikhdam al Aradi* (Water Geography and Over Exploitation), Riyadh, Maktabat Al Rushd, 1998.

Abu Ghanima, Ziyad, *Al Haraka al Islamiyya wa Qadhiya Filistin* (The Islamic Movement and the Palestinian Question), Amman: Dar al Farqan lil Nashr wal Tawzi, 1985.

Abulfadil, Mahmoud, 'Al-Tashkilat al-Ijima'iah wa al-Takuyn al-Tabaqi fi al-Watan al-Arabi' (Social Formation and the Class Emergence in the Arab Homeland), *Al-Mustaqbal al-Arabi*, vol. 115, Sept. 1998.

Abu Talib, Hassan, 'Asus Al-siassa al Kharijiya Asa'udiya', *Al-Siassa al-Dawlya*, vol. 90, Oct. 1987.

Ahmed, Mahmoud, *Israil wa al-Miyah al-Arabiya* (Israel and the Arab Water), Beirut: Dar al Mustaqbal al Arabi, 1991.

al-'Alam, Jalal, *Qadat al-Gharb Yaquluwn* (Western Leaders Say), Al-Ain: UAE Student Union, 1979.

Ali, Hussein Fathi, 'Al-Miyah fil Mufawadat Muta'dida al-Atraf' (Waters in the Multiparty Negotiation), *Al-siassa Al-Dawlya*, April 1992, vol. 108, pp. 210–5.

al-Alkim, Hassan Hamdan, Challenges facing the Arab world in the twenty-first century: an overview, *Contemporary Arab Affairs*, Vol. 1, No. 3, July 2008, 417–444

al-Alkim, Hassan Hamdan, 'Al-Suhywniah al-Yahwudiah al-Amirikyah wa Tathiraha 'Ala Siassat al-Wilayat al-Mutahidah al-Kharijiah Tijah al 'Alim al-Arabi' (American Jewish Zionism and its Impacts on the US Policy towards the Arab World), *Shu'un Arabiah* (Tunis), vol. 56, Dec. 1988, pp. 212–26.

al-Alkim, Hassan Hamdan, *The Foreign Policy of the United Arab Emirates*, London: Saqi Books, 1989.

al-Alkim, Hassan Hamdan, *The GCC States in an Unstable World: Foreign Policy Dilemmas of Small States* , London: Saqi Books, 1994.

al-Alkim, Hassan Hamdan, "Azmat al-Miyah fil Watan al-Arabi' wa al-Harb al-muhtamilah (Water Crisis in the Arab Homeland and the Potential of War)', *Journal of Social Science* (Kuwait), vol. 23, no. 3, Autumn 1995, pp. 7–31.

al-Alkim, Hassan Hamdan, Azmat al-Ghitha fi al-Wattan al-Arabi: al-Tahdiat wa Afaq al-Mustaqbal (Food Crisis in the Arab Homeland: Challenges & Prospects) Al-Siassa al-Dawlya, no. 123, January 1996, pp. 8-26.

al-Alkim, Hassan Hamdan, Al- Salam Bin al- Arab wa Israil: Drasa Istrafiyah (Peace between the Arab & Israel: A Futuristic Study) Journal of the Social Sciences, vol. 24, no. 4, winter 1996, p.p. 73-106.

al-Alkim, Hassan Hamdan et al., *Qadhaya Islamiyya Mua'sira*, Cairo: Centre for Asian Studies, Cairo University, 2nd edn, 1997.

al-Alkim, Hassan Hamdan, Bi'at Sun'a al-Qarar al-Kharijy al-Saudi (The Environment of the Saudi Foreign Policy-Making), *Arab Journal of Political Science*, No. 7, November 1992, pp.39-71.

Allan, J. A., and Mallat C., *Water in the Middle East*, London: British Academic Press, 1995.

Amın Jalal, *al-Mashriq al-Arabi wa al-Maghrib* (The Arab Mashreq and the Maghreb), Beirut: Centre for Arab Unity Studies, 1981.

Aras, Bulent, 'Post-Cold War Realities: Israel Strategy in Azerbaijan and Central Asia', *Middle East Policy*, vol. 5, no. 4, Jan. 1998, pp. 68–81.

Aryis, Riyad Najeeb, *Riyah Asumuh* (Western Winds), London: Riyad Arees lil Kutub wal Nashr, 1994.

Asultan, Abdullah, *Ethiobia: Al-Bahr al-Ahmar wa Siraa' al-Arabi al-Israili wa Tanafus Bayn al-Istratijiyeen* (Ethiopia: The Red Sea and the Arab Israeli Conflict), Beirut: Centre of Arab Unity Studies, 1984.

Bakr, Hassan, 'Al-Mandhur al-Miyah lil Sira' al-Arabi al-Israili' (Water Perspective in the Arab–Israeli Conflict), *Al-siassa Al-Dawlya*, vol. 104, April 1991, pp. 132–44.

Balaqziz, Abdulilah, 'Muqadimat litahlil al-Khitab al-Siassi al-Arabi' (Introduction to the Analysis of the Arab Political Speech), *Al-Mustaqbal al-Arabi*, vol. 123, May 1989.

Barakat, Nizam Mahmoud, "Al-Istitan wa Sira' al-Arabi al-Isra'ili: Al-Janib Asiassyi', *Journal of Social Science* (Kuwait), vol. 23, no. 1, Spring 1995, pp. 153–94.

al-Barsan, Ahmed, 'Masadr al-Quwah al-Arabiah wa al-Siassa al-Kharijiah al-Amrikyah' (Sources of Arab Power & the American Foreign Policy), *Arab Journal of Political Science*, No. 13, winter 2007

al-Bayyati, Adnan Hiza', 'Attasahur wa Azmat al Ghida fil Watan al Arabi' (Desertification and Food Crisis in the Arab Homeland), *Shu'un Arabiya*, vol. 74, 1993.

Beernaerts, Sophia, 'Economic, Political and Legal Aspects of Cooperation between the European Economic Community and the Countries Parties Charter of Cooperation Council for the Arab States of the Gulf', Dissertation presented to the Institute of European Studies, Université Libre de Bruxelles, 1989.

Al-Biyati, Adnan Hiza', 'Attasahur wa Azmat al Ghida fil Watan al Arabi' (Desertification and Food Crisis in the Arab Homeland), *Shu'un al Arabiya*, vol. 74, 1993.

Blum, William, *Rogue State*, Monroe, IL: Common Courage Press, 2005.

Bustani, Basil, *al-Tanmiah al-Bashariyah al-Mustadamah* (Human Sustainable Development), Beirut: Arab Unity Study Centre, 2009.

Calabrese, John, China and the Persian Gulf: Energy and Security, *Middle East Journal*, vol. 52, no. 3, summer 1998, pp. 351-66.

Chubin, Shahram, 'Iran and Regional Security', *Survival*, vol. 34, no. 3, Autumn 1992.

Chubin, Shahram, and Green, Jerrold, 'Engaging Iran: A US Strategy', *Survival*, vol. 40, no. 3, Autumn 1998, pp. 153–69.

Clapham, Christopher (ed.), *Foreign Policy Making in Developing States*, Saxon House, 1977.

Cohen, Avner, *Israel and the Bomb*, New York: Colombia University Press, 1998.

Cordesman, Antony H., *The Gulf and the Search for Strategic Stability*, Boulder, CO: Westview Press, 1984.

Cordesman, Antony, '*Al Quadrat al 'Askaria al-Iranyah*' (Iran's Military Capabilities), Dirasat 'Alamiah, Abu Dhabi: Emirates Centre for Strategic Studies and Research, 1996.

Dahl, Robert A., *Democracy and its Critics*, Yale University Press, New Haven and London, 1989.

Dakroub, Abdul Amir, 'Mustaqbal Al-Sira'a Huwla al-Miyah fi al-sharq al-Awsat', *Al-Fikr al Arabi*, vol. 76, Spring 1994, pp. 212–32.

Dervis, Kemal, and Shafik, Nemat, 'The Middle East and North Africa: A Tale of Two Futures', *Middle East Journal*, vol. 52, no. 4, Autumn 1998, pp. 505–16.

Dhahir, Mas'aud, 'Al-Fadha' al-Arabi wa Ma'zaq al-Ta'wun ma' Duwal al-Juar al-Iqlimi fi Matala' al-qarn al-Wahd wa al-'Ashrin" (Arabs and the Problem of Cooperation with Neighbouring Countries in the 21st Century), a paper presented to the conference on the Arab in the 21st Century, Amman, Jordan, 7–8 Nov. 2001 (unpublished).

Feldman, Shai, 'Missiles and CBW Proliferation: The Middle East', Proceedings of the American Association for the Advancement of Science Annual Meeting Symposium, New Orleans, 19 Feb. 1990.

Finer, Herman, *Dulles over Suez*, Chicago: Quadrangle, 1964.

Gause, F. Gregory, 'British and American Policies in the Persian Gulf 1968–1973', *Review of International Studies*, vol. 11, no. 4, Oct. 1985.

Green, Stephen, *Al-Inhiyaz: 'Alaqat Amrika al-Sirriya bi Isra'il* (Taking Sides: America Secret Relations with Israel), Cyprus: Mu'asasa Adirasat Filistiniya, 1985.

Haass, Richard N., 'What to Do with American Primacy', *Foreign Affairs*, vol. 78, no. 5, Sept./Oct. 1999.

Habashinah, Sadah, 'Al-Siassa al-Urbiah Tijah al-Arab Munthu Harib 1973 Hta Mutamar Barcelona al-Thani 2005' (The European Policy towards the Arabs from the 1973 War to Barcelona Second Conference 2005), *Mu'atah*, vol. 22, no. 5, 2007.

Hasso, Tawfiq, *Wa'd Balfur wal Halqa al-Mafquda* (The Balfour Declaration), Al Ain: Dar al Kitab al Jami'I, 1986.

Hasso, Tawfiq, (ed.), *Qadhaya Duwliya Mu'asira* (Contemporary International Issues), Al-Ain: Mu'asasa al Ain lil Nashr, 1989.

Herzl, Theodor, *The Jewish State*, trans. Sylvie d'Avignon, London, NP., 1967.

Hill, William, 'Siassat Turkia al-Kharjiah fi 'Asr ma Ba'd al-Harb al-Barida wa al-Sharq al-Awsat' (Turkey Foreign Policy in Post Cold War Age and the Middle East), *The Arab Researcher*, vol. 48, July–Oct. 1998.

Hillal, Ali Edin, and Matter, Jamil, *Al-Nidham al-Iqlimy al-Arabi* (Arab Regional Order), Beirut: Centre of Arab Unity Studies, 1979.

Holden, David, and Johns, Richard, *The House of Saud*, London: Pan Books, 1983.

Huntington, Samuel P., 'The West Unique, Not Universal', *Foreign Affairs*, vol. 75, no. 6, Nov./ Dec. 1996, pp. 28–46.

Huntington, Samuel P., *The Clash of Civilizations*, London: Free Press, 2002.

Hurst, David, *The Gun and the Olive Branch*, London: Faber & Faber, 2nd edn, 1984.

Hussein, Taha, *Mustaqbal al-Thaqafah* (Future of Culture), Beirut: Dar al-Kitab al-Libnani, n.d.

al- Hut, Ali, Al-Iqtrab al-Thaqafi. Cultural alienation, *Majallat al-Wihda*, no. 39, December 1987, 137–147.

Indyk, Martin S., 'Ma Wara Tawazun al-Quwwa: Khiyar Amrika fi al-sharq al-Awsat', *Silsilat Maqalat Ma'raba 2*, Beirut: Markaz Adirasat al Istratijiya wa al-Bahuth wa Tawthiq, 1992, pp. 7–20.

Indyk, Martin S., 'Siassat Idarat Klintun Hiyal al-sharq al-Awsat', *Dirasat Filistiniyah*, vol. 15, Summer 1993, pp. 196–205.

Isaacs, Stephen D., *Al-Yahud wa Siassa Al Amrikiya* (The Jews and the American Policy), Beirut: Dar al Ittihad, 1987.

Ismael, T., *The Middle East in World Politics*, New York: Syracuse University Press, 1974.

Jabiri, Mohammed Abid, 'Ishkaliat al-Assalah wa al-Hadathah fi al-Fikr al-Arabi al-Mua'sir: Sira' Tabaqi awu Mushkilat Thaqafah' (The originality vs. modernity dilemma in contemporary Arab thought: a class struggle or cultural problem?) In: *Al-Turath wa Tahadiat al-A'sr fi al-A'alam al-Arabi* (Heritage and challenges of the age in the Arab world). Beirut: Centre for Arab Unity Studies, 1985, pp. 29–33.

Jalal, Mohammed Numan, 'Atughayurat al Jadida fil Ittihad Asufiyati wa Athruh ala Sharq al Awsat' (The New Changes in the Soviet Union and its Implication on the Middle East), *Al Bahith al Arabi* (The Arab Researcher, London), vol. 12, June 1987.

al-Jamal, Sira, *al-Khitab al-Tarikhy al-'Arabi ma bin al-Harbin al-'Udhmiyn* (The Historical Arab Speech between the two World War), *Al-Mustaqbal al-Arabi*, vol. 123, May 1989.

Kelly, J. B., *Arabia the Gulf and the West*, London: Weidenfeld & Nicolson, 1980.

Khoury, Enver, *The Saudi Decision-Making Body: The House of Saud*, Washington, DC: Institute of Middle Eastern and North African Affairs, 1978.

Korany, Baghat, and Dessouki, Ali H., *The Foreign Policies of Arab States,* Boulder, CO: Westview Press, 1984.

Kostiner, Joseph, 'Saudi Arabia and the Arab- Israeli Peace Process: The Fluctuation of Regional Coordination', *British Journal of Middle Eastern Studies*, vol. 36, no. 3, December 2009, pp. 417- 429.

Lacey, Robert, *The Kingdom*, London: Fontana Paperbacks, 1982.

Laqueur, W., *The Struggle for the Middle East*, New York: Macmillan, 1969.

Lewis, Bernard, 'Rethinking the Middle East', *Foreign Affairs*, vol. 74, no. 4, Autumn 1992, pp. 2–15.

Lewis, Bernard, 'The West and the Middle East', *Foreign Affairs*, vol. 76, no. 1, Jan./Feb. 1997, pp. 114–30.

Libiszewski, Stephan, 'Water Disputes in the Jordan Basin Region and their Role in the Resolution of the Arab–Israeli Conflict', Centre for Security Policy and Conflict Analysis, Swiss Peace Foundation, 13 Aug. 1995, www.mideastweb.org/mew_water95.pdf

Maynes, Charles, 'The Middle East in the Twenty-First Century', *Middle East Journal*, vol. 52, no. 1, Winter 1998, pp. 9–16.

Mottale, Morris Mehrdad, *The Arms Buildup in the Persian Gulf*, New York: University Press of America, 1986.

Mubaideen, Mekhled Obaid, 'Al-Syn al-Sha'biah wa Imkaniat Tahwlah ila Qutb Dawli Fa'il' (China and the Probability of Becoming an Effective International Power), *Al-Manarah* (Jordan), vol. 15, no. 2, 2004.

Muqalled, Ismail Sabri, *Al-Illaqat al-Syassya al-Dawlya* (International Political Relations), Kuwait: Thaat al Salasil, vol. 5, 1978.

'Al-Muqif al-Amiriki Tijah al-Barnamj al-Nawawi al-Irani' (The American Attitude towards the IranianNuclear Programme), *Dirasat* (Jordan), vol. 34, 2007.

'Al-Muqif al-Amiriki Tijah al-Barnamj al-Nawawi al-Kuri al-Shimali' (The American Attitude towards the North Korean Nuclear Programme), *Mu'tah* (Jordan), vol. 23, no. 3, 2008.

Mufti, Malik, 'Daring and Caution in Turkish Foreign Policy', *Middle East Journal*, vol. 52, no. 1, Winter 1998, pp. 32–50.

Muslih, M., 'The Golan: Israel and Syria Strategic Calculations', *Middle East Journal*, vol. 47, no. 4, 1993, pp. 611–32.
Mustafa, Nadia, *Uruba wal Watan al Arabi* (Europe and Arab Home Land), Silsilat Athiqafa al Qawmiya, 8, Beirut: Markaz Dirasat al Wahda al Arabiya, 1987.
Nafi', Bashir, 'Ittifaq Ghaza-Ariha: Nuqat al-Da'af wa al-Quwwa', *Shu'un Asharq al-Awsat,* vol. 24, 1993, pp. 17–31.
al-Naqrash, Abdulla, "Al Andhimah al Siassia al- Arabia wa al- Nidham al-Arabi" (Arab Political Regimes & The Arab Regional System) *Arab Journal of Political Science*, vols 3 and 4, Sept. 1989.
Niblock, Tim (ed.), *State, Society and Economy in Saudi Arabia*, London: Croom Helm, 1982.
Niblock, Tim (ed.), *Iraq: The Contemporary State*, London: Croom Helm, 1982.
Nixon, Richard, *Beyond Peace*, trans. Malak Abbas, Amman: Al-Ahliya lil Nashr wa al-Tuwzi', 1995.
Nu'aman, 'Asam, 'Nahwa Mashru'a Distur Itihadi 'Arabi' (Towards an Arab Federal constitutional Project), *Al-Mustaqbal al-Arabi*, vol. 123, May 1989.
Nufal, Ahmed Said, et al., *Al-Qadayah Al-filistiniyah* (The Palestinian Question), Beirut: Markaz Dirasat al Wahda al 'Arabiya, 1989.
Omar, Mahjoub, *Al-Sıra' al-Arabi al-Isra'ili wa Sidam al-Hadharat, fi Sidam al Hidharat*, Beirut: Markaz Adirasat al Istratijjiya wa Bahouth wa Tuwthiq, 1995.
Patai, Raphael (ed.), *The Complete Dairies of Theodor Herzl*, trans. Harry Zohn, New York: Herzl Press and Thomas Yoseloff, 1960.
Peres, Shimon, *Ma'rakat Al-ssalam: Yuwmiyat* (The Battle for Peace: Diary), trans. Ammar Fadhil wa Malik Fadhil, Amman: Al-Ahliya lil Nashr wa al-Tuwzi, 1995.
Peterson, John E., Saudi Arabia and the Illusion of Security, Adelphi Paper 348, London: the International Institute for Strategic Studies, 2002.
Postel, S., *The Last Oasis: Facing Water Scarcity*, London: Earthscan Publications, 1993.
Prestowitz, Clyde, *Al-Dawlah al-Mariqah* (Rogue Nation), trans. Fadhil Jatkar, Beirut: Al-Hiwar al-Thaqafi, 2003.
Qassim, Abbas, 'Al-Amtaa' bil-Miyah al-Arabiya wa Ab'aduha Ajiyulitikiya', *Al-Mustaqbal al-Arabi*, vol. 174, Aug. 1993, pp. 25–52.
Quant, William, *Saudi Arabia in the 1980s*, Washington, DC: Brookings Institute, 1981.
Rabi', Mohammed Mahmoud, *Manahij al-Bahath Fi 'alm Al-Siassa* (Methodology of Research in Political Science), Kuwait: Maktaba al Falah, 1987.
Riyadh, Mahmoud, *Al Bahth 'an Aslaam wa Sira' fi Asharq al Awsat 1948–1978* (The Search for Peace and the Struggle in the Middle East), Beirut: Al-Mu'asasa al-Arabiya lil Dirasat wa Nashr, 1981.
Sabhi, Majdi, 'Azmat al-Miyah fi al-Mufawadat Muta'dida' (Water Crisis in the Multiparty Negotiations), *Al-siassa Al-Dawlya*, vol. 114, Oct. 1993, pp. 124–30.
Safran, Nadav, *From War to War: The Arab–Israeli Confrontation*, New York: Pegasus, 1969.
Safran, Nadav, *Saudi Arabia: The Ceaseless Quest for Security,* Boston, MA: Belknap Press of Harvard University Press, 1985.
Said, Mohammed Sayyed, 'Mustaqbal Anizam al-Iqlimi al-Arabi' (The Future of the Arab Regional System), *'Alam al-Ma'rifa* (Kuwait), vol. 158, Feb. 1992.
Salama, Ghassan, 'Al-Ta'adadiah wa al-Tahyyid al-Mutabadil: Al-Illaqat al-Arabia-al-rabiah fi al-Rahyn wa al-Muhtamal' (Pluralism and the Interdependent Neutralism:

Contemporary Inter-Arab Relations and the Potential), *Al-Mustaqbal al-Arabi*, vol. 115, Sept. 1988.

Salama, Ghassan, 'Al-Arab wa Isra'il wa Amrika wa al-Mufawadat' (The Arabs, Israeli and America and the Negotiations), *Al-Mustaqbal al-Arabi*, vol. 172, June 1993, pp. 4–12.

Salama, Ghassan, 'Afkar Awaltya 'an Asuq Asharq Al-Awsatiya' (The Initial Thought of the Middle East), *Al-Mustaqbal al-Arabi*, vol. 179, Jan. 1994, pp. 67–89.

Samman, Nabil, *Israil wa al-Miyah al-Arabiya: Harb al-Miyah min al-Furat ila al-Nil* (Israel and the Arab Water from the Nile to Euphrates), NP., 1990.

Sardar, Ziauddin, and Devies Merry Wyn, *Why do People Hate America*, trans. Ma'ain al-Imam, Riyadh: Obeikhan Publishers, 2005.

Seaver, Brenda M., 'The Regional Sources of Power-Sharing Failure: The Case of Lebanon', *Political Science Quarterly*, vol. 115, no. 2, Summer 2000, pp. 247–71.

Serfaty, Simon, 'Europe and the United States in the Persian Gulf,' *Middle East Journal* 52, no. 3, Summer 1998, pp. 334-350.

Shamir, Yitzhak, 'Israel's Role in a Changing Middle East', *Foreign Affairs*, Spring 1982.

Shayf, Za'if, 'Al-Maksab al-Istratiji li Isra'il wa al-Urdun' (The Israeli–Jordan Strategic Benefit), *Dirasat Filistiniya*, vol. 20, Autumn 1994.

Sindelan, Richard, and Peterson, J. E. (eds.), *Cross Current in the Gulf*, New York: Routledge, 1988.

Starr, J. R, 'Water Wars', *Foreign Policy*, vol. 82 (Spring 1991), pp. 17–36.

Stoessinger, John G., *Crusaders and Pragmatists: Movers of Modern American Foreign Policy*, New York: W. W. Norton Co., 1979.

Subhi, Majdi, 'Azmat al- Miyah fi al- Mufawadhat al-Muta'adidah' (Water Crisis in the Muti Parties Negotitations), *Al-Siassa Al-Dawlya*, no. 114, Oct. 1993, pp. 124- 130.

Al Suwaidi, Jamal S. (ed), *Iran and the Gulf: A Search for Stability*, London: I. B. Tauris, 2002.

al-Tahir, Hamdi, *Mustaqbal al-Miyah Fil al-'am al-Arabi* (Water Prospect in the Arab World), NP., 1991.

Tahsin, Khalid Ali, 'Azmat al-Ghitha wa al-'Amal al-'Arabi al-Mushtarak' (Food Crisis and the Joint Arab Work), *Al-Mustaqbal al-Arabi*, vol. 123, May 1989.

Talbott, Strobe, 'Democracy and the National Interest', *Foreign Affairs*, vol. 75, no. 6, Nov./ Dec. 1996, pp. 47–63.

Tani, Jalal, *Al Ikhwa al Za'ifa* (The False Brotherhood), trans. Ahmed al Bazuri, Beirut: Mu'asasat al-Risala, 1983.

al-Thanyan, Abdatniyan, *Al-Aman al Ghida'i wal 'Amal al 'Arabi al Mushtarik* (Food Security and the Arab Joint Work), Beirut: Dar al Fikr al Mu'asir, 1990.

Tripp, Charles, 'Iraq and the Gulf States', *Survival*, vol. 34, no. 3, Autumn 1992, pp. 43-61.

Wild Abah, Abdullah, 'Al-Taswiya fi al-sharq al-Awsat wa Mustaqbal al-nizam al-Arabi' (Peace Settlement in the Middle East and the Prospect of Arab System), *Al-Mustaqbal al-Arabi*, vol. 192, Feb. 1995.

Wildstrand, C., *Water Conflict and Research Priorities*, Oxford: Pergamon Press, 1980.

Wilson, Harold, *The Labour Government 1964–1970: A Personal Record*, London: Weidenfeld & Nicolson, 1971.

Woodward, Bob, *State of Denial*, London: Pocket Books, 2007.

Zahlan, Rosemary, *The Origin of the United Arab Emirates*, London: Macmillan, 1978.

Media

Al-Arab (Newspaper)
Al-Islah (Journal)
Al-Kifah al-Arabi (Journal)
Al-Nahar (Newspaper)
Al-Quds Al- Arabi (Newspaper)
Al-Rai al- 'Am (Newspaper)
Al-Safir (Newspaper)
Al-Sha'ab (Newspaper)
Al-Shuruq (Newspaper)
Al-Siassa (Newspaper)
Al Usbu' al Arabi (Newspaper)
Al-Wafd (Newspaper)
Al-Wa'i al- Islami (Journal)
Al-Waqt (Newspaper)
Al-Wattan (Newspaper)
Arab Parliament (Journal)
al-Bayan (Newspaper)
Daily Mail
Daily Telegraph
Financial Times
Gulf News (Newspaper)
al-Hayat (Newspaper)
International Herald Tribune
al-Ittihad (Newspaper)
Khaleej (Newspaper)
Los Angeles Times
Majallat al- Muhandis al- Arabi (Journal)
Middle East Economic Digest
Middle East Economic Survey
Middle East Insight
Middle East Monitor
New York Times
Washington Post
Yemen Post

Periodicals

Al-Siassa Al-Dawlya, Cairo: Centre for Political and Strategic Studies, Al-Ahram Press Establishment *Arab Human Development Report 2009*, UNDP
Arab Journal of International Studies
Arab Journal of Political Science
Arab Knowledge Report 2009
Arab Record & Report
Arab Strategic Report 2007- 2008, Cairo: Centre for Political and Strategic Studies, Al-Ahram Press Establishment, 2008
Ataqrir al-Iqtisadi al-Arabi al-Muwahad, Arab Monetary Fund

British Journal of Middle Eastern Studies
Contemporary Arab Affairs
Critique
Foreign Affairs
Foreign Policy
Gulf Strategic Report, Sharjah: Dar al-Khaleej for Press & Publications
Human Development Report, UNDP
Journal of Social Sciences
Middle East Journal
Middle East Policy
The Military Balance, London: The Institute of International & Strategic Studies

Index